COMMON LAW AND
LIBERAL THEORY

COMMON LAW AND LIBERAL THEORY
COKE, HOBBES, AND THE ORIGINS OF AMERICAN CONSTITUTIONALISM

JAMES R. STONER, JR.

UNIVERSITY PRESS OF KANSAS

For my parents, Lois and James Stoner

Published by the University Press of Kansas (Lawrence, Kansas 66049), which was organized by the Kansas Board of Regents and is operated and funded by Emporia State University, Fort Hays State University, Kansas State University, Pittsburg State University, the University of Kansas, and Wichita State University

Library of Congress Cataloging-in-Publication Data

Stoner, James Reist.
   Common law and liberal theory : Coke, Hobbes, and the origins of
American constitutionalism / James R. Stoner, Jr.
     p.   cm.
   Revision of thesis (Ph.D.)—Harvard University, 1987.
   Includes bibliographical references (p.   ) and index.
   ISBN 0-7006-0532-0 (cloth)   ISBN 0-7006-0630-0 (pbk.)
    1. Common law—England—History.   2. United States—Constitutional
law.   3. Judicial power—United States.   4. Liberalism—History.
5. Coke, Edward, Sir, 1552–1634.   6. Hobbes, Thomas, 1588–1679.
I. Title.
KD671.S76   1992
342.73—dc20
[347.302]   91–40787

British Library Cataloguing in Publication Data is available.

Printed in the United States of America

10 9 8 7 6 5 4 3 2

Produced digitally by Lightning Source Inc.

CONTENTS

ACKNOWLEDGMENTS

A custom is said to be good at common law when it is thought to exist "from time immemorial," that is, for so long that "the memory of man runneth not to the contrary." Though modern historians have often enough improved on custom's memory, one who has been at work on a project for a decade or more finds human meaning in the phrase "time immemorial," or at least accumulates more debts than he is able to recollect. At the risk of omission, let me attempt acknowledgment.

Professor Harvey C. Mansfield, Jr., of Harvard University supervised the dissertation from which this book developed with infinite patience, sound suggestion, and gentle encouragement, then helped me secure the leisure that made possible its revision. As another of his students has written, Professor Mansfield teaches with the virtue of example as well as with his words, and though the world knows well, or should, his words, to have had the benefit of the example has been a special fortune. In its early stages, my research was saved from certain traps by the guidance of Professor Judith Shklar. When circumstances made it impossible for her to serve as second examiner on the dissertation, Shannon Stimson generously accepted the task and gave it a thorough and probing reading, with almost unimaginable dispatch. Nor can I neglect to thank Professors James Q. Wilson, Harry Hirsch, and R. Shep Melnick, for their exposition of contemporary quandaries in the doctrine and practice of American courts, and Professor Michael Walzer, whose interpretation of Hobbes became more cogent to me each time I reread the texts.

Many friends and colleagues over the years have taken an interest in my study of common law and its relation to American constitutionalism, and their conversation, queries, and criticism helped me focus my thoughts. Allow me to mention Jean Baker, Jack Chapin, Jack Fruchtman, Marianne Githens, Ralph Hancock, Bill Hedges, Chris Kelly, Charles Kesler, Matt Lalumia, Bill Lasser, Harold Levy, John McNeill, Grant Mindle, Peter Minowitz, James Shapiro, Rogers Smith, Rob Vipond, and Chris Wolfe. As every teacher knows, the interest and questions of one's students are often the sharpest prod to thought, and mine—at Harvard University, Goucher College, and now Louisiana State University—wonderfully met the challenge. My colleagues at the latter, especially Professors Cecil Eubanks and Ellis Sandoz, gave me the support—intellectual and administrative—that helped bring the crop to harvest.

I was first introduced to the study of the American Founding and of political philosophy by Professor Murray Dry at Middlebury College. With sure judgment and liberal encouragement, he has remained my teacher long after I earned my first degree, reading not only multiple drafts of individual chapters but several versions of the entire manuscript. His steady reassurance of the worth of my study more than once gave me the courage to continue, as his invitations to lecture at the college gave me more concrete incentive to prepare parts of the book. Nor can I omit a word of thanks to his colleague, also my teacher, Professor Paul Nelson, who first taught me to wonder at the philosophy of Thomas Hobbes.

The John M. Olin Foundation of New York generously provided a year's fellowship, which gave me the chance to revise the dissertation into a book. Earlier, an invitation courtesy of Ellis Sandoz to the conference "Magna Carta and the Ancient Constitution," sponsored by the Liberty Fund of Indianapolis, helped to supplement my lonely study of English legal history. In the first stages of its conception, and then again in its final weeks, my work was supported by the generosity of the Earhart Foundation of Ann Arbor.

To the staff of the University Press of Kansas, especially Fred Woodward, Michael Briggs, Cynthia Ingham, and Susan McRory, I am much obliged for the genuine interest they have taken in the book. The readings they secured, by Robert Clinton and another, anonymous reviewer, made useful suggestions for improvement of my still imperfect text.

One's greatest debts are most personal and must remain by and large unwritten. Still, I would say that without the great faith and trust of my bride, Jill Landry, I cannot imagine having seen this book through to completion. And the dedication expresses a debt for benefits about which my memory truly "runneth not to the contrary."

INTRODUCTION

It is a maxim of common sense that a definitive biography cannot be written until its subject has breathed his last. Character might show early promise, and great deeds manifest themselves, but we hesitate to grasp the full significance of a life until we can judge it as a whole. Even then, we doubt the adequacy of our perspective, at least if we remember that the reach of a person's influence often spans generations, that genius can go almost unrecognized in a lifetime, and that great genius often does. Historiographers, of course, will add that we can never be sure of the completeness of the data available, and they may even lead us to wonder whether reputation is as insecure after one's demise as it is during one's lifetime, at least so long as those who judge have their own purposes and the standards for judgment stay open to debate.

Perhaps something similar in the life of a regime or constitution helps explain the variety of interpretations given to the American Founding, for the principles enunciated in the Declaration of Independence still frame our political discourse, and the institutions established by the Constitution of 1787 still govern our political life. Even apparent innovations in principle and institution—not to mention amendments to the Constitution itself—are often ambiguous in their import for the whole: Do they repeal an original understanding, or work out the logic of a founding idea, or settle a choice left open at the outset for later resolution? When we write about the Founding, in other words, we cannot avoid passing judgment on its legacy as we know it today, and what we say will be only as definitive as our confidence in the latter judgment and our presumption that all the possibilities of the regime have been disclosed.

If these last reflections have merit, then we cripple ourselves in trying to understand contemporary American politics or political institutions without reference to the Founding. I do not mean to claim that the Founders' understanding of the regime they established was clairvoyant, nor do I assert that we must bend our minds to theirs. Rather, since some continuity of principles and institutions is a fair supposition, and since it is well known that those principles were not lightly declared nor those institutions formed without conscious design, it is as foolhardy of the contemporary student to dismiss the Founders' insight and intentions as it would be to assume that these alone explain our politics today or teach us all we need to know of how to act.

I undertook the present study with a hope to shed light on the contemporary practice of judicial review—the power of courts to declare void and refuse to enforce acts of the legislature or the executive that they determine violate the Constitution—through an inquiry into its place at the Founding. In this book, though I conclude with an account of the anticipation of judicial review voiced at the Philadelphia Convention and with an examination of the case made on its behalf in *The Federalist Papers,* I devote the bulk of my attention to authors who wrote in the century or two before the American Constitution was devised, most of whom never saw the New World. For this too is true of the Founding: It is not only a mirror in which to see ourselves but also a window that opens on vistas of thought and learning that came before and made it possible. Judicial review as we know it is a peculiarly American institution in many ways; indeed, it has sometimes been thought the distinctive contribution of American constitutionalism as a whole. But like our constitutionalism, the elements from which it is formed are not indigenous, even if colonial experience and Revolutionary deliberation provided its kiln.

For at least the past century, the practice of judicial review has been a matter of continuous controversy.[1] Particular rulings of the Supreme Court have often been the source of complaint, but sometimes dispute has widened to call into question the legitimacy of the function itself, or at least the whole way of thinking that judges bring to its exercise. Most obviously, the right of an appointed judiciary holding office for life to void acts passed by popularly elected bodies has seemed anomalous in a system of government now called democratic, and the arguments from bench or book seeking to reconcile judicial review and democracy—or purporting to show actual harmony in result—have thus far rather deflected than defeated the doubt.[2] Nor has the matter been solved by mere reference to the statements of its first defenders, for these seem paradoxical to the modern mind, linking the power of judicial review to the fact of a written constitution, though the power itself must be inferred from, as it is not declared in, the Constitution's text.[3] The pragmatic spirit of modern America has generally been willing enough to live with judicial review, provided courts exercise the power with moderation, and various parties rarely hesitate to invoke it when they can to their advantage. But pragmatic use is not the same as principled defense, and the latter might be expected of a practice that claims to follow the logic of justice and rights, rather than, like administration or legislation, aiming to prosecute a public interest or fashion common good. Besides, our fabled pragmatism, or at least our practical sense, should not at the outset be supposed an independent virtue, uninstructed by our ways at law.

Much academic debate in recent years has been among various competing theories of judicial review, each purporting to offer a method for resolving constitutional disputes. Attempts a decade ago to classify theories as interpretive or noninterpretive have been superseded by advanced theories of interpretation; and theories based upon postulated personal or moral rights have been joined by theories centered on property rights and economics, supplemented by theories based upon inference from constitutional structure.[4] During the presidency of Ronald Reagan and especially through the confirmation hearings of Judge Robert Bork, public attention was directed to the jurisprudence of original intention, a doctrine that constitutional texts ought to be interpreted according to the intentions of their framers. Observers have increasingly recognized, however, that this doctrine serves rather to encourage an attitude of judicial restraint than to provide an alternative theory for judicial decision, in part because determining original intent in any particular case is notoriously difficult, in part because the doctrine has little practical to say concerning settled precedents established on different assumptions.[5] In the polity at large, or at least in the press and among many political scientists and law professors, it is simply taken for granted that judges inevitably bring their political orientation to the exercise of judicial review, though an occasional "anomalous" opinion gives pause. Judge David Souter's surprising success in winning almost unanimous confirmation to the Supreme Court may indicate a latent aspiration toward constitutional consensus in the polity, though his hearings offered no elaborated account of what an "objective" constitutional jurisprudence would entail;[6] the bitter inquisition of Judge Clarence Thomas suggests that partisan passions in constitutional matters still seethe.

One point of emerging consensus is that the character of judicial review has changed significantly since the early years of the republic. Generally scholars now divide constitutional legal history into three eras: the antebellum years, the age of the laissez-faire Court, and the modern era, dating from the "Constitutional Revolution" of 1937. Alexander Bickel, perhaps the most influential commentator on the Court in a generation, wrote a book in the aftermath of the Warren era arguing that the modern Court had, while initially devoted to undoing the discredited activism of its predecessor, unwittingly repeated it, though in different form.[7] Bickel had little to say about the Marshall or Taney Court; but his account was refined by Rogers Smith, who argues that changes in constitutional doctrine parallel developments in American liberalism, and by Christopher Wolfe, who contrasts Chief Justice Marshall's constitutional jurisprudence with what he calls "modern judicial review," in both its laissez-faire and libertarian-egalitarian forms. Wolfe's thesis has recently been seconded by Robert Clinton's work on *Marbury v. Madison,* which argues that judicial review as we often conceive it—as the power of courts to sit as final judges of the constitutionality of legislation—is almost entirely a development of the past one hundred years, the original power of courts to void legislative acts having been strictly limited to "cases of a judiciary nature."[8]

In the pages that follow, I hope to show that judicial review and the constitutionalism of which it forms a part can be illuminated by an awareness of the sources of the Founders' understanding in two different, indeed sometimes directly opposing schools of legal and political thought: on the one hand, the tradition of the English common law; on the other, early liberal political philosophy. I begin by examining the legal thought of Sir Edward Coke, the seventeenth-century English judge and parliamentarian whose opinion in *Doctor Bonham's Case* (1610) was once seen as a precedent for the modern practice. Coke still receives attention from legal historians, but his work is not well known today among political scientists interested in constitutionalism, despite the fact that to the generation of Americans who made the Revolution and wrote the Constitution he was an authority, not a curiosity. I turn next to the political philosophy of Thomas Hobbes, the source of many of the principles, if not conclusions, of modern liberalism, who in the *Leviathan* and other works explicitly disputes Coke's doctrines. As Coke and Hobbes display in sharpest relief the distance between the ways of thinking about law and judging characteristic of the common law mind and liberal political theory, I accord them the most extensive treatment—though it must be noted at the outset that Hobbes is much better known, not to mention respected, by political theorists today than he would have been to Americans at the time of the Founding. But Hobbes indeed was known, openly corrected, and quietly adopted by authors who developed the versions of liberalism that more directly influenced the Founders, and I devote chapters to the thought of three: John Locke, Montesquieu, and William Blackstone, the last of whom gradually replaced Coke as the authority on common law. I close with a few essays on law, liberties, and judging at the Founding, which do not pretend to be definitive but rather illustrate the relation between liberalism and common law.

My argument, then, is preliminary to any account of American constitutional history, not to mention any doctrine of contemporary adjudication, though I think it should prove useful in establishing the larger context of the origin of judicial power in the United States and in explaining the course of its subsequent alteration. As an account of the sources of American constitutionalism, it perforce joins a number of scholarly debates. What Thomas Pangle has called the "old orthodoxy" of constitutional development, based upon a faith in historical progress and telling a story of the evolution of modern liberalism out of the constitution of medieval England, has largely given way to different schools of thought that stress the novelty of liberal politics, though they differ as to its source and its opposition.[9] Since the publication of Bernard Bailyn's *Ideological Origins of the American Revolution* and Gordon Wood's *Creation of the American Republic,* historians have often framed debates over the Founding in terms of a dispute between civic republicanism, which they trace back through the radical Whigs in Britain, and an emergent liberalism, indebted to the Enlightenment and to the pressures of modern commercial life; the typical drift of their analysis has been to attribute the Revolution principally to the first and the Constitution to the second.[10] This framework has been accepted by some political theorists; others, finding the roots of modern liberalism in the thought of such seventeenth-century philosophers as Hobbes and Locke or even in the works of Niccolo Machiavelli, draw the critical line between classical and modern republicanism, counting liberalism within the latter and thus attributing even more exclusively to modern influence the inventive spirit of the Founding as a whole.[11]

This quick summary does not presume to do justice to the subtlety and complexity of the positions involved (some of which I will treat in more detail later), but it does indicate a certain consensus and allows me to locate my own study for the reader reluctant to travel without a map. The consensus is that the American regime has come to take its bearings from modern liberalism and that the source of this orientation can be discovered in the Founding, even though it is usually acknowledged that elements of earlier forms of thought and practice—most notably, those associated with Christianity— persist and play an ancillary role in American political life.[12] My intention here is not to gainsay the hegemony of modern liberalism over American politics today nor to deny the importance of liberal thought in informing the American Founding, but to propose that, for the understanding at least of the judicial branch and its capacity to expound the Constitution as originally conceived, the recovery of forms of thought besides modern liberalism is not ancillary but decisive. I mean to suggest, in other words, that the division of function behind the separation of powers permits or perhaps requires very different ways of thinking about politics and government. Harvey Mansfield has ingeniously shown that the American presidency owes a special debt to the development of the concept of executive power in modern political theory, but his argument does not preclude that the judicial branch taps a different root, particularly as he finds in the American "taming" of the modern executive an Aristotelian echo, if not a voice.[13] And while the modern exercise of judicial review may have allowed liberal influences to eclipse other moments, the crisis of modern liberalism—to which, in one way or another, all the alternatives to the "old orthodoxy" respond—recommends the wisdom of restoring a sense of the alternatives available within the regime.

My aim is first to bring to life the way of thinking about politics, law, and liberty characteristic of the common law mind, and then to show how

liberalism could be interpreted to seem assimilable to common law, not destructive of it. It would be misleading to describe the first task as providing a
theory of the common law, however, for it is characteristic of the common
law mind to collect and gather, rather than to theorize—or at least to resist
any theory that would too quickly reduce the multiplicity of phenomena to
strict distinctions and abstract causes. This habit of common lawyers and
their friends maddens the modern liberal intellect, but the latter has a lesson
to learn about itself from taking patience—indeed, a lesson about its own
strength. For the strength of liberalism is not in its ability to provide an
account of the whole—here it notoriously fumbles—but in its keen analytical
insight into specific matters put before its probe. In one way or another this
was known to those whom we now call the early liberals and forgotten by
most of their successors in the nineteenth and twentieth centuries—the first
actually to call themselves "liberals" and their doctrine "liberalism," we
should recall.[14]

To any reader familiar with the common law it is obvious by now that I do
not mean to use the term in its technical sense, and to any student of the
federal judiciary in the United States its use in any sense relevant to federal
courts might seem anachronistic; so a few words of explanation are in order
at the start.[15] Since the famous lectures of Oliver Wendell Holmes, Jr., scholars and lawyers have tended to think of common law as judge-made law, but
this definition has become so familiar as to lose the ring of paradox it had for
ears still attuned to the distinction between judging cases and making law.[16]
Nor ought the term be limited to the ancient and unwritten law of England.
One never can and never should forget the source of American common law,
nor should one ignore that its spirit pays homage to the wisdom embedded in
tradition. At the same time, one must remember that it is characteristic of
common law to survive the abandonment of particular customs and that by
the time of Independence common law had grown sufficiently at home in the
American colonies to withstand the shock of severance from the mother-root.
In defining common law, it is better to begin by noting that, in the time of
Coke as in our own, common law is said to exist wherever precedents have
the force of law, although traditionally precedents are seen to indicate common law, not create it. Precedents as well as statutes have the force of law, not
to encourage stubbornness or thwart improvement, but simply because justice demands that similar cases be similarly disposed of. Common law typically proceeds by the forms implied in the ancient phrase "due process," many
of which are still familiar today, most especially trial by jury. In contrast to
systems of Civil Law, based upon a code and employing a professional
magistracy, common law courts not only draw their law from precedent but
draw their judges from the practicing bar, as they draw their juries from the
community at large. Without doubt the common law has changed over time,

but as J. W. Gough has noted in a slightly different context, it is characteristic of common law to be oblivious to changes in itself and then even to erase the evidence of transformation.[17]

Common law differs from statutory law—and what I call the common law way of thinking differs from legal positivism—not merely in its source or its ground, but more essentially in its perspective. It is law seen from the point of view of a judge faced with a controversy, or a jury seeking to arrive at a verdict, not from the point of view of a sovereign monarch faced with an unmanageable people, or a sovereign people faced with civil war. To judge and jury, law need not begin with a statute, which in turn began with a sovereign authority, which began in consent; popular consent, after all, is given for a reason, and in a democracy it is given by the same sovereign that a jury represents. In court, statutes are law when statutes are there, but new cases come up which statutes do not cover, and, of course, what statutes themselves mean for a case requires interpretation. From the standpoint of the legislator, case law fills gaps between statutes, for new gaps open as circumstances change; but from the standpoint of the judge, statutes themselves fill gaps and revise precedents, though they are neither as comprehensive nor as precise as their authors might imagine.

Now common law and constitutional law are obviously not identical. Common law is unwritten law, while the most evident characteristic of American constitutionalism is its insistence on written constitutions. Moreover, common law and constitution are strictly speaking opposites in the hierarchy of kinds of law: Statutes override common law, while constitutions can override statutes. But to limit common law to its technical sense, as these objections would have it, obscures the deeper relations between common law and constitution. The Constitution of 1787 was formed in the midst of a common law tradition—not the least element of which was a habit of declaring fundamental law in written documents, such as Magna Charta, the Petition of Right, and the English Bill of Rights—and it established a judicial power that was expected, in certain fundamentals, to follow the familiar form of judging. Whatever the disposition of the delegates at Philadelphia on this matter, the adoption in the federal Bill of Rights of numerous protections and practices from common law (including, in the Seventh Amendment, mention of common law itself) made that intention clear. There were of course many particulars to be worked out once a federal judiciary was established, arising partly from the continued existence of competent common law judiciaries in the several states, partly from the conjunction of law and equity in a single set of courts; debates about the existence of a general federal common law in the strict or technical sense continued well into the present century.[18] Any thorough account of the development of the judicial power in the United States of course must treat these matters, but for my purposes here what is noteworthy is that, taking the wider definition, one sees the color of common law in their very settlement; in other words, they are settled by thinking through what Alexander Hamilton called "the nature and reason of the thing," in the context of particular cases where the questions were put to judgment.[19] For cases that arise within their jurisdiction, federal judges have authority to interpret all the various sorts of relevant law, and in such interpretation similar forms of reasoning are involved, since the particular cases and controversies, not the technically different forms of law, provide the beginning point of judicial analysis.[20] Specifically, since precedent operates in constitutional decisions, even if it operates in a limited way, the forms of constitutional adjudication itself entail a sort of common law. In short, if the marks of a common law judiciary include attention to the rule of precedent, trial by jury, a bench drawn from the bar, and the like, the federal judiciary qualifies, or at least deserves the presumption of probable cause, which is all that the author of an introduction needs to claim.

I have suggested that the spirit of common law includes a way of thinking about political liberty, not simply settling cases in court, and this suggestion might seem particularly inapt when one encounters the origin of common law in English monarchy. How can any sort of political liberty consistent with the republican principle of the sovereignty of the people, which the Constitution announces in its first words and which popular elections seem to reinforce, be attached to inherited law that preserves a certain independence from popular will? The modern liberal, of course, appeals to private rights privileged against infringement by the public power, though often enough when pressed to define those rights the liberal has recourse to a principle so expansive that little remains for political decision outside the juridical realm. In any event, this response is foreclosed to one who would plead for attention to the common law, for the distinction between public and private, or at least between public and private law, derives from the Civil Law, which the traditional common lawyer believed a foreign system of thought. That we often take the distinction between public and private for granted today is some indication how far we have moved from a common law background; but before we give its importation a hero's welcome, we might pause to consider whether that distinction has not more often sacrificed the rights of individuals to the state, or hidden oppression from common view, than it has preserved personal integrity against state power or lawless force.

In a sense it is the burden of this entire study to give a satisfactory answer to the question of the relation of popular sovereignty to political liberty anchored in common law. At the outset let me simply appeal to an observation of Alexis de Tocqueville, who wrote in 1835 at the height of Jacksonian Democracy: "Up till now no one in the United States has dared to profess the maxim that everything is allowed in the interests of society, an impious maxim apparently invented in an age of freedom in order to legitimize every future tyrant."[21] At the close of this brutal century we are no longer innocent of tyrannical slogans, but I take it as axiomatic in a constitutional regime that this claim remains impious to the public mind, and I take it as a point of departure for the political scientist to wonder why in the United States this still holds. I do not think the answer is judicial supremacy: This is not what the Constitution meant to establish, and it is not in fact what we have. There is something sovereign about judging in the United States, but it can be understood only by paying attention to the influence of common law in American political culture or constitutionalism, and to the impetus and form it gives to judgment, not only by a detached observer, but by citizens of the regime.

PART ONE
THE COMMON LAW JUDGMENT
OF SIR EDWARD COKE

Scholars today typically dismiss an older orthodoxy that held Sir Edward Coke's opinion in *Doctor Bonham's Case* an early precedent for judicial review, but in the pages that follow I argue that summary judgment on the case is an error caused by two related misunderstandings: The case has been misread, and what it might have signaled has been mistaken. *Bonham's* offers no comfort to the partisan of courts that sit as general censors upon the constitutionality of acts of other agents of government; but then, it has recently been argued, neither does *Marbury v. Madison*. Read without a predisposition to fit Coke's reasoning into modern categories, *Bonham's* is far more coherent than most scholars have allowed, and the possibility that it guided early American thought on the matter is much less remote. To amend the predisposition of the modern reader and to unfold the logic of the case, there is no better way than to engage Coke's legal thinking as a whole. For if *Bonham's Case* deserves notice as a precedent for *Marbury* and, say, *McCulloch v. Maryland*, it is not as an isolated instance but as representative for an entire mode of thought.

1
COKE'S LIFE AND LAW

In the preface to the eighth part of his *Reports*, Sir Edward Coke asks, what is the text of the common law? His answer includes mention of statutes, writs concerning common pleas, and forms of indictment and judgment in criminal cases, supplemented by four hundred years of yearbooks and records that are "commentaries and expositions of those laws." But in the American colonies, far from the seat of justice at Westminster and the Inns of Court, lawyers had to rely on printed law books, and by the late colonial period, in addition to the various Abridgments that summarized important cases, the "text of the common law" was above all the works of Edward Coke himself, supplemented and then later supplanted by the *Commentaries* of William Blackstone. Thomas Jefferson, who in his student days had once referred to Coke as an "old dull scoundrel" but who in later years saved his venom for Blackstone and his followers, testifies: "Coke Lyttleton was the universal law book of students, and a sounder Whig never wrote, nor of profounder learning in the orthodox doctrines of the British Constitution, or in what was called British liberties."[1] Of Coke's *Institutes* as a whole he wrote: "This work is executed with so much learning and judgment, that I do not recollect that a single position in it has ever been judicially denied. And although the work loses much of its value by its chaotic form, it may still [1814] be considered as the fundamental code of English Law."[2] Parts of Coke's *Reports*, meanwhile, had apparently first come to America on the *Mayflower*, and in 1647 the Massachusetts General Court had sent an order to England for a complete set.[3]

Cases from the *Reports* were also known to colonists through the Abridgments, and it was from one of these that James Otis, in his argument in *Paxton's Case of the Writ of Assistance*, cited Coke's famous remark in *Doctor Bonham's Case* that at one time was generally thought to have first formulated the doctrine of judicial review.[4] In upholding Bonham's suit for false imprisonment against the London College of Physicians, who claimed they acted under authority of a royal grant subsequently confirmed in Parliament, Coke wrote:

And it appears in our books, that in many cases, the common law will controul acts of parliament, and sometimes adjudge them to be utterly void: for when an act of parliament is against common right and reason, or repugnant, or impossible to be performed, the common law will controul it, and adjudge such act to be void.[5]

Much has been written about the adequacy of Coke's precedents, about whether his decision in *Bonham's Case* invoked higher law against parliamentary statute or merely involved statutory interpretation, and about the subsequent influence of the case and its doctrine in English as well as American law. From a reading of the case itself and of Coke's other writings this much is clear: To assess the meaning, much less the influence, of *Doctor Bonham's Case* for judicial review in the United States, one must delve into Coke's legal thought as a whole.

Coke's outlook on the law and on what we now call the constitution is in many ways foreign to American doctrine. The common law he describes is distant not only from contemporary American law but also from American law at the time the Constitution was drafted. Coke's common law is the law of England, determinedly insular in many respects and fervently national. It is principally concerned with feudal tenures, the subject of Littleton's treatise—the commentary upon which makes up the first, longest, and most commonly cited of Coke's *Institutes*.[6] The criminal law he discusses is replete with crimes of felony, with heresy, witchcraft, and sodomy included alongside treason, murder, rape, and robbery, all of which were punished by hanging—except those thought so heinous as to deserve burning at the stake. As the mention of heresy suggests, Coke's law has little room for the principle of religious liberty as we understand it (Jews and especially Catholics receive his scorn), and one modern commentator has charged Coke with originating prosecution for seditious libel, contrary to later American doctrines of freedom of speech and press. Coke discusses Parliament in the context of an account of the courts of the realm and their jurisdiction, but in the volume on jurisdiction he has no chapter on the office of the king, lacking the notion of separate legislative, executive, and judicial power which we Americans so take for granted.[7] In addition, his writing itself so offends modern standards of scholarship and method as to challenge the patience of even the most painstaking historian. It is medieval in its citation of numerous authorities, from the Bible to ancient authors to English law books; apparently chaotic in its organization, as Jefferson noted; variable even in its language, moving sometimes almost at random among English, Latin, Law French, Saxon, and ancient Greek; and, according to one modern scholar, obscurantist in its utter disregard for historical accuracy.

But one cannot dismiss the many features of Coke's writings that make him seem to us, as Blackstone said hardly a century after Coke's death, a bit pedantic and rather quaint,[8] at least without first seeing whether these qualities are thoughtless adornment now happily abandoned or considered and thus meaningful parts of Coke's thought. Nor, given the testimony of Coke's influence from Founders such as Jefferson, should he be dismissed without a hearing. Moreover, Coke's importance in the development of English law has been celebrated even by those historians who have done much to discredit his particular theories. The most glowing praise bestowed on him comes from the encyclopedic historian of English law, William Holdsworth: "What Shakespeare has been to literature, what Bacon has been to philosophy, what the translators of the Authorized Version of the Bible have been to religion, Coke has been to the public and private law of England."[9] Others are less effusive, but even Maitland, himself the most celebrated of the legal historians, acknowledges Coke's role in the simultaneous preservation of medieval law and its transformation to fit the modern world. Without prejudging the question of historical influence, Coke's thought is worth the work of unraveling, for it contains, amid the vast learning in law and the unequivocal devotion to English liberties, reflections on the nature of law and judging that transcend a particular time and place—though, ironically, precisely because they eschew transcendence.

AN ACTIVE FIGURE

Edward Coke was born in 1552 and lived until 1634.[10] A lawyer's son, he attended Cambridge, then trained for the bar himself and became a distinguished member at a young age. In 1593, sitting in his second Parliament, he was made Speaker of the House of Commons; the next year Elizabeth I appointed him attorney general (in preference to Francis Bacon), a post he kept when James I acceded to the throne in 1603. Three years later James made him chief justice of the Court of Common Pleas; after six years in that office, he was promoted (though this appears to have signaled the triumph of his enemies at court or the displeasure of the king) to be chief justice of the King's Bench. In 1616, James evidently became exasperated at Coke's various attempts to limit royal prerogative and dismissed him from his post and from London, but Coke was back on the Privy Council (where he had sat while a justice) one year later, after apparently forcing his daughter to marry the brother of the royal favorite. Elected to the Parliament of 1621, Coke was imprisoned in the Tower of London for his activities there but was released within the year and sat in the Parliaments of 1624 and 1625. He was excluded from the Parliament of 1626 by his selection by Charles I to be sheriff of Buckingham.[11] Elected to the Parliament of 1628, he played a leading role in drafting and guiding to passage the Petition of Right. After this Parliament, at the age of seventy-six, he went into retirement to complete his *Institutes,* the first part of which was published the same year. Eleven volumes of his *Reports* had appeared during his years as attorney general and chief justice; he evidently saw his *Institutes* as a continuation of these, for in the preface to the *First Institutes* (often called *Coke upon Littleton*), he thanks God for assisting him in bringing "this twelfth Worke to an end: In the eleuen Bookes of our *Reports* we haue related the opinions and iudgements of others; but herein we haue set downe our owne." The remainder of his works appeared posthumously. Seized by the Crown as Coke lay on his deathbed, the *Second, Third,* and *Fourth Institutes* were not published until 1642-44, and then at the order of the Long Parliament; the two final volumes of his *Reports* appeared in the 1650s, though modern scholars have expressed doubts as to their authenticity.[12]

The variety of Coke's career and the jumbled appearance of his writings provide scholars with a ready explanation for the many contradictions they find in his life and work. Even his loyal defender, biographer Catherine Drinker Bowen, reconciles his ruthless prosecution of Sir Walter Raleigh for treason with his own pronouncements from the bench and later from the floor of Parliament in favor of limiting the king's prerogative by saying, "Coke was above all a fighter, a born advocate who loved to feel the courtroom floor beneath his feet."[13] Others, skimming quickly or not knowing where to look, dispute the reading of *Bonham's Case* as a precedent for judicial review by noting its absence from the *Institutes'* commentary on Parliament. But in fact, *Bonham's* appears in the *Institutes* at least four times, at points that appear entirely logical once one understands the case and is attuned to Coke's way of reasoning. Moreover, as the quotation above suggests, Coke himself thought his work possessed a certain integrity, if not simple unity; he cites his *Reports* throughout the *Institutes* and refers in each part of the *Institutes* to the other parts.

If one assumes that Coke's works contain, as he suggests, a certain order and that their reputed lack of method, as we understand method, owes more to their author's choice than to his carelessness, one acquires a key by which to unlock his thought. One gleans some sense of his own approach to authorship from what he says of Thomas Littleton's *Tenures*:

Hee hath left this Booke, as a figure of that higher and nobler part (that is) of the excellent and rare endowments of his minde, especially in the profound knowledge of the fundamentall Laws of this Realm. He that diligently reads this his excellent Worke, shall behold the child and figure of his mind, which the more often he beholds the visiall [usual?] lines and well obserues him, the more shall he iustly admire the iudgement of our Author, and increase his owne.[14]

In a subsequent paragraph he calls the book "the most perfect and absolute Worke that euer was written in any humane Science," but precedes this with the assertion, "Certain it is that when a great learned man (who is long in making) dyeth, much learning dyeth with him." In short, Coke suggests that no text can do more than collect learning and place it before a student; learning lives in the student himself, in the judgment formed and the knowledge gained, rather than in books alone. Several pages later Coke explains that he calls his writings *Institutes* "because my desire is, they should institute, and instruct the studious, and guid him in a readie way to the knowledge of the nationall Lawes of England." In the epilogue to the commentary on Littleton, he notes that he leaves to the student the task of compiling an index, since "Tables and Abridgements are most profitable to them that make them." In the preface to his first volume of *Reports,* after explaining his practice of seeking out the "right reason and rule of the Judges" in the cases he documents, scorning those who "stuff their studies with wandering and masterless reports," Coke outlines the elements of legal education:

> In troth, reading, hearing, conference, meditation, and recordation, are necessary I confess to the knowledge of the common law, because it consisteth upon so many, and almost infinite particulars: but an orderly observation in writing is most requisite of them all; for reading without hearing is dark and irksome, and hearing without reading is slippery and uncertain, neither of them truly yield seasonable fruit without conference, without meditation and recordation, nor all of them together without due and orderly observation: *scribe sapientiam tempore vacuitatis tuae* [a scholar's wisdom comes from ample leisure], saith Solomon.[15]

Though writing and reading are critical, they are only steps in the larger activity of learning the law. The treatise has its purpose, but it is rather propaedeutic than definitive.

As author, then, Coke remains the man of action, for the knowledge he conveys is a practical science, which achieves its end in forming the judgment of one who studies. In fact, Coke's attitude to learning defines not only his understanding of texts but his understanding of the law itself. In the epilogue on Littleton, Coke comments favorably on Littleton's remark that the *Tenures* contains passages that

> are not altogether Law, yet such things shall make thee more apt, and able to vnderstand and apprehend the Arguments and the reasons of the

Law, etc. For by the Arguments and Reasons in the Law, a man more sooner shall come to the certaintie and knowledge of the Law.[16]

Citing the adage *Ratio est anima legis* [reason is the soul of the law], Coke proceeds to elaborate upon Littleton's text:

For then are we sayd to know the Law, when we apprehend the reason of the Law, that is, when we bring the reason of the Law so to our own reason, that we perfectly understand it as our own, and then and never before we have such an excellent and inseparable propertie and ownership therein, as we can never lose it, nor any man take it from us, and will direct us (the learning of the Law is so chayned together) in many other Cases.

The law, to Coke, is thus a science in something like the Aristotelian sense of a practical science, joining reason and knowledge of particulars, yet contained not in books as a body of knowledge but in the minds of those who can use it.[17] This is why, despite Coke's insistence on recording cases, documenting legal developments, and studying old books, the common law itself remains unwritten. It comes as no surprise that he ends the volume by invoking the classical virtues: "And for a farewell to our Jurisprudent I wish unto him the gladsome light of Jurisprudence, the loueliness of Temperance, the stability of Fortitude, and the soliditie of Justice." Aristotle had described the virtuous man as completing his virtue with prudence though he saw legislative and political prudence as two among several kinds of prudence, and located judging as a further subdivision of political prudence.[18] Though Coke apparently agrees with Aristotle in his understanding of the nature of prudence as a whole, he takes Aristotle's claim that justice is the *Architectonica Virtus* to mean that true prudence is jurisprudence and that the completely virtuous man must be a judge, or at least a man of judgment.

WHAT COMMON LAW IS AND IS NOT

After what has been said, it will come as no surprise to learn that Coke nowhere develops a systematic definition of what we today would call the concept of law. He does define law several times by citing Latin maxims: *Lex est ratio summa, quae jubet quae sunt utilia et necessaria, et contria prohibet* [law is the perfection of reason, which commands what is useful and necessary, and forbids the contrary], or *Lex est sanctio justa, jubens honesta, et prohibens contraria* [law is a just sanction, commanding what is right, and prohibiting the contrary].[19] But it is typical of these citations both that they differ slightly from one formulation to another and that they arise in the course of commentary upon particular statutes, cases, or legal texts. From these various definitions, and more especially from Coke's commentaries upon the law, one can usefully collect the following propositions: (1) Law is concerned first of all with right and wrong, not simply with policy, as we tend to assume today; (2) the law Coke is concerned with is English law, especially English common law, not universal law, and it is characterized above all by land law and due process, which together form the basis of English liberties; (3) while it belongs to one land, law has a variety of sources, many of which are in the distant past, though the question of law's origin is altogether secondary to the question of its rightness; (4) law is rational, though one must take special care to understand what Coke means by legal reason; (5) finally, what is law remains to some extent a question that can never be definitively answered, though the tentativeness or openness of law itself is worthy of notice. Each of these propositions merits discussion in turn.

(1) The concern of the law with right and wrong is evident in the Latin quotations above and was self-evident to Coke and most of his contemporaries. It is not a point to which he devotes much discussion, but it is assumed at every step. Property rights are not simply useful conventions for dividing up social wealth; the many rights in and about what we call property are for Coke ancient and vested privileges, and it is of the utmost importance to him that they be justly settled. Likewise, crimes are not defined as conduct society has simply chosen to forbid. Rather, Coke speaks of crimes as moral wrongs, and though he occasionally notes the severity of a penalty and, at the end of the *Third Institutes,* devoted to criminal law, stresses the importance of preventing crime as well as punishing it, he leaves no doubt of his opinion that convicted felons get what they deserve.

In the preface or epilogue of each part of the *Institutes,* Coke invokes God's blessing, and he frequently cites the authority of the Bible: He apparently takes it for granted that divine authority lies behind the law. At the same time, like his predecessors Sir John Fortescue and Christopher St. Germain, he distinguishes English law from both the law of the Pentateuch and natural law.[20] He refers to Moses as "a Judge, and the first writer of Law," more a model for himself than a divine authority.[21] He occasionally mentions natural law—his most celebrated discussion is in *Calvin's Case*—but his purpose in referring to it there is quite restricted: It is not the theoretical basis of all law but a useful reference in discovering the law in relation to birthright and allegiance.[22] As an attorney, a judge, and a commentator, Coke insisted upon maintaining a sharp distinction between ecclesiastical jurisdiction and the jurisdiction of the king's courts, so as to protect the latter from infringement by the former. The law Coke discusses may refer to God and nature, but the authority of its judges is altogether independent of clerics and priests.

(2) Canon law was foreign to the common law not only because it was clerics' law but because it was based upon the principles of Civil Law. Although Coke sometimes cites Justinian and indeed borrows Justinian's title for his *Institutes,* he presents common law and Civil Law as opposite sorts of law.[23] It is difficult to judge whether Coke's conviction of the inherent superiority of common law to Civil Law leads him to exaggerate the purely English character of the former or whether his English patriotism leads him to exaggerate the independence of common law from Civil Law. In either case, Coke insists that the common law is the very essence of English justice. In the preface to the third volume of his *Reports,* he shows himself willing, though not without doubt, to accept that the origin of English law is the legendary King Brutus, who fled Troy for Britain in the twelfth century B.C.; he considers it firmly proven that early English laws were written in Greek. Throughout history the ancient laws were often lost, then often recovered; indeed, English history in his hands is largely shown in this pattern. He refuses to acknowledge the Norman Conquest as such, much less to admit that English law owes anything substantial to practices introduced by the Conqueror; William simply asserted a legal claim to the throne, as many did before and after him, and the similarity between English law and Norman custom is due to the incorporation of the English into the Norman, not the reverse. Even the use of French in the courts of law proves nothing for Coke, since the English kings also held territory in France. Moreover, he argues that the political institutions of England descend, like the law, from time out of mind; he finds evidence not only of sheriffs but of Parliaments before 1066.[24] The common law, in short, may be a standard of right and wrong that respects God's preeminence, but it is as nearly indigenous to England as one can imagine.

What J. G. A. Pocock has called the insular character of Coke's legal thought appears also in the phrase from the twenty-ninth chapter of Magna Charta that Coke did so much to celebrate: The common law is "the law of the land." Though this has come to mean "the law of England," its most elementary meaning deserves attention, for common law was first of all the law that governed the possession and use of the soil.[25] Pocock argues that Coke overlooks the feudal nature of English law, in particular its origin in feudal practice established on the continent and imported to Britain with the Norman Conquest. Yet whatever might be said of Coke's neglect of similar institutions on the continent and his failure to derive many particulars from the practices of conquering tribes, the law he describes does include such feudal notions as enfeoffment, tenancy, homage, and service. Those who argue the modernity of Coke's work note the emphasis he places on non-feudal forms of property, such as the copyhold and the freehold. What is less noted is the fact that Coke of course does not acknowledge a fundamental distinction between feudal and modern forms of ownership. The law he describes is not built upon the distinction between public and private so integral to our own thinking. Indeed, as I suggested previously, the distinction between public and private law descends from Civil Law, not common law. Fealty, for Coke, defines the relation of all subjects to the king. But the embodiment of its principles in law shows its affinity to what we now call citizenship; Coke, who draws no sharp distinction between feudal practices and those of either the ancient or his contemporary world, treats the rights and duties of public and private life interchangeably.[26]

That Coke does not restrict the "law of the land" to land law, however, is apparent in his commentary on the twenty-ninth chapter of Magna Charta, in which the phrase occurs. Historians credit Coke with reviving Magna Charta from the obscurity into which it had fallen under the Tudors; his praise of it shows he holds it second to none as a declaration of fundamental English law. To the twenty-ninth chapter he gives an especially broad reading: It extends to all free men *and* women; it guarantees due process in all criminal proceedings—including the right to indictment by grand jury instead of accusation by information, the right to trial by jury, the right to answer one's accusers, and the privilege of habeas corpus; it even forbids royal grants of monopoly, for "generally all monopolies are against this great Charter, because they are against the liberty and freedome of the Subject, and against the Law of the Land."[27] Indeed, the term *liberties* itself receives a broad stroke from Coke's brush. While liberties can refer more specifically to the freedom of subjects from interference in basic pursuits, it is also used to comprehend the whole of the fundamental laws of the realm, so that Magna Charta is sometimes styled "the Great Charter of the Liberties of England, so called of the effect, because they make men free."[28] As Coke offers no philosophic discussion of law, he refrains from any precise definition of liberty or liberties. One might conjecture that he sees liberties as the obverse of the laws; the same respect for particularity implicit in his embrace of the municipal character of law and his celebration of its infinite particulars can be found in the respect accorded individuals by English law in Coke's hands. Whether these forms of respect can be grounded in the doctrines of divine providence on the one hand and man's free will on the other, Coke the legal scholar does not say. It is clear that the liberties he describes are not necessarily political, though he does include as liberties the privileges of members of Parliament.[29] But neither are they limited to a right to be left alone and ignored by the larger world.

(3) In part because of its antiquity, there is no single code of the common law, in contrast, of course, to the Civil Law accepted not only on the continent but in several kinds of English courts. As noted, Coke lists some of the sources of law: statutes, writs, legal forms, records of cases.[30] What is

remarkable about this list, and indeed about the common law itself, is the fluidity of these sources—the inability of one unlearned in the law to know a priori where the law to any given case is likely to be found. To be sure, rules govern how each source of law is to be applied, but these rules themselves are diverse. Moreover, the law as Coke presents it includes many maxims as well as particular rules, and these maxims have a certain force in law, as Coke's judging and reporting makes plain, not least in the celebrated *Bonham's Case*.

Most apt to confuse the modern reader is Coke's treatment of statutes as sources of law, for we today often take for granted the priority of legislation and therefore of statutory law. Some scholars claim that Coke and the medievals generally had no concept of legislation but thought that law was only found, never made.[31] Though not incorrect in noticing that Coke does not share the modern concept of legislation, this claim exaggerates the matter by forcing earlier thought to conform to modern distinctions. Coke clearly acknowledges that statutes can correct the common law and thus that they take precedence over the common law rules they revise. At the same time, he would never admit that the only purpose of legislation is to make new law: Statutes sometimes simply declare what the law already is, rather than change it into something different.[32] Even the correction of abuses by statute may serve to reinstitute the good old law that had been abrogated by evil design or foolish innovation. Coke's celebration of the antiquity and the excellence of the common law makes it difficult to deny his conservatism, but he himself is not averse to all change, provided it be a clear improvement. Even leaving aside the many instances in which legal historians credit him with transforming the law while claiming merely to follow precedents, he acknowledges in the *Institutes* the novelty of writing in English and considers the plan of the later *Institutes*—providing a complete table of common law crimes and an analysis of all the courts of England—to be altogether new.[33] Indeed, Coke's texts belie the rigid traditionalism so often attributed to him. At the end of the preface to the *First Reports* he cites a favorite proverb, that "out of the old fields must spring and grow the new corn," and he concludes the epilogue to the final part of the *Institutes* by asking future scholars to correct his errors, assuring them, "Blessed be the amending hand."

THE REASON OF THE COMMON LAW

(4) From the standpoint of judicial review, as suggested by the earlier quotation from *Doctor Bonham's Case,* the most significant principle in Coke's understanding of the law is his insistence upon the equation of law and reason. Over a century later, in the midst of the Enlightenment, Blackstone

would claim that the assertion that the law is reasonable meant only that unreasonable precedents have been excluded from it.[34] This captures something of Coke's earlier meaning, but something is lost as well. Coke certainly did not think that law could be constructed by reason alone, like geometry, from a few axioms. The reason Coke describes is neither so pure, so comprehensive, nor so authoritative.

In one of his most famous passages (and personally his favorite, for it echoes throughout his works), Coke writes:

> For reason is the life of the Law, nay the Common Law it selfe is nothing else but reason, which is to be understood of an artificiall perfection of reason gotten by long studie, obseruation and experience and not every mans naturall reason, for *nemo nascitur artifex* [no one is born skillful]. This legall reason *est summa ratio* [is the highest reason]. And therefore if all the reason that is dispersed into so many severall heads were united into one, yet could he not make such a Law as the Law of England is, because by many succession of ages it hath beene fined and refined by an infinite number of graue and learned men, and by long experience grown to such a perfection for the gouernment of this Realme, as the old rule may be iustly verified of it *Neminem oportet esse sapientiorem legibus*: No man (out of his owne private reason) ought to be wiser than the Law, which is the perfection of reason.[35]

Reason is not original and comprehensive; rather, it takes what is given and works upon it, improves it. It does this by bringing to bear not logic alone, but logic together with wide learning. The reason Coke appeals to is not a theoretical but a practical faculty. It is certainly not mere discretion, but neither is it logic devoid of experience. It is a trained way of thinking, not arbitrary but also not apodictic.

This definition of the word reason is confirmed by the several different uses to which Coke puts it. In the preface to the *First Institutes,* he mentions "these two faithfull witnesses in matters of Law, Authority, and Reason," suggesting a distinction between them; likewise, in the epilogue to the same volume, he comments upon the passage in Littleton, quoted previously, by admitting that reasons for laws "are not altogether Law." But the melding of authority and reason pervades Coke's work. In the preface to the *Second Institutes,* he distinguishes his commentaries from the glosses and interpretations made upon the text of the Civil Law by many "Doctors of equall degree and authority." As advocates, the civilians produce what are "in a manner private interpretations," introducing further uncertainty into law, so that "the professors of that noble Science say, That it is like a Sea full of waves." In contrast, the commentaries of English lawyers consist of "the resolutions of Iudges in

Courts of Justice in judiciall courses of proceeding, either related and reported in our Books, or extant in judiciall Records." The work of the commentator is to collect what has been adjudged with authority and, by his collection, to produce certainty, "the Mother and Nurse of repose and quietnesse, and . . . not like to the waves of the Sea." The commentator's reason evidently performs the work of collection, silently discovering order in multiplicity but making no independent claims. At the same time, judicial decisions as well as legal commentaries enhance their authority over time as, amid the "infinite, several, and divers cases," "sweet consent and amity" among judges becomes apparent.[36]

Coke also speaks of reasons in the plural in several contexts, and these confirm the practical and particular connotation in his use of the term. In the preface to the *Third Reports,* he speaks of the need, in "cases of importance and difficulty," to report not only the judgment in the case but also the reasons upon which the judgment is founded. "Wise and learned men do before they judge, labour to reach to the depth of all the reasons of the case in question, but in their judgments express not any," for this would create records like *"Elephantini libri* of infinite length, and in mine opinion lose somewhat of their present authority and reverence" (as the experience of our own century amply illustrates). Still, when it is necessary to give reasons, Coke's advice is "that then he set down all authorities, precedents, reasons, arguments, and inferences whatsoever that may be probably applied to the case in question, for some will be persuaded or drawn by one, and some by another, according as the capacity or understanding of the reader or hearer is."[37] The multiplicity and particularity of reasons appear likewise in the interpretation of statutes, for it is imperative to know "whether the statutes were introductory of a new law, declaratory of the old, or mixt, and thereby perceive what was the reason and cause of the making of the same, which will greatly conduce to the true understanding thereof."[38] Reasons thus are presumed to lie behind all law, whether grounded in statutes or judgments in court, though knowing the reason for any law may require study and learning. At the same time, once the reason is uncovered, one has a key to knowing what the law is and therefore how it is to be applied to a case at hand.

But for the interpretation of *Doctor Bonham's Case* and for the subsequent history of judicial review, the most interesting use of the term *reason* occurs in those passages where Coke comments on laws that are "against reason." This phrase appears a number of times in Littleton's *Tenures,* and Coke draws attention to it repeatedly in his remarks, even cross-referencing its various occurrences.[39] Apparently it first surfaces in section 80 of Littleton's treatise, when, in the context of admitting the variety of customs of tenancy on different manors, the author qualifies the acceptance of local customs: "Whatsoeuer is not against reason, may well bee admitted and allowed." Coke notes simply what he later elaborates in the passage quoted earlier at length: "This is not to be understood of euery unlearned mans reason, but of artificiall and legal reason warranted by authority of Law: *Lex est summa ratio*."[40]

In the subsequent passages, Littleton speaks more directly about interpretations of law that cannot be admitted because they would be "against reason," or, as he usually adds, "inconvenient." In section 138, where Coke meets the argument "against reason" with the lengthy passage on the artificial perfection of reason in law, he treats the argument from inconvenience separately: "An argument drawne from inconuenience is forcible in Law as hath beene obserued before, and shall bee often hereafter. *Nihil quod est inconvenient est licitum* [nothing that is inconvenient is lawful]. And the Law that is the perfection of reason cannot suffer anything that is inconuenient."[41] An inconvenience in law appears to be a general rule that would conflict with other rules of law, going against the web of consistency the law weaves. In the passage under discussion, Coke proceeds to distinguish an inconvenience from a mischief: "It is better saith the Law to suffer a mischiefe (that is particular to one) then an inconuenience that may prejudice many." The actual difficulty Littleton is discussing makes clear that the widespread mischief in question is not a physical harm but a violation of feudal principle; for at issue is the kind of service a tenant must render to his lord, and the inconvenience Littleton imagines is a form of tenancy that would involve no service whatsoever, thereby undermining the principle that lords deserve some service from their tenants, or the more general principles of hierarchy or reciprocity. Several other uses of the term *inconvenience* occur in analogous passages in Littleton, where the legality of a practice is determined by appeal to its consistency with law as a whole. Indeed, the literal meaning of the term, from the Latin and the French, is "inconsistency."[42]

Coke often simply equates the argument from inconvenience with the argument "against reason."[43] In one of the passages he cross-references to the discussions of inconvenience but in which only the term *against reason* appears, Littleton repeats his earlier claim that local customs against reason are void; but as in the instances of inconvenience, the violation of reason under examination is a violation of the order of feudal rank.[44] At other points in the *Institutes*—for example, in a discussion of the interpretation of general language in a statute governing inheritance—Coke appears to use *reason* to refer not to a first principle but to a guarantor of consistency in the law as a whole: When "the words of the statute are generall, . . . the construction thereof shall be according to the reason of the Common Law."[45] And in a section reminiscent of *Bonham's Case*, Coke draws attention to a passage in which Littleton declares void, "because it is against reason," a prescription that would make a lord his own judge in a case of distraint: "And so such prescription, or any other prescription used, if it be against Reason, this ought not, nor will not be allowed before Iudges, *Quia malus usus abolendus est* [because a bad custom is to be abolished]."[46]

Except perhaps in this last instance, Coke seems to use the term *reason* in a sense that corresponds with and indeed clarifies his notion of an artificial perfection of reason in the law. Reason is not the sole cause of law; it takes much for granted, from custom, perhaps, or from authority. But reason permeates the law: testing whether any proposition advanced conforms to the law as a whole, determining when law must be reformed to meet abuses, explaining authorities and thus preparing them to serve as precedents in future cases that may arise. It serves to "fine and refine" the law, to complete and perfect it, but only through the common work and experience of many learned men, little by little over a long time. Reason is the life of the law, as Coke often says, because it is through the action of reason that law grows to meet new cases. Its action makes the law a tradition, built on the assent of many learned men over many generations, though it is reason that elicits assent, not assent that defines reason.

(5) These remarks lead to the fifth general proposition about law: The law remains open not only in regard to its sources but also in regard to its future. This observation about law, or at least law in a common law environment, would be widely recognized today by legal scholars of many descriptions, but not necessarily in Coke's sense. Legal realists consider law open-ended because they see in it the reflection of the ruling opinions or interests of society at large; as these change over time, the law must change with them. Critics of realism, such as Ronald Dworkin, see the open-endedness of law not only over time but at every moment; law, Dworkin argues, is essentially controversial, always willing to yield to the most cogent party (or judge).[47] For Coke, the incompleteness of law implies neither a fundamentally shifting basis nor a host of rules ever at the mercy of the cleverest suitor. Law is incomplete because new cases arise, new mischiefs develop, and new reasons are discovered. Still, law always strives for completion, for perfection, and Coke appears to assume that the law must be approached not only as though it wants to be perfect but as though it almost is. This is why his writings simultaneously exude confidence and profess modesty. It would personalize the law in a way foreign to Coke's thought to say that law itself is always striving for a perfection it approaches; at the same time, he insists upon this attitude in the student of law—and the lawyer and judge. Repeatedly, Coke describes his labors in writing as opening windows on the law: improving perspective or letting in light, but never conquering or capturing their object.[48] Coke seems to think that the law—and thus a learned judge, who is, after all, the voice of law in court—can answer any question put to it, but at the same time he is aware that not every question has been asked.

CONSTITUTION, KING, AND PARLIAMENT

THE MISSING CONSTITUTION

As a background to understanding Coke's contribution to judicial review, one would suppose that an outline of his general thoughts about law should be followed by a discussion of his constitutional theory. One has begun to understand Coke only when one comes to see how mistaken it would be to assert that he had such a theory at all. Modern commentators readily note that Coke has but a rudimentary concept of a written constitution, that he antedates the modern doctrine of the separation of powers, and that he appears not to accept the modern concept of legislation, much less the concept of the sovereign as the source of all law. What they often fail to observe is that Coke not only seems ignorant of the modern political science his contemporaries and immediate successors began to develop, but he also apparently rejects much that the classical political science available to him might have offered.

In his influential article on *Doctor Bonham's Case,* Theodore F. T. Plucknett argues that Coke was more than a lawyer or "an antiquary of great distinction. . . : for to all this he added the character of a political philosopher."

> Urged by a presentiment of the coming conflict of Crown and Parliament, he felt the necessity of curbing the rising arrogance of both, and looked back upon his country's legal history to find the means. . . . [F]rom [the Year Books'] forbidding mass of obsolete technicalities [he] raised a harvest of political theory which was destined to be the food of far-distant states to which he had never given a thought.
>
> The solution which Coke found was in the idea of a fundamental law which limited Crown and Parliament indifferently.[1]

But if Coke indeed possessed what could be called a political theory, he kept it scrupulously hidden in the background. For he never addressed systematically, or even explicitly, the question fundamental to political theory—who rules?—even to answer it by saying, the laws. His question is always, rather, what is law? And his responses make clear that politics is an activity either within law or beside law, rather than that law is a product of politics.

In the third book of the *Politics,* which Coke occasionally cites, Aristotle discusses the different forms of constitution or regime (*politeia*). At one point he asks whether the rule of law might comprise a further regime and concludes it does not, since the laws in every city reflect its regime, for those who rule make the laws.[2] Aristotle returns to this question at the end of Book III, however, discussing absolute kingship and whether it is better to be ruled by law or by the best man.[3] The passage is complex and difficult, since Aristotle presents arguments on both sides, suggesting that godlike men might rule absolutely but that usually it is best that authority be exercised through law. Law and virtue each seem incomplete without the other for Aristotle, and it remains unclear whether they can be made neatly to complement each other or whether one must always assert priority to the other's neglect.

Despite Coke's familiarity with Aristotle, he does not discuss the different forms of regime or address the question of the problematic relation of law and political rule. He once raises the issue, noting that in making new laws one must consider "under what form of commonwealth the law-makers be governed; for one consideration is requisite where the government is monarchical, another when it is aristocratical, and a third when it is democratical." Yet this is the extent of his comment and, as far as I can determine, all he ever had to say on the matter.[4] When he speaks of what we call political institutions, it is always in the context of law. Indeed, in his systematic account of English institutions of government, he sets out to treat them all as different courts, and he specifies that he means by the term *court* not the entourage around the monarch but "a Tribunall, or Court of Justice." His question is not which is sovereign but what is the jurisdiction of each. He speaks of their "admirable benefit, beauty, and delectable variety," not their composite form. Coke appears to accept Fortescue's distinction between a kingdom ruled regally and one ruled regally and politically—between a king's absolute rule and his rule in concert with others—and he would agree with Fortescue that England is an example of the latter. But while Fortescue emphasizes the determinative influence of the regime for the prosperity of the country and for its laws, Coke gives no priority to the form of regime.[5] For him, the body politic is a part of the laws, not the laws a part or consequence of the body politic.

This is not necessarily to say, however, that Coke takes issue with Aristotle on the question of whether the rule of law can be a distinct form of regime. Again, he hardly addresses the matter. But even to ask the question is perhaps already to decide the issue in favor of the priority of the regime and hence of politics. It is to look at the political world from the detached perspective of the political philosopher or from the engaged perspective of a citizen considering political change. Coke's perspective, at least in his writings if not in his own mind, is always from within the realm, within the law, within a tradition of learning. To the political philosopher or the revolutionary citizen, this viewpoint is partial. But to the learned lawyer, the perspective of the political theorist is condemned to distortion, for it is the claim of a single, imperfect mind to comprehensive vision. For Coke even to have formulated a theory of fundamental law would require of him a perspective he avoids; he does indeed speak of fundamental law or laws, but not as something that could be distinctly marked, much less enthroned. The common law is clearly fundamental; Magna Charta is a fundamental statute of the realm; the form of Parliament seems fundamental, though like the common law, it is not unchangeable.[6] But more fundamental is the whole that all of these comprise. If in Aristotle the regime is the whole that explains the many facets of political life, for Coke it is the law.

To circumscribe all politics by law might seem to deprive political life of both its spontaneity and its urgency; law, after all, involves obeying due process, and that means following regular patterns and taking one's time. It is certainly true that Coke promotes political action that proceeds by deliberation and avoids arbitrariness. But one must recall that Coke does not see law as so mechanical or bureaucratic a force as do we. The prudence of the judge is not the same as the rule-mindedness of the bureaucrat; it is at once freer and more responsible, for it is the judgment of a living mind, not the mandate of an impersonal rule-book.[7] Nor should one dismiss the priority Coke assigns to law as the characteristic myopia of a lawyer. In his career, he had held many different places in English government, whose contemporary American equivalents are found in all three branches. Moreover, the law was not his exclusive concern in any of his posts. On the Privy Council, his advice was reputedly much valued on matters of trade. In Parliament, even while leading the effort to secure the Petition of Right, he served on several other committees, chairing the committee on grievances, where he heard the complaints, for instance, of London brewers, and from the floor he spoke on issues ranging from the East India trade to the navigability of rivers.[8] He was a man of wide experience and ability, whose concentration on the importance of law is more profitably viewed as an informed choice than as a reflex of professional loyalty.

THE KING AND THE LAW

Though not a constitutional theorist, Coke did attach special importance to the king and to Parliament, and his views on their rights and functions deserve examination. From the American perspective of judicial review, as well as from the British perspective of parliamentary sovereignty, Coke's statements on the power of Parliament are especially interesting; but from his own perspective, and that of the century he helped set in motion, it is proper to begin with his view of the monarch. Despite his fierce loyalty to Queen Elizabeth, Coke's quarrels with James I when he was chief justice and his subsequent activities in Parliament have gained him the reputation as a forebear of the English revolutionaries. Several memoranda he had kept which were published in the posthumous volumes of *Reports* apparently confirm the picture of a bold defender of the law against the claims of prerogative.

The first item, recorded as *Prohibitions del Roy,* describes a famous meeting of the king with all the judges on Sunday, 10 November 1608.[9] James sought confirmation of an opinion given him by the archbishop, which would sanction the king in taking certain cases away from the courts and deciding them himself "in his royal person." Coke reports that he answered,

> in the presence, and with the consent of all the Judges of England, and Barons of the Exchequer, that the King in his own person cannot adjudge any case, either criminal, as treason, felony, etc. or betwixt party and party, concerning his inheritance, chattels, or goods, etc. but this ought to be determined and adjudged in some court of justice, according to the law and custom of England.

After Coke recited the precedents, James responded "that he thought the law was founded upon reason, and that he and others had reason, as well as the Judges," to which Coke replied:

> that true it was, that God had endowed his Majesty with excellent science, and great endowments of nature; but His Majesty was not learned in the laws of his realm of England, and causes which concern the life, or inheritance, or goods, or fortunes of his subjects, are not to be decided by natural reason but by the artificial reason and judgment of law, which law is an act [art?] which requires long study and experience, before that a man can attain to the cognizance of it: and that the law was the golden met-wand [measuring rod] and measure to try the causes of the subjects; and which protected his Majesty in safety and peace: with which the King was greatly offended, and said, that then he should be under the law, which was treason to affirm, as he said; to which I said, that Bracton saith, *quod Rex non debet esse sub homine, sed sub Deo et lege* [the king ought to be under no man, but under God and the law].

Historians doubt whether in fact Coke stood up to the king quite so brashly: A letter written by one present at the scene has James in "high indignation," "Which the Lo. Cooke perceaving fell flatt on all fower; humbly beseeching his Majestie to take compassion on him and to pardon him if he thought zeale had gone beyond his dutie and allegiance." Coke holds to his opinion on the question in the *Institutes,* not only quoting the passage on the artificial reason of law and the metaphor of the golden met-wand in other contexts but speaking directly, if discreetly, to the matter at issue in the chapter of the *Fourth Institutes* on the Court of King's Bench: "The King hath wholly left matters of judicature according to his lawes to his Judges."[10]

Another case in the posthumous *Reports* has Coke and his colleagues rejecting the chancellor's argument in support of novel proclamations by the king prohibiting construction of new buildings in London and the processing of wheat starch. The chancellor had asserted that "every precedent ought to have a commencement":

> To which I answered, that true it is that every precedent hath a commencement; but when authority and precedent is wanting, there is need of great consideration, before that any thing of novelty shall be established, and to provide that this be not against the law of the land: for I said, that the King cannot change any part of the common law, nor create any offence by his proclamation, which was not an offence before, without Parliament.[11]

In this case, the judges ruled that the king's prerogative of proclamation extended only to prohibit beforehand dangers "which it will be too late to prevent afterwards," and that beyond this, there were "divers precedents of proclamations which are utterly against law and reason, and for that void." In sum, "the King hath no prerogative, but that which the law of the land allows him." Still, despite the accusation made in the course of his dismissal as chief justice that he had interfered with the royal prerogative, another case in the *Twelfth Reports* shows Coke's consistency in squaring prerogative and law, this time upholding the monarch's claim. In the *Case of Non Obstante, or Dispensing Power,* Coke notes that "No Act [of Parliament] can bind the K.[ing] from any Prerogative which is sole and inseparable to his Person, but that he may dispense with it by a *non obstante*"; hence, for example, "the King could not be restrained by any Act to make a Pardon; for Mercy and Power to Pardon is a Prerogative incident, solely and inseparably to the Person of the King."[12]

Coke's insistence on the legal boundaries of prerogative is illustrated as well by his treatment of what came to be called the prerogative courts, such as the High Commission and the Star Chamber, which had grown so hateful to Parliamentarians by the time of the Civil War. Coke acknowledges the legitimacy of these courts, but he is careful to restrict their jurisdiction according to law. He insists that the Star Chamber, whose establishment historians attribute to the Tudors, is an ancient court, dating back at least to the reign of Henry III. Though Coke says that "it is the most honourable Court, (our Parliament excepted) that is in the Christian world," he notes the limits to its ability to punish those brought before it and advises its members that "novelties without warrant of presidents [precedents] are not to be allowed."[13] Through a lengthy discourse on the interpretation of general words in statutes, he draws boundaries to the jurisdiction of the High Commission, the court charged with policing offenses against the English church. More generally, Coke's practice of issuing prohibitions to ecclesiastical courts, thereby staying proceedings that he thought belonged in common law courts, together with his charges of praemunire against ecclesiastical judges who proceeded in cases in which he thought they were not authorized, earned him many enemies. And his struggle to limit the jurisdiction of the Chancery—by his insistence that the court of equity could not disturb decisions of common law courts—likewise demonstrates his commitment to restricting the various courts besides the common law courts and of course further explains his fall from favor.[14]

Holdsworth considers Coke's defense of common law against new courts that were tools of royal aggrandizement one of his great achievements.[15] What is most remarkable to us today is not that Coke would limit the jurisdiction of competing courts but that he seems to leave little room for political activity that takes place in a nonjudicial setting. For instance, in the *Fourth Institutes,* in which he undertakes to define the jurisdiction of all the courts of the commonwealth—a task as novel as freshly breaking ice, Coke claims, and as complex as "the raising of [a] great and honourable building"—he includes the "Councell Board" (the Privy Council) among them, not in their capacity as judges in the Star Chamber, but in their function to "consult of, and for the publique good, and the honour, defence, safety, and profit of the Realm."[16] Leaving private cases to be decided by the "Kings Courts of Justice," the council members are "the profitable Instruments of the State." Coke speaks of the character necessary in "councellors" and of their duties as laid down in their oath; and he recounts the charges brought in Parliament against the Spencers, who, as privy counsellors in the reign of Edward I, had sought to make themselves effective rulers of England by drawing a distinction between the king and the Crown. From Coke's silence one can infer that the council does not proceed by strict forms and precedents as do the other courts; his "rules of Councell" are rather suggestions for how advice ought to be sought and how greeted, not procedures for running a meeting. The Privy Council is for Coke a deliberative body, and its functions are surely political. But its inclusion among the courts suggests that Coke considers political choice to take place in a setting in which questions are raised and considered, then judgment rendered, as in court—and perhaps also that deliberation and concern for broad matters of what is today called public policy were not altogether removed from the province of the courts of law.

The account of the Privy Council, at least when taken in conjunction with the chapter on Parliament which immediately precedes it, is the closest Coke comes in the *Institutes* to describing the political work of the monarch. In contrast to Blackstone, who will write a chapter describing the king's prerogative, Coke apparently treats the prerogative as a matter that is by definition apart from law, though he mentions the prerogative at points where it sets limits to law, or is limited by law. This emphatically does not mean that for Coke the king is a minor player in the government; it is a measure rather of the limits of law than of the preeminence of the king.[17]

Nowhere do Coke's views on monarchy become more clear than in his report of *Calvin's Case,* which he describes as "the greatest case that ever was argued in the hall of Westminster," "the longest and weightiest that ever was argued in any court, the shortest in syllables, the longest in substance."[18] In this case, decided by all fourteen judges of the two common law courts and the Exchequer, together with the lord chancellor, and argued by the king's attorney general and the solicitor general, Coke was in the majority, agreeing with earlier antagonists such as Lord Ellesmere and Francis Bacon, with whom he would again afterward clash. Though many judges argued the case, each with his own "peculiar method," Coke claims to restrict himself to a summary and assumes for himself "that which of right is due to every reporter, that is, to reduce the sum and effect of all to such a method, as, upon consideration had of all the arguments, the reporter himself thinketh to be fittest and clearest for the right understanding of the true reasons and causes of the judgment and the resolution of the case in question."[19]

The facts of the case and the question presented are, as Coke says, simple. In 1603, upon the death of Queen Elizabeth, James VI of Scotland inherited as well the throne of England. Soon afterwards Robert Calvin was born in Edinburgh; while still an infant he was disseised of a freehold to which he was heir in the English town of Haggard, and his guardians brought a complaint to recover his right. Since aliens were prohibited by law from owning property in England, at issue in the case was whether young Calvin was an alien in England, having been born in Scotland during the reign of a king who also wore the English crown.

Coke divides his treatment of the case under five headings: ligeance (i.e., allegiance), laws, realms, alienage, and legal inconveniences. For the purposes of this study, Coke's account of ligeance is most revealing, because he insists that, since ligeance is defined by natural law, it is part of the law of England. The crux of the argument concerning ligeance is the proof that the bond between subject and king is personal and natural, not abstract or political. On the subject's side this is shown by the fact that ligeance is determined as a matter of birthright and requires obedience and service; on the king's side, it appears from his reciprocal duty—which of course he too acquires by birthright, by inheritance of the crown—to protect and govern his subjects, "as well in time of peace by justice, as in time of war by the sword."[20] As the subject's duties and the king's aims in time of war make plain, ligeance is not dependent upon place but upon the persons. Together with faith and truth, ligeance is a quality "of the mind and soul of man," Coke argues; "ligeance of the subject was of as great an extent and latitude, as the royal power of the King."[21] Thus, since "the protection and government of the King is general over all his dominions and realms," a person is subject to the king generally, so that a subject in one dominion is subject also in any other dominion under the same king.[22]

In the course of arguing the natural character of allegiance, Coke confronts two arguments that help situate his understanding of kingship. First, while acknowledging the distinction between the natural and the politic bodies of the king, he makes clear how restricted the latter is. Indeed, he refers to it as a consequence merely of "the policy of the law," to avoid a few inconveniences; the fiction of the politic body, for instance, allows acts to be taken in the name of a king during his minority, and it ensures that royal lands descend along with the crown, as to a queen, not by the usual law of inheritance, which excludes women in different ways. Second, he rejects the distinction between the Crown and the person of the king, advanced by the Spencers (and, incidentally, accepted today); the king is fully king before his coronation, by natural descent, the crown being "but a royal ornament" and "an hieroglyph of the laws, where justice, etc. is administered."[23] In short, what we would call the political functions of the king—making war, administering justice—belong to his natural person, while the "politic" king exists only in a few corners of the law. And this is true even though the king makes war through his generals and admirals and does justice through his judges. As the substantive law of the land that Coke reports owes much to the logic of feudalism, so his account of kingship describes, in form if not in function, a feudal king.[24]

Coke then proceeds to assimilate the natural character of ligeance to natural law, and thence to the law of England. Perhaps the latter step in the argument is most easily grasped: If the law of nature is of universal obligation, surely nothing in English law could abrogate it. To establish that ligeance itself is a matter of natural law, Coke calls upon the philosopher whom he immediately before has dubbed "nature's secretary":

And Aristotle [Book] I *Politicorum* proveth, that to command and to obey is of nature, and that magistracy is of nature: for whatsoever is necessary and profitable for the preservation of the society of man is due by the law of nature: but magistracy and government are necessary and profitable for the preservation of the society of man; herefore magistracy and government are of nature.[25]

The jump in the reasoning from Aristotle's statement that the polis exists by nature to Coke's conclusion that ligeance is nature's form of government is, typically, made with the help of history:

And certain it is, that before any judicial or municipal laws were made, Kings did decide causes according to natural equity, and were not tied to any rule or formality of law, but did *dare jura* [give right/law].

After citing Fortescue and quoting Vergil and Cicero, he continues:

Now it appeareth by demonstrative reason, that ligeance, faith, and obedience of the subject to the Sovereign, was before any municipal or judicial laws. 1. For that government and subjection were long before any municipal or judicial laws. 2. For that it had been in vain to have prescribed laws to any, but to such as owed obedience, faith, and ligeance before, in respect whereof they were bound to obey and observe them.

Natural law is thus prior to ligeance, but ligeance is prior to the particular laws of any realm. While appealing to the ancients, Coke's argument here is medieval: Not the regime but the bond of ligeance underlies the laws. And to any particular man, though ligeance can be altered by conquest or naturalization, it is in the first place determined by nature, by the birthright of both subject and lord.

With this Coke has Calvin's argument clinched: His subjection is to James, to whom he owes ligeance and from whose protection he is entitled to benefit in any of James's realms; so he gets to keep his land. Coke's subsequent arguments in the case simply meet the objections raised: The generality of allegiance does not destroy the separateness of realms, so England and Scotland can share a king but each maintain their own laws; one born under a king can be no alien in any of the king's domains since he can never be an enemy to his fellow subjects; and finally, the legal inconveniences alleged evaporate on closer inspection, for the subject who owns land in a realm different from his homeland is bound by that realm's law regarding that land.

What seems more difficult to reconcile is Coke's apparent elevation of royalty over law in this case with his usual insistence that law is paramount to the king. But the apparent contradiction is lessened, if not dissolved, by two considerations. First, it ought to be recalled that, as Coke is not averse to reminding his readers, law determines the path of descent of the crown. In this way, at least in ages that follow the first king or that follow the king who first makes the law of succession, law governs the course of ligeance. Though ligeance may be personal, a dispute over succession is a dispute in law, even if not resolvable in ordinary courts.[26] Second, ligeance as Coke describes it cuts both ways: The subjects owe obedience, but the lord ought to protect. Coke hedges here a little, for obvious reasons; who, after all, could force the king to meet his obligations, without himself thereby becoming king to the king or breeding civil war? But the duties of the king suggest perhaps that he ought not in all things to act alone, and through this recognition laws might come to establish bodies of men with whom or through whom he must act, such as Parliament and the royal judges.

The priority of ligeance is not, for Coke, a political statement determining the form of government. Rather, it is an acknowledgement that before one can specify what the law is to a person, it ought to be established whether he has an obligation to obey it. Coke ascribes this principle to natural law, but it results in the opposite of what we today, like certain clerics in his own time, might call a strong natural law teaching. Instead of saying that obedience is mandated only in that regime whose laws conform to a universal standard of goodness, it makes obedience to a particular government the first instance of a man's obedience to law. This is consistent with what was argued before about Coke's view of the law: He begins with the assumption that the law he shall speak of is English law; he begins within the realm, then develops how the law might be perfected or refined.

Though Coke never treats the king's prerogative systematically, he does begin the final chapter of the *Institutes,* "Of the precedency of the great Officers, Nobility, and others of this Realme," with the following sentence: "At the Common law, the King by his Prerogative royall might give such honour, reputation, and placing to his Counsellors and other his subjects, as should be seeming to his wisdome, which Prerogative was so declared by Act of Parliament."[27] Though he goes on to discuss how Henry VIII, "though standing as much upon his Prerogative as any of his Progenitors, yet finding how vexatious it was to himself, . . . was content to bind and limit his Prerogative by Act of Parliament concerning the Precedency of his great Officers, and of his Nobility," it appears that for Coke the role of the king is to serve as the anchor of ligeance and the source of honor, rather than as ruler of the country, at least in matters of property and in time of peace. Even in this role the king is circumscribed: "And by the Lawes of England as all the degrees of nobility and honour were derived from the King as the fountaine of honour: so all the Lands in England were originally derived from the Crowne of

England, and are holden of the same mediately or immediately."[28] But conversely, as English land is governed not by the king's will but by the law of the land, so the nobility has a certain independent standing. Coke's king is a feudal lord, but one who lives in modern times and is bound, except perhaps in matters of warfare, by law. The king as chief of the feudal hierarchy anchors the polity but, like an anchor, has little freedom to move.

"THE HIGH AND MOST HONOURABLE COURT OF PARLIAMENT"

The account thus far perhaps draws Coke's king too much in the image of the modern constitutional monarch, who reigns but does not rule. While there is some resemblance, it should be borne in mind that Coke never denies the king's participation in ruling, and in foreign affairs and matters of warfare he had a relatively free hand. But within the realm his rule was to be exercised, Coke argues, with "the high and most honourable court of Parliament." Coke's discussion of Parliament in the *Institutes* is not the first expression of the great extent of its powers; one ought to compare the statements in *De Republica Anglorum,* by Elizabeth's secretary of state, Sir Thomas Smith.[29] Still, Coke's words— "Of the power and jurisdiction of the Parliament, for making of laws in proceeding by Bill, it is so transcendent and absolute, as it cannot be confined either for causes or persons within any bounds"— serve as the basis for Blackstone's subsequent account of parliamentary sovereignty.[30] They also vex American constitutional historians who seek to assimilate such sweeping pronouncements with Coke's apparent willingness, in *Doctor Bonham's Case,* to void a parliamentary act.

The leading attempt to reconcile the statement in the *Institutes* on Parliament's power with a reading of *Bonham's Case* as an exercise of judicial review is Charles Howard McIlwain's *The High Court of Parliament and Its Supremacy,* first published in 1910. McIlwain argues that until the Long Parliament demonstrated legislative omnipotence, the English had no concept of legislative sovereignty. In fact, Coke "never recognized the antithesis between legislation and adjudication by which the moderns have interpreted him."[31] Wholly within the tradition of medieval thinking about law, Coke thinks of Parliament as a court, not as a legislative body. Its function is to declare the law, *jus dicere,* not *jus dare,* to create it. When Coke calls Parliament's power absolute, he means only that its word is final, that from it there is no appeal; it can no more govern at its pleasure than can, say, the United States Supreme Court, though the latter too has the last word, at least case by case.

McIlwain's thesis of what he calls the fusion of legislative and judicial powers in the minds of the Elizabethan English was certainly a useful corrective to those who saw no difference between Coke and Blackstone, and his eloquent reminder to the critical historian bears repeating.

> The stream of political thought in one sense is the converse of what we find in nature. As we follow it back toward its sources we find that instead of narrowing, it becomes ever wider. Institutions that are now narrow and definite become as we trace them back indistinguishable from others that we have always considered equally definite. To ignore this fact is fatal. To read the same definiteness into earlier institutions is not necessarily to put words into men's mouths which they never uttered, but to put ideas into their heads that they never dreamed of.[32]

Still, the assumption that history drifts out of cloud to clarity can itself obscure. Coke surely does not conceive a separation of powers like the American system, which draws sharp lines between legislation and adjudication and assigns the tasks to different institutions. At the same time, he by no means thinks that all political activity is merely declaring the law, either in particular cases or in general. He certainly does not lack the concept of legislation—the idea that new law of human making can be introduced. We have seen already his mention in *Calvin's Case* of the nature of governance before laws were made, when kings were indeed able *jus dare*. That he thinks Parliament is empowered in later ages to do the same is evident from his preface to the volumes of the *Institutes* treating statutes and penal laws. As noted earlier, he explains there that in discussing statutes he will determine the state of the common law before the statutes were made, so that the reader might "thereby know whether the Statute be introductory of a new Law, or declaratory of the old, which will conduce much to the true understanding of the Text it selfe."[33] In the expositions of numerous statutes that follow, there is plenty of new law discerned, though Coke does insist that Magna Charta, the greatest of statutes, is declaratory of ancient common law, not the invention of King John's angry barons. Again, in the preface to the *Fourth Reports*, he treats explicitly the points to observe in making new laws, though characteristically he adds that the same are to be followed in correcting old laws— suggesting perhaps that making new law and correcting old are essentially the same activity.

What Coke does deny is that new legislation is often desirable. In the same preface just mentioned, he asserts this most forcefully.

> For any fundamental point of the ancient common laws and customs of the realm, it is a maxim in policy, and a trial by experience, that the alteration of any of them is most dangerous; for that which hath been

refined and perfected by all the wisest men in former succession of ages, and proved and approved by continual experience to be good and profitable for the commonwealth, cannot without great danger and hazard be altered or changed.[34]

Not only a conservative temper and concern for the reverence that comes with antiquity are at work here; Coke is often quite blunt, despite his celebration of Parliament, about the ignorance of some of its members. In an early preface, he decries "acts of parliament, overladen with provisoes and additions, and many times on a sudden penned or corrected by men of none or very little judgment in law." Even in the *Institutes,* written in his parliamentary years, he notes the care that judges must take in expounding an act "whereof many of the makers are Lay and unlearned men."[35] He denounces various attempts that kings have made to exclude lawyers from Parliament, saying of a Parliament from which Henry IV shut out the profession that "this Parliament was fruitlesse, and never a good law made thereat, and therefore called *Indoctum Parliamentum,* or Lack-learning Parliament."[36]

But Coke's resistance to legislation is not nearly so rigid as many of his modern commentators have supposed. In fact, in the area of penal law, Coke strikes the pose of a reformer. In the preface to the *Fourth Reports,* after warning against changing common law, he continues:

And yet concerning certain of our penal statutes, to repeal many that time hath antiquated as unprofitable, and remain but as snares to intangle the subjects withal; and to omit all those that be repealed, that none by them be deceived. . . . To make one plain and perspicuous law divided into articles, so as every subject may know what acts be in force, and what repealed, . . . so as each man may clearly know what and how much is of them in force, and how to obey them, it were a necessary work, and worthy of singular commendation.[37]

The same concern that criminal law be regularized so that it will be clearly and generally understood is expressed in the preface to the *Third Institutes* and embodied in that volume itself, in which Coke defines the various crimes in English law. Most remarkable is the volume's epilogue, where he speaks of the importance not only of punitive justice but also of "preventing Iustice." After noting the common failure of what we would call deterrence in law, since "the frequency of the punishment makes it so familiar as it is not feared," Coke outlines the elements of preventive justice, including education both in religion and in vocational skill, so as to prevent idleness and "by honest trades cause them to become good members in the Commonwealth." These are not the words of a narrow legalistic mind.[38]

To question the wisdom of innovation in matters of law is not to deny its possibility. Still, McIlwain's reading of Coke's view of Parliament as a court rather than a law-making body derives some plausibility from an examination of the chapter of the *Fourth Institutes* on Parliament. It is no accident that Coke begins the volume on courts with Parliament, just as it is no accident that he begins the volume on statutes with Magna Charta or the volume on crimes with treason—or, for that matter, the *Seventh Reports* with *Calvin's Case*. But within the chapter, the order in which topics are considered is much less clear.[39] He begins, logically enough, with the persons who comprise the body: "the Kings Majesty sitting there as in his Royall politick capacity, and . . . the three Estates of the Realm: *viz.* . . . the Lords Spirituall, . . . The Lords Temporall, . . . [and] the Commons of the Realme whereof there be Knights of Shires or Counties, Citizens of Cities, and Burgesses of Burghes . . . and these represent all the Commons of the whole Realme, and trusted for them."[40] After discussing their number and something of their history, he describes, in a passage that is either quaint or ironic, "what properties a Parliament man should have" and concludes that they are the same as the properties of an elephant: to have "no gall"; to be "constant, inflexible, and not to be bowed"; to be "of a ripe memory"; to be "sociable, and go in companies," unlike "Beasts that walk solely, or singularly, as Bears, Foxes, etc. [and] are dangerous and hurtfull."[41] Then follow sections on the records and summons of Parliaments; the sort of expert advisors they may have (the justices serving as advisors to the Lords); how a session of Parliament begins (with the "Royall presence" and a speech); how a Speaker of the Commons is elected and presented to the king, and how, after protesting his unworthiness, he is to request of the king the privileges of free speech and no arrest for members of Commons, and access to the royal person for himself on their behalf.

Having come to the privilege of free speech, Coke pauses to examine "the matters of Parliament," beginning with a list:

> 1. Touching the King. 2. The state of the Kingdome of England. 3. The defence of the Kingdome. 4. The state of the Church of England: and 5. The defence of the same Church. . . . And these words (the state and defence of the Kingdome) are large words, and include the rest. And though the state and defence of the Church of England be last named in the Writ, yet it is first in intention.[42]

Leaving aside what this passage suggests about Coke's views on the relation of church and state—characteristically, he pays homage to the church while including it as part of the kingdom, not the reverse—this list is no mere enumeration of objects of government, as, for instance, Article I, section 8, of the American Constitution appears to be. Moreover, coming soon after a terse mention that the king in his opening speech shall "shew the causes of the calling of his High Court of Parliament," the passage clearly indicates that the king does not alone determine the body's agenda. Coke's digression to discuss "an excellent law" from the time of Edward III requiring annual sessions of Parliament reinforces his claim that Parliament is and ought to be treated as a body of independent stature, not a mere creature of the king, and the subsequent sections on the unalterability of writs of election, on the receipt of petitions in Parliament, and on the appointment of committees of grievances pursue the theme. The point is sealed by a lengthy discussion, including reports of several cases, of the law and custom of Parliament, designed to show that the rules by which the body proceeds, and the behavior of its members during its sessions, are policed by itself and not subject to any other, necessarily inferior court.[43]

In this context, Coke treats of the judicial power of Parliament, speaking first of writs of error to the House of Lords, giving many examples, then of "other matters of Judicature in the Lords house, and of matters of Judicature in the house of Commons," comprising what we now call impeachment and policing the behavior of members. "After Judicature," he returns to the question of members' privileges, and only then does he proceed to examine "Statutes, or Acts of Parliament": their different kinds, their several forms, how they are proclaimed or published, and the relation between royal assent to bills and the manner in which sessions of Parliament come to an end, adding a note to show the complexities of prorogation, since "the House of Commons is to many purposes a distinct Court."[44] Thus, though Coke refers to Parliament and its houses as courts (as McIlwain notes), he explicitly distinguishes their adjudicative from their statutory activities (as McIlwain does not).[45] Again, in discussing the kinds of parliamentary acts, Coke differentiates between those "introductory of new law" and those "declaratory of the ancient law."

There follows a lengthy commentary on the various forms of subsidies and customs that Parliament could lay upon the realm, which Coke interrupts once to observe that good bills in Parliament eventually pass, if not at one session, then at a subsequent one. After mentioning that parliamentary acts can confirm letters patent of the king (as did the acts in question in *Doctor Bonham's Case*, incidentally), Coke considers how the Lords and Commons vote. As mention of the privilege of free speech leads to a discussion of Parliament's business, so mention of technical matters of voting here changes the tenor of the account from rules to politics. Coke relates in one section:

> It is observed by ancient Parliament men out of Record, that Parliaments have not succeeded well in five Cases. First, when the King hath been in displeasure with his Lords, or with his Commons. 2. When any of the

Great Lords were at variance between themselves. 3. When there was no good correspondence between the Lords and the Commons. 4. When there was no unity between the Commons themselves. 5. When there was no preparation for the Parliament before it began.[46]

He discreetly limits himself to distant examples, concentrating particularly, in his schoolteacher's way, on the importance of preparing well for the start of the session and of appointing a select committee to review bills left unpassed at the end of the previous session. Finally, after a brief section on the "honour and antiquity of the Parliament," in which he refers his readers to earlier writings, he proceeds to the famous passage on "the power and jurisdiction of the Parliament."

I have meandered toward this passage, partly to establish its context, partly to give example of Coke's manner. For once one sees that Coke typically addresses larger issues circumspectly, often in the context of more technical legal questions, one finds his discussion of Parliament's power less surprising. After the ringing initial sentence ("Of the power and jurisdiction of the Parliament . . ." quoted above) and quotations from Fortescue and Vergil, Coke offers several examples of what Parliament can do by bill. As has been noted by commentators, all the examples appear to involve private bills, not general legislation: causing heirs to inherit during the ancestor's lifetime, judging a minor to be of full age, attainting a man of treason after his death, naturalizing an alien, bastardizing a child legitimate by law, and legitimating children born bastards.[47] One bill, representative of the last sort, is printed and discussed; since it involves the children of John of Gaunt, Duke of Lancaster, from whom Henry VII and thus the royal line in Coke's time traced their lineage, it is a matter of no small importance, especially since Coke proceeds to call into question Henry's title through this line, at least had the crown not been entailed to him by act of Parliament. As subsequent British history was to show, the power of Parliament to settle a claim to the crown was hardly an insignificant issue, though it remains a particular, not a general, bill. The principle of parliamentary power is asserted in full voice, but the examples, while not trivial, do not confirm the assertion. After all, Coke certainly had at his fingertips statutes from the reign of Henry VIII, such as the Act of Supremacy and the act dissolving the monasteries, that he might have cited to illustrate a Parliament with real muscle.

But then, it hardly appears to be his purpose to show a muscular Parliament. Despite having insisted earlier in the chapter upon the privileges of Parliament, he now seems more intent on curbing its pretensions than expanding its claims. Moving past the tepid examples in one section after another, Coke concentrates on the limits upon Parliament, not its power— or, more precisely, on the limits it is bound to respect despite its power. The precedents here tend to be from the reigns of Richard II, Henry VII, and Henry VIII. The first case, appearing still in the section on power and juris-diction, is the attainder for treason of Thomas Cromwell by Parliament with-out having called him to answer the charges. Coke recounts at some length a story, told him by a senior judge, of Henry VIII's inquiries of his chief jus-tices (ironically, through Cromwell himself) before the fact, on whether an attainder in Parliament could be made without summoning the accused to answer:

> The Judges answered, that it was a dangerous question, and that the High Court of Parliament ought to give examples to inferiour Courts for proceeding according to justice, and no inferior Court could do the like; and they thought that the High Court of Parliament would never do it. But being pressed by the expresse commandment of the King . . . to give a direct answer: they said, that if he be attainted by Parliament, it could not come in question afterwards, whether he were called or not called to answer.[48]

Though Coke would have had the judges cite chapter 29 of Magna Charta, he admits that their opinion was according to law, for "the act of Attainder being passed by Parliament, did bind." Still, he goes on to list numerous passages from the Bible where people were called to answer for crimes, and to denounce as evil an earlier instance of attaint without answer.

In subsequent sections, Coke gives other examples of parliamentary acts that he considers illegitimate, though binding. After showing some proper writs for calling men to answer charges in Parliament, he further criticizes attainders for treason made in general words, without specific complaints, saying again, in his own name, that Parliament "ought to give example to inferiour Courts." He saves a more vehement denunciation for an act in the time of Henry VII substituting accusation by information for indictment by grand jury, which allowed royal officers "to commit upon the Subject unsuf-ferable pressures and oppressions." Still, though the law in question illus-trates the "dangerous inconveniences" upon altering "any Maxime, or Fun-damentall law of this Realm," Coke does not deny its force before its repeal: He recites the matter "to the end, that the like should never hereafter be attempted in any Court of Parliament."[49]

In the next part, however, Coke does meet acts that "bind not." The exam-ples concern principally acts that would deprive future bodies of the power to do precisely what those who make them are doing. Thus Coke notes with satisfaction the repeal of a law made by a Parliament under Richard II that would have forbidden any future Parliament from undoing its ordinances. Likewise, he remarks that the last will and testament of Richard II, which made the inheritance of his domains dependent upon observing forever the acts of one of his Parliaments, "was holden unjust and unlawfull, for that it restrained the Soveraign liberty of the Kings his successors." Also "abnichaled [annihilated], and made void," this time by an act of Parliament, was an earlier act that would have forbidden suit for pardon in certain cases, for it was "unreasonable, without example, and against the law and custome of Parliament." Coke adds, in a similar vein, that the power of Parliament to review petitions cannot be committed to a small number of members, though here he says not that the action would be void but that it would go against "the dignity of Parliament" and thus "ought" not to be taken.[50]

The longest example in the section involves a law passed during the time of Henry VIII by which speaking against the king's claim to supremacy in the Church of England was made a form of treason. Coke's objection to the act does not rest on grounds of natural law or fundamental right, at least not directly. Instead, he claims that proponents of the act "closely cowched" the text into a bill where other treasonable offenses were detailed rather than including it in the Act of Supremacy, which would have been its "proper place" but where it would have had "little hope" of passage. "All laws," Coke asserts, "especially penall, and principally those that are penall in the highest degree ought to be so plainly and perspicuously penned, as every Member of both Houses may understand the same, and according to his knowledge and conscience give his voice."[51] At the end of the section on nonbinding laws, Coke considers only the sort of fault with which he began, the attempt by one Parliament to bind its successors. He now says of any such project that "they could never effect it," "for it is a maxime in the law of the Parliament, *quod leges posteriores priores contrarias abrogant*" [subsequent laws abrogate prior laws to the contrary].

Does this concluding statement mean that acts of Parliament that violate fundamental maxims in the law are void? Surely that would give the particular issue under discussion a wider meaning than it need assume. Is the problem of whether or not an absolute power can bind itself and thus renounce its absoluteness a peculiar logical difficulty inherent in the notion of absolute power? Perhaps, but if absolute power must be limited in one way, why can it not be in others? In fact, the limits to Parliament's control over its own succession are ambiguous, for if Coke denies that kings can alter the writs of summons to a Parliament, he allows that an act of Parliament *can* do so. Moreover, he notes even of the limiting acts that they were repealed, not simply ignored, suggesting, as before in the discussion of Cromwell's attainder, that right and force in parliamentary actions do not always coincide. Perhaps the example of deceit in the legislation on treason provides a clue: The call for honesty in legislating is an appeal to the wisdom of Parliament, and the logic of wisdom requires openness to improvement every bit as much as the logic of absolute power requires openness to change. Indeed, very early in the chapter Coke had suggested a distinction between power and wisdom, in a simile comparing the natural and politic bodies:

> As in the naturall body when all the sinews being joined in the head do join their forces together for the strengthening of the body, there is *ultimum Potentiae* [highest power]: so in the politique body when the king and the Lords Spirituall and Temporall, Knights, Citizens, and Burgesses, are all by the Kings command assembled and joined together under the head in consultation for the common good of the whole Realm, there is *ultimum Sapientiae* [highest wisdom].[52]

To know what ought to be void, or what ought to be repealed, or what ought not to be done is the part of wisdom; whether one is in a position to effect wisdom is another matter. The law, partaking of both wisdom and force, remains necessarily ambiguous when the two are at odds. But it is not fatal to law as Coke conceives it that it cannot solve every problem; what would be fatal would be to renounce the aspiration to right.

Ten pages remain in this chapter from the *Fourth Institutes,* and in them Coke returns to somewhat more technical matters—how acts of Parliament are registered in other courts, that all members of Parliament ought to attend, who is eligible to sit in Parliament, how much members of Commons are paid, who elects them, who can avoid service. A final remark about Parliament's role in consultations concerning the navy makes clear, as if it were ever in doubt, that parliamentary purview is not limited to local grievances. Coke concludes with a discussion of the records of Parliament, mentioning not only the unreliability of the printed versions but also the need to supplement what one reads with a knowledge of the history of the times. In typical fashion, he thus reminds us that his own work is both encyclopedic and tentative. His account of Parliament, for all its sweeping phrases, is not a comprehensive doctrine of parliamentary form and power; it is a reading from the records of what Parliament has been, together with suggestions as to what it might become. Again, if this seems to transcend our views of what a legal treatise ought to do, it says more about the narrowness of our own understanding of law than about the confusion of Coke's work.

No discussion of Coke's views on Parliament can be complete without some mention of his own parliamentary career, for he had become, by the time he authored the *Institutes,* perhaps the greatest "Parliament man" of his generation and something of a mentor to the generation that went on to sit in the Long Parliament.[53] There can be little doubt that Coke himself saw the passage of the Petition of Right in 1628 as his greatest parliamentary achievement. The story of the petition is well known: It arose after Charles I had imprisoned several gentlemen and attempted to force from them a loan, and after the courts, in the *Five Knights' Case,* had refused relief to one of those imprisoned.[54] The petition reaffirmed the liberty of subjects from arbitrary arrest, from the forced quartering of troops, and from taxation without parliamentary consent. Coke served on nearly every committee of the Commons concerned with the grievances that led to the petition. On the floor he appears to have been instrumental in insisting that remonstrance to the king be made by the form of a petition of right—that is, by a form of bill, not by informal correspondence or a petition of grace—and again in certifying the form of the king's assent that would ensure the petition's status in law. The petition declares, with the clear mark of Coke's influence, that the rights detailed are ancient liberties being confirmed, not new ones being introduced. The twenty-ninth chapter of Magna Charta is cited, and the principle of due process explicitly invoked.

In the course of debate, as Commons was considering an amendment proposed by Lords that would have added to the petition an assurance of Parliament's "due regard to leave entire that sovereign power wherewith your Majesty is trusted for the protection, safety, and happiness of your people," Coke delivered a much quoted and, it seems, misquoted speech. Coke rose to speak against the amendment and its "saving" of "sovereign power." It would, he argued, "overthrow all our petition":

> Look into all the petitions of former times. They never petitioned for the King's sovereignty, as if the subjects would save it. I know the prerogative is part of the law, but "sovereign power" is no parliament word in my opinion. It weakens Magna Carta and all other statutes, for they are absolute without any saving of sovereign power; and shall we now add it, we shall weaken the foundations of law, and then the building must needs fall. . . . Magna Carta is such a fellow as he will have no saving. I wonder this saving was not in Magna Carta or in the confirmation of it. By implication we give a sovereign power above all these laws. Power in law is taken for a power with force. The sheriff shall take the power of the country. What is meant here God only knows. It is repugnant to our petition, that is a petition of right grounded on acts of parliament. . . . We must not admit of it; and to qualify it, it is impossible. Let us hold our privileges according to the law. That power that is above this is not fit for the King and people to have it disputed further. I had rather for my part have the prerogative acted and I myself to lie under it, than to have it disputed with. When it was in former times it ever bred ill spirits.[55]

Evidently Rushworth's *Historical Collections* misprinted a crucial sentence as follows: "Magna Carta is such a Fellow, that he will have no *Sovereign*," and scholars who comment on the speech have accepted this version. But the speech as a whole, especially its closing lines on the prerogative, reveals how less likely such a reading is.[56] Like John Pym, who spoke before him, Coke would readily acknowledge the sovereign person of the king; other versions of the speech quote Coke explicitly distinguishing the sovereign prerogative.[57] What he denies is that sovereignty is a power that stands above and determines law. Again, law and force are distinguishable. Coke certainly recognizes the necessity of force in political life, but he refuses to allow this necessity to overturn the claims of law.

DOCTOR BONHAM'S CASE AND LAWYERS' HISTORY

INTERPRETING THE LAW OF *DOCTOR BONHAM'S CASE*

One myth about *Doctor Bonham's Case* ought to be dispelled at the outset: that Coke's voidance of a statute in *Bonham's* can be squared with his assertion of parliamentary supremacy in the *Institutes* simply by taking into account the different stages of his career.[1] There are indeed some differences of style and tone between the *Reports* and the *Institutes,* attributable perhaps to the composition of the latter in English, rather than the Latin and Law French of the original *Reports*. The change of language is hardly insignificant. In the preface to the *Third Reports,* Coke apparently sees a need to avoid writing law "in the vulgar tongue, lest the unlearned by bare reading, without right understanding, might suck out errors, and trusting to their own conceit, might endanger themselves, and sometimes fall into destruction." Explaining the shift to English in the preface to the *First Institutes,* Coke speaks of the importance of making the law accessible to "any of the Nobilitie, or Gentrie, or of any other estate, or profession whatsoeuer"—some of whom, after all, could well find themselves in Parliament.[2]

Still, there is no evidence that with regard to *Bonham's Case* we ought to abandon our presumption of continuity in Coke's works. That Coke makes no mention of *Bonham's* in the chapter of the *Institutes* on Parliament may help us interpret both the case and the chapter, but it is no sign of a change of mind on Coke's part. He cites the case at least three times in the margins of the *Second Institutes*—twice when discussing statutes listed in the case as examples of acts of Parliament discarded by the courts as void and inconvenient, once when discussing a statute interpreted so it would not violate fundamental law.[3] Then in the *Fourth Institutes,* in the chapter on the courts of London, Coke handles the question of the jurisdiction and authority of the College of Physicians simply by referring "the studious Reader" to *Bonham's Case* in the *Reports*.[4] That Coke makes no mention of *Bonham's* in other places may indicate that he does not think the case involves a unique constitutional principle. But that seems to have been his opinion of the case from the beginning. Though in the *Seventh Reports* he mentions the weightiness of *Calvin's Case* in the preface and covers it first, in the *Eighth Reports* he gives *Bonham's* neither prefatory mention nor special place. Even so, his lengthy report of the case is certainly some evidence of his opinion of its importance.

Briefly, the facts of the case are as follows.[5] Thomas Bonham, "doctor in philosophy, and in physic," graduate of Cambridge, brought an action of false imprisonment against the president and censors of the London College of Physicians, alleging that the latter had taken and imprisoned him "for a long time, that is to say, by the space of seven days, against the law and custom of this kingdom of England." In April 1606 Bonham was found practicing medicine in London without a license and summoned by the president and censors to appear before them for an examination. He did, but he "answered less aptly and insufficiently in the art of physic" and thus was forbidden to practice in London for longer than a month. Bonham, however, continued to work, and so, "for his said disobedience and contempt," was fined one hundred shillings and again commanded to cease, "under the pain of being cast into prison." The following October he was found to be still at work, was again summoned for an examination, but this time did not appear, whereupon the censors decided to fine him ten pounds "for his disobedience and contempts" and to arrest him and deliver him into custody. The death of the president of the college seems to have interrupted proceedings for a week or two, but on 7 November Bonham appeared before the censors (evidently having been arrested), refused to be examined, and promised to continue his practice, charging that the college had no authority over him, since he was a graduate of the university.[6] He was immediately jailed. Throughout, the president and censors relied on the authority given them to regulate the practice of medicine in London and its environs by letters patent of Henry VIII, confirmed by act of Parliament. Bonham rejoined by citing another clause of the same act, which restricted the practice of medicine throughout England to those who had passed an examination before the college or had earned a medical degree at Oxford or Cambridge.

The suit was brought before the Court of Common Pleas, where Coke was chief justice; since the five justices expressed their opinions seriatim, and since the several reports of the case differ somewhat and vary in their degree of completeness, there is some uncertainty about exactly how the vote went and for what reasons.[7] It is clear that Bonham won his suit, though by a close margin; it is also clear that he did not win on the grounds he pleaded. Justice Foster read the prohibition against unlicensed practice in London literally, so Bonham was not excused from examination as a university graduate; and since he failed the exam, he could be punished for continuing to practice without a license. Justice Walmesley agreed that no exception for university graduates was intended by the statute for London (as opposed to countryside) practitioners, and he gave the court the right to punish Bonham for contempt, as any court may do. So much for the dissenters, whose individual positions Coke only summarizes, succinctly but apparently with accuracy. Justice Daniel thought good Bonham's claim that as a university graduate he was exempt from the college's authority, while Justice Warburton joined the dissenters on this point; but both of them joined Coke in finding for Bonham, on other grounds. A manuscript report recently discovered by Charles Gray shows some variance among the three on precisely what those grounds were, though there seems to have been agreement on the main points. In his own account, Coke notes the disagreement between Daniel and Warburton on the status of university graduates before the college—he himself does not address this issue, finding other grounds sufficient[8]—and then subsumes their views in his. As his remarks in reporting *Calvin's Case* revealed, Coke considers this altogether within the prerogative of a reporter.

Coke's Analysis of the Case

Coke outlines his argument with precision, though the numbers in the text sometimes obscure the clarity of the organization.[9] Bonham wins the case on two grounds, either of which is sufficient alone: (I) "the said censors had not power to commit the plaintiff for any of the causes mentioned in the bar," and/or (II) "admitting that the censors had power by the act, . . . they had not pursued [their authority]." In other words, either the act of Parliament gave the censors no power to imprison Bonham (I), or if it did, they had not followed its provisions in their actions against him (II). To establish the first point (I), Coke adduces five reasons, the fourth of which is the famous passage, quoted at the outset of the first chapter, which is often taken as authority for judicial review; then he sums up the reasons in two maxims (one report of the case considers this a move from reasons to authorities); finally, he raises and refutes three objections to his argument. The second point (II) is met more expeditiously: Six reasons are given, then one objection raised and refuted. There follows a brief discussion of a technical issue of pleading, apparently because the court finds for Bonham on grounds other than those he had pleaded. Coke concludes by "observ[ing] seven things for the better direction of the president and commonalty of the said college in the future," summarizing the practical effect of his arguments.[10] He mentions as a sort of afterword that he "acquainted Sir Thomas Fleming, Chief Justice of the King's Bench, with this judgment and with the reasons and causes of it, and he well approved of the judgment which we had given," a fact made relevant by simultaneous proceedings against Bonham in Fleming's court.[11]

Again, scholarly controversy has centered upon Coke's fourth reason for his first ground of decision. The key issue has been whether Coke announces a maxim of statutory interpretation or a principle supporting judicial invalidation of statutes that violate higher law. Still the most succinct presentation of the former view is a 1938 article by Samuel Thorne; the most recent assertion of the latter comes from Raoul Berger.[12] Several scholarly attempts have been made to avoid a choice between stark alternatives. The latest is Gray's article, which suggests that in announcing his opinion from the bench Coke spoke the idiom of statutory construction, but that later, in preparing the case for press, he added the phrases "that could indeed support a doctrine of 'judicial review,' though he had obviously not thought out the implications of such a doctrine."[13] Long before, in an especially fine article, R. A. MacKay had argued that Coke's assertion was of "a right of strict construction in the courts," but that "the only reason for the existence of this power is to bring the statutes into general conformity with the fundamental law."[14]

Now all historians of law are aware of the danger of importing into earlier ages ideas and even issues familiar to us but unknown to those under study, and all who treat *Bonham's Case* are on special alert, for even to frame the issue as judicial review versus statutory construction is to introduce modern terminology. Hence, the various interpretations of *Bonham's* strive to show how Coke's manner of argumentation accords either with seventeenth-century standards of judicial construction, which were apparently rather broad in comparison to modern practice, or with doctrines of fundamental or natural law, which were very much alive in Coke's time, however much they disappeared from English political and legal thought in the eighteenth century. Often overlooked is how much can be gleaned from Coke's opinion itself, read in conjunction with his other works. Coke's own principle of "artificial reason" in the law justifies modern scholars' collecting and incorporating the ideas of his contemporaries in their attempts to understand his opinion. But since that artificial reason was no abstract Zeitgeist but the property of a professionally trained and experienced legal mind, and since the collections accrue evidence on both sides, Coke's arguments bear close attention, though one ought to keep in mind that Coke advocates listing all relevant reasons for a judgment, since different minds are differently persuaded.

In the establishment of the first major ground of the judgment (I), one thing is clear: All five reasons are given in the context of supporting a certain construction of the statute in question. The argument, in brief, is that the statute distinguishes the college's authority over unlicensed practice from its authority over malpractice, allowing a fine of five pounds for practicing a month without license but permitting fines and imprisonment at discretion for malpractice; the college had mistreated Bonham by invoking its authority over malpractice, though his offense was at most that he had no license. After summarizing, Coke moves to his five reasons, which, he says, "had their vigour and life from the letters patent, and the act itself; and the best expositor of all letters patent, and acts of parliament, are the letters patent and the acts of parliament themselves, by construction, and conferring all the parts of them together." True to this principle, he proceeds in his first reason (1) to comment directly upon the text, noting that the two clauses "were two absolute, perfect, and distinct clauses, and as parallels, and therefore the one did not extend to the other." This can be seen, first, by the introduction of the second clause with the word *praeterea* (moreover), and second, by the contrast between the definite specification of the penalty for unlicensed practice and the discretion left in punishment for malpractice, presumably so that the penalty could be tailored to be proportionate to the damage done.

Though his next three reasons (2-4) support the distinction between unlicensed practice and malpractice, they do not comment upon the text of the statute or the letters patent. Rather, they show different grounds for separating the two offenses and for punishing them in different ways; and not only the famous fourth, but every one of these arguments makes explicit reference to reason itself. The second (2) states that since the harm of malpractice is to a patient's body, "it is *reasonable* that the offender should be punished in his body, *sc.* by imprisonment," but the same cannot be alleged of unlicensed practice, for that "is not any prejudice to the body of man." The third (3) explains that unlicensed practice can be punished only after a period of one month so as to allow "divers nobles, gentlemen, and others" to bring their personal physicians with them when they visit London (as, for instance, the earl of Shaftesbury was later shadowed by John Locke), without bothering them with an examination before the college board. Coke notes that "the law hath *great reason* in making this distinction."

Common Right and Reason: No Judging One's Own Cause

In this context, Coke presents the argument that has become controversial:

> 4. The censors cannot be judges, ministers, and parties; judges to give sentence or judgment; ministers to make summons; and parties to have the moiety of the forfeiture, *quia aliquis non debet esse Judex in propria causa, imo iniquum est aliquem suae rei esse judicem* [a person ought not to be judge in his own cause, rather it is wrong for a man to be judge in his own matter]; and one cannot be judge and attorney for any of the parties. . . . And it appears in our books, that in many cases, the common law will controul acts of parliament, and sometimes adjudge them to be utterly void: for when an act of parliament is against common right and reason, or repugnant, or impossible to be performed, the common law will controul it, and adjudge such act to be void.[15]

Before discussing the larger implications of this passage, it would be worthwhile to consider precisely how it supports the particular argument in which it is embedded. The president and censors of the college did indeed serve as judges, ministers, and recipients of the fines in relation to Bonham. This alone would show that the principle of not judging one's own case was violated, and thus if all that mattered was the violation of justice, the case would be over. But the question at this stage is not how the college behaved—that comes later (II)—but what the law is and, particularly, how the statute is to be read. Do the letters patent and the confirmatory statute allow this way of proceeding? More precisely, are the clauses concerning unlicensed practice and malpractice distinct? The first clause, on licensing, includes the provision for splitting the fine between king and college, but it says nothing about where the issue should be tried. The second clause makes no mention of fine-sharing but gives the college broad authority of "supervision and scrutiny, correction and government" over all doctors in London, "and punishment of them for their faults" in malpractice, though it does not explicitly constitute the college as a court of law. Somewhat later in the case Coke makes clear his opinion that indeed the college does not constitute a court, only an "authority." At this point, however, he does not need that distinction. To separate the clauses concerning unlicensed practice and malpractice, he has only to demonstrate that if the clauses are allowed to spill over one into the other, party and judge (or authority) will be confounded, against a basic maxim in law. If Coke can show that statutes ought to be construed to avoid contradiction with legal maxims, he has his fourth reason for interpreting the two clauses as separate—and Bonham was wrongly imprisoned for an offense that deserved at most a fine.[16]

To establish this is the burden of the famous passage and of the four precedents and one hypothetical that Coke next introduces to support it. The crucial sentence itself (the last one in the quotation) is usually broken down as follows. First, it is noted that Coke attributes to the common law two powers regarding parliamentary acts: to control them, and to adjudge them void. "Control" is usually read as a synonym for "construe," while "adjudging void" is taken to signify embryonic judicial review. But thus to dichotomize Coke's terms is misleading: As MacKay has pointed out, "void" did not connote for Coke the stark constitutional confrontation it calls to our minds.[17] More important, Coke twice couples "control" and "adjudge void," both times with "and," not "or." The implication of the language itself seems to be that voidance of a statute is the extreme case of construction or "control," not an alternative to it. The form of reasoning was one, the consequence variously strong or modest.

The second phrase that is usually analyzed gives the causes for which the common law may control and void: "when an act of parliament is against common right and reason, or repugnant, or impossible to be performed." Here the issue is generally thought to turn on the distinction between "common right and reason" on the one hand, and repugnancy and impossibility on the other. Both of the classic critics of *Bonham's Case*—Ellesmere, who was Coke's contemporary and James's chancellor, and Blackstone, who might be called Coke's successor—admitted that parliamentary acts that were repugnant (that is, internally contradictory) or that commanded impossibilities were of themselves void, at least if all reasonable attempts to provide a consistent or plausible construction failed. What they could not abide was the authority over statutes Coke apparently claimed for the common law judges on the basis of "common right and reason."[18] The question thus becomes, what does Coke mean by this term?

From my previous discussion and from the examples Coke cites here, I think it is evident that, whatever the opinion of his critics, Coke drew no sharp distinctions between different forms of inconsistency in law. "Against common right and reason," "inconvenient," "impertinent," "repugnant," "absurd," "impossible"—these are all shades on a continuum to Coke, sometimes distinguished, sometimes not. In the sentence in question, Coke joins the three terms he uses with the disjunctive "or," but he would have the common law act similarly in all three cases: "control" and "sometimes adjudge void." This is not to deny Coke's passion for precision. He notes, and in his voluminous writing certainly illustrates, the infinite particularity of matters of law, and he clearly insists that each case be determined not on the basis of some loose theory but according to the particular rules that apply. This might explain, as Gray points out, why Coke refuses to accept Bonham's claim that university graduates are excepted out of the statute by implication: So loose a reading squares much less well with Coke's scrupulous mind than the strict reading the statute eventually gets in his hands.[19] Still, when what is at issue are not legal rules, which are many, but legal reason, which is one, precision takes on a different meaning. We today have become quite sophisticated in distinguishing the different mental operations involved in legal reasoning, even as we harbor a passion for simplification of the rules of law.[20] Coke's perspective is in some respects the reverse: He accepts the immense multiplicity of legal rules but thinks that through the art of legal reason they can be joined into a whole.

Precedents

In Coke's use of precedents to support his fourth reason in *Bonham's Case*, his way of thinking becomes clear. Two observations are in order right away. First, it is surprising that Coke even draws upon precedents at this step in the argument in *Bonham's,* for as we have seen, he had begun the larger section (I) by stating that statutes are best interpreted in their own terms, without outside help. The first three reasons (1—3) are internal, if not dependent on the mere language, but for the next two (4, 5) he looks to other parts of the law; his admonition to interpret statutes in their own terms is thus the starting point of construction, but not the whole story. Second, one ought to recognize Coke's own thoughts on the use of precedents. His modern commentators typically mention that statutory interpretation in his era, but more especially in the centuries preceding him, was much looser than is usual in our century.[21] They ignore his own remarks upon a similar trend already discernible in the use of precedents. In the preface to the *Tenth Reports,* he writes:

> The ancient order of arguments by our Serjeants and apprentices of law at the bar is altogether altered. 1. They never cited any book, case, or authority in particular as is holden in 40 E. 3 etc. but *est tenus ou agree in n're liures, ou est tenus adjudge in termes,* or such like, which order yet remains in moots at bar in the Inner Temple to this day. Then was the citing general, but always true in the particular; and now the citing is particular, and the matter many times mistaken in general. 3. In those days few cases in law were cited, but very pithy and pertinent to the purpose and those ever pinch most; and now in so long arguments with such farago of authorities, it cannot be but there is much refuse, which ever doth weaken or lessen the weight of the argument. This were easily holpen, if the matter (which ever lieth in a narrow room) were first discerned, and then that everyone that argueth at the bar would either speak to the purpose or else be short.

Coke's preference for the traditional ways in matters touching legal practice—as illustrated, for instance, by his praise of the old reporters and his distrust of innovation even in judicial dress[22]—suggests he thinks the old way of using precedents ought at least to be given its due. He certainly does give particular citations in the modern fashion, but he is not willing to grant precedents only their narrowest authority in cases where his legal judgment determines that general principles of law are properly invoked. Again, Coke does not confuse the precise and the narrow: Narrow construction is imprecise when general principles are at issue. He proceeds in the passage just quoted to apologize for the length of some of his reported cases, but he notes that "he may be a good miner, that followeth the main veins"—while yet insisting that "he that wrested or misapplieth any text, book, or authority of the law against his proper and genuine sense, yea.though it be to confirm a truth, doth against distributive justice, which is to give to every one his own." The "narrow rooms" in which particular cases lie nevertheless open upon a common passageway and permit straight reasons to enter.

Plucknett's analysis of Coke's precedents in *Bonham's Case* is the reigning account, so a brief rehearsal of his argument is in order.[23] Coke cites four precedents for the assertion that the common law can control a parliamentary act: *Tregor's Case, Cessavit 42, Annuity 41,* and *Strowd's Case.* In the first case, Plucknett finds Coke to have seriously misquoted the opinion by Justice Herle. While Herle says, "There are some statutes made which even the maker would not wish put into effect," Coke writes, "Herle saith, some statutes are made against law and right, which those who made them perceiving, would not put them in execution."[24] Plucknett allows, however, that *Cessavit 42* is a good precedent, though in that case the court simply ignored the act of Parliament in question, while Coke explains that "because it would be against common right and reason, the common law adjudges the said act of parliament as to that point void." *Annuity 41* presents a different problem: The report gives only the judges' debate on the point in question, not their judgment— though Plucknett notes that since the report was printed along with clearly decided questions, this subtlety was not likely to have been noticed in Coke's day. Although the judges did say the statute was "impertinent," they did not say explicitly, as Coke does, "void, for it is impertinent to be observed." Finally, *Strowd's Case,* which involves changing "rent services" in a statute to "rent charges" when they are owed by the king, so as not to offend his prerogative, is "merely the expounding of the statute," argues Plucknett; surely, he thinks, the simple change of a word does not deserve Coke's characterization that "the common law controuls [the statute], and adjudges it void as to services, . . . for it would be against common right and reason that the King should hold of any, or do service to any of his subjects." Plucknett, in short, has Coke batting one for four, though he acknowledges that contemporary scorers would have also counted *Annuity 41* as a hit.

From the standpoint of modern scholarship, Plucknett concludes that Coke could make for his contemporaries "a fairly convincing case in which the weak points were by no means obvious to an uncritical mind"; but

> the theory which he believed to be [its] legal foundation must be credited to his own political thought rather than to that of his mediaeval predecessors upon the Common Bench. . . . Coke's work is therefore in the nature of an antiquarian revival of obsolescent law with a view to applying it to current needs, an attitude towards history which was characteristic of the age, and which can be illustrated from the controversial literature of all parties.[25]

However, Plucknett has attributed to Coke a certain political theory of judicial review to which Coke does not necessarily subscribe and then has counted Coke's precedents according to their support of this imagined theory. Suppose one reads more narrowly the meaning of "control and adjudge void," so that it refers not to the outright disallowance of a statute but more generally to a course of reasoning whereby the judge seeks to accommodate the statute to the law as a whole, perhaps by giving the statute a strict interpretation, perhaps by finding it inapplicable, or void, in the case at bar. Then *Tregor's Case* and *Strowd's Case* assume new light. Herle's statement in *Tregor's,* which occurs in the course of a debate over interpreting a statute, certainly does not foreclose Coke's interpolation, for if Coke is within the realm of construction, his citation of the case no longer appears so arbitrary.[26] Though *Strowd's* involves construction, it is hardly irrelevant, for it also involves striking a word and replacing it with another in certain circumstances. *Cessavit 42,* on the other hand, the "one clear and incontestable precedent in his favor," according to Plucknett, receives a narrower reading in Coke's hands than in the theory Plucknett would attribute to him: Coke voids the act only "as to that point" which was particularly in question (the right of heirs to make a certain recovery for arrearages in the time of their ancestor), much as in *Strowd's Case* rent services were voided only when applied to the monarch.

Finally, the hypothetical case Coke devises ought to show most clearly his meaning, for he has in it the total control of authorship: "So if any act of parliament gives to any to hold, or to have conusans [cognizance or jurisdiction] of all manner of pleas arising before him within his manor of D., yet he shall hold no plea, to which he himself is party; for, as hath been said, *iniquum est aliquem suae rei esse judicem* [it is wrong for a man to be a judge in his own cause]."[27] But surely here Coke is giving to judges only the power to except out of general words a situation in which a maxim of common law would be violated; there is no reason to say that this cannot count as statutory interpretation every bit as much as in the precedents he cites.

In sum, Coke's precedents seem much less inadequate for his purpose when it is not presupposed that he is claiming a general power to void unconstitutional legislation. Two precedents, *Cessavit 42* and *Strowd's,* cover instances where statutes were voided as to particular circumstances, a course of reasoning practically indistinct from excepting those circumstances out of the statute by construction. The hypothetical case illustrates the same. *Annuity 41* is the oddity here, since it involves a statute whose wording is taken to be "impertinent" or "impossible"—in the account of the case in the *Institutes,* Coke adds "inconvenient."[28] Yet the uniqueness of *Annuity 41* is evident from Coke's own words in *Bonham's,* for he uses "impertinent" only in discussing this case; furthermore, *Annuity 41* is the only one of the cases in which he does not claim a violation of right. Nor is it accidental that Coke begins with Herle's remark in *Tregor's Case,* denying that statutory language by itself is sacrosanct, even while finding a way of construing the statute so it yields a legitimate meaning: That is precisely what Coke does in the case at hand.

To read the famous sentence in *Bonham's* as an instance of "mere" statutory construction is too narrow an interpretation. Such a concept would likely appear unintelligible to Coke, for it presumes a distinction between construing statutes and voiding them that he does not acknowledge. The question to Coke in any case at bar is, what is the law? Clearly statutes help provide an answer to this question in many cases, as does the common law. But in every case, it is the trained reason of the judge that pieces together the different sources of law to discover how *the* law—our idiom preserves the sense of wholeness in law that Coke elaborates—would answer the question posed. This is no "mechanical jurisprudence," but neither, in Coke's mind, is it the rule of discretion, much less of will or whim.

More Reasons

The role for legal reason here described is illustrated repeatedly throughout the remainder of Coke's opinion in the case. The sentence discussed at length, it will be recalled, belongs to the fourth (4) of five reasons supporting the first (1) ground of the decision, namely, that the college lacked authority to imprison Bonham since the statutory grants of authority over licensing and malpractice are distinct. The fifth (5) reason is much briefer, though divided into two parts. If the clauses are not distinguished, Coke argues, "two absurdities should follow": One could be punished many times for the same offense, violating both a divine saying and a legal maxim, and the limitation to a five-pound fine for a month's unlicensed practice would be undermined by the general authority to fine without a time limit. In short, echoing the violation of "common right and reason" that would occur in relation to judge and party if the statute were read other than as Coke reads it, an absurdity—that is, an utter violation of reason—would ensue in relation to the time limit on fines from the same misreading.

Coke then summarizes: "All these reasons were proved by two grounds, or maxims in law."[29] Both maxims are unambiguously concerned with statutory interpretation. In discussing one of them Coke writes, after giving an example from property law, "if it be so in a deed, *a fortiori,* it shall be so in an act of parliament, which (as a will) is to be expounded according to the intention of the makers." To the objections raised, he provides a close reading of the supervisory authority granted in the second clause, drawing again on an argument from absurdity in his interpretation; then establishes that the college was not constituted as a court, so could not punish for contempt of court; and then determines that even if the college were a court with authority to punish contempt, Bonham had committed no contemptuous action, "for he only shewed his case to them, which, he was advised by his counsel, he might justify."[30]

The second major ground of decision (II)—that even assuming the college possessed the authority it claims, the president and censors did not properly execute their statutory charge—rests on six reasons. Again, Coke begins with the strictest sort of statutory construction: The president and censors of the college had fined Bonham, but the statute gives that authority to the censors alone. He then moves to interpretations of the statute based upon much more than the words themselves. For instance, the fines should have been paid to the king, since no grant was made (at least under the second clause) of half the fine to the college, and it is evidently assumed unless otherwise stated that fines belong to the king. Then, "by construction of law," imprisonment should have been made immediately after judgment, not delayed for several weeks; "construction" here refers to a settled practice or presumption made when the act in question is silent, for the benefit of the convicted. Again, the college held their proceedings by parol, not by record, but "regularly they who cannot make a record, cannot fine and imprison." Finally, Coke allows the courts to intercede for Bonham, despite the authority to imprison and deliver out of prison granted to the college, for "reason requires that [this grant] should be taken strictly, for the liberty of the subject (as they pretend) is at their pleasure." Indeed, he says, Parliament itself has shown how narrowly the power to imprison ought to be read, for it thought it necessary to add a statute requiring jailers to receive those committed by the college "because they had authority to do it without any Court." As surely as in the fourth reason for the first ground above, Coke here invokes the reason of the common law—this time not to control an act of Parliament, but with a "judgment of parliament" on his side.[31]

The Verdict on Bonham's

The celebrated statement in *Bonham's Case* thus fits by the logic of the overall argument into a judicial act of interpreting, not striking down, a statute, and the principle it invokes pervades the case as a whole. Still, it is hard to deny that the modesty of the judicial form belies somewhat its larger meaning. Coke was fond of saying that Magna Charta was like Alexander the Great, *magnum in parvo* (a great thing in small form), and one is tempted to apply his adage to his own words in *Bonham's*.[32] The apparent disproportion between the principle and its use is no doubt what Gray has in mind when he notes the change from what Coke apparently said at the time the decision was rendered to the broad statement in his own report of the case. From the bench Coke clearly intended no more than statutory interpretation, but his report suggests a broader meaning. The same observation is certainly behind the arguments of those scholars who see in Coke's words the invocation of higher law. As noted above, MacKay suggests that if the form of Coke's argument is statutory construction, the cause behind the construction is a notion of fundamental law.[33] Moreover, the particular maxim on behalf of which Coke would "control" the statute is no technicality, but a great principle that lies behind the very idea of constitutional government. If no man ought to be judge in his own cause, absolute government is *ipso facto* illegitimate. The principle resonates in Coke's words to James, explaining why the king does not judge in his own person but through his judges; it lies behind his insistence that law rests on the authority and work of a long tradition, expressed perhaps through one mind (though his suggestion that judges ought to give many reasons to convince different hearers qualifies even this) but certainly not created by any one will. "Common right and reason" and *iniquum est aliquem suae rei esse judicem*, like "the common laws," Magna Charta, "fundamental law," and "the artificial perfection of reason," are phrases that for Coke embody the majesty of law. They are no less majestic for serving the cause of construing a statute, rather than ruling in their own name.

But is the invocation of such principles, even indirectly in statutory construction, an exercise of what we today consider judicial review—the overturning by judges of an official act of another government authority? Some of Coke's contemporaries certainly thought this was the gist of *Bonham's Case*. In a speech he gave at the swearing in of Henry Montague, who was made chief justice of the King's Bench upon Coke's dismissal and who was himself the grandson of a chief justice, Chancellor Ellesmere listed his objections to Coke's rulings, half obliquely, by pointing out to the grandson what the grandfather did not do. The last admonition is a clear reference to *Bonham's*: "He challenged not power for the Judges of this Court . . . to judge Statutes and Acts of Parliament to be void, if they conceived them to be against common right and reason; but left the King and Parliament to judge what was common right and reason. I speak not of impossibilities or direct repugnances."[34] Sorting through the double negatives, it appears that Ellesmere's objection to Coke's doctrine parallels Judge Gibson's objection to Chief Justice Marshall's opinion in *Marbury v. Madison*: not that illegitimate statutes would be valid, but that it is the business of others, not of judges, to determine when a statute is illegitimate.[35]

That Coke agrees with Ellesmere that the king or the Parliament can find statutes void is evident from the discussion in the previous chapter: The king can prevent encroachment upon his prerogative by dispensing with the offending statute, and Parliament can always repeal a statute it finds objectionable. The question, then, is not whether Coke thinks the judges are exclusive guardians of fundamental law; it is not whether judges are even principally responsible for maintaining fundamental law, for he surely gives that role to "the high and most honourable court of Parliament." It is whether judges are bound always to read statutes only on their own terms or whether they are to interpret them in light of a common law strong enough "sometimes [to] adjudge them void," at least with regard to certain cases.

Phrased in such a way, it seems clear that Coke believes this is within the authority of judges. Lest this be confused with modern American doctrine, several qualifications are in order. First, Coke's precedents and his entire corpus of writing about the law suggest that from his point of view the innovation would have been to argue that judges must restrict themselves to the mechanical application of statutes whenever possible.[36] It is not clear that statutes are always susceptible to such application: In *Bonham's Case,* even without the fourth reason, Coke constructs a persuasive case that the college had assumed authority far beyond what the words of the statute could fairly be taken to authorize. Even leaving aside the question of the unavoidable ambiguity of statutory language, especially in the face of particular cases not imagined by the legislators, historians do well to remind us that in Coke's day legislation was hardly conceived as the preeminent source of law, as we today conceive it. They go too far who assert that Coke lacked the idea of legislation or new law; but it is clear from his writings that legislation comes about to fill in the gaps in common law, not the reverse. In sheer volume, the legislation that an entire generation might produce in Coke's era was small in relation to the law as a whole, and when one accepts that many statutes were understood to declare common law, not to introduce new law, the significance of legislation further recedes. Coke might indeed state the duty of the judge more generally and more boldly than had his predecessors: This was his innovation. But he faced a much greater innovation in the assertions by James and his supporters of the authority of the monarch.[37]

Second, one should recall the limited meaning Coke attaches to the judges' invocation of common right and reason. However majestic the law is that Coke envisions, *Bonham's* gives judges authority to invoke it only as they go about their business of determining the law in a specific case—for instance, through the form of construing a statute. No censors are given jurisdiction to roam at large through the statute books, excising what they doubt. The authority of judges comes only in the particular case and in the context of interpreting a particular statute. Coke's citations of *Bonham's Case* in the *Institutes* support this reading. It is not cited as a limit on the power of Parliament, or even as a claim to independent power or jurisdiction in the King's Bench or Common Pleas; rather, it is cited when the actual statutes and precedents it interprets themselves merit discussion. Moreover, one might develop a re-stricted reading of *Bonham's* by categorizing it as a question of jurisdiction. As the statute at issue in *Marbury* concerned the jurisdiction of the Supreme Court and thus might merit special attention from that Court, the claim of the college in *Bonham's Case* was that it too was a court of law, and the thrust of Coke's opinion is to refute this pretension.[38]

Finally, the most important limit to *Bonham's Case* as a precedent for mod-ern judicial review is the character of Coke's legal thought as a whole. His question, as we have seen, is always first and foremost, what is law?—not, who rules? In the final part of the *Institutes,* he does distinguish the jurisdic-tion of various courts. In this way he addresses the issue of who has say over what the law is in diverse matters, and he admits how important a question this can be. But his thought is not primarily institutional, his perspective not that of a political scientist. The priority of law itself over the particular bodies that enforce it appears a fixed principle in Coke's understanding. It is implied in his defining jurisdiction by law, rather than defining law by its source. It is consistent with his stress on the importance of learning in law: Not where one sits, but what one knows ultimately counts most. And it may even explain the shift in emphasis away from the common law courts to Parliament as Coke's career moves from one to the other: If authority follows wisdom, and if Coke thought himself the most learned lawyer in England (as even his enemies had to grudgingly concede), then a Parliament filled with lawyers of the stamp of Edward Coke, John Eliot, William Prynne, and others surely was a more reliable source of knowing what was law than a judiciary packed with Stuart courtiers. Coke gives no indication of holding *Bonham's Case* to be a source of what we today would call constitutional principle. But it does indeed testify to his principle of the power and the reason of the law.

OBJECTION AND APOLOGY: COKE'S HISTORY

The interpretation of Coke's legal thought offered in the preceding pages stipulates coherence in a mind as capable as Coke's until the reverse be shown. Nevertheless, it has to confront the following objection: Even if one can excuse Coke's somewhat quaint and pedantic style, even if one can tolerate the pride much noted by his peers and still evident in his pages, one must admit that as a historian Coke has been proven inadequate, not only by sub-sequent research but even by the standard and achievements of some of his near-contemporaries. Modern historians have found Coke guilty of cement-ing into English law numerous palpable fictions. His credulity seduced him to accept as authentic and cite as authoritative the *Mirror of Justices,* a "lavishly fantastic" account of English institutions since King Arthur, concocted in the reign of Edward II but pretending merely to revise a much earlier tract. His stubborn attempt to minimize the impact of William the Conqueror made him blind to continental influences on English law, especially the importation of feudalism.[39] The same historians, however, typically admit that Coke's lack of historical sense was the secret of his great achievement: preserving and indeed revitalizing common law in the age of absolutism, invisibly remaking medieval ideas so that they might prove adequate to the modern world.[40] And since Coke was a preeminently practical man, it is by his achievement that he ought to be judged. Still, his work was not merely "dogmatizing the results of the middle ages," as Maitland would have it; it was illustrating and expounding a certain way of thinking about the law. Coke was concerned not just with the particulars of law but also with the reason that fits them into a whole, into a science. His historiography, then, is integral to his legal thought. If it proves insufficient, the entire edifice is undermined.

The most thorough account of Coke's view of history is in J. G. A. Pocock's *The Ancient Constitution and the Feudal Law*. Treating Coke as the "truly representative genius" of the common law mind, Pocock writes, "His historical thought could be founded on the presumption that any legal judgment declaring a right immemorial is perfectly valid as a statement of history." The flawed or primitive historiography that characterized "the common-law interpretation of English history, the predecessor and to a large extent the parent of the more famous 'Whig interpretation,'" he continues, "arose essentially from latent assumptions governing historical thinking, which had been planted deep in the English mind by centuries of practice of a particular form of law; but it possessed also a political aspect, the need to make a case for an 'ancient constitution' against the king."[41] Pocock's book examines the history of English historiography and aims to document the development of historical consciousness, the understanding that societies and social structures exist in time and thus change over time, with the corollary that "law is a product of history."[42] From his perspective, the matter to explain is what inhibited and then what finally caused the development of this consciousness in England. His finding: The common law mind was the inhibition, while the discovery of the sources of English law in the feudal relations introduced by William the Conqueror broke the stranglehold of belief in the antiquity or immemorial character of English law, thus preparing the way for geniune historical insight, as well as self-conscious political change. My concern here is in a way the obverse: Leaving aside his contemporaries, why did a writer of the stature and talents of Sir Edward Coke insist so fervently, in a manner that apparently foreclosed all evidence to the contrary, upon the antiquity of English law?

Pocock says of Coke that he "read[s] history backwards," deciphering the past in the light of the present rather than trying to accept it on its own terms.[43] This phrase nicely captures the attitude of the common lawyer at work: He begins from the case before him and searches out its precedents in cases decided in the past. If the precedents are honestly read, the result is not necessarily dyslexic. Even finding in a case a meaning only dimly foreseen by its author need not be unhistorical; surely historical development, on any reading, must involve continuity as well as change. Still, the case-by-case search for precedents, which comprises so much of Coke's historical work, does rest on certain assumptions that modern historians understandably question; most especially, it assumes either that the story of the particulars of law can be traced one by one, without examining at every step changes in the whole, or that the whole, while in principle changeable, has remained constant. As the discussion of *Bonham's Case* has shown, Coke's adeptness at collecting precedents has sometimes been wrongly impugned. But Pocock objects to Coke's historiography not for his treatment of particular lines of precedent in themselves but for his complacency about the whole into which they fit: Coke fails to see that the "infinite particulars" he finds in English law are in fact divergent streams from a single, simple fountain—the feudal law imported from the continent by William—and he fails because he has fallen prey to myths about the antiquity of England's fundamental law and political institutions.

Why is Coke vulnerable to historical error? The first point to note is that Coke's insistence is a little less adamant than Pocock's account would make it appear.[44] Though Coke speaks of the fundamental laws as immemorial, he does not assert that law, like gold, cannot be made afresh but simply awaits discovery. Indeed, as we have seen in his discussion of penal law, there is in him something of the reformer, though he would add, no doubt, that his concern for an open and readily knowable criminal law derives from his respect for the fundamental principles of due process, embodied in the twenty-ninth chapter of Magna Charta and declared again in the Petition of Right. His most sweeping claims of the antiquity of English law appear in the prefaces to the *Reports,* beginning in the *Third* and continuing in nearly every subsequent volume, as he pursues his dispute with unnamed critics—though, as Pocock notes, the reliance on the questionable *Mirror* colors his entire oeuvre, for it is cited throughout the *Institutes* as well. It is not altogether clear that Coke expects his claims about the antiquity of the law to be taken strictly. As Pocock admits, Coke expresses skepticism about the mythical King Brutus even as he recites the myth. He does not pretend that unfortunate events—principally the conquest—did not occur, even if he does try to put them in their best light.[45] He tells numerous stories of attempts to subvert or fundamentally alter the laws, though he finds the ancient laws, happily, always restored or confirmed sooner or later. At least once his words suggest that his reading of history is not without a further purpose: In the preface to the *Fourth Institutes,* in speaking of the advantages of writing in English rather than Law French, he adds, "And (to speak what we think) we would derive from the Conqueror as little as we could." Finally, when recounting English history broadly (as opposed to when he examines particular cases or statutes and the circumstances surrounding their origin), Coke constantly says that he is proceeding with a "light touch," suggesting, perhaps, the inconclusiveness of what he writes.[46]

Still, Coke does start from the assumption of continuity in the law. He is not uncritical as an historian, but he is too easy on those sources, such as the *Mirror,* that support continuity, while skeptical of those, such as the writings of Polydore Vergil, that postulate change.[47] In this, again as Pocock notes, Coke follows a tradition of common law thinking; indeed, when discussing the antiquity of English law, he typically cites like-minded assertions from Fortescue and others. What must be recognized is that the presumption of continuity over change is perfectly reasonable for someone like Coke, who accepts divine support for justice and takes seriously the notion of fundamental law as a limit on human willfulness. If justice is not a creation of human will, and if fundamental law can somehow make justice actual, fundamental law ought not to be changed, for justice itself would seem unchangeable.[48] Certainly Coke's expressed belief that God is the source of justice is reason enough for his opinion of its permanence, but the same can be gleaned, if only in a limited way, from one of the most formal and simple principles of justice: that similar cases ought to be similarly decided. This principle, together with a recognition of the importance of predictability in law, holds as good in our time as in Coke's. Moreover, though we Americans take a more positivist view of fundamental law than did Coke, finding it written in our Constitution rather than between the lines in ancient rolls, we are still, despite Article V, apt to regard its most fundamental points—for example, the First and Fifth Amendments—as beyond alteration. The step Coke makes that modern historians would not is to move from the principle that fundamental law ought not to be altered to the historical presumption that it has not been.

Coke takes this step in good conscience because, in the end, the question of law's origin is of secondary importance for him. Paradoxically, despite the great emphasis he seems to place upon the antiquity of law, despite his persistent search for ancient precedents and his research in old records, his understanding of law is in a way more oriented toward the present and the future than is modern theory: Coke presumes historical continuity rather than historical change because he thinks the wisdom of the law has a higher authority than its origin. The importance of wisdom over origin in law helps explain what otherwise appear to be strange quirks in Coke's history. For instance, at the beginning of the chapter on Parliament in the *Fourth Institutes,* immediately after recounting the various names given to Parliament in its distant past, Coke jumps to the Bible to show that parliaments had been held in ancient Israel. His grounds for inferring the authority of the past for the present appear in the passage quoted earlier about the "artificial reason of the law," "fined and refined" over many generations. Pocock treats Coke's "artificial reason" as a "sophistication and extension" of a general presumption of the wisdom of custom, but the difference is not superficial: It seems less irrational to assume wisdom in practices developed by those who in their own time were reputed wise and trusted with authority than to assume wisdom in anything that has merely survived.[49] And even in matters of law, the claim of antiquity serves as a presumption, not a proof, of wisdom: If reason can show the presumption mistaken in a particular case, the law can be revised. What Coke insists is that "no man ought to take it upon himself to be wiser than the laws."[50] Such a notion would not only cause trouble for society; it would most likely be purely and simply mistaken.

Coke's attitude toward wisdom in law and his consequent approach to history complement the absence in his thought of the concept of regime or constitution. Modern historiographers such as Pocock stress the embeddedness of all political thinking in the idiom of its age and in the intellectual tradition of its milieu, but for Coke, thinking within a tradition was less an unavoidable necessity than a wise choice. As noted before, the concept of regime, at least on the classical understanding, entails the priority of the question, who rules?, over the question, what is law? It gives precedence to prudence over jurisprudence, and to the statesman over the lawyer. Coke's view, in contrast, is that the wisdom of any single ruler is impoverished beside the wealth of experience collected in the law and given effect through one who is learned in the law. This seems due as much to the limits of the human mind as to weaknesses of human nature: Ruling requires knowledge of a multitude of particulars that is beyond the capacity of even the wisest to comprehend. Rule by many, collecting their knowledge, still would not surpass the law in wisdom or dispense with its necessity; many minds are as apt to disagree as to complement one another, and an accepted principle of harmony among them would already be law. Despite his frequent references to Aristotle and his participation in the custom of calling him simply "the philosopher," Coke's embrace of the laws and neglect of the concept of regime is more Platonic than Aristotelian. Aristotle wrote of different kinds of regimes, some good although imperfect, while Plato speaks of regime in the precise sense as rule by a philosopher-king, in whose absence the second best scheme involves a turn toward laws.[51] Coke differs from Plato, of course, not only because he never raises the possibility of rule by a divine philosopher, but also because he makes the law an object less of reverence than of scientific study.

Still, Coke does not deny the need for veneration of the law. Indeed, one might say he takes it for granted, for even his legal science, with its presumption of the law's wisdom, puts respect before criticism; this certainly accords with his ready use of numerous authorities and his unwillingness to scrutinize too closely their authenticity. He is explicit about the need for lawyers themselves to cultivate respect. In an age known for its corruption, Coke was reputed to be a scrupulously honest judge, and he had no sympathy for judicial officers who accepted presents for giving justice.[52] In fact, in the preface to the *Tenth Reports,* he links reverence and robe:

> Their ancient reputation is (I assure myself) the better continued, because they without the least alteration continue the ancients habits and ornaments belonging to their state and degree: for most commonly the ancient reverence of any profession vanisheth away with change of the ancient habit, albeit the newer be more costly, courtly, and curious.[53]

One is tempted to wonder whether the "light touch" of ancient English history that Coke adds to his analysis of law is not in fact an "ancient habit" of dressing the law in reverential garb. But Coke seems ill suited to play costumer: He is too earnest, and he lacks the flair for disguise. In the same preface, defending the study of antiquity against those who condemn it "as a withered and back-looking curiosity," he praises the light it brings to understanding, as well as its "great grace and ornament." Though he certainly borrows ancient quotations, not only from law and Bible but from "the philosophicall poet" (Vergil) and "our English poet" (Chaucer), his own style of writing bears a quaintness that goes well beyond what can be attributed, as Blackstone thought, to his times —as even a cursory comparison with the legal writings of his contemporary and rival Bacon makes plain.[54] Certainly his many, clumsy invocations of truth make it unlikely that he meant his celebration of the law's antiquity merely as a salutary myth. Even Coke's "light touch" seems heavy-handed, lacking in irony as much as grace. But perhaps this is attributable less to the temper of the man than to the character of law itself.[55]

Coke recognizes that the obscurity of the origin of common law is in some respects the secret of its success: It makes the law in its most fundamental points unwritten and thus leaves it always dependent upon reason for its discovery, confirmation, and elaboration. Still, the obscurity of law's origins is accidental for any society. If a country has had the good fortune of continuous peace and uninterrupted succession, together with the loss of ancient records, perhaps the myth of near perpetuity can grow out of the fact of long endurance. But few modern societies enjoy such political luxury; the origin of their laws is within memory, or at least a matter of record. Of course, Coke too had to face a country in whose recent as well as distant history he found much to deplore. Still, the English kings' ancient habit of professing that they merely confirmed ancient laws was a happy circumstance—and, incidentally, indicates that Coke's view that they lacked the authority to act alone is not entirely without foundation.[56] It cannot be presumed that the ancient laws of all countries are good laws, or good enough to require mere adjustment instead of deeper transformation. The artificial reason of the law was a blessing to England, but others have been less fortunate. The real insularity of Coke's thought is not his lack of familiarity with other systems of law; these he thought he knew well enough to distrust.[57] It is the inability of his rich elaboration of law to serve, without recasting, any society other than England and its progeny—and perhaps even them once the chain of continuity had been severed. The power of Coke's writing for England was its ability to assimilate that which it found into a whole of law. Its weakness is its inability to start fresh—or to meet a drastic change in fortune.

PART TWO
THE SOVEREIGN REASON
OF THOMAS HOBBES

There is no surer stumbling block for scholars who would trace the origins of American constitutionalism in the tradition of the English common law than the current recognition on the part of political theorists of all stripes that one cannot dismiss as eccentric or anomalous the political theory of Thomas Hobbes. Years ago Edward Corwin could give Hobbes only passing mention in a story that moved from Coke, to the mid-seventeenth-century Parliamentarians, to John Locke, and thence to the American Founders; now it seems clear that the radicalism Locke sought to temper, if temper he did, was not only the political radicalism of the Roundheads but the philosophic radicalism of his older contemporary. The awareness today of Hobbes's importance comes partly from the insight of scholars who have returned to his work or to its context, partly from the uncanny ability of his theory to speak to our time—as if Hobbes had better understood, or at least more frankly foretold, the logic of the modern world he helped inaugurate than did his more celebrated successors.

Hobbes has long been recognized as a founder of the modern legal positivism that came to dominate legal thought in the nineteenth century, and thus he is known as a forerunner of Jeremy Bentham and John Austin. Overlooked was the extent to which his doctrine of law is at the center of his political thought and of a piece with his entire philosophy. Moreover, though scholars acknowledge that Bentham's critique of Blackstone was the source of his life's project, few appreciate that the quarrel between utilitarian theory and common law had been rehearsed over a century before in the censure of Coke and common lawyers that runs through Hobbes's works and culminates in the posthumously published *Dialogue between a Philosopher and a Student of the Common Laws of England*. No doubt Hobbes's battles with the clergy, always the principal site of his reputation, have eclipsed his battles with the lawyers; and perhaps his ultimate success with the latter healed earlier wounds. Still, in order to see the paradox involved in tracing the roots of American constitutionalism at once to the common law and to its declared enemy, Hobbes's political theory demands our attention. And in the course of this examination, especially through discovery of his scientific analysis and its limits, we gain a clue as to what the liberal project was and was not intended to achieve.

4

THE SCOPE OF SCIENCE
AND THE FOCUS OF LAW

No one with the research skills of a freshman or a textbook younger than his grandparents could overlook the importance to the development of political and legal thought ascribed today to the philosophy of Thomas Hobbes. Even if his claim to have invented political science is not accepted without complaint, his contribution is judged invaluable. He introduced the concept of power into political discourse, gave accounts of such ideas as natural right and sovereignty that have become classic, invented or at least justified the morality of modern commercial society, and sewed together these threads with a rigor that challenges contemporary logicians and in a pattern that still lures the politically acute. Among legal theorists and philosophers he is acknowledged as the father of legal positivism—the doctrine that all law is the command of a sovereign authority—and even in circles where positivism is no longer accepted, it is still considered the opponent to flog.

Yet to an educated American of the generation that wrote and adopted the Constitution or that saw the establishment of judicial review, the notion that Hobbes's philosophy lay behind American constitutionalism would have appeared preposterous. Leaving aside the obvious preference for monarchy Hobbes expresses in his various works, he could hardly be interpreted to countenance anything like an independent judiciary, much less one empowered to set aside legislative acts. He insists throughout his works that sovereignty cannot in any form of government be divided, and it is essential to sovereignty that it include both the power to legislate and the power to judge. When he speaks of fundamental law, it is as a moral command to seek peace or as a grant of power to a sovereign, but not as an enforceable bar to the exercise of authority. Turning from text to historical record, there is little evidence that Hobbes's works were widely known or read by the Framers. His books were apparently absent from early American libraries, so it is not surprising that one recent study of the frequency of citations to authorities in the pamphlet literature of the Founding era weighs Hobbes in well behind Montesquieu,

Blackstone, and Locke, behind even the rather technical Coke—and does not mention whether Hobbes was cited as authority or rogue.[1]

Of course, the frequency of citation or even the self-understanding of the Framers is not decisive if the question of Hobbes's influence is treated not from a narrowly historical but from an analytical point of view—as, incidentally, Hobbes himself would have wished it measured. Those who claim Hobbes as a forebear of American constitutionalism trace his influence through the media of Locke and Samuel Pufendorf, or even Montesquieu and Blackstone: Not his writings but his concepts were indispensable, concepts he formulated with such singular clarity and force that they needed shielding by more prudent minds and blunting by gentler pens before they could face the test of practice.[2] That Hobbes deserves to be considered the founder of modern liberalism I will not dispute, although the interpretation is itself controversial. That, I believe, is because his theory is not constitutionalist, though it seems liberal, and this perplexes modern liberals who think the marriage of liberalism and constitutionalism unproblematic. In any event, modern liberalism is not the only parent of the American regime, and thus Hobbes must share the ancestral shrine, not only with his intellectual progeny, but even with some of those he vigorously opposed. What is undeniable is that Hobbes thought radically about politics and law. His importance either as father of liberalism or grandfather of American constitutionalism cannot be assessed until his thought is understood.

Understanding Hobbes's political philosophy, however, is a tall order, as suggested by the prodigious number of recent books and articles attempting it. The only matter on which there is universal agreement is that Hobbes's theory is riddled with inconsistencies.[3] Of a lesser thinker—or in a more intuitive philosopher—inconsistency is expected, but Hobbes insists with perfect self-confidence that his originality lies precisely in the rigor with which he moves from proposition to proposition: Grant him his premise, and no one who reasons rightly can avoid his conclusion. One might be excused the thought that the repeated efforts of modern scholars to explain or resolve the inconsistencies they think they find in his writing betray a lingering doubt that perhaps after all his boast was warranted. In this chapter, in the context of Hobbes's legal doctrine, I will discuss his doctrine of science, which is not only a solvent for some of the inconsistencies commentators find in his theory but also a key to his liberalism—indeed, to liberalism simply. In the next, I will look at the fundamentals of his political science, with an eye toward both his scientific method and his view of law. There follow some thoughts on Hobbes's efforts to apply his theoretical concepts to particular circumstances, specifically to the English polity. Finally, I will examine in some detail Hobbes's book devoted to common law, showing, I hope, how it fits into his

larger theory and how it sharpens his opposition to the common law understanding of Sir Edward Coke.

A NEW DEFINITION OF LAW

Hobbes refers to his political teaching, or at least to certain parts of it, by a
variety of names: civil science, moral philosophy, doctrine of politiques, civil
philosophy, even "doctrine of Subjection."[4] Although, for reasons that will
soon be apparent, he never calls it a jurisprudence, the importance of the
theme of law to his thought is evident throughout his works. He entitled the
first version of his theory *The Elements of Law,* ending the volume with a
thematic discussion of law. The subsequent versions, *De Cive* and *Leviathan,*
conclude with discourses on religious matters, but these follow chapters on
law, and it is characteristic of Hobbes's treatment of the relation of religion to
politics that he defines religion in terms of law, not the reverse. Hobbes devotes three chapters of *Leviathan* to law, crime, and punishment (chapters
26–28), introducing the first by comparing himself explicitly to Plato,
Aristotle, and Cicero, and concluding the last with an explanation of the
book's title. Even the bulk of his discussion of the state of nature is devoted to
law—to what he calls "laws of nature," though with a peculiar twist.

But if law is a critical theme in Hobbes's political thought, it is no accident
that it is a theme toward which he builds, not one with which he begins. His
work—in spite of its scientific form, or perhaps because of it—is a polemic
against a number of schools of thought, most prominently the clerics and
their fellows in the universities; but also among his opponents are the English
common lawyers, and most prominent among these is Sir Edward Coke.[5]
Twice in *Leviathan* Hobbes criticizes Coke by name, accusing him of supporting flagrant injustice in the name of law. More frequently, he challenges
the way of thinking characteristic of common lawyers, of reasoning from
precedents and other authorities. The common lawyers, like their counterparts in the clergy, typify the mentality which in the context of the latter
Hobbes brands "Aristotelity," and he intends by his science to dissolve it.[6]
Indeed, the central concepts of Hobbes's political theory—the state of nature
and the sovereign—are designed precisely to undermine the claims to political authority not only of the clergy but of those versed in the common law.

Hobbes thinks that, strictly speaking, all law must be civil law, and he
leaves no doubt how that ought to be defined: "CIVILL LAW, Is to every
Subject, those Rules, which the common-wealth hath commanded him, by
Word, Writing, or other sufficient Sign of the Will, to make use of, for the
Distinction of Right, and Wrong; that is to say, of what is contrary, and what

is not contrary to the Rule."[7] From this definition he draws a number of consequences: The sovereign, who represents the commonwealth, is its legislator; since it can make and unmake laws, the sovereign can be bound by no law; custom is law only through the tacit consent of the sovereign; neither a parliament that sits at the pleasure of a monarch nor a learned lawyer writing commentaries can be said to have the legislative power. Moreover, laws must be promulgated, and they need interpretation to be applied to particular cases; as the key to interpretation is knowing the intent of the lawgiver, authoritative interpretation is properly the office of the lawgiver itself. In short, Hobbes defines law as the product of a legislative power, but precisely because the sovereign legislator is the source of all law, it must also be the supreme judge.

The union of judging and the legislative power in Hobbes's doctrine is further secured by his remarkable statement that "the Law of Nature, and the Civill Law, contain each other, and are of equall extent."[8] It is no surprise that Hobbes's law of nature should envelop the civil law. The third law of nature, "justice," requires that covenants be kept and therefore, when the covenant is to obey a sovereign, it follows that the civil laws must be obeyed. However, that the civil law contains natural law is a bit less obvious and has been the subject of extensive scholarly dispute. Hobbes says that the existence of a sovereign power transforms what in the state of nature were merely the counsels of reason into commands to be obeyed: The laws of nature become the sovereign's law, too.[9] This happens automatically, as it were, without the sovereign's having to invoke them, but in practice natural law enters civil law most obviously when judges must decide cases which no written law seems to determine. These must be decided by equity, Hobbes insists, which is among the laws of nature he details, rather than by precedent, for precedents might be in error, and "No mans error becomes his own Law; nor obliges him to persist in it." The principle of equity and the command of the sovereign are perfectly complementary; "the Intention of the Legislator is always supposed to be Equity."[10]

From this quick account of Hobbes's definition of law and the functions of the sovereign as legislator and judge, one can discern already the difficulties in relating his theory to the American doctrine of judicial review. A sovereign in Hobbes's view must by definition be absolute, and therefore it must be a single man or a single body of men. He cannot allow a separation of powers, and without separation at least of the judicial power from the legislative, there can be no judicial voiding of legislative acts. In fact, though he sometimes hints to the contrary, Hobbes leaves no place in his theory for a constitution in the sense of a fundamental law, because the only fundamental law is that "without which the Common-wealth cannot stand," and for Hobbes this means only the grant of power to the sovereign, which of course includes the power to make all laws.[11] Rather than supply a foundation for American doctrine, Hobbes's theory would appear to justify its critics. But such assertions must remain preliminary until a more thorough exploration of his thought is undertaken.

THE LOGIC OF HOBBESIAN SCIENCE

Picking up afresh Hobbes's *Leviathan,* or indeed any of his political works, one is immediately struck by how far away from politics they seem to start. *The Elements of Law* and *Leviathan* begin with chapters on human sensation—the second chapter of *Elements,* condensed in *Leviathan,* is devoted to optics—and even *De Cive,* which Hobbes introduces as the final part of a complete philosophical system, begins with his famous abstraction, the state of nature. As commentators have observed, Hobbes's strategy of beginning with the pieces of human nature and only afterwards moving toward the state is in some way or another central to his intention. His resolutive-compositive method, which analyzes wholes into their elements and then reassembles them as complexes of those elements, not only lends his work its format but permeates its conclusions.[12] Disputes that have arisen in the scholarly literature over whether Hobbes's basic intention is political, with the method serving as a rhetoric toward political ends, or whether the method is primary and the politics derivative, somewhat miss the point. Hobbes's science is of a piece with his politics; indeed, he thinks it is the key to his politics—or at least, it is his solution to politics as it has typically been practiced.[13] In any event, to get to Hobbes's theory of law through his politics requires that one examine in what kind of enterprise he thinks himself engaged.

Those who read Hobbes's method as rhetoric are on strongest ground when examining his treatment of religious matters, for the usefulness of Hobbes's scientific method in combatting the doctrines of the divines is in one sense indisputable. Presenting his method as a hypothetical construct of reason frees Hobbes from the need to start with theological authority; then finding his conclusions perfectly consonant with Scripture, properly interpreted, allows him to eat his cake and have it too. Or rather, Hobbes invites the proverb's admonition, for he thoroughly chews and digests the case for reasoning from authority in the scientific sections of his writings, then argues that scriptural authority blesses the meal. Indeed, it is difficult to see how anyone not inclined to doubt could be seduced by Hobbes's rhetoric, for his purpose is transparent from the start. For instance, in the second chapter of *Leviathan,* concerning imagination, he inserts a lengthy discussion of how people can mistake dreams for waking thoughts, hinting in no uncertain terms that this explains the visions prophets allege. At the end of the lengthy third part, in which he reinterprets Scripture so that it coincides with his philosophy, he reminds the reader that "it is not the bare Words, but the Scope [intention] of the writer that giveth the true light, by which any writing is to bee interpreted," recommending perhaps that the twelve previous chapters be read with a wink.[14]

Hobbes's attitude toward religion and its place in his political theory have been sources of continuing debate among commentators. This is not the place either to review that debate or to reweigh the evidence on which it depends; my interpretation of Hobbes supposes that his notions of the unknowability of God and of the unreliability of divine accounts philosophically undermine—as indeed he meant them to—his occasional appeals to Christian authority. What should be noticed for the purpose of understanding Hobbes's legal teaching is that in many passages he clearly assimilates religion to his general analysis of man and society. In his discussion of belief and its causes, and throughout his work, Hobbes treats prophetic or ecclesiastical authority as a particular sort of the more general category of authority and thus treats belief and faith within the more general category of opinion.[15] Subsuming Christian doctrine under general categories accords with his project of giving every divine mystery a natural explanation; but he thinks himself engaged in an even broader critique, aimed not only at clerics but at the pagan moral philosophers—because he considers their works flawed in themselves and easy prey for churchmen—and at modern rhetoricians and others who found in such authors fuel for their own flames.

As the natural philosophy of the ancients was "rather a Dream than Science," "Their Morall Philosophy is but a description of their own Passions," and their politics just a registry of what they saw.

> In these westerne parts of the world, we are made to receive our opinions concerning the Institution, and Rights of Common-wealths, from *Aristotle, Cicero,* and other men, Greeks and Romanes, that living under Popular States, derived those Rights, not from the Principles of Nature, but transcribed them into their books, out of the Practice of their own Common-wealths, which were Popular; as the Grammarians describe the Rules of Language, out of the Practise of the time.[16]

Hobbes has been accused of distorting Aristotle's political science, but the charge misfires, once it is recognized that his objection is not simply to Aristotle's conclusions but to his whole mode of inquiry.[17] Classical political thought makes a point of starting from practice, prejudice, and passion—in sum, from opinion—then tries, dialectically, to rise beyond it. According to Hobbes, such a way of proceeding is doomed from the start, captivated by its origin and thus incapable of solving the problems it encounters. To accept the

authority of classical authors is merely to thicken the fog, for literary authority is only an opinion in the reader of the virtue or wisdom of the author—or
perhaps of the teacher who instructed the reader in the author.[18] Opinion
bolstered by opinion, prejudice confirmed by prejudice: This, for Hobbes, is
the character of all previous political thinking. Of little value in itself, its chief
use is by ambitious men, who promote their own purposes while confusing
ordinary people's common sense, or in Hobbes's language, their "naturall
Prudence."[19]

When Hobbes defines science, it is in contrast not to authority or
divinity—though it is certainly distinct from them—but to prudence, to
what passes for unassisted human wisdom among most men, indeed among
even those who claim to speak scientifically. Prudence is "a *Praesumption* of
the *Future*, contracted from the *Experience* of time *Past*." It seems to be the
sum of the processes of natural thought, according to Hobbes, collecting the
freight of the "Trayn of regulated Thoughts" as it runs in two directions:
"when of an effect imagined, wee seek the causes, or means that produce it,"
and "when imagining any thing whatsoever, wee seek all the possible effects,
that can by it be produced; that is to say, we imagine what we can do with it,
when wee have it." Hobbes calls prudence also a natural act of the mind, not
an acquired skill; it depends upon memory, and thus those are most prudent
who have the longest memories (or what is the same thing for Hobbes, the
most experience); and it is particular to that realm of experience in which a
man is versed, so that "A plain husband-man is more Prudent in affaires of his
own house, than a Privy Counseller in the affaires of another man."[20] Prudence is subject to error—for knowledge confined to particulars cannot distinguish surely enough when new circumstances are different from previous
ones—but its faults, like its powers, are confined to particulars. Prudent men
might be wrong in their predictions, but they are at least immune to systematic error or absurdity.[21] Since, however, even a particular error of judgment in the governance of one's life (or one's commonwealth) can lead to dire
consequences, something better than prudence is needed (though this is not
to say that there is not something worse).

That something better, of course, is science, acquired by the steady work of
reason, which itself is "nothing but *Reckoning* (that is, Adding and Subtracting) of the Consequences of generall names agreed upon, for the marking and
signifying of our thoughts." Science is thus "a knowledge of all the consequences of names appertaining to the subject in hand," or "knowledge of
Consequences, and dependence of one fact upon another."[22] Since it consists
in the proper ordering of language, and since language is invented by human
beings as a way of remembering their own thoughts and sharing them with
one another, science is not, like prudence, a natural possession; it depends on
human industry, first in "apt imposing of names," then in the reckoning of

their consequences. Indeed, reason itself, since it works upon language, is not entirely a natural faculty, according to Hobbes, though he often refers to "natural reason," especially in contrast to religious thought. The reckoning of cause and consequence is a natural function of the mind, but naturally human beings perceive only particular things, so the fullest natural knowledge of cause and consequence can be no more than memory of particulars—that is, prudence. Language, however, enables men to invent general names for things that seem alike to them and thus to develop a general science of cause and consequence. It is precisely in the distinction between accounting only for particulars and knowing general relations that the distinction between prudence and science lies.[23]

Of course, not only science and prudence are differentiated by the relation of particular and general, for when speaking of human things, the relation of individuals to the generality is what politics—and law—are about. In *Leviathan,* Hobbes explains the distinction between proper and common names:

> Of Names, some are *Proper,* and singular to one onely thing; as *Peter, John, This man,* this *Tree*: and some are *Common* to many things; as *Man, Horse, Tree*; every of which though but one Name, is nevertheless the name of divers particular things; in respect of all which together, it is called an *Universall*; there being nothing in the world Universall but Names; for the things named, are every one of them Individuall and Singular.

This passage is often cited to illustrate Hobbes's nominalism, but the paragraph immediately following appears to counter its thrust:

> One Universall name is imposed on many things, for their similitude in some quality, or other accident: And whereas a Proper Name bringeth to mind one thing onely; Universals recall any one of those many.[24]

If the similitude is in the things named, then the things themselves, not just their names, partake of universality. Since Hobbes insists that careful definition is the root of all science, it seems critical to be clear whether he thinks general names are human creations or are bestowed in recognition of natural kinds.[25] The dichotomy dissolves, however, if one recalls the psychological basis upon which he is building: Accidents, which Scholastic philosophers defined as nonessential characteristics of things, are according to Hobbes given their names to indicate not properties in things themselves but our conceptions of things, and the origin of our conceptions is in sense. Hobbes gives an account of the cause of sensation, to be sure, and thus an account of how it is that actual (if unknown) properties in bodies make us aware of themselves, but like all natural philosophy, this must remain to some extent conjectural: An account of sensation, like an account of the motions of the heavens, offers possible causes only. Moreover, in the description Hobbes gives, sensation is not mere receptivity but the mutual action of organ and object. Assigning common names is not done at random, according to Hobbes, but that does not make naming any less an arbitrary act.[26] Like necessity and freedom, conceiving and naming are as consistent to Hobbes as cause and consequence: The apparent opposition between something caused (conceiving) and something free (naming) arises only because the train of thoughts runs in two directions, because human beings can look both forward and back.

This last remark deserves elaboration, for Hobbes's reconciliation of liberty and necessity is at the heart of his theory, in its epistemological as well as political moment. According to Hobbes, the term *free will*, taken literally, is nonsense. Freedom is the absence of external impediments to the movement of bodies; voluntary actions that are unimpeded are free, but also necessary,

> because every act of mans will, and every desire, and inclination proceedeth from some cause, and that from another cause, which causes in a continuall chaine (whose first link is the hand of God the first of all causes) proceed from *necessity*. So that to him that could see the connexion of those causes, the necessity of all mens voluntary actions, would appear manifest.[27]

Whether or not any man can see every connection between sense and thought and deed is a matter that will be of some importance later—Hobbes seems to think it more or less possible in oneself, but not necessarily in another—but in either case, the argument here is unaffected. Actually, Hobbes considers it no loss, and perhaps a gain, that men be disabused of vain mystique about the autonomy of their wills. Knowing the cause of will might satisfy the curious and even prove politically useful, but Hobbes clearly thinks the more interesting form of knowledge proceeds in the opposite direction—not back to find why we have done as we have, but forward to figure the future results of our present actions. Moreover, the latter sort of knowledge is the more certain for Hobbes, since we have greater control over effects when the causes are in our power. The question of the origin of man's conceptions is of interest to the biologist and anthropologist, but the surer knowledge is of the consequences of the names we assign to give those conceptions steady form. Though the logic of Hobbes's position requires that the causes of assigning names be themselves subject to study—this, no doubt, is the business of etymology, which Hobbes now and again pursues—the consequences of names can be known independent of etymological inquiry, provided the definitions are clear. The direction of study along the chain of consequence, in other words, depends upon one's interest; there is no inherent need to grasp the whole in order to calculate the links.

These observations ought to help resolve certain difficulties that appear to arise concerning Hobbes's account of scientific reasoning, in particular whether he regards scientific truth as analytical ("consequences of names") or empirical ("consequences of facts"). In *Leviathan* he says both, as we have seen—though he denies that there can be scientific knowledge of the consequences of things, or as post-Kantians say, of "things-in-themselves."[28] In his more strictly philosophical treatises, *De Corpore* and *De Homine,* he distinguishes between deductive and inductive reasoning and the degrees of certainty they possess. Geometry and other sciences that proceed from humanly constructed definitions to conclusions strictly by means of syllogism yield certain knowledge, while physics, which studies things whose causes are not in our power, must involve some speculation as to causes—though it can use geometry in working out its theories.[29] Yet again, even the break between the deductive and speculative sciences does not seem decisive for Hobbes: Though optics and harmonics belong to physics as he conceives it, what we would call mechanics belongs to a science of motion that he thinks can be developed a priori. The beginning of all science is experience or sense, and what is crucial for science is that everything studied be treated with consistency in naming, precision in distinguishing, and thoroughness in the calculation of consequences. The different directions of our reasoning, even the differences in the things studied, depend upon our purposes. As science itself results from human industry working upon a continuous universe of bodies in motion, so its various parts do not mimic natural kinds but answer to the various questions researchers decide to ask. As Hobbes says of the division of categories of law, so he would say of distinguishing the sciences: "It is a thing that dependeth not on Nature, but on the scope of the Writer; and is subservient to every mans proper method."[30]

SCIENCE'S PURPOSE AND POLITICS' SCIENCE

Where, then, in Hobbes's scheme does his political science belong? This turns out, not surprisingly perhaps, to be a difficult question, and one on which his several works seem equivocal. At the beginning of *De Corpore,* in a general introduction to his system of philosophy, he writes:

> The principal parts of philosophy are two. For two chief kinds of bodies, and very different from one another, offer themselves to such as search

after their generation and properties; one whereof being the work of nature, is called a *natural body,* the other is called a *commonwealth,* and is made by the wills and agreement of men. And from these spring the two parts of philosophy, called *natural* and *civil.*[31]

But he divides the sciences somewhat differently in *De Homine,* where he compares "politics and ethics (that is, the sciences of just and unjust, of equity and inequity)" to geometry. As demonstrable knowledge is possible in geometry because "the generation of the figures depends on our will," so politics and ethics "can be demonstrated a priori; because we ourselves make the principles—that is, the causes of justice (namely laws and covenants)—whereby it is known what justice and equity, and their opposites injustice and inequity, are."[32]

The comparison between civil philosophy and geometry runs through *Leviathan* as well; in its chapter on reason and science, Hobbes notes that "Writers of Politiques, adde together *Pactions,* to find mens *duties.*"[33] After the excerpt from *De Corpore* quoted above, he proceeds with another refinement: "Civil philosophy is again divided into two parts, whereof one, which treats of men's dispositions and manners, is called *ethics*: and the other, which takes cognizance of their civil duties, is called *politics,* or simply *civil philosophy.*" This might explain the passages that appear to limit civil philosophy to the science of man-made covenants: Those elements of the doctrine that do not fit the bill, most notably the state of nature, natural right, and natural laws, apparently belong to ethics or moral philosophy, which is only a part of the whole. But this solution—though it corresponds to the division between parts of *Leviathan* and the chart in its ninth chapter—is inadequate, not only because Hobbes structures the division somewhat differently in each of his works but also because he insists that both the right and laws of nature persist in civil society.

A further complication appears from the preface to *De Cive.* Explaining why he was able to expound the third part of his philosophical system before the composition of those parts logically prior—why, despite the rigorous order of proof he appears to demand of science, he could write about politics without having first explained the principles of body and motion and then the psychology of man—he asserts that the part of the system on politics, "grounded on its own principles sufficiently known by experience, . . . would not stand in need of the former sections." Indeed, shortly before this claim he had established the state of nature and natural right with these words: "I set down for a principle, by experience known to all men and denied by none. . . ." In the introduction to *Leviathan* he again asks his readers to start from their own experience, but apparently at a different level; that is, from reflection on their own thoughts and passions. Later he treats the "naturall condition of mankind" as an "Inference, made from the Passions," though he immediately shows "the same confirmed by experience" directly. When he treats the passions systematically, however, he begins not with experience, either private or collective, but with his theory of "endeavor," a biological hypothesis about animal motion rooted in his general theory of motion.[34]

In short, though Hobbes clearly signals a special place for politics in his philosophy, his attempts to distinguish political science by the source of its principles seem riddled with ambiguity. But to announce contradiction or muddle would again be premature, for the definition of science given thus far—that science is knowledge of consequences of names or facts—is incomplete. It tells how the scientific mind proceeds, or in Hobbes's terms, what reason does, but it omits what for Hobbes is, as we have seen, indispensable: what is science's end or scope. This he usually defines in reference to philosophy, which he considers synonymous with science.

> The *end* or *scope* of philosophy is, that we may make use to our benefit of effects formerly seen; or that, by application of bodies to one another, we may produce the like effects of those we conceive in our mind, as far forth as matter, strength, and industry, will permit, for the commodity of human life. For the inward glory and triumph of mind that a man may have for the mastering of some difficult and doubtful matter, or for the discovery of some hidden truth, is not worth so much pains as the study of Philosophy requires; nor need any man care much to teach another what he knows himself, if he think that will be the only benefit of his labour. The end of knowledge is power: and the use of theorems (which, among geometricians, serve for the finding out of properties) is for the construction of problems; and, lastly, the scope of all speculation is the performance of some action, or thing to be done.[35]

Human beings—our needs, our benefit, our ends—are the hook from which all scientific thought is suspended; or rather, since Hobbesian philosophy is industrious rather than contemplative, human beings are the switchyard through which all trains must run. The centrality of the human in Hobbesian science does not make his discourse humanistic in the sense in which we use the term today. His principal image is the mechanism. When in *Leviathan* he makes a simile between the human body and the state, he describes the body as itself a mechanism, not mechanism as something organic.[36] What Hobbes remembers but we tend to forget is that the machine is not our opposite but our creature, designed for human purposes. Indeed, thinking in terms of cause and consequence is not simply a human characteristic; for Hobbes, the ability to see oneself as the cause of consequences, not just a link in the chain of causation, is what distinguishes human beings from other animals.[37]

Nothing would be further from the spirit of Hobbes's thought than to dwell too long on what is distinctive about human beings, however. Though he admits that thought may have in curiosity its spur, constant attention to its end must be its bit and bridle, or the mind gets lost in proud or vain speculation. The orientation of science by its ends can serve as a solvent for the difficulties that precipitate when Hobbes's writings are subjected to analysis that begins with distinctions Hobbes himself would never admit. He insists upon precision, as any philosopher must—certainly any philosopher who finds in geometry the model of all rigorous thought. But though he thinks the edifices he constructs to be sound and solid, he makes no pretense that they are anything splendid or grand, much less comprehensive or definitive. His political doctrine of the leviathan-state has been treated by some commentators as a sort of utopia, but this goes beyond Hobbes's own intention. He recognizes, and in *Leviathan* writes repeatedly, that human affairs "can never be without some incommodity or other." Moreover, his doctrine of science itself contains hints of a similar modesty, as when he writes of language that "words are wise mens counters, they do but reckon by them: but they are the money of fooles, that value them by the authority of an *Aristotle*, a *Cicero*, or a *Thomas*, or any other Doctor whatsoever, if but a man."[38] Hobbes has great expectations of the scientific project which he saw beginning around him and to which he made his signal contribution, but he gave to science a limited task: not to weave in man the pattern of the universe or lift him out of time, but simply to address his needs. Today many accept the limited scope of the sciences but expect of philosophy a deeper ambition. Hobbes, who admits no distinction between philosophy and science, exasperates those who would force him to plumb what he thinks are obscure, or indeed illusory, depths.

Nowhere is the limited role for science in Hobbes more evident than in his civil philosophy. In *De Corpore*, Hobbes details some of the arts and thus benefits which science makes possible, then adds: "But the utility of moral and civil philosophy is to be estimated, not so much by the commodities we have by knowing these sciences, as by the calamities we receive from not knowing them."[39] The negative task of politics (almost the definition of liberalism, by the way) perfectly complements Hobbes's assumption that the ends of politics are so obvious as not to require extended argumentation or to legitimate political debate: Whether one begins with the theory of motion, with the practice of introspection, or with the experience of civil war, one arrives at the natural right of self-preservation and the natural law to seek the peace which promises safety. As his most perceptive commentators have noted, Hobbes presupposes rather than concludes that the human good is defined by human passions and by nothing else. Yet this presupposition is coincident with every step of his science, since he thinks the very capacity—

not to mention the motive—to inquire into cause and consequence is constituted by the principle that every action of a human being aims at some good to himself. Hobbes grounds this principle too on experience, confident he can by his logic interpret away any apparent counterexample. Since all experience is irreducibly individual experience, individualism, the hallmark of liberal thought, is the beginning at once of Hobbes's science and his politics. His science, in a sense, is always political or practical science because it is individualistic at its core.[40]

AGAINST THE COMMON LAWYERS

From this sally into Hobbes's theory of science, it must be clear that the manner of thinking characteristic of the common lawyer belongs rather to the drunkenness of the old moral philosophers than to the sobriety of scientific reason. Hobbes does not leave this to the reader's inference. In the chapter of *Leviathan* devoted to what he calls "civill lawes," he takes issue directly with

> (as Sr. Ed. Coke makes it,) an *Artificiall perfection of Reason, gotten by long study, observation, and experience,* (as his was.) For it is possible long study may encrease, and confirm erroneous Sentences: and where men build on false grounds, the more they build, the greater is the ruine: and of those that study, and observe with equall time, and diligence, the reasons and resolutions are, and must remain discordant: and therefore it is not that *Juris prudentia,* or wisedome of subordinate Judges . . . that maketh Law.[41]

Not only what passes for learning among common lawyers receives Hobbes's scorn, but also the principle that precedents have authority. He cites a lengthy passage from Coke as an example of a rule "wherein mens Judgements have been perverted, by trusting to Precedents."[42] The common lawyers' reliance on precedent is consistent with their manner of practical reasoning, their juris*prudence,* and Hobbes's science of politics is designed to make such thought superfluous. Though he admits that to his doctrine "The greatest objection is, that of the Practise," he concludes:

> But howsoever, an argument for the Practise of men, that have not sifted to the bottom, and with exact reason weighed the causes, and nature of Common-wealths, and suffer daily those miseries, that proceed from the ignorance thereof, is invalid. For though in all places of the world, men should lay the foundation of their houses on the sand, it could not thence be inferred, that so it ought to be.[43]

In an earlier passage, in discussing what he calls the manners of men that incline them to irascibility or peaceableness, he makes clear that the common lawyers' appeal to precedent belongs to such ignorance and contributes to the consequent misery.

> Ignorance of the causes, and originall constitution of Right, Equity, Law, and Justice, disposeth a man to make Custome and Example the rule of his actions; in such manner, as to think that Unjust, which it has been the custome to punish; and that Just, of the impunity and approbation whereof they can produce an Example, or (as the Lawyers which onely use the false measure of Justice barbarously call it) a Precedent . . . grown strong, and stubborn, they appeale from custome to reason, and from reason to custome, as it serves their turn; receding from custome when their interest requires it, and setting themselves against reason, as oft as reason is against them: Which is the cause, that the doctrine of Right and Wrong, is perpetually disputed, both by the Pen and the Sword.[44]

Hobbes's answer to the common lawyers, then, is his entire doctrine of the "originall constitution of Right, Equity, Law, and Justice." Houses built on sand cannot be secured by fresh siding or even a few buttresses; the foundation needs rebuilding, and that is no simple task. To be sure, Hobbes does not propose beginning English law again from scratch. Statutes are clearly law by his definition—indeed, they are the very pattern of law—and even custom can remain, provided its authority be derived from the sovereign's tacit consent in leaving it unaltered, rather than from any independent source. Still, to understand the full extent of Hobbes's attempt to transform the law, we must glimpse at the political doctrine he thinks his scientific method has established. Law, it turns out, is not only the system's product but at work in its process as well.

5
THE ORIGINAL CONSTITUTION OF RIGHT

One of the paradoxes in interpreting Hobbes's "doctrine of politiques" is that, in relation to the political thinking of his contemporaries, it is at once completely different and hardly new. That this philosopher, a "radical in the service of reaction,"[1] was no conservative, much less a faithful partisan of Restoration, was not lost on members of his sovereign's court, who distrusted him and sought his prosecution for heresy. Yet Hobbes thought that the marriage of a radically modern science to unswerving support for established sovereignty was perfectly sound, theoretically and politically. Indeed, without a new foundation, the ancient edifice was sure to tumble, as of course Hobbes and his countrymen witnessed before their eyes. In laying this foundation, Hobbes was willing to use old stone, but he insisted it be cut afresh: His language, unlike that of the modern social scientists he helped beget, is not newfangled, but novelty sparkles in the definitions he struck.

For the contemporary scholar who has any acquaintance with the prodigious secondary literature on Hobbes, however, the difficulty in approaching his political philosophy is apt to be almost the reverse. We have necessarily lost much of the context in which Hobbes argued and thus lack a clear sense both of the traditions he meant to oppose and of the novelty of his stance; but we have seen his definitions and concepts subjected to minute and exacting scrutiny, until their lustre is mostly gone. The review here offered of a few central concepts of Hobbes's political theory—the state of nature, natural law, natural right, covenant, and sovereignty—makes no pretense to great originality, unless in proceeding with a somewhat lighter touch than is sometimes applied. The intention is to recollect the scheme of Hobbes's theory to aid in the elucidation of his views on law and particularly on one of the traditions he set himself against, or sought to remake: the common law.

A SCIENTIFIC MODEL OF POLITICS

Whatever the beginning of Hobbes's chain of scientific reasoning in general, the beginning of his politics is the state of nature, or as he calls it in *Leviathan,* "the Naturall Condition of Mankind, as concerning their Felicity, and Misery."[2] As everyone who has ever heard the name Hobbes probably knows, the state of nature is, according to his theory, a state of war, indeed "such a warre, as is of every man, against every man."[3] Between felicity and misery in this condition there is no contest. Human felicity eludes even definition, according to Hobbes, but human misery is self-evident, as the most famous sentence in his writings declares:

> In such condition, there is no place for Industry; because the fruit thereof is uncertain: and consequently no Culture of the Earth; no Navigation, nor use of the commodities that may be imported by Sea; no commodious Building; no Instruments of moving, and removing such things as require much force; no Knowledge of the face of the Earth; no account of Time; no Arts; no Letters; no Society; and which is worst of all, continuall feare, and danger of violent death; And the life of man, solitary, poore, nasty, brutish, and short.[4]

The question of what sort of theoretical construct Hobbes's state of nature is has invited much discussion among scholars. Hobbes calls it an inference from the passions, as we have seen; since he proceeds generally by the resolutive-compositive method, the state of nature ought perhaps to be understood as an image of a political world that, having been taken apart to its causes, is now reassembled. More precisely, it is a reconstructed image of civil war, though it is Hobbes's opinion that even many states that appear sound are in fact on the brink of battle—as seen from his reference to ancient republics as "the Greek and Roman anarchies,"[5] as well as from his critique of European states where political and ecclesiastical authority are in separate and independent hands. Indeed, the best-constituted state is never far enough from the state of nature as not to feel its pinch. Hobbes gives as evidence that we lock up our private possessions (and sometimes go out armed); and it is a much-noted point in his teaching that the sovereign remains in a state of nature vis-à-vis its subjects, in the same way, more obviously, that sovereigns stand one to another.

The crucial presupposition of the state of nature, which Hobbes declares plainly in every version of its exposition, is human equality, and the decisive proof of equality is apparently that every human being is at once vulnerable to being killed and capable of killing.[6] He makes this claim with perfect equanimity, though he hints he is not unaware how shocking a statement it is likely to seem to people who believe in, or believe they have, a conscience, not to mention those who think death a passage, not a stop. His grounds for the claim are difficult to pinpoint, but without doubt it is sewn into the whole fabric of his thought. The assertion of equality depends on the overwhelming finality of death; that death is decisive is confirmed by Hobbes's scientific materialism and his theory of motion; that human beings can be understood in terms of such a science, as objects in motion, seems already to presume equality, or the individualism that is coincident with it. Since equality of mind becomes crucial if one admits that, in the matter of killing and being killed, a clever wit can overcome any disadvantage in bodily strength, Hobbes argues for it based upon his critique of prudence—his firm conviction that no one is prudent enough to foresee everything he would have to foresee to secure himself among his enemies.[7] The additional proof he adds in *Leviathan,* that the equality of wits is confirmed by each man's deep-seated satisfaction with his own wisdom, is evidently a jest borrowed from the first paragraph of René Descartes's *Discourse on Method*; but, characteristically, in Hobbes the play turns deadly serious, for each man's pride in his own wisdom, if too weak to quell the fear of dying, is strong enough to give him mettle to kill.[8]

In discussing the equality of mental faculties in *Leviathan,* Hobbes raises, only to set aside, science, "which very few have, and but in few things."[9] This dismissal merits pause, however, for if science is power, or is becoming powerful, why could scientists not discover so irresistible a science of controlling human behavior as to make themselves invulnerable and their fellows their slaves? Hobbes's response to this query might follow the more general argument he makes against attempting to seize the state: Success is impossible without the help of others' errors, "which errours a man cannot reasonably reckon upon as the means of his security."[10] However determined men's thoughts and actions seem to be in Hobbes's system, he anticipates no science of mental causation so thorough that it could flawlessly manage human thought, or at least another's thought; Hobbes has confidence in the irreducible privacy of the individual mind.[11] Paradoxically, the limit to behavioral science might be said to depend as well on the similarity of human minds and the simplicity of human reasoning. Reason is not so much a faculty as an activity, the elementary activity of adding and subtracting, and success in science is the reward of industry, not the gift of nature.[12] Again, in contrast to prudence, science is easy to share and hard to arrogate to oneself; scientists know their discoveries are no private property of their own, however proud they may be of their efforts and however anxious to see that they are properly credited by a grateful public. Hobbesian science, in capacity as well as intention, promises important things but retains a sort of modesty that makes it politically safe. The diffident Hobbes apparently trusts in the benevolence or public-spiritedness of science: He says that the end of knowledge is both power and the benefit of mankind, without a hint that the two might ever conflict. Hobbes's political science, though it rests on a calculus of passion, betrays its decency, its public-spiritedness, by its reliance on visibility and speech.[13]

But these comments jump ahead of the story. The innocence Hobbes remarks on in the state of nature belongs not to science but to ordinary human nature. Recognizing that his depiction of nature as a condition of utter distrust and universal enmity "may seem strange to some man, that has not well weighed these things" (not to say impious, to one who has), Hobbes insists that he does not "accuse mans nature in it. The Desires, and other Passions of man, are in themselves no Sin. No more are the Actions, that proceed from those Passions, till they know a Law that forbids them: which till Lawes be made they cannot know." Indeed, this point he underlines with repetition: "To this warre of every man against every man, this also is consequent; that nothing can be Unjust. The notions of Right and Wrong, Justice and Injustice have there no place. Where there is no common power, there is no Law: where no Law, no Injustice."[14] In the exegesis of Hobbes's writings, however, this statement, though it seems central to his whole intention, poses a riddle. For after denying that there is either right or law in nature, Hobbes on the very next page of *Leviathan* defines the concepts of natural right and natural law.

THE LAW AND RIGHT OF NATURE

In every version of his political theory, Hobbes insists upon the distinction between right and law, *ius* and *lex*.[15] Right is liberty, law is obligation, and these are as opposite as sea and shore. Where law ends, liberty begins, according to Hobbes, although this formula does not altogether do justice to the tenor of the doctrine. In general, laws cover what they must, and in all things on which laws are silent human beings are free to do as they please; but there are a few limits set by right or liberty to what the legislator can command, or at least, having commanded, can expect to see obeyed. Of these limits, more later. For the present, the point to grasp is that in Hobbesian vocabulary, right and law—typically equated not only by common lawyers but by much of the legist tradition—are both contrary and complementary.

Hobbes defines the right of nature as "the Liberty each man hath, to use his own power, as he will himselfe, for the preservation of his own Nature; that is to say, of his own Life; and consequently, of doing any thing, which in his own Judgement, and Reason, hee shall conceive to be the aptest means thereunto." How far this liberty in the choice of means extends becomes quickly apparent: In the state of nature, "every man has a Right to every thing; even to one anothers body." It is the right of war, indeed of a war without rules. In contrast, the law of nature is the rule of peace: "A LAW OF NATURE, (*Lex Naturalis*,) is a Precept, or generall Rule, found out by Reason, by which a man is forbidden to do, that which is destructive of his life, or taketh away the means of preserving the same; and to omit, that, by which he thinketh it may be best preserved." The "Fundamental Law of Nature" is "to seek Peace, and follow it." Nearly twenty further rules are built upon this, all of them specifying practices that would induce, or at least maintain, a peaceful condition of mankind and all summarized by Hobbes's rewritten golden rule: "Do not that to another, which thou wouldst not have done to thy selfe."[16]

Hobbes answers the riddle of how there can be law in a lawless condition quite explicitly. The laws of nature are, strictly speaking, not laws, but men's "conclusions, or Theorems concerning what conduceth to the conservation and defence of themselves."[17] Accordingly, they do not oblige in deed, only in endeavor, for otherwise they might undermine their basis:

> The Lawes of Nature oblige *in foro interno*; that is to say, they bind to a desire that they should take place: but *in foro externo*; that is, to the putting them in act, not alwayes. For he that should be modest, and tractable, and performe all he promises, in such time, and place, where no man els should do so, should but make himselfe a prey to others, and procure his own certain ruine, contrary to the ground of all Lawes of Nature, which tend to Natures preservation.[18]

Though in civil society, under a sovereign's protection, natural laws have full force, in the state of nature they bind only to the desire to get out. This is suggested even more directly by the second natural law, which urges men to make the covenant that would establish society, and by the third law, which is, "That men performe their Covenants made." The conclusions of reason add up to a science of natural law, which Hobbes calls moral philosophy, obviously intending it to replace what has previously passed by that name. Like the old moral philosophy, it speaks to human passions and seeks in a way to form them—but by changing the object of endeavor, not by recommending their abeyance.

Hobbes calls this philosophy moral rather than civil or political because it is directed toward the individual, or rather, it is what every individual could work out for himself thinking only about his own preservation in the company of men. Commentators, including many in our own day, who condemn the doctrine as not moral but prudential have missed Hobbes's point. He too would distinguish the moral from the prudential, because the former is general, not particular; that is why, after all, natural law can become a science and why it can become enforceable law once there is a common power to enforce it. Any other attempt at the distinction, especially one that defines morality as denial that a man's actions aim at some good to himself, would be classed by Hobbes as "insignificant speech."[19] What confuses or perturbs Hobbes's readers, in his own time as much as in ours, is that his moral law, though general, is not common, in the sense of being anchored in the mores or customs of a community. Custom, like prudence, is too uncertain a ground for human action according to Hobbes, too much like sand, unless of course it is later fixed by a sovereign's notice.

The riddle of how there can be right in a state where there is no right or wrong is more difficult to answer. To be sure, Hobbes equates right and liberty, then defines liberty in what appears to be an altogether amoral way, as "the absence of externall Impediments." As commentators have noted, the external impediments to which Hobbes is referring are moral or legal ones, as he makes more explicit in the chapter of *Leviathan* "Of the LIBERTY of Subjects," where he describes laws as artificial chains; indeed, the state of nature Hobbes depicts is so far from lacking in impediments that all men there seem to be but so many impediments to one another.[20] Hobbes's use of the term *right,* then, seems intended less to show something men have than to free them from preconceived notions. Natural right, he explains in *The Elements of Law,* is "blameless liberty";[21] rhetorically, it is a concept that liberates men from praise and blame, or rather, from claims that nature provides any standards by which men can hold one another to account. Not appearing in *Leviathan* until after Hobbes has described the natural condition, the right of nature seems designed to show not what the state of nature must be but what natural law is not. More precisely, it expresses the state of nature itself, as it appears not to the detached imagination but to the individual in it as he contemplates himself and his predicament.[22] As the state of nature remains always imminent, so the right of nature is inalienable, but the inalienability of the right of self-defense for Hobbes seems rather to testify to the brute fact of individual recalcitrance than to any inherent dignity of human being.[23] Privacy of mind is for Hobbes a natural condition, even a theoretical supposition; it is not, however, a virtue, at least not a virtue Hobbes is willing to defend theoretically.

If this interpretation of natural right is correct, then it follows that Hobbes's use of the term *natural right* does not imply the existence of natural wrong, though commentators have occasionally argued that it does.[24] Since Hobbes holds that necessity in the state of nature knows no bounds, no action there can be categorically denounced, but without doubt certain intentions or attitudes can violate the laws of nature. He says explicitly, for example, that the ninth law of nature is made "against pride," and there are others against cruelty, contumely, and arrogance. Still, to violate natural law is not to violate natural right, though the two can only be understood in relation to each other. What leads to the view that natural right can be wronged is Hobbes's definition of the right in terms of self-preservation: If by nature men have a right to preserve themselves, then it must be wrong to endanger one's own safety. But as the definition quoted before shows, the prohibition against self-destruction belongs to natural law, not natural right. The mention of self-preservation in the definition of the right of nature merely indicates the finding of Hobbesian science as to the direction in which human action—indeed, all motion, as the principle of inertia would have it, or at least all animal motion, as Hobbes's biological theory posits—is bound to go. Without reason, we human beings show our ignorance in the contradictory objects our passions seek; however simple our basic motives, the complexity of human nature leaves us constantly thwarting ourselves. In a sense, this is what the image of the state of nature makes vivid. The work of reason issues in natural law, the doctor's cure for our fever. Natural right gives it room to work, if also work to do.

There is, however, one positive implication of the term *natural right,* which is confirmed by Hobbes's subsequent use of the term *right*. Natural right is the liberty of exercising one's own will or judgment or reason. It expresses the individualism presupposed by Hobbes's theory, and precisely in so doing, it shows each individual what it is about himself that enables him to escape the natural predicament. For right—again, will or judgment or reason—is the coin with which individuals can purchase security. In Hobbesian science, right is the name given to private judgment from the perspective of one who would see it bettered. Since natural right is not wholly alienable, private judgment of the means to one's own preservation can never be completely abandoned, even as the privacy of thought cannot be successfully invaded. Still, proximate matters may be placed in expert hands, and this men can do by covenant, by transferring right and thus by consenting to the right of a sovereign.

COVENANT AND SOVEREIGN

In *Leviathan,* Hobbes devotes the bulk of the first of two chapters on the laws of nature to a discussion of contracts and covenants, then considers at greatest length in the sequel the law of nature that commands justice, that is, that covenants be kept. The importance of covenant and justice—what Hobbes sometimes calls the science of just and unjust—to his political theory as a whole is often overlooked. Scholars who hold, against Hobbes's own statements, that his natural laws are really laws find the discussion of covenant tangential, as do those who think that the account of authorization and representation in *Leviathan* is meant to supplant it.[25] To be sure, Hobbes himself warns against assigning to covenants too much consideration; he was fond of his pun that "covenants without swords are but words," which of course points beyond covenants to a sovereign power. But beginning with a natural right of private judgment in all things and with natural laws that are not really laws because they in no way abridge this right, Hobbes needs the theory of covenant to move from lawlessness to law, from anarchy to justice. Only through covenant is the state of nature transcended, for without it, even a man with the strength to be sovereign remains just another enemy among enemies, holding a power always open to assault.

Covenants are mutual promises, Hobbes writes, and are a form of contract, which is the mutual transfer of right. Since by nature all men have the right to all things, it might seem odd that men would seek to acquire additional rights, but Hobbes explains that to transfer a right to a man involves that one "onely standeth out of his way, that he may enjoy his originall Right."[26] To transfer a right is to create a bond or to put oneself under an obligation to the person to whom the right is transferred. As all men have by nature perfect right to all things, there is "no Obligation on any man, which ariseth not from some Act of his own."[27] Though this seems to leave men enormous freedom, it turns out that there are limits on what sorts of contracts men can make. In particular, no man can contract away his preservation, for that right is, in Hobbes's word, inalienable; no one can can contract to do anything impossible; and no one can contract away a right that has already been transferred. Moreover, covenants are impossible between beings that cannot share speech, so there are no covenants with animals or, barring "Revelation supernaturall," with God.

As these last remarks make plain, covenants become possible through language, though Hobbes points out in his discussion of inalienable right that speech cannot always be taken at face value: Covenants that are impossible to make do not suddenly become possible when one turns a happy phrase. As words are marks for our thoughts, by Hobbes's theory, so they are also signs of our wills. As by speech we fix the flux of thought, so by covenant we settle our wills in relation to one another. Indeed, since Hobbes defines will as the last appetite in an alternate chain of appetite and aversion called deliberation, not as a faculty of mind or soul, there seems to be no other way for human beings to fix their wills in relation to one another except through covenant.[28] The importance of speech in covenant appears again in Hobbes's much-noted remark that relates justice, defined as the keeping of covenants, to the principle of noncontradiction.

Injury, or *Injustice,* in the controversies of the world, is somewhat like to that, which in the disputations of Scholers is called *Absurdity.* For as it is there called an Absurdity, to contradict what one maintained in the Beginning: so in the world it is called Injustice, and Injury, voluntarily to undo that, which from the beginning he had voluntarily done.[29]

In the absence of such a settling of wills, men remain in the state of nature toward one other, where no act can be unjust.

But covenant alone proves insufficient to draw men out of the state of nature, at least until its terms are straight. Logic requires that men keep their covenants lest they contradict their wills, but since the steadiest of all wills is toward self-preservation, and since the right thereto cannot be renounced, there is no contradiction in breaking one's promise so as to save one's skin. Of a covenant made in "the condition of meer Nature," Hobbes writes that "upon any reasonable suspition, it is Voyd," and since every man in that state is his own judge of what is reasonable, this release is no small matter. Yet he immediately adds: "But if there be a common Power set over them both, with right and force sufficient to compell performance; it is not Voyd."[30] Covenant is only one step on the way out of the state of nature. It must be accompanied by the establishment of a common power, of a sovereign. Though the definition of justice is given by the logic of covenant, Hobbesian law is a covenant plus a sword.

The twist, as many of Hobbes's commentators have discovered, is that, while the sovereign is needed to make covenants secure, a covenant is needed to create the sovereign. Such a compact, after all, is what Hobbes recommends in the second law of nature: Every individual who would leave the state of nature agrees with every other to transfer their rights to govern themselves to some person, who thereby becomes, not a member of the covenant, but sovereign authority over all who are. Hobbes even provides the form of words: "as if every man should say to every man, I Authorize and give up my Right of Governing my selfe, to this Man, or to this Assembly of men, on this condition, that thou give up thy Right to him, and Authorize all his Actions in like manner."[31] What has troubled Hobbes's critics is, first, how a sufficient power can be created merely by the negative act of renouncing right and agreeing to stand out of the way, rather than by some positive action, such as swearing allegiance; and second, in what order the steps from the state of nature are taken, since covenant and sovereign apparently presuppose one another.

The second question is perhaps the more easily answered: Covenant and sovereign work together like the parts of a watch, which must all be in place for the mechanism to run. The art of building a watch is in some respects a distinct business from describing its dynamic, and so perhaps is the art of founding commonwealths from the analysis of how they stand. Of Hobbes's two accounts of the origin of states, institution and acquisition, only the former presents an issue of sequence. Conquest in practice seems well enough understood, though Hobbes must interpret the cessation of resistance to a conqueror as a tacit covenant to join his entourage. Even if conquest is the more common origin of states, institution needs to be explained, since conceptually Hobbes assimilates acquisition to institution, not the reverse, and since conquering states themselves had an origin, perhaps not always in an individual's strength. Hobbes's clue here is his account of free gift and the fourth law of nature, which commands gratitude to the giver of gifts, without which, "if men see they shall be frustrated, there will be no beginning of benevolence, or trust; nor consequently of mutuall help; nor of reconciliation of one man to another; and therefore they are to remain still in the condition of War." In running the state, "The Passion to be reckoned upon, is Fear," but in setting it up, something is apparently needed of that "Generosity too rarely found to be presumed on." From the perspective of a founder, this prescription might seem too exacting, but it must be remembered that Hobbes is more concerned to address those who would shore up extant commonwealths than those who would begin afresh. The rarer a successful beginning, the more reasonable attachment to the existing order will appear.[32]

As to the first question—how a sovereign made by covenant can be sufficiently strong for the tasks Hobbes gives it—he himself must have thought it crucial, for he spends no small proportion of the second part of *Leviathan* instructing sovereigns in how to keep their strength. First and foremost in every part of this treatment is clarity about the absoluteness of their right within the commonwealth: No part of their sovereignty may be given away; sovereignty must not be divided among branches of government or especially between state and church; subjects must be instructed in their duties and in their sovereign's rights; pernicious doctrines must be suppressed; and so forth.[33] All this, after all, is implied by the transfer of right, which appears a small thing only to one who fails to consider just how extensive the right of nature really is. At the same time, once a commonwealth and its subjects are clear about the placement of rights, Hobbes thinks it in the interest of both the people and the sovereign that substantial liberty be allowed, especially in economic matters but also in education (if not political education) and perhaps even in religious worship.[34] When peace is established, Hobbes's sovereign must be strong enough to keep it, but this does not have to take immense resources, if minds are set aright. The sovereign's laws, first described as chains, turn into hedges, once subjects lose their desire to break for the woods.[35] As for foreign wars, Hobbes leaves no doubt that these ought to be pursued only for defense, not for the prince's glory; and to shore up defense, he adds a natural law—"that every man is bound by Nature, as much as in him lieth, to protect in Warre, the Authority, by which he is himself protected in time of Peace"—though he clearly prefers an enlisted army to a draft.[36]

"THE CONSTITUTION OF A CIVILL POWER" AND FUNDAMENTAL LAW

The sovereign just described seems more a benevolent behemoth than a fierce leviathan. Hobbes "reckons upon fear" both in his account of the state of nature, which ought to remind men what it is to be afraid, and in his picture of the sovereign, who is to be a visible cause of fear in the recalcitrant. But it is important to remember that to the law-abiding, the sovereign is supposed to put the fear of nature to rest; Hobbes's insistence that covenants made in fear in the state of nature are valid is meant to allay fear, not extend it, since his point is that by agreeing whom to fear, we free ourselves from terror. If a government that holds potential criminals in awe can nevertheless in most of civil life appear gentle, why does Hobbes apparently think it impossible, even in civilized states where subjects have learned their duties, for a covenant itself to serve the place of the sovereign, defining right and wrong, just and unjust, and providing perhaps a few ministerial offices where details can be worked out? In other words, if the sovereign is likely in many states to be a reformed warlord, why can the course of political development not proceed beyond the sovereign-leviathan to constitutional government?

That Hobbes allows no such evolution is beyond doubt: His description of the basic covenant makes it clear that it merely specifies who will be sovereign, without enumerating the sovereign's rights or duties, much less any legal limits on the sovereign. When Hobbes speaks of "the Constitution of a Civill Power," he refers merely to its establishment, not to some fundamental charter; the only fundamental law he recognizes "is that, by which Subjects are bound to uphold whatsoever power is given to the Soveraign, whether a Monarch, or a Soveraign Assembly, without which the Commonwealth cannot stand, such as is the power of War and Peace, of Judicature, of Election of Officers, and of doing whatsoever he shall think necessary for the Publique good." Nor does the fundamental law of nature—to seek peace— appear to limit the sovereign power, since the sum of its advice to "masterlesse men" is: Get a sovereign.[37]

Although Hobbes's mention of fundamental law may appear to be a piece of rhetoric aimed to invert the term's previous meaning, in fact it is a doctrine that merits serious attention. The definition of fundamental law just quoted is a slender thread from which to hang an incipient constitutionalism, but it does have an important consequence: It provides a principle by which to judge the legitimacy of grants from the sovereign power. Hobbes, who teaches that a sovereign can by definition do no injustice to subjects, since they have authorized all the sovereign's acts—and who says explicitly that the sovereign cannot be subject to civil law—nevertheless does not hesitate to criticize those sovereigns who have parted with any of their power, leaving sovereignty apparently weakened or divided.[38] Indeed, he considers such concessions the first of "those things that Weaken, or tend to the DISSOLU-TION of a Common-wealth." In the chapter on the rights of sovereignty, he treats grants as not merely foolish but invalid:

And because they are essentiall and inseparable Rights, it follows neces-sarily, that in whatsoever words any of them seem to be granted away, yet if the Soveraign Power it selfe be not in direct termes renounced, and the name of Soveraign no more given by the Grantees to him that Grants them, the Grant is voyd: for when he has granted all he can, if we grant back the Soveraignty, all is restored, as inseparably annexed thereunto.[39]

Hobbes does not say who is to declare such concessions void, though it must presumably be the sovereign itself, in claiming back its rights.

This limit upon the sovereign's power to limit itself reflects another fence built into the structure of Hobbes's theory: the inalienability of the natural right of self-preservation. As we have seen, the fact of the inalienability of self-preservation, like the fact of sovereign indivisibility, overrides any words to the contrary. Hobbes justifies inalienability on the grounds of natural necessity, introducing it as an observation of the behavior of criminals on the way to the gallows, but he then proceeds to unfold a surprisingly broad set of consequences.[40] Inalienable natural right allows the privilege against self-incrimination, indeed against any testimony that would endanger one's fam-ily or other benefactors; it recommends against torture, since it gives the tortured a right to lie; it condones the attempt to avoid military service, at least when a substitute can be found. Most startling, it permits, if not a right to revolution, a right to continue a rebellion once begun, at least until the guarantee of pardon. Of rebels, Hobbes writes: "There was indeed injustice in the first breach of their duty; Their bearing of Arms subsequent to it, though it be to maintain what they have done, is no new unjust act. And if it be onely to defend their persons, it is not unjust at all."[41] He proceeds to explain that "The Greatest Liberty of Subjects, dependeth on the silence of the Law," and liberty of this sort can of course be justly limited when the lawgiver chooses to speak. Still, the echoes in American constitutionalism of Hobbes's language of inalienable right and of some of its permissions are unmistakable.

The parallels between inalienable natural right and indivisible sovereign right are not accidental in Hobbes's theory, since he thinks that the sovereign's right is in fact his natural right, though now applied in a situation where most of the human beings around him have agreed with one another to accept his word as law. That the sovereign's right is anchored in his natural right becomes explicit in Hobbes's treatment of punishment, which is "not grounded on any concession, or gift of the Subjects," but merely remains from the natural condition.[42] Consequently, the natural right that persists in subjects is no abridgment of the sovereign's right to punish; it merely shows that in the moment of inflicting hurt, there is a resumption of the natural war.

Besides the matter of indivisibility, the only limits upon the sovereign of which Hobbes speaks directly are those placed on him by the law of nature. Since laws of nature are precepts of reason about the means to one's preservation, and since the sovereign's situation regarding his own preservation is no longer that of a man surrounded by enemies, it follows that what a sovereign would rationally endeavor differs somewhat from what an ordinary individual ought to do. The sovereign is bound by the original natural laws, but in addition it is his office or duty to see to "the procuration of *the safety of the people*; to which he is obliged by the Law of Nature, and to render an account thereof to God, the Author of that Law, and to none but him."[43] Procuring the safety of the people is a legitimate demand of natural law, Hobbes thinks, because their safety and prosperity are perfectly coincident with the sovereign's, rightly understood. At the same time, for the sovereign to be subject to natural law means he is held to obey in conscience only, *in foro interno*; there is no one on earth who can hold the sovereign to account, for then that person would himself be sovereign, and so on in infinite regress. To be sovereign is to be bound by a somewhat broader natural law than is the individual by nature, but jurisdiction apparently remains in the same court.

THE POWERS AND LIMITS OF SOVEREIGN REASON

These remarks show Hobbes's answers to the objections constitutionalists might raise to his doctrine and also highlight some indications of constitutionalism in Hobbes's theory. It is worth noting that those hints generally point away from, not toward, a written constitution. Judging void any grant against the fullness of sovereignty, finding an inalienable natural right in every individual, holding the sovereign accountable only to a natural law of which he himself can be the sole earthly judge— these all demonstrate rather the limits of the written word than its power. Indeed, Hobbes's short answer to the query posed earlier—why the covenant cannot itself be taken for fundamental law, with a sort of police officer hired to enforce its provisions—is that "All Laws, written, and unwritten, have need of Interpretation," and that interpretation is no ministerial task but "dependeth on the Authority Soveraign."

> No written Law, delivered in few, or many words, can be well under-
> stood, without a perfect understanding of the finall causes, for which the
> Law was made; the knowledge of which finall causes is in the Legislator.
> To him therefore there cannot be any knot in the Law, insoluble; either
> by finding out the ends, to undoe it by; or else by making what ends he
> will, (as *Alexander* did with his sword in the Gordian knot,) by the Legis-
> lative power; which no other Interpreter can doe.[44]

The case for authoritative interpretation works as well against any attempt to call upon natural law to limit sovereign power. The sovereign is bound by natural law, but to hold him to account requires that that law be interpreted, the interpreter thus becoming sovereign—and the problem of infinite regress recurs.

The inability of law to speak for itself, its inadequacy without interpreta-tion, is again characteristic of Hobbes's doctrine of speech and reason. Words have no authority in themselves for Hobbes, and there is no surer path to-ward foolishness than to think they do. They are marks and signs of human thoughts and intentions. Thoughts and intentions are, according to Hobbes, the most private of things: Neither can we read them in one another nor are we always willing to share them with one another. This, of course, is not surprising in a being that aims above all at its own good and whose thoughts are not ideas with independent substance but the phantasms of decaying sense. For words to serve as reliable signs, their meaning must be agreed upon; this Hobbes makes clear in his discussion of definition. Yet the prob-lem of agreement—which is, after all, what covenant aims to solve—arises before language, or at least before shared language. Hobbes's commentators tend to notice this difficulty in historical form: How can society depend upon a contract if the language human beings need for contract itself depends upon the prior existence of society? What they fail to see is that Hobbes not only anticipates the historical objection by raising it in analytical form but answers it with his doctrine of sovereignty. Language consists of marks and signs, but Hobbes thinks that marking is more fundamental than signing. This makes a certain intuitive sense—how can one use a word to express a thought if one is not already clear about its meaning oneself?— even though it is common enough that we say and hear things the meaning of which we know to be uncertain. The priority of marking also accords with the fundamental indi-viduality of thought: The private word, like the private thought, comes first. Indeed, if thoughts are essentially private and if marks follow thoughts, how can a system of signs ever be agreed upon?

Here Hobbes gives a remarkable account, early in *Leviathan,* which quite clearly foreshadows the doctrine of sovereignty he subsequently unfolds. After defining reason as reckoning, noting the tendency of men to err in calculation but affirming that "Reason it selfe is always Right Reason," Hobbes proceeds:

> But no one mans Reason, nor the Reason of any one number of men, makes the certaintie; no more than an account is therefore well cast up, because a great many men have unanimously approved it. And therfore, as when there is a controversy in an account, the parties must by their own accord, set up for right Reason, the Reason of some Arbitrator, or Judge, to whose sentence they will both stand, or their controversie must either come to blowes, or be undecided, for want of a right Reason constituted by Nature; so is it also in debates of what kind soever: And when men that think themselves wiser than all others, clamor and demand right Reason for judge; yet seek no more, but that things should be determined, by no other mens reason but their own, it is as intolerable in the society of men, as it is in play after trump is turned, to use for trump on every occasion, that suite whereof they have most in their hand.[45]

In the defining of words and then in the development of their consequences, the absence of natural standards leads men to point out a man they can see and then accept his verdict, not because that verdict is necessarily right but because there is no other way to avoid anarchy or war.[46]

Hobbes would agree that human beings ought to be ruled by reason, but since he defines reason as a process, not as a faculty that perceives an invisible order, his principal question is not, what does reason teach? but, whose reason is to count?[47] The sovereign does not gain its authority from its own reason, though its reason must become authoritative in order for it to settle controversies and to take the place of that private judgment which men have by natural right and which they must renounce in the covenant by which they make a sovereign. The private nature of thought makes it impossible for men to agree on a fundamental covenant that would do the work of reason; even if they could nod in accordance with a series of sounds or scrawls, they could never be sure their minds have met. But they can point to some body and then let it do the thinking. This is why, in drawing the image of the state as artificial man, Hobbes equates the covenant with "that Fiat, or Let us make man, pronounced by God in the Creation"; only then can one make of that "man's" or sovereign's *"Equity* and *Lawes,* an artificiall *Reason* and *Will."*[48]

The sovereign, of course, is not only an arbiter or judge, not only a reasoner. Awards and judgments need execution; sovereign reason must be backed by sovereign force. Still, it is characteristic of Hobbes's doctrine both that there is no sharp distinction drawn between judgment and enforcement and that Hobbes shows far more interest in the former than the latter—for instance, in devoting the bulk of even the chapter on crimes to a discussion of circumstances that extenuate or excuse them.[49] Hobbesian reasoning is always about cause and consequence; Hobbesian science always takes its cue from human purposes. This means that there is little room for a gap between what reason says and what people do, at least when they are exercising their reason, which Hobbes believes they can easily enough be trained or frightened into doing. By defining science as he does, Hobbes aims to close the breach between theory and practice. Reason that is never more than a step away from human passions and purposes is, he thinks, reason that effectively can rule.

Defining the sovereign as an artificial right-reasoner harmonizes Hobbes's doctrines of the privacy of individual thought and the sovereign's power over what may be taught in the commonwealth. Though the sovereign is censor of education, at least of political and religious education, minds themselves, if strong enough to resist what they hear, stay free. Without contradiction, Hobbes can describe the sovereign as right reason and at the same time privately undertake to develop political science. He means, of course, not in any way to confuse his science and the sovereign's authority; he assures readers of this explicitly in *Leviathan,* again in the context of the question of legal interpretation.

> The Interpretation of the Lawes of Nature, in a Common-wealth, dependeth not on the books of Morall Philosophy. The Authority of writers, without the Authority of the Common-wealth, maketh not their opinions Law, bee they never so true. That which I have written in this Treatise, concerning the Morall Vertues and of their necessity, for the procuring, and maintaining peace, though it bee evident Truth, is not therefore presently Law; but because in all Common-wealths in the world, it is part of the Civill Law: For though it be naturally reasonable; yet it is by the Soveraigne Power that it is Law.[50]

Obviously he has in mind that some sovereign might have the wisdom to put upon his work the stamp of authority, that is, to assign that it be taught—or, as Hobbes says less modestly, to "protect . . . the Publique teaching of it"[51]—in the universities, which Hobbes thinks the ultimate source of what we call public opinion. Indeed, his opinion of the power of universities further confirms the strength he finds in human reason as a cause of human action, for reason acts person by person, not through any natural whole.

Hobbes compares both his labor to Plato's and what he asks of sovereign reason to Plato's philosopher-king, but it is no accident that he distances himself from the Platonic image. Hobbesian science makes no claim to rule in its own name; though one who reasons rightly might see the superior consistency of Hobbes's thought to that of some established sovereign, still the inevitable arbitrariness of naming leaves any science itself, even if certain in its coherence, without sure bedrock. As Hobbes says in the introduction to *Leviathan,* the ultimate demonstration of his doctrine depends upon the individual reader finding in himself the traits Hobbes posits in human beings generally. Even in science, then, there is a sense in which consent is the foundation of authority. The Hobbesian philosopher, unless elected independent of his degree, can only advise a sovereign; however great his wisdom, he can raise no claim to be king.

6

FROM GENERAL SCIENCE
TO SINGULAR CASE

In the Epistle Dedicatory to *De Cive*, Hobbes assures his patron, the earl of Devonshire, not only of the innocence of his "appendage . . . concerning the regiment of God" but of the absence in his civil science of ordinary political polemic: "I have also been very wary in the whole tenour of my discourse, not to meddle with the civil laws of any particular nation whatsoever; that is to say, I have avoided coming ashore, which those times have so infested both with shelves and tempests."[1] Whether because the tempests had calmed or, as his recent editor Joseph Cropsey has suggested, because he intentionally delayed its publication until he was beyond earthly reckoning, Hobbes's *Dialogue between a Philosopher and a Student of the Common Laws of England* appears to meddle precisely where before he had abstained. The preface to the *Dialogue*'s first edition, apparently written by Hobbes's publisher William Crooke, presents this as the book's intention, if at the same time its liability: "Herein he [Hobbes] has endeavoured to accommodate the general notions of his politic to the particular constitution of the English monarchy: a design of no small difficulty; wherein to have succeeded deserves much honour; to have perchance miscarried, deserves easy pardon."[2]

Hobbes's recent commentators, when they have not pardoned the effort by their neglect, have honored it with criticism: "Windy, inept, and unpersuasive" is the epithet of one. Meanwhile, those who give the *Dialogue* serious philosophic attention find that, rather than merely applying general theory to particular case, Hobbes substantially modifies some basic tenets of his thought.[3] Specifically, Hobbes appears in this late work to grant to Parliament a much greater role in the English polity, suggesting an alteration not only in his account of the English constitution but in his doctrine of the knowledge necessary in rulers and thus also of the nature of sovereignty itself. The weight of these claims, to say nothing of the subject matter of the *Dialogue*, makes an examination of the text and its themes imperative for an understanding of the implications of Hobbes's political theory for Anglo-American constitutional law.

Before turning to the text of the *Dialogue,* however, it is worth considering what, on the basis of Hobbes's earlier works, one might have expected of an endeavor "to accommodate the general notions of his politic to the particular constitution" of England. This is not so straightforward a matter as might at first be supposed. Hobbes is aware that his new political science abstracts from the self-understanding of actual political entities; that, after all, is part of its strength in his eyes, since existing political ideas breed instability. By abstraction Hobbes makes his theory universal, but he thereby complicates its application to any actual regime. While this means that actual polities cannot dispense with prudence, it also insulates his theory from any charge of revolutionary tendency or subversive intent.

FORMS AND SOVEREIGNS

The inquiry into how Hobbes, in the frame of mind in which he wrote his scientific works, would have extended his political science to a particular civil society need not be altogether speculative, since there are plenty of passages in them that speak more or less directly to English politics, even in the era of its disarray. In particular, *Leviathan*—which is dedicated to an English commoner and "willingly expose[d] . . . to the censure of my Countrey"[4]—comments frequently on English common law and common lawyers, and it addresses the correct relationship between king and Parliament as well as the cause of the Civil War. More important, though Hobbes seeks a new basis for political life in such abstractions as right of nature, laws of nature, covenant, and sovereign—in the terms, that is, of what I have referred to thus far as his science of politics—he cannot ignore the question of how the science of general causes and consequences translates into the particularity of political life, precisely because he intends "to convert this Truth of Speculation, into the Utility of Practice."[5] Solving theoretically the political predicament is not enough; the lessons ought to work here and now. To refer again to the construction metaphor of which he was so fond, if Hobbes denied that laying a new foundation required tearing down the old house to build afresh, he nevertheless thought the discovery of sound architectural principles had implications for superstructure as well as cellar.

Beginning his political theory with the state of nature and the concepts it contained or generated meant not beginning with what had seemed to both partisans and theorists the central political question: the form of government or regime.[6] In all versions of his political science—and this distinguishes that science from his one prescientific political commentary, the introduction to his translation of Thucydides[7]—Hobbes makes clear, both by order of treatment and by explicit statement, that the question of the form of government is strictly secondary to the question of the power of the sovereign. Though he follows the traditional division of "kindes of Common-wealth" into monarchy, aristocracy, and democracy, he insists that their differences "consisteth not in the difference of Power; but in the difference of Convenience, or Aptitude to produce the Peace, and Security of the people; for which end they were instituted."[8] All forms of government have the same end, and in all the sovereign power must be absolute, whether placed in one man, in an assembly of a few, or in an assembly of all.

Moreover, Hobbes considers the attempt of classical political science to distinguish regimes not only by number but by goodness to be especially pernicious. Since tyranny and oligarchy "are not the names of other Formes of Government, but of the same Formes misliked,"[9] the science that gives them separate names encourages rebellion against inferior forms on the basis of private opinion, thus negating the end of government, whatever its form. For Hobbes, the basic political choice is not between this or that form of sovereignty, but between sovereignty and anarchy. Indeed, precisely because he finds the choice between peace and war so obvious, he is able to develop a rigorous science of politics; the secret to the science is the substitution of what one commentator has called the indirect question of consent and representation for the direct question of which regime is better or worse, just or unjust.[10]

In all his works, Hobbes makes no secret of his preference for monarchy, but in *De Cive* he says of his argument supporting this view that it is the "one thing alone I confess in this whole book not to be demonstrated, but only probably stated."[11] The merely probable character of the argument for monarchy is also clear in *Leviathan,* where he details the advantages of monarchy as well as its liabilities, principally the problem of succession. On the question of governmental form, conveniences and inconveniences are apparently to be weighed by the original democracy that congregates to institute a government; in government established by conquest, of course, the conquest itself concludes the matter, or the conqueror makes the choice. Between the state of nature and sovereignty, in contrast, there is nothing to deliberate—although Hobbes admits that there are incommodities in every civil society, making the case for joining a covenant somewhat less than perfect, even if compelling. Because the choice between regimes is of secondary importance and subject to uncertainty, Hobbes thinks there is nothing serious ever to be gained by changing forms; hence he makes the first lesson in his civics curriculum that subjects "ought not to be in love with any forme of Government they see in their neighbor Nations, more than with their own."[12] To flourish, "obedience, and Concord of the Subjects" are needed, not this or that form. Hobbes's admitted inability to prove the superiority of one type of government to another is thus not an accidental shortcoming of his science to be repaired by more research: To mandate one form above another, when forms in fact differ in the world, would undermine the doctrine of sovereignty itself.

To apply Hobbes's doctrine of sovereignty to a particular country requires that one be able to identify that country's sovereign. This may seem obvious enough, but it is hardly trivial. Given the extensive rights Hobbes attributes to the sovereign and the importance he attaches to its visibility, doubt over who is sovereign is simply intolerable. Hobbes's science includes plenty of clues on how to find the sovereign in a state—for instance, that it must be one man or one body of men—but he is certainly aware that the question may not always be so easy to answer, not the least because sovereigns have often ignorantly chartered away certain of their rights. Hobbes's insistence that such charters are void does not solve the issue: Someone must declare them void and convince others it is so. Hobbes aims to provide sovereigns with tools to repair the imperfections in their states, without disturbing their foundations; though in theory an imperfect sovereign is no sovereign at all, Hobbes hardly recommends a return to the state of nature and a fresh start. The paradox is genuine: Hobbes would not criticize the form of government in any existing state, and yet any form in which sovereignty is imperfect must somehow be corrected. Applying these observations to the English case in particular, the Civil War may be seen—as in a sense Hobbes sees it—as a dispute over the question of who is sovereign in England. Though he is convinced that it is not Parliament, Hobbes's adoption of the generally accepted formula "Rex in Parlamento" illustrates his quandary, for he must use the established form of words even though his theory would seem to require he say simply, "the king."[13]

FROM SOVEREIGN TO SUBJECT: THE ROLE OF THE JUDGE

The problem of translating universal political science to a particular country finds at once a parallel and a step toward resolution in the problem of extending a sovereign's rule to individual lives, of applying general authority to particular cases. Here too Hobbes's attempt to remove from politics the question of regime makes his task more difficult. By eliminating the regime issue, he aims to dissolve partisanship within the state, but partisans or parties or classes typically serve as intermediate wholes between sovereign and subject.[14] In one respect Hobbes seems to think the relation of sovereign and subject a direct one: The sovereign is a visible power whom each subject fears. He emphasizes this characteristic of sovereignty throughout *Leviathan*, but never more surely than when he writes of that

> Errour of Aristotles Politiques, that in a wel ordered Common-wealth, not Men should govern, but the Laws. What man, that has his naturall Senses, though he can neither write nor read, does not find himself governed by them he fears, and beleeves can kill or hurt him when he obeyeth not? or that beleeves the Law can hurt him; that is, Words, and Paper, without the Hands, and Swords of men?[15]

On the parallel plane of science and nation, this might seem to suggest that a particular country is subject only to its established institutions, not to abstract principles of a universal political science, and there is a sense in which for Hobbes this is true. Still, one who would rule more than a small band of illiterates needs to rely upon speech and law, not only in the creation of his right but in its exercise, even if he can never dispense with the sword. Similarly, a political science for a large and complex state must not only establish the need for a single authority at its center but must show how its power extends through its realm.

Attention to the channels that run between the general and the particular, between the sovereign and the subject, characterizes the string of chapters in *Leviathan*, numbers 21 – 25, that have no chapter-length counterparts in the earlier works. The first of these, "Of the LIBERTY of Subjects," might be said to illustrate limits to the whole problem by making explicit Hobbes's view that, despite the unrestrained nature of the sovereign's power, there are plenty of matters on which the law can afford to be silent. Economic affairs are the chief among these and indeed form a principal concern of the chapters in question, especially chapter 24, "Of the NUTRITION, and PROCREATION of a Common-wealth," and the chapter on bodies politic or corporations, where Hobbes works out the logic of risk and responsibility in joint commercial ventures. From the point of view of the sovereign, what is crucial is that property rights be understood strictly as a protection afforded subjects against one another, never against the sovereign's power to tax. Once this is settled, Hobbes seems decidedly of the opinion that prosperity is best secured, not by orders from above, but by allowing the particulars to pursue their own ways.[16]

If the problem of the relation of sovereign and subject is cushioned on the one side by the limited scope of the sovereign's concerns, it is met on the other by Hobbes's account of the importance of promulgation in the making of law. One common criticism of Hobbes's command theory of law is that commands are particular directives to individuals while laws are generally phrased, but Hobbes anticipates this objection by insisting that the sovereign bring his commands to all ears. As put succinctly in the marginal note in *Leviathan,* "Law made, if not also made known, is no Law."[17] The minimal meaning of the requirement of promulgation is that "Over naturall fooles, children, or mad-men there is no Law, no more than over brute beasts," but Hobbes carries the argument further. Since the origin of civil law is legislation, subjects cannot know by what laws they are bound unless those laws are announced and made available to them—indeed, not only made available but with sufficient signature so each subject can know that the words he reads are in fact those his sovereign uttered. In making the covenant, the subject agrees to give over so much of his right of self-governance as the sovereign determines it needs to keep the peace. In promulgating laws, the sovereign's commands replace the rational self-direction that individuals abandoned. As Hobbes often says, subjects creating a sovereign agree to authorize its acts as their own; receiving the dictates of law, they learn what it is they have taken upon themselves to do. If, as noted before, the limits on the sovereign are unwritten, the limits it imposes on its subjects, Hobbes thinks, should be written down.[18]

Of course, the question arises whether positive law that is not promulgated remains valid law. (Natural law, which can be known by anyone with ordinary reason and which is presumed to become obligatory when a sovereign exists to enforce it, binds without promulgation.) Hobbes's answer would seem to be both that an unannounced command is not law and that there is no one who can declare it invalid. This is suggested most clearly in the discussion of punishment, where Hobbes writes "that the evil inflicted by publique Authority, without precedent publique condemnation, is not to be stiled by the name of Punishment; but of an hostile act; because the fact for which a man is Punished, ought first to be Judged by publique Authority, to be a transgression of the Law."[19] Since the sovereign's right is unlimited, unpromulgated commands and hostile acts cannot destroy it, in Hobbesian theory. However, a sovereign who follows the law of nature rules by law and hurts subjects only through punishments after trials at law; since natural law is the law of reason, which in turn aims only at a man's own good, the sovereign who ignores it is himself a fool. Rule by law is not a right subjects can demand, but it is the efficient way to bridge the gap between the sovereign's intentions and people's acts.

Promulgation of laws proves so efficient a manner of governance precisely because all subjects are equal. As the covenant was made among human beings on terms that were entirely reciprocal, so they are all bound by the same laws. In a state founded upon a hierarchy of classes, the distinctions among men would be built into the laws; the commands of the state must then mean different things to different people, if they are to be legitimate. By contrast, since Hobbes's theory admits of no fundamental political difference except that between sovereign and subject, law can speak to subjects with one voice. This is not to say that there can be no distinction of classes in the Hobbesian state, only that all hierarchy of rank under the sovereign depends altogether upon the sovereign, not only for its initial creation but for its continued existence. Since everyone enters political life as an abstract individual giving up identical rights through a perfectly reciprocal covenant, the law speaks to every individual even when it speaks abstractly. Obedience to promulgated law, in a Hobbesian commonwealth, is thus a rather straightforward obligation: Once one knows what the law says any similarly situated person must do, one has all the reason needed to act.

Still, human equality, like all general characteristics applied to particular things, is a loose fit. Hobbes does not deny that specific circumstances are subject to almost infinite variety and thus that the application of general law to particular individuals is not automatic—though he certainly thinks some people, seeking their private advancement, exaggerate the variety of circumstance and the difficulty of application. To close the gap between general law and particular subject, laws need interpretation; to prevent the need for interpretation from unravelling the whole of the law, judicature is as inseparable from sovereignty as legislation. And unless the sovereign is never out of the subjects' sight, and they never out of his—and perhaps even when they are visible to one another, since a man's mind is never fully revealed—the interpretation of the laws in order to apply them to the many particular cases must be the work of a number of judges.

Hobbes writes a great deal about judges in *Leviathan*— about their function, their characteristics, their authority. The last of these always comes first for Hobbes and indeed receives first treatment: Judges are public ministers who represent the sovereign person in matters of judicature.[20] As representatives of the sovereign, of course, their authority is not their own but derivative from his. This is no mere fiction for Hobbes. The sovereign, it seems, has power of appointment over judges, or at least the power to specify who will appoint, and in addition, the decisions of subordinate judges may be appealed to the sovereign or his agent. Moreover, Hobbes defines a judge as an "Interpreter of the Law," not as a settler of disputes or a giver of justice; he does settle disputes and administer justice, but first and foremost through application of established law. As a judge "ought to take notice of the Fact, from none but the Witnesses; so also he ought to take notice of the Law, from nothing but the Statutes, and Constitutions of the Soveraign, alledged in the pleading, or declared to him by some that have authority from the Soveraign to declare them."[21] A judge, in short, represents the sovereign twice, by receiving authority directly from the sovereign and by ruling according to the sovereign's command. Obviously, judges, as ministers of the sovereign, have no independent authority over against him, either to bring him to the bar of judgment or to establish law—through precedent—by their own decisions.

Several comments Hobbes makes about judges deserve special mention. First, despite his frequent scorn for things that common lawyers praise, Hobbes too has good words for the English jury. Juries are not witnesses of fact, he notes, but judges, both of fact and of right. What Hobbes commends is the manner of their selection, their "excellent constitution": Not only are lords judged only by their peers, but the common jury is analogously chosen from men of the vicinity, with the parties allowed to make exception against jurors they do not wish, "So that having his own Judges, there could be nothing alledged by the party, why the sentence should not be finall."[22] Though some of Hobbes's praise evidently results from the efficiency of such a system, he also appears pleased that the arrangement allows the parties to consent to their judges. This surfaces as well in a remark on what to do should a dispute arise between a judge and an ordinary subject. Such a controversy,

> because they be both Subjects to the Soveraign, ought in Equity to be Judged by men agreed on by consent of both; for no man can be Judge in his own cause. But the Soveraign is already agreed on for Judge by them both, and is therefore either to heare the Cause, and determine it himself, or appoint for Judge such as they shall both agree on.[23]

Consent in the covenant to obey the sovereign remains fundamental, but no harm is done, and probably even some good, if it is reinforced by the exercise of further, more immediate consent.

The second point to notice in Hobbes's remarks about judging is hinted at in the paragraph just quoted and mentioned directly many times: The essential ingredient in making a good judge is *"A right understanding of that principall Law of Nature called Equity."* The knowledge of equity in judges allows them to fill in the gaps in the interpretation of statute law, where the law is either silent or ambiguous. All interpretation of the letter of statutes ought to follow the intention of the legislator, but where this is not otherwise indicated (as by a preamble), "the Intention of the Legislator is always supposed to be Equity: For it were a great contumely for a Judge to think otherwise of the Soveraigne."[24] In fact, Hobbes intends the natural law of equity—which he defines in an earlier chapter as "the equall distribution to each man, of that which in reason belongeth to him"—not only to patch holes but to set the tone of a judge's work, for he thinks judges are permitted, "if the Word of the Law doe not fully authorise a reasonable Sentence, to supply it with the Law of Nature." Again apparent is the working of the principle that the civil law and the law of nature "contain each other, and are of equall extent," and one finds here yet another reason why legislation and judicature must be in the same hands.[25] Every bit as much as he is a legislator, the sovereign has to be a judge.

One body is more easily made legislator than jurist, however; legislation, with its general language, seems precisely the idiom of sovereignty. There is no easy way of calculating the size of a country that can be subjected to a single legislature; indeed, in Hobbes's theory, there is in principle no limit to size, at least within the reach of promulgation, as there is no upper limit on the number that can be admitted to a covenant. A judge, in contrast, must necessarily hear controversies one at a time; even identical cases must be certified as such before they can be taken concurrently. If appeals are few enough, a sovereign may well be able to handle them personally or appoint a single deputy, but in general, it seems, the sovereign has no alternative but to rely upon the public ministers of his justice. Equity at first seems to grant individual judges wide discretion but in fact helps ensure uniformity in an extensive sphere: Its very principle of treating subjects equally points in this direction. Moreover, as a part of natural law, equity requires no feats of erudition, only the clear and careful natural reason of an individual.

As Hobbes's praise of the jury seems to endorse a sort of renewal of original consent in the act of submitting to judgment, his emphasis on equity in the act of judging seems to recall the equality of the state of nature and the equal terms of the transfer of rights in the covenant. The latter observation has led one recent commentator to argue that for Hobbes equity is in fact more fundamental than justice, since the terms of the covenant itself are governed by equality, while justice enters only later to insist that the covenant be kept.[26] Though it seems true enough that equality precedes justice for Hobbes, equity is defined from the start with reference to a third party who is judge in relation to other parties. Since by nature every man is his own judge and thus in no position to deal impartially, equity, like justice, depends upon prior covenant, namely, the covenant to submit a dispute to arbitration and to accept the arbitrator's word for its resolution. As the legislative task of the sovereign is somewhat eased by Hobbes's recommendation that the law can afford silence on many matters, so his judicial task is made less complicated because both the end of equity (peace, as of all natural laws) and its principle (equal dealing) are uniform. This makes the unavoidable delegation of the power of judging safe to the sovereignty. The similarity of men's basic powers of reasoning and the coincidence of their goals keep in line the discretion that must be given to individual judges—though of course it also helps that judges have the sovereign's statutes for definition of the basic outlines and his presence behind them as court of appeal.

FROM SOVEREIGN TO SUBJECT, AGAIN:
COUNSEL AND EDUCATION

The problem of connecting particular to general in the relation of sovereign and subject runs in two directions, like so much in Hobbesian theory. Through judicature one sees the relation of the general sentence of the sovereign to the particular cases of individuals. But from the reverse perspective, the sovereign's will is particular and yet must be fashioned for a multitude of circumstances. The question of how the sovereign's will is formed and informed is in Hobbes's idiom the question of counsel. In every version of his theory, but at greatest length in *Leviathan,* he distinguishes between counsel and command. People typically confound these, he finds, not only because both are delivered in the imperative voice but because most political and legal thinkers, beginning as they always do from opinion, lack the concepts needed to separate command and counsel. Perhaps Hobbes would add that they lack also the desire to distinguish them, since they flatter themselves when others take their counsel as command.

According to Hobbes, the difference between the two terms is straightforward:

> COMMAND is, where a man saith, *Doe this,* or *Doe not this,* without expecting other reason than the Will of him that sayes it. From this it followeth manifestly, that he that Commandeth, pretendeth thereby his own Benefit: For the reason of his Command is his own Will onely, and the proper object of every mans Will, is some Good to himselfe.
>
> COUNSELL, is where a man saith, *Doe,* or *Doe not this,* and deduceth his reasons from the benefit that arriveth by it to him to whom he saith it. And from this it is evident, that he that giveth Counsell pretendeth onely (whatsoever he intendeth) the good of him, to whom he giveth it.[27]

In *The Elements of Law* and *De Cive,* Hobbes explains the distinction at the beginning of the chapter on law, and for good reason: As noted previously, he defines civil law as the command of the sovereign, while natural law is the counsel of reason, made command only when there is a sovereign to give reason some force. Though counsel and command are discrete, they can certainly be related, as the incorporation of natural law into civil law makes plain.

Moreover, though the sovereign's command intends by definition some good to himself, natural law counsels the sovereign that his own good is perfectly coincident with the good of his people. The intention of distinguishing command and counsel is to remind people that in forming the covenant they have transferred their right to be judge of good and evil to the sovereign, so that henceforth his will is to count for theirs. At the same time, the right of the sovereign to command ought not to make him think counsel useless; on the contrary, since natural law imposes on him the care of his people, he is apt to need quite a bit of advice. The distinction establishes that giving counsel is not a right the counsellor can insist upon, since another's good is at issue, and no man has a right to dictate another's good without his consent. However, once the difference is understood and thus the matter of right clearly settled, counsel can be safely offered and welcomely received.

What sort of thinking is involved in giving counsel, according to Hobbes? This turns out to have no simple answer. In the metaphor of the state as artificial man, he writes that *"Counsellors,* by whom all things needfull for [the state] to know, are suggested unto it, are the *Memory,"* implying that the wisdom of the counsellor is prudence, since prudence depends on experience and experience is "much memory."[28] In the chapter on counsel, it appears, as one might expect, that Hobbes hardly means to discount science by reviving prudence. Characteristically, the first virtue of a good counsellor that Hobbes lists is good intention—that is, that an advisor really aim by his advice at the good of the state, not merely his own advancement. But then Hobbes turns to the intellectual skills required:

> The wit required for Counsel . . . is Judgement. And the differences of men in that point come from different education, of some to one kind of study, or businesse, and of others to another. When for the doing of any thing, there be Infallible rules, (as in Engines, and Edifices, the rules of Geometry,) all the experience of the world cannot equall his Counsell, that has learnt, or found out the Rule. And when there is no such Rule, he that hath most experience in that particular kind of businesse, has therein the best Judgement, and is the best Counsellour.[29]

Since he has often enough compared the political science he is developing to geometry, it is tempting to see here Hobbes's nominating himself for king's counsel; but perhaps his silence about his role tells a different tale. In other passages he expresses his confidence in having found certain rules of political order, but here he leaves open whether the art of ruling depends principally on scientific knowledge or on experience and common sense.

Of course, one reason for Hobbes's reticence may be his refusal to allow anyone (and so, even a scientist) to claim a right to counsel, much less a right to command. Certainly Hobbes does not hesitate in what he actually writes to offer plenty of counsel to whoever would read, nor does he leave unexpressed his hope that sovereigns will read his books. As he states his intention in a slightly different context, "Any man that sees what I am doing, may easily perceive what I think."[30] But one ought to resist the conclusion that Hobbes thinks, but only slyly says, that political science is all a sovereign needs to know or the political scientist the only counsellor he wants. There is surely much a sovereign can learn from Hobbes: for instance, about his rights, office, religion, what to legislate in general, what ought to be taught, and the like. But Hobbes's lessons are in the form of principles and precepts. These often enough may serve a sovereign well, but general principles, as much as laws, need interpretation to be applied. It is not sufficient, for instance, to know that a sovereign ought to make only such laws as are needful and perspicuous, unless one also knows what the times demand and what the people will think clear.[31] In other words, universal political science, though indispensable to settle matters of right, cannot do the whole work of advising. It must be supplemented by the counsel of those whose knowledge is less of abstract cause and consequence and more of concrete fact.

There is, however, one sort of business in which Hobbes apparently thinks his science can provide precisely what sovereigns need, and that is in the business of education. "Any man that sees what I am doing" easily means that Hobbes intends his *Leviathan* to become required reading in the universities, from whence its doctrines will be dispersed throughout the realm at large, in exposition and in action, both by the learned of the community and by those who are more specifically charged with the education of the people, namely, the clergy. Precisely how Hobbes expects a sovereign's protection for the teaching of his books to gain them a following in the schools is not entirely clear. Surely he does not try to win scholars by flattery, for his criticism in *Leviathan* of the universities is unrelenting. As Cropsey has noted, "At one and the same time [Hobbes] nominated the clergy to be indoctrinators of the many and himself to be the indoctrinator of the clergy, while he instantly and violently alienated that order of men in ways and to a degree that the world knows well."[32] Perhaps similar reflections have led another recent commentator to the conclusion that Hobbes aimed not merely at a reformed clergy that would then propound a version of faith that endorsed the sovereign's right, but rather at a more widespread "cultural transformation" from faith to enlightenment that would "transform men and women into the rational and predictable beings they would have to be before his vision of political society could ever be realized"[33]—apparently to be achieved through the literary power of *Leviathan* itself, Hobbes's rhetorical *tour de force*.

Hobbes seems to expect success for his project—if indeed he would allow it to be called his—through channels whose workings are extremely uncertain. A sovereign might allow the books in print, even see them assigned in the schools, but Hobbes as author must rely on his own devices for his books to persuade, and these include, at least by the time he wrote *Leviathan,* a marriage of rhetoric and demonstration.[34] Though a sovereign can control what people hear, and though for most people "faith comes by hearing," human beings cannot give up to the sovereign their judgment over what they find persuasive; the inevitable anarchy of intellectual influence, then, is a consequence of the inalienable privacy of thought.[35] Perhaps his recognition of this anarchy explains why Hobbes tried so many different versions of his political science and why he declined to announce the primacy of any one of them. Besides, in light of Hobbes's famous observation that "the Felicity of this life, consisteth not in the repose of a mind satisfied," it would be strange to expect a final word from a mind in "continuall progresse of the desire, from one object to another."[36] In any event, after the Restoration, in addition to answering critics and trying his hand at autobiography and a translation of Homer, Hobbes put *Leviathan* into Latin and wrote two dialogues, both of which were published posthumously: *Behemoth,* a history of the English Civil War whose publication the king refused to certify, and *A Dialogue between a Philosopher and a Student of the Common Laws of England,* to which I now turn.

THE *DIALOGUE* AND COMMON LAW

PHILOSOPHY CORRECTS THE REASON OF COMMON LAW

The *Dialogue* provides fuel for scholarly dispute not only in its text but in the story of its composition. There is some evidence supporting a presumption that the *Dialogue* is incomplete and was never intended for publication: the absence of a remaining manuscript; a letter from Hobbes to his admirer and biographer John Aubrey reporting that his "treatise De Legibus, at the end of it is imperfect, . . . nor shall Mr. Crooke himselfe get my consent to print it"; and the rather abrupt ending of the text. Joseph Cropsey suggests that Hobbes did indeed finish the *Dialogue,* whatever might be said of the "De Legibus" referred to in Hobbes's letter. He notes that Hobbes did not dispute Crooke's notice, several years before the philosopher's death, of an intent to publish the piece; that Aubrey, though a great defender of his friend, apparently never complained of its publication; and that the *Dialogue* begins as abruptly as it ends.[1] Cropsey's case is strengthened by the fact that, like the manuscript of *The Elements of Law* some thirty years before, the *Dialogue* evidently was circulated in manuscript form during Hobbes's lifetime, for it received a careful (if also apparently incomplete) response from Sir Matthew Hale, who was chief justice of the King's Bench and a posthumously acclaimed historian of the common law—indeed, in many ways the proper heir to Sir Edward Coke.[2] If *Leviathan* was directed to commoners and intended for use in reformed universities, perhaps the *Dialogue* was written for lawyers who skipped university to study directly at the Inns of Court.

To the modern student familiar with Hobbes's works of political philosophy, what is immediately striking about the *Dialogue* is precisely its dialogic form. Though to my knowledge Hobbes never explains why he chooses to write his late works as dialogues, commentators who criticize his dramatic powers have both caught his flavor and missed the point.[3] In *Leviathan* and elsewhere, as we have seen, Hobbes describes science as demonstrative, and as Michael Oakeshott has pointed out in describing those earlier works, the literary form proper to demonstrative science is the treatise.[4] If Hobbes's dialogues lack Platonic drama, perhaps that is because they are not written with Platonic intent. In each case, one of the speakers apparently carries the author's voice, but of course this can only be conjectured; the other seems, as commentators have noted of the *Dialogue,* to serve a variety of purposes, urging the authorial character to make his case, but providing commentary, asking occasional questions, answering requests for information, and the like.[5] The aim does not appear to be dialectical, with the characters discovering a path toward wisdom through conversation. Rather, Hobbes seems to have a case to make, but it is somewhat clouded, perhaps because the nature of the material makes clarity impossible in principle or dangerous in practice. As both dialogues Hobbes writes concern English politics in his time and include arguments only partially mediated by abstract scientific categories, there is reason to suspect that the choice of form reflects the peculiar practical complications of the matter.

To a lawyer of Hobbes's time, however, the most immediately striking aspect of the *Dialogue's* form would not be how it differs from Hobbes's other works but how it resembles and subtly departs from the frequently cited work written a century and a half before by Christopher St. Germain, *Dialogues between a Doctor of Divinity and a Student in the Laws of England.* Even at a cursory glance, the parallels and differences between the two works are conspicuous and, to one familiar with Hobbes's thought, not surprising. The substitution of philosopher for doctor of divinity is evident already in the titles. While St. Germain begins with a chapter on the eternal law and then moves to the law of reason, Hobbes begins immediately with a section entitled "Of the law of reason." St. Germain allows the doctor to establish a general, Thomistic classification of the kinds of law, then has him ask the student for details about the human or positive law of England, though the student also has something to say about the law of reason in English law. Generally speaking, the dialogue has the characters take turns questioning each other, as each is ignorant of law as understood and taught in the other's field.[6] Unlike his counterpart the doctor, Hobbes's Philosopher seems in control of the conversation and its course, rarely yielding to an objection from the Lawyer and nearly comprehensive in his knowledge. Though the Lawyer often reads aloud passages from Coke's *Institutes* or cites statutes, the Philosopher seems always to know what to expect, having himself, he announces at the outset, just spent several months reading the English statute books and a few commentaries on common law, including Littleton and Coke.[7]

If the difference in interlocutors between St. Germain's *Doctor and Student* and Hobbes's *Dialogue* is readily noted from the divergent titles, a further difference is easily overlooked: St. Germain undertakes to consider the laws of England generally, while Hobbes explicitly focuses on the common law. In the text of Hobbes's *Dialogue* it becomes clear beyond a doubt that the target of the work, from start to finish, is Sir Edward Coke.[8] Already by the third page he takes up Coke's doctrine of the "artificial perfection of reason" in the common law, which he disputes just as he had in *Leviathan*: The reason of the common law can be nothing other than natural reason, available to any thoughtful person, not the special treasure of a single guild.[9] In every section of the work, this point is driven home, as one after another of Coke's doctrines fail whenever they rely upon judicial custom in any way that is derogatory of sovereign power or opposed to common sense. The common law cannot impose on the king limitations that are enforceable by judges; the common law judiciary must accept that its decisions can be appealed to the king's chancellor in the court of equity; the definition of crimes and the specification of their punishments must be the work either of natural reason or statute law, not of judicial custom.

Indeed, repeatedly Hobbes attacks the doctrine of precedent by which the common law stands or falls. As he argued in *Leviathan* and elsewhere, customs obtain their character as law only through the tacit consent of the sovereign. This also applies to customary judicial practices, for they remain always subject to reversal on appeal as well as alterable by statute. The independence of the common law judiciary from chancellor and even king, which Coke appears in some respects to claim, is insupportable.[10] As the Philosopher defines it, "A Law is the Command of him, or them that have the Sovraign Power, given to those that be his or their Subjects, declaring Publickly, and plainly what every of them may do, and what they must forebear to do."[11] The identity with the definition of law in chapter 26 of *Leviathan* is evident. The *Dialogue* takes as its subject the common law examined in its particulars, but it shows Hobbes no reason to modify the central principles of his political or legal thought. After the Philosopher states, "It is not Wisdom, but Authority that makes a Law," the Lawyer objects, "You speak of the Statute Law, and I speak of the Common Law"; but the Philosopher admits no fundamental gulf between them, for he replies simply, "I speak generally of Law."[12] The problem of the *Dialogue*, then, is how to tame the common lawyers so that they respect and understand the sovereign's law.

If Hobbes would gladly dispense with much of what Coke claims for the common law judiciary, he nevertheless retains the phrase *common law* and the principle, with which Coke would agree, that there can be nothing in the common law that is against reason.[13] Of course when Coke states this maxim, he understands by reason the "legal or artificial reason" that Hobbes deplores, the practical reason of a learned and experienced lawyer and judge. It is, as we have seen,[14] a sort of reason that relies upon the strength of tradition, that at once presumes wisdom in those who went before and yet obliges successors to think long and hard to bring order to the rich legacy left behind. Beginning with the experience of enormously varied particulars, it builds toward certain principles of unity but does not presuppose them nor find them readily; it draws upon numerous legal maxims, but these are rather collected than systematically derived. Common law reason, in short, is typically more impressed by the almost infinite differences in kind among human things than by the claim that they may be subsumed under general categories.

Hobbesian reason, as should be obvious by now, has precisely the opposite genius, seeking always to clarify and simplify, to deal in certainty, not nuance. Hobbes's rhetorical strategy in the *Dialogue* is to preserve the term *common law* but see its definition "first snuffed, and purged from ambiguity,"[15] so that nothing except reason itself remains. As the Philosopher emphasizes in the opening section, "Remember this that I may not need again to put you in mind, that Reason is the Common Law."[16] Despite the admonition, he does not hesitate to reformulate the principle, as for example when he says, "the more General and Noble Science, and Law of all the World is true Philosophy, of which the Common Law of *England* is a very little part."[17] As he concludes in a later passage, "the Common-Law is nothing else but Equity"—and equity belongs to natural reason and the science of what in the earlier works was called natural law.[18]

The snuffing and purging of the definition of common law and its equation with equity demands of Hobbes not only a general critique of judicial custom and precedent but also denial that due process of law is the exclusive province of the common law courts. Hinting at the matter several times, the Philosopher takes it up directly with the Lawyer in response to the latter's distinction, much insisted upon by Coke, between a court of justice and a court of equity.

> But perhaps you mean by Common-Law, not the Law it self, but the manner of proceeding in the Law (as to matter of Fact) by 12 Men, Freeholders, though those 12 Men are no Court of Equity, nor of Justice, because they determine not what is Just, or Unjust, but only whether it be done, or not done; and their Judgment is nothing else but a Confirmation of that which is properly the Judgment of the Witnesses; for to speak exactly there cannot be any Judge of Fact besides the Witnesses.[19]

The drift of the statement is not in derogation of the jury but against the attempt to so exalt process by jury as to forbid the reexamination in the Court of Chancery, which was the court of equity, of a jury verdict. As Cropsey points out, Hobbes's aim in the section "Of Courts," and again in the section "Of Premunire," is to establish the Chancery as the highest ordinary court of the realm and the place to which decisions of the common law judges may be appealed.[20] Since the chancellor is keeper of the great seal and thus the king's clear agent, finding the Chancery the supreme court confirms the doctrine expressed in the *Dialogue*'s only subheading, that "The King is the Supream Judge."[21] It likewise confirms the principle of *Leviathan* that the sovereign legislator must also be a sovereign judge.

PHILOSOPHY REFORMS COMMON LAW CRIME

The substance of the common law receives Hobbes's attention not so much in reference to property law (though that is the subject of Littleton's *Tenures* and Coke's *Commentary,* the two books the Philosopher mentions at the start), but for what it has to say about crime and punishment. Property is treated briefly toward the very end of the *Dialogue,* apparently to illustrate the distinction between the politic and the natural capacity of the king, though the king's power to tax subjects for support of his troops is a theme that surfaces regularly from the second section on. But consistent with Hobbes's principle of putting safety first, his primary attention is devoted rather to criminal than to civil matters. Coke, as noted earlier, fancied himself something of a reformer in criminal law; he considers his effort to collect in writing what acts are crimes an original achievement, and he concludes the volume of the *Institutes* on criminal law with a plea for attention to the prevention of crime, not only its punishment.

Hobbes, however, finds Coke's accomplishment marginal and his whole approach misguided. Again, the culprit is the notion of judicial custom or common law as Coke understands it. Coke determines what are crimes by listing examples. As Hobbes's Philosopher notes with evident contempt, "He no where defineth a Crime, that we may know what it is: An odious name sufficeth him to make a Crime of any thing."[22] Hobbes does not deny that there are common law crimes, that is, criminal violations of reason. His principal example of such a crime is treason, which he defines as hostility to the sovereign power and its purpose, the people's safety.[23] In the language of *Leviathan,* common law crimes are the crimes against natural law. Beyond this, however, nothing can make an act a crime except the sentence of the sovereign; crimes not obviously against reason must be specified by statute. Hobbes illustrates the role of statute in determining crime in the case of several of the forms of treason in English law—which he says are treasonous not in themselves, but only by virtue of the statute that made them so—and even more vividly in the case of heresy, wrongly listed by Coke as a common law crime when in fact only the sovereign's establishment of a religion and forbiddance of other doctrine can make a crime of heresy, defined by Hobbes simply as "singularity of Doctrine, or Opinion."[24]

Not only Coke's catalogue of crimes but his specification of punishments earns Hobbes's rebuke. Though some acts can be found criminal by natural reason, reason alone cannot decree the appropriate penalty; that must be the work of some particular reason, and so in a state, the determination of appropriate punishment is the task of the sovereign power.[25] In *Leviathan* Hobbes had counted among the natural laws that punishment look forward to the good to be attained by the hurt done, not backward in the spirit of vengeance, and the treatment of punishment in the *Dialogue* appears intended to the same end. As Cropsey points out, Hobbes seeks to mollify the harshness of punishment at common law, a harshness that tends to turn men against the law itself.[26] Coke may have spoken of preventive justice, but the criminal law he endorses is plainly vindictive. Hobbes opens the door for serious reform of criminal law through which his successor, Jeremy Bentham, would later march.

In the critique of Coke on crime and punishment, Hobbes's Philosopher saves some of his sharpest words for the various ways Coke undervalues the desire for self-preservation and the right of self-defense. The Philosopher's discovery of Coke's shortcomings here is no surprise, since the *Dialogue* exposes quite early Coke's failure to distinguish law and right, a distinction we know to be central to Hobbesian legal thought.[27] The criticism in question appears in the discussion of suicide, which Coke apparently includes as a felony, provided the suicide is of sound mind, or in the legal phrase, *compos mentis*. The Philosopher objects to the Lawyer's statement of the crime, even though it is backed by statute.

> I conceive not how any Man can bear *Animum felleum,* or so much Malice toward himself, as to hurt himself voluntarily, much less to kill himself; for naturally, and necessarily the Intention of every Man aimeth at somewhat, which is good to himself, and tendeth to his preservation; And therefore, methinks, if he kill himself, it is to be presumed that he is not *compos mentis,* but by some inward Torment or Apprehension of somewhat worse than Death, Distracted.[28]

Beneath the classic Hobbesian argument recognizable here, one sees Hobbes's redefined common law—that is, equity or reason—working to limit statute law where Coke's common law reason merely confirmed it.

Later, Hobbes takes Coke to task for allowing that a killing excused because in self-defense nevertheless can require the forfeiture of the killer's goods; the Lawyer calls it custom, prompting the Philosopher to say, "You know that unreasonable Customs are not Law, but ought to be abolished" —a maxim that Coke too finds in common law, though he would not apply it here.[29] Most decisively, Hobbes's Philosopher derides Coke for the doctrine that demands forfeiture of even an innocent man's goods, if he had made himself a fugitive from justice when first accused: "O unchristian, and abominable Doctrine!" he declares. The attack on this passage of Coke's—the same passage, incidentally, skewered in chapter 26 of *Leviathan* as an example of precedent that ought to be ignored—is especially striking, since Coke himself cites the matter only in passing: The forfeiture is an example of an instance where the common law admits no proof against a presumption in law (here, apparently, that one who flees an indictment is guilty as charged), though the general rule is that a legal presumption stands only until the contrary be proven.[30] Hobbes, who makes escape from threat an inalienable natural right and who proudly proclaimed himself the first of those who fled the English Civil War, could hardly be expected to allow the presumption of customary law to override the right of nature. Moreover, Coke's allowance of exceptions to a legal maxim cuts against the whole logic of Hobbes's version of a common law of reason: "There can be no exception to a general Rule in Law, that is not expresly made an exception by some Statute, and to a general Rule of equity there can be no exception at all."[31] In short, without undoing the whole structure of English courts but with the benefit of scientific analysis, Hobbes thinks he can purge English law of both errors in process and substantive mistakes.

As Hobbes makes clear in the *Dialogue,* in *Leviathan,* and in his other works, private individuals who reckon their opinions authoritative independent of the sovereign's endorsement are usurpers of public authority. Cropsey quite correctly notes that Hobbes directs this charge against the common lawyers in the *Dialogue* as surely as he did against the clergy in *Leviathan*—a book intended, if not for the clerists themselves, at least for those who have listened to them. But as Hobbes does not hesitate in *Leviathan* to adopt the clerics' term *natural law* and apply it to principles discovered by his own science, so here he does not shrink from taking the term *common law* and applying it to the faculty of natural reason. As the passages just examined suggest, Hobbes hardly thinks established law above a need for repair. Part of his recommended reform is what one might call his jurisprudence of equity—his confidence that judges who apply to the law their natural reason will slice through the tangles of contradictory and pernicious custom that have developed under the rubric of common law.[32] Not that equity can replace, much less override, statute law; Hobbes repeats in the *Dialogue* his definition of law as sovereign command, and he adds to the consequent requirement of promulgation the suggestion that there should be "as many copies abroad of the Statutes, as there be of the Bible."[33] But as promulgation puts the law within the reach of every man, so equity puts it within his grasp, because its principles are simply those of common reason. Equity is to guide judges in the interpretation of statute law; although "It cannot be that a

Written Law should be against Reason: For nothing is more reasonable than that every Man should obey the Law, to which he hath himself assented to,"[34] written laws are often obscure, requiring a clear-headed judge to bring them to light. Giving extensive room to judges chosen rather for their reasoning powers than their legal learning does not, for Hobbes, reinstitute a private-minded judiciary, if the legislative authority of the sovereign is well established and the sovereign sits as supreme judge in a court of appeals. After all, philosophic reason, while posing no threat to authority, can apparently do the king service, not only as counsellor but as that public minister called judge.

PARLIAMENT GETS REINTERPRETED, BUT SOVEREIGNTY REMAINS INTACT

In the various doctrines of the *Dialogue*'s Philosopher reviewed thus far, there appears to be almost nothing at odds and much in common with the teachings of *Leviathan* and Hobbes's earlier works. Plenty of other congruities can be signaled. For instance, the Philosopher, while discussing the potential danger of a sovereign wasting money upon a favorite, remarks in passing, that "To think that our Condition being Humane should be subject to no Incommodity, were Injuriously to Quarrel with God Almighty for our own Faults"; or again, the Philosopher comments, in only his second speech, that in reading English statutes, "I did not much examine which of them was more, or less rational; because I read them not to dispute, but to obey them, and saw in all of them sufficient reason for my obedience, and that the same reason, though the Statutes themselves were chang'd, remained constant."[35]

Still, in a number of passages having to do less with common law than with statute law and Parliament, recent commentators have uncovered sentences that seem to revise Hobbes's doctrine of the absolute authority of sovereign power, or at least to suggest that Parliament, though a collective body, has a larger role to play in the English polity than he had been willing to allow in *Leviathan*. Cropsey, who aims to link such a revised doctrine of the role of Parliament to the material on Coke and the common law, apparently finds in the *Dialogue,* if not a novel precept, at least "a difference of emphasis." This he sees indicated by the Philosopher's silence regarding the state of nature and his new moderation, expressed in the view that "the true rationality of law inheres not simply in the reason of the sovereign doctrinairely insisted upon but in the endurability of the laws as that is signified or imparted to them through the assent of the people in Parliament."[36] Susan Okin, who "dissent[s] from the extreme aspects of [Cropsey's] interpretation," nevertheless follows his lead and finds Hobbes in the *Dialogue* struggling with what she calls "the unresolved problem of absolutism"—namely, that the coincidence between the public good and the sovereign's private interest is unstable, especially in the case of a mad king. However, she concludes that the *Dialogue* at once contains "a radically different attitude toward Parliament from that expressed in *Leviathan* and other earlier works" and yet "does not constitute a radical break with Hobbes's theory of absolutism."[37]

The passages that lead both Cropsey and Okin to find at least "a difference of emphasis" between the *Dialogue* and *Leviathan* are of several sorts. First, both characters in the *Dialogue* frequently acknowledge that in England statutes are typically made by the king in Parliament, that is, by the king with the concurrence of the Lords and Commons.[38] Since in *Leviathan* Hobbes had acknowledged sovereignty in England to lie with Rex in Parlamento, there need be nothing new in these references to Parliament's assent. The crucial question in interpreting the phrase "the king in Parliament" is whether such a sovereign is one man or one assembly. Exactly as in *Leviathan,* Hobbes in the *Dialogue* has his Philosopher insist that sovereignty lies with the king in person, understanding the assembly that gathers at his call to come to offer advice, not to make law on its own authority. The Philosopher's position is clarified by his comment on royal proclamations: When the Lawyer hesitates to accept the general definition of law as the sovereign's command because it would apparently give proclamations the full force of law, against the teaching of Coke, the Philosopher replies simply, "Why not? If he think it necessary for the good of his Subjects."[39]

But Hobbes does not leave the matter of Parliament's role and its relation to the monarch to the reader's inference. In the brief account of the history of Parliament with which the text concludes, he offers the following exchange:

> La. . . . But by those Laws of the *Saxons* published by Mr. *Lambert,* it appeareth that the Kings called together the Bishops, and a great part of the wisest and discreetest Men of the Realm, and made Laws by their advice.
> Ph. I think so; for there is no King in the World, being of ripe years and sound mind, that made any Law otherwise; for it concerns them in their own interest to make such Laws as the people can endure, and may keep them without impatience, and live in strength and courage to defend their King and Countrey, against their potent neighbours.[40]

If the sovereign has the right to legislate alone, still it is foolish to try to do so. Again, the king needs counsel; as the Philosopher adds, since "It is a hard matter to know who is wisest in our times," it is reasonable enough to leave the choice to the inhabitants of boroughs, who "can take notice of the discretion, or sufficiency of those they were to send to Parliament."

What makes the doctrine seem at odds with the teaching of *Leviathan* is that Hobbes appears to accept that useful counsel can be given in an assembly, not just individually.[41] In *Leviathan* and even more emphatically in the earlier versions, Hobbes inveighs against the dangers of oratory in collective bodies, against the vanity of orators whose eloquence is such "seeming prudence" not only to others but to themselves that they think they are actually entitled to rule.[42] Yet here two observations are in order. First, Hobbes's recommendation to sovereigns that they take their counsel in small doses is itself a piece of counsel, not a rule of right; it certainly cannot override an established form of government, and more to the point, it need not upset a long-settled practice in a particular state. Second, and in a way more important, the danger of orators is obviated once the question of who is sovereign is clearly settled in favor of the king. While the Long Parliament sat and the issue of right was disputed, parliamentary oratory fueled the fire, and Hobbes saw a duty to put it out. But if Parliament can be tamed on the matter of right, as Okin suggests the Cavalier Parliament was, then Hobbes might welcome its participation without a change of principle, since there had been a change of fact.[43]

The passages in the *Dialogue* that give real pause to the case for continuity are those that seem to hold parliamentary participation not merely to be wise but to be legally required. Several of these which appear to grant Parliament special say on matters involving the determination of a scale of punishment and a distribution of property can easily enough be read to suggest at most a custom of consultation or a counsel of special need for advice, and of course neither custom nor counsel makes law for Hobbes.[44] The most serious counterexample is the exchange, at the end of the section "Of Soveraign Power," concerning the Act of Oblivion by which offenses committed during the Civil War were declared unknowable and hence unpunishable at law. The Philosopher admits that while the king may pardon crimes against the peace, in matters where other individuals are hurt "it [is] great reason that the parties endammaged ought to have satisfaction before such a pardon be allowed."[45] This leads the Lawyer to exclaim, "You see by this your own Argument, that the Act of Oblivion, without a Parliament could not have passed." The Philosopher's ensuing "I grant it" leads Okin to construe Hobbes as yielding an essential point of sovereignty to parliamentary control.[46]

In fact, this conclusion is not only unnecessary but unwarranted, for the Philosopher's "concession" is followed immediately by a distinction between an Act of Oblivion—something altogether new in England, having been borrowed from two ancient examples, in Athens and in Rome—and a general pardon in Parliament, a traditional practice in English law. The latter is a statute like any other and subject to the same sort of interpretation, but the Philosopher makes clear that the Act of Oblivion is unique. Such an act puts an end to civil war, and it excuses generally all offenses there committed. But "civil war" in Hobbes's language is the concrete political condition that corresponds to the abstract state of nature. Since in the state of nature all offenses are excused, it would be inequitable, once civil society is reestablished, to punish what was not blamable at the time it was done. Moreover, it would be impossible for people to agree to restore civil society after civil war if they were then to be tried for what they had done when they were left unprotected. The Act of Oblivion, in other words, is nothing less than a clause in the covenant reinstituting a sovereign after civil war. Since the covenant is meaningless without consent, the Act of Oblivion needs the approval of the people—given, in this case, through a Convention Parliament, a body different in status from the usual assembly called at the direction of the king for his information.

Hobbes does not explicitly rehearse this argument, but he does explicitly make the Philosopher insist upon the distinction between a Parliament pardon and an Act of Oblivion. The matter is dropped when the Lawyer initially fails to understand but then the question is revived some 150 pages later, where the Philosopher gives a clearer explanation, even if in the end to deaf ears.[47] If my interpretation is correct, then one can hardly call the role assigned to Parliament in the *Dialogue* radically different, unless perhaps in the moment of Restoration, a point Hobbes never would have denied. As Okin notes, despite the greater visibility of Parliament in the *Dialogue,* "the king's essential sovereignty is not impugned."[48] In the end, there is simply a "difference in emphasis" from the early works.

Cropsey too is reluctant to admit to finding more than a subtle shift, but it is not obvious how important he thinks a digression by Hobbes would be.[49] As noted before, he finds the shift registered by Hobbes's refusal to mention in the *Dialogue* his concept of the state of nature—which apparently signals abandonment of the project of winning over the clergy—and he sees the shift result in a substitution of parliamentary assent for "the reason of the sovereign doctrinairely insisted upon."[50] Since Cropsey believes the key to understanding Hobbes's project is to grasp that Hobbes is seeking to restore the political world against those bands of private men, especially clerics and legists, who have arrogated public authority to themselves, a change in the character of Hobbes's notion of the public—from public indoctrination to public assent—is no small matter. In a previous essay on Hobbes's earlier works, Cropsey traces to Hobbes "the ideological characteristic of modern thought," but now he finds in the *Dialogue* "a teaching of moderateness in popular politics that is edifying in all times and places."[51] He apparently considers the change signaled if not effected by Hobbes's reconciliation with the philosophy of Francis Bacon, who, Cropsey notes, as chancellor under James I became "the only philosophic man of first rank to have come so close to regality as in fact to have sat vicegerent while the monarch was absent from the realm."[52] According to Cropsey, the meeting of minds between Hobbes and his former master was triggered by the device of John Aubrey, who apparently stimulated Hobbes's interest in writing about English law by giving him a copy of Bacon's *Elements of the Common Laws of England.* Hobbes, reflecting again on the role of the common lawyers in precipitating the Civil War, evidently then decided to take up the cause of Bacon against his rival, Sir Edward Coke, at once demolishing (so he hoped) Coke's reputation and learning a lesson in politic writing from the almost-was philosopher-king.

If this is indeed the case Cropsey is suggesting, it encounters two difficulties. First, the circumstances need not tally to Cropsey's sum. Perhaps Hobbes's failure to have his Philosopher admit to having read Bacon's *Elements* is indeed only what any prudent man would do in conversation with an admirer of Coke; it is, after all, clear enough that Hobbes takes the part of Chancellor Bacon against independent-minded common law judges. On the latter point, the Philosopher finds even the precedents are "flatly against Sir Edw. Coke, concerning the Chancery," and he goes so far as to propose that the writ of praemunire, intended to run against those who appealed from king to pope but borrowed by Coke in an effort to stop appeals from common law courts to Chancery, ought rather to have run against Sir Edward himself.[53] But later, in the discussion of Parliament with which the *Dialogue* concludes and in his last substantive reference to Coke, Hobbes's Philosopher suggests that on the issue of whether "the Parliaments of the old *Saxons,* and the Parliaments of *England* since are the same thing, . . . Sir *Edw. Coke* is in the right."[54]

This remarkable admission of Coke's authority on a parliamentary matter should be coupled with the fact (which Cropsey neglects to mention) that Bacon met his demise by impeachment in Parliament. If Hobbes means for the *Dialogue* to be a vindication of Bacon, one might have expected from the Philosopher a critique of Parliament's impeachment power to accompany the assertion of the chancellor's judicial authority.[55] Surely if the king deserves control of judicature through the Chancery, his ministers ought not to serve at the pleasure of an advisory body. Still, though impeachment cuts against Hobbes's theory of sovereignty, he appears to condemn it only by neglect. Indeed, this seems to be his strategy toward the whole quasi-judicial status of Parliament. In contrast to Coke's *Institutes,* where the High Court of Parliament is treated first and at greatest length in the volume on courts, Hobbes practically ignores Parliament in the section of the *Dialogue* on courts. As far as I can tell, the old style "High Court of Parliament" occurs only twice in the

Dialogue, and the Philosopher's sole use of the term is in a complicated and imperfectly printed speech that begins by asserting the power of the king in Parliament to distinguish the jurisdiction of (other) courts; within five pages the same character asserts flatly, "The Highest ordinary Court in England is the Court of Chancery."[56] Whatever might be concluded on these matters, the point at present is that if the *Dialogue* aims both to enhance the role of Parliament and to pursue Bacon's case, it joins together causes that were historically once at odds.

The second difficulty with Cropsey's interpretation raises the question of Hobbes's intention as a whole. If the shift from *Leviathan* to the *Dialogue* involves a move from a public doctrine of sovereign right to a legal order built on public opinion, the ground of Hobbes's political science itself is shaken, and the mere "difference of emphasis" in fact demands revision of his whole project. To replace the leviathan-sovereign with a monarch whose philosophic chancellor whispers in one ear while a public deliberative body speaks to the other, with none of the three openly dependent upon the theory of natural chaos and artificial salvation, would indeed be to assume the risks of prudence in order to avoid the incommodities of absolute power. The *Dialogue*—Hobbes's "testament," Cropsey calls it[57]—would then not only evade the sovereign but torch the patrimony, at least if the scientific spirit of the earlier works is not thin air. But as the arguments in the previous chapter and in this one were intended to show, so revisionist a reading is neither demanded by the *Dialogue*'s text nor required if *Leviathan*'s implications are drawn out.

There is nothing in the *Dialogue* that goes against the doctrine of *Leviathan* in principle and little or nothing that conflicts in detail. Likewise, there are many indications in *Leviathan* that application of its theory to the particulars of the English constitution would produce a description both of English courts and the English Parliament similar to that which surfaces in the later work. Hobbes requires in both places that there be a single, identifiable sovereign that is the ultimate locus of public decision and the focus for social engagement of naturally disparate, indeed disputant, individuals. Once a sovereign is in place, however, though his rights are great, their exercise can be modest. Any sovereign, to govern wisely, needs ministers to work his will and counsellors to inform it. As sovereigns whose rights are in dispute quite properly show reluctance to grant much discretion to ministers or much say to assembled advisors, so the clear settlement of the sovereign's right makes it reasonable for him to trust them both. Indeed, settling the question of right liberates the minds of counsellors and ministers to concentrate their efforts on their public business, not on matters of their public status, for the latter has been well defined. Similarly, science itself, or the public enlightenment that it engenders, can cleanse the minds of judges and parliamentarians of that jumbled mixture of opinion and maxim that has passed for practical reason, replacing these with a neat compound of Hobbesian moral philosophy and prudent common sense. If what Cropsey means is that in writing in different times and to different audiences, Hobbes adjusts his words, the point is well taken: Against clerics in the midst of civil war, the fierceness of the leviathan-state deserves emphasis; addressing lawyers in time of peace, one ought to stress its benevolence. Perhaps the *Dialogue* should be considered analogous to the third part of *Leviathan,* to be read not as a redesigned political science but as a rhetorical supplement to science that imports scientific conclusions into the language and the texts of a guild.

In the end, the question of whether the greater visibility of Parliament in the *Dialogue* reflects revision of basic Hobbesian doctrine turns on the distinction Hobbes so often belittles in the earlier works but has his Philosopher raise directly toward the end of the *Dialogue*: the difference between king and tyrant. After recounting the biblical story of Nathan's parable to King David concerning the rich man and the lamb, in which David pronounces a sentence of death upon the rich man (who, when the parable is interpreted, is himself), the Philosopher asks, "Was it a Royal, or Tyrannical Judgement?"[58] The Lawyer is reluctant to condone an arbitrary punishment but is hesitant to denounce it in the case of one reputed to be a good king. So he changes the subject to the clergy's right to distinguish good kings from evil ones, prompting the Philosopher to reiterate the Hobbesian doctrine that clergy receive their authority to teach from the king, not he his right to rule from their judgment of his character. The Philosopher then explains that he cited the parable to illustrate that before Magna Charta, by which the king promises to go against criminals only by the law of the land, offenses without specified punishment were left to the king's judgment. Apparently the Philosopher is showing that the distinction between king and tyrant can be made in principle—though he does not indicate whether the tyranny is in punishing without precedent law or in punishing excessively. At the same time he passes over any application of the distinction in practice, since the direction of the argument is toward shoring up, not tying down, the monarch's power. The difference between king and tyrant, in other words, is like the difference in *Leviathan* between a just law and a good law.[59] Not all laws are good—for instance, those that are obscure or meddlesome—but all laws are just and therefore ought to be obeyed; not all kings are good—some may act tyrannically—but all who can protect should be obeyed.

Cropsey discerns the issue of the royal versus tyrannical surfacing again in the *Dialogue*'s closing pages, in the consideration of whether the Norman Conqueror and thus the English kings hold their lands in their politic or natural capacity. The Philosopher concludes it must be in the latter, since they gave them away without parliamentary consent.[60] This seems to raise the possibility of distinguishing certain matters in which the king rules on his own from matters in which he is bound to act in Parliament; that is, the Philosopher seems to make room for Fortescue's distinction between regal rule and political rule, two moments in the authority of one king.[61] But in the *Dialogue* this suggestion quickly falters. Though the political acts of a sovereign assembly are separated easily enough from the private acts of its members, the natural and political acts of a monarch are continuous, for "his publick Commands, though they be made in his politick Capacity, have their original from his natural Capacity."[62] Again, the distinction between natural and politic capacities, like that between tyrant and king, might work in principle, but it could never be judged with certainty enough in practice to make it worth risking the chaos tyrannicide would unleash.

Cropsey concludes his introduction with the thought that Hobbes "aimed at restoring the politic as distinguished from the merely private in its clerical, legalistic, and tyrannical manifestations."[63] Though the pairing of clerical and legal is appropriate, as the two orders share styles of thought, pose similar dangers, and thus earn analogous treatment from Hobbes's pen, the problem of the tyrant-king is different in kind and, in Hobbes's opinion, less urgent. Clerics and lawyers must have their whole way of thinking revolutionized by Hobbes's scientific criticism, but the tyrannical king need only be enlightened as to the true nature of his interest (namely, that it is coincident with the interest of his people), and this can be the work both of ministers and counsellors, provided the king feels secure in his rule. In other words, the private reason of the sovereign, precisely because it repeats the reason of every individual in the state of nature, can be universalized and thus made truly public. This is not so, in contrast, for the private reason of the churchmen and common lawyers, which lives always in some mysterious body of the profession, residing among individuals but never in the full possession of a single one. What makes the clerical and common law mentalities dangerous is that their adherents, because they find their forms of thought in company, mistake their own opinions for common knowledge. The tyrant is tamed by his loneliness, while the rebellious are encouraged by their solidarity. Hobbes's sovereign partakes of neither characteristic, though he is closer to the individual tyrant: The tyrant at least both admits and reveals his own desires, while the clerics and lawyers pretend some common standard as they hide, even from themselves, the private interests that make them tick.

A REJOINDER FROM THE COMMON LAW

The "almost imperceptible" praise of aristocracy and "dim view . . . of a collaborative regime" that Cropsey discovers in Hobbes's *Dialogue* thus show not a change of heart but an appropriate reconciliation with a tamed Parliament and an effort, consistent with his theory, to reinvent common law. That the *Dialogue* was not viewed by common lawyers as a concession of any sort either to their view of law or to the understanding of parliamentary authority integral to that view is evident in the response it provoked from Sir Matthew Hale. Left in manuscript, like so much of Hale's work, at its author's death in 1675 and remaining unpublished until 1921, the "Reflections by the Lrd. Cheife Justice Hale on Mr. Hobbes His Dialogue of the Lawe" is rough in spelling and syntax but confirms the sureness of mind and integrity of character typically attributed to its author. It was such traits that allowed him, sitting as chief justice under both Oliver Cromwell and Charles II, to maintain the continuity of common law while the regime itself was in dispute.[64] Though apparently unfinished, Hale's "Reflections" treat of the themes of the first two sections of the *Dialogue*—in his words, "In Caput Primum of Laws in Generall and the Law of reason," and then "Of Soveraigne Power." There is a sense in which the tract, however fragmentary, does not seem incomplete, for Hale cuts to the core of Hobbes's project—to redefine legal reason and sovereign power— and offers a defense both of the practical reason of the common lawyer and the limits on the royal prerogative in the English constitution.

Hale's piece wastes so few words that it defies adequate summary. He meets Hobbes's critique of the "artificial perfection of reason" in common law by distinguishing the mere faculty of reason, either theoretical or prudential, from the use of the term *reason* "taken complexedly when the reasonable facultie is in Conjunction wth the reasonable Subject, and habituated to it by Use and Exercise."[65] Habituated reason is the knowledge of one skilled in some art; moreover, "Of all Kind of subjects where about ye reasoning Facultie is conversant, there is none of So greate a difficulty for the Facultie of reason to guide it Selfe and come to any Steddiness as that of Laws, for the regulation and Ordering of Civill Societies and for the measureing of right and wrong, when it comes to particulars."[66] The immense complexity of circumstances—so great that "Scarce two Morall Actions in the world are every way commensurate"—makes rational certainty in human affairs virtually impossible, so that those who seek a Euclidean demonstration of "an unerring Systeme of Laws and Politiques" "deceive themselves wth Notions wch prove ineffectual, when they come to particular application." Indeed, what Hobbes would substitute for the learned and experienced reason of the common law judge is an "Arbitrary and uncertaine rule wch Men miscall ye Law of reason."[67] Practice, not philosophy, is the key to justice in the law:

Long Experience makes more discoveries touching conveniences or Inconveniences of Law then is possible for the wisest Councill of Men att

first to foresee. . . . Laws . . . are the Production of long and Iterated
Experience wch, tho' itt be commonly called the mistriss of Fooles, yett
certainly itt is the wisest Expedient among mankind, and discovers those
defects and Supplys wch no witt of Man coud either at once foresee or
aptly remedye.[68]

In the judgment of particulars, in knowledge of the details of law, even in the
exposition of statutes, the simple faculty of natural reason Hobbes proposes
is, in Hale's judgment, a skinny waif beside the rich experience of a common
law judge.

Hale's critique of Hobbes's sovereign follows necessarily. As Hobbes can
suggest so absolute a sovereign because he has cut through the Gordian knot
of human passion to find its principles, so Hale must examine sovereign
power according to the study and experience available through common law.
After mentioning the various forms of sovereignty and allowing, unlike
Hobbes, the legitimacy of mixed sorts, Hale turns to consider the sovereign's
powers, not by deducing them as Hobbes did from the right of nature but, in
the manner of a common lawyer, by listing the king's prerogatives as "fixed in
the Crown of England." His most prominent point concerns the relation of
king and Parliament: "Though the Legislative Power be in the King, So that
none but he can make Laws oblidgeing the Subjects of this Realme, yett there
is a Certaine Solemnitie and Qualification of that Power, namely with the
advice and assent of the 2 houses of Parlemt, wthout which no Law can be
made. And therefore Proclamations cannot make a Law."[69] After citing the
precedents that support this view, Hale proceeds to assert the doctrine that
had anchored so much of Coke's thought—that the liberties that Englishmen
have by statute are mostly "but Restitucons of those very Liberties wch by the
Primitive and Radicall Constitution of the English Governmt were of Right
belonging to them." To deny the liberties of subjects and Parliament while
exaggerating the powers of the king would undermine "the Mutuall Confidence that the Governors have in the people as to point of Duty and obedience and that the Governed have in their Governors as to point of Protection." The same collapse would follow the acceptance of these propositions:
that the prince is not bound by prior law; that subjects' properties depend on
the monarch's pleasure; that laws that seem to establish the opposite im-
plicitly reserve the king's absolute power, so that "when he Judgeth itt fitt he
may Suspend or abrogate them"—all views easily found in Hobbes's work.
Hale pointedly concludes: "Such a man that teacheth Such a doctrine as this
as much weakens the Soveraigne Power as is imaginable and betrayes it wth a
Kisse."[70]

William Holdsworth, the English legal historian who brought the manuscript to print, suggests that "Hale had obviously misunderstood Hobbes's

theory of sovereignty. . . . Because Hale was a common-lawyer, his political conceptions were naturally of a somewhat mediaeval type."[71] But this rather underestimates Hale's achievement. Hale knows what Hobbes means a sovereign to be, but he refuses to admit this is what the English king is, much less what every government needs. Hobbes's error, in Hale's view, is to take his bearings by the extreme case: "It is a Madness to thinke that the Modell of Lawes or Governmt is to be framed according to Such Circumstances as very rarely occurre. Tis as if a Man should make Agarike and Rhubarb his Ordinary Dyett, because it is of use when he is Sicke wch may be once in 7 yeares."[72] Hale agrees with Hobbes that "Itt is not possible for any humane Constitution whatsoever to be so perfect as to answere exactly to every Circumstance of affaires," but he casts his lot the other way.[73] Experience shows, he thinks, that English government as traditionally constituted is fit enough for emergencies. Not stubbornness in the face of exigency, much less arrogance and ignorance, but rather just resentment against arbitrary threat to liberties and properties explains why Parliament men resisted the innovations of King Charles. The common lawyers, as represented by the moderate Hale, remain firm in their defense of an Aristotelian practical reason, unpersuaded by Hobbes's dire analysis of human conflict and unrepentent of their position in the years before the troubles of Cromwell's age.

HOBBES AND AMERICA

If the contrast between Hobbesian science and the common law is as thoroughgoing as the studies thus far have made it seem, how can such opposite understandings of law and government fit together in the constitutionalism of the American Framers? The essays that follow aim in part to address that question, by tracing the development of liberalism in several major political philosophers and by suggesting how Americans of the founding generation drew their political principles and practices from liberal and from common law sources. It is worth pausing, though, to shoot a quick glance ahead at certain elements of American political life and discourse that Hobbes's political science seems to illuminate. The concepts of equality, natural rights, representation, and others have long formed a part of American political speech, and though there is no insurance that we use our words as Hobbes defined them, the sense of familiarity and even immediacy one gets in reading *Leviathan* today sets Hobbes's thought apart from that of so many of his contemporaries. Indeed, what is remarkable about Hobbes's political science is how it seems better to describe our world than his, or than the world of the 1770s and 1780s. Surely Hobbes's immense popularity in our time, in contrast to the time of the Framers, is some measure not only of changes of fashion but of the power of his insight—and maybe the reach of his influence. One sees this even in his psychology, for while many are apt today to call his account of human being shallow, people often seem content enough to think themselves as radically individual and competitive as the beings he describes in the state of nature—and as much in need of a way to escape. Likewise, though the definitions he gives of science are more analytical than usually fits the modern empirical taste, the basic tenor of his outlook—the concentration on cause and consequence, the emphasis on explanation of relations rather than description of form, the ubiquity of the concept of power—is thoroughly recognizable to contemporary American political scientists, even if they find little place in their scientific work for the urgency of his concern for secure peace or the steadiness of his dedication to justice.

On the matter of law, once again it might be said that Hobbes's concepts jump ahead across tradition. Americans today tend to take for granted that the origin of law is statutory, and we consider even our fundamental law to be statutory in form. Likewise, state and federal law has in this century generally assimilated common law and equity so that they are hardly distinct in anything but the most technical circumstances. To be sure, this trend was begun with Article III of the Constitution, which established a single federal judiciary to handle cases of equity and law; but that alone cannot explain the modern willingness to urge judges to use their equity powers to do simple justice in particular situations, then give their ruling precedential force. Indeed, the chasm that separates the different approaches to constitutional jurisprudence today—between those on the one hand who urge judicial restraint in the face of legislative will and strict adherence to the intent of constitutional Framers, and those on the other who urge the use of theoretical reason to settle rights and equities directly—results from the separation of the functions of judicature and legislation, as Hobbes thought impossible to do, with each party pursuing the logic of one strand of his thought. From this perspective, the impasse between the partisans of judicial supremacy and those of fundamental legislative will vindicates Hobbesian logic. The problem of ultimate authority and the concept of sovereignty Hobbes devised to solve it, recognized and accepted quickly enough in his homeland but never quite in the United States, has now caught up with Americans, at least if we persist in defining law in a Hobbesian way.

PART THREE
INVENTING
CONSTITUTIONAL PRUDENCE

It is one of the ironies of thought that in every contradiction there is a point of common reference, so that in authors sharply opposed there is some matter of tacit agreement. Between Coke and Hobbes, for all the differences in their conceptions of law and of the nature of the reason that informs it, there is in common an aspiration toward a legal whole where law can be known with tolerable certainty and justice can be exact. In the authors to whom I now turn, Hobbes's conceptions of law and reason are at once adopted and tempered, at some cost to exactness and certainty, but in exchange they earn wider acceptance or use. One recognizes the spirit of modern liberalism in the attitude of tentativeness, tolerance, or compromise these authors adopt, or rather, one recognizes the characteristic ambivalence of the modern liberal: as certain as Hobbes about the sovereignty of reason and the absoluteness of individual liberty, but cautious in the face of a recalcitrant world.

Locke, Montesquieu, Blackstone, and others who share their purpose make liberalism politic by making it constitutional, that is, by seeking to weave liberal principles into the fabric of law and government they find around them, reinforcing institutions they admire even as they reinterpret them, all the while discarding what they thought the noxious remnants of barbaric times. Locke quietly moves the locus of sovereignty to the people while saving the outward form of British government; Montesquieu draws attention to judicial practices that buffer individual security; Blackstone seeks to fit together the best of both. With each step there is an advance not only in the practicability of liberalism but in liberal thought itself, at least insofar as a modification in the liberal way of thinking itself contributes to improved security and to the sort of liberty that that enables. Between Hobbes and the others, one sees the much-noted passage from rationalism to empiricism, but it is important to recall that this is rather a change in emphasis than in principle. Rationalism and empiricism are not antagonistic, but complementary modes of the modern scientific outlook: Reason agrees to accept no principles whose evidence is not available to universal human experience, while the senses defer to the logic of discovery for advice on where to look and verification of what they see.

Hobbes was well aware in theory of the need to accommodate his doctrines to accepted opinion—hence his attempts at redefining the natural law of the clergy and the common law of the bar—but his confidence in the power of human reason and perhaps a certain generosity of spirit that his theory does not explain led him to eschew obscurity in his writings, at no small cost to his reputation among his contemporaries. His successors were less haunted by obscurity, perhaps in part because Hobbes's outspoken treatises remained available as a ready point of reference. Still, in reconciling their doctrines to the world, they took the risk implicit in every genuine compromise: that the principle tolerated might revive and eventually triumph. Even in Hobbes— whose political doctrine does not pretend to be an account of the whole but a rigorous solution to the political problem sharply put—early liberalism, though based on principles deeply at odds with the world it would replace, nevertheless strikes a modest pose. Though its ultimate intention may have been to undo that world, it seems to come bearing only counsel, as if it were the classical voice of prudence and not a modern despotism of command.

8
THE REVOLUTIONARY CONSTITUTIONALISM OF JOHN LOCKE

Like the tourist in a distant port who hears the cadence of his native tongue, the student of American constitutionalism, in first encountering the *Second Treatise* of John Locke, recognizes at once a friendly voice. Of course, there is plenty about Locke's book that strikes the modern reader as a little odd: the companion *First Treatise,* with its polemic against the long-forgotten doctrine of patriarchalism, for instance, or Locke's earnest denunciation of "absolute, arbitrary power" and his branding of its subjects as slaves. Still, only a pupil who skipped the reading or a scholar of great erudition could fail to recognize the obvious echoes of Locke in our Declaration of Independence, not only in the theory of the origin of government and the legitimacy of change spelled out in the famous second paragraph but in the very words that move the text from theory to deed.

Locke's influence on the constitutionalism of 1787 is perhaps less apparent than his hand on the script of 1776, but again the echoes are unmistakable. Like the American Framers who followed him, Locke articulates the parts of government, not by depicting a mixed form that accompanies a division of society into estates, but according to a principle of separation of powers, including a legislative power composed of the people's deputies and an executive that can be much stronger than at first seems.[1] Furthermore, though the Preamble to the Constitution catalogues a series of purposes sought by the new government, its spirit as a whole—not to mention the practical effect of several, more particular clauses—seems congruent to Locke's insistence that the end of government is the protection of property, broadly understood; James Madison's well-known gloss in *Federalist* No. 10 certainly admits of such a Lockean interpretation, and the importance allowed the principle of taxation only by consent further supports this reading. More generally, Locke uses the term *constitution* in something approaching what would become the

American sense, to describe the standing rules agreed upon by the people in establishing the legislative power, rules by which the people could hold its rulers to account and which the people could decide to change in the event they failed to work their purpose.

Yet the mention of correspondences between the theory of government outlined in Locke's *Second Treatise* and the frame of government assembled by the Philadelphia Convention highlights one striking difference: the absence in Locke's account, and the presence in the Constitution, of a separate and independent judicial power. It is not that Locke forgets about the need for "indifferent and upright judges"; on the contrary, he considers their absence a principal shortcoming of the state of nature. Nor was the thought that the powers of government could be analyzed as legislative, executive, and judicial unavailable to him. Recent scholars have found intimations of such a scheme in several constitutionalist tracts Locke undoubtedly read, and he himself at one point describes the tasks of governance according to this pattern.[2] Still, almost as certainly as his near-contemporary Thomas Hobbes made the judiciary one with the sovereign, Locke places it squarely in the service of the executive and thus leaves little or no room in his scheme for anything resembling judicial review. When he faces the issue of who determines what we might call constitutional questions, he asserts, "The People shall be Judge."[3]

As this last comment suggests, however, the matter of judging is not peripheral to Locke's theory but at its very core. Not only does government require "indifferent and upright" judges, but the state of nature is defined as the condition in which each man is his own judge. Moreover, when Locke speaks of revolution or rebellion, it is rarely by name; rather, he typically describes the situation with a judicial metaphor, as an "appeal to Heaven," and he repeatedly asks the question, "who shall be judge?" The constitutionalism of Locke's *Second Treatise* is neither oblivious of the supremacy of judging nor supportive of a supreme judiciary.[4] To explore how this may be so is the burden of the remarks that follow.

JUDGING ONE'S OWN CAUSE

Having in the *First Treatise* disposed of Sir Robert Filmer's argument that the origin of political power is inheritance from God's grant to Adam, Locke begins the *Second Treatise* (alternatively titled *An Essay Concerning the True Original, Extent, and End of Civil Government*) with a definition of political power and an examination of the state of nature out of which, he thinks, government was formed. No quick recounting can do justice to the subtlety of Locke's text, but for purposes of exposition, a sketch is needed. Locke defines political power as "*a Right* of making Laws with Penalties of Death, and consequently all less Penalties, for the Regulating and Preserving of Property, and of employing the force of the Community, in the Execution of such Laws, and in the defence of the Common-wealth from Foreign Injury, and all this only for the Publick Good."[5] The state of nature is a condition of "perfect Freedom" and "perfect Equality"[6] and so contains no political power, but the elements of political authority do appear in embryo. Though there is no legislative power, each individual is bound by the law of nature, which, Locke explains, is reason; its command is to preserve oneself and, "when his own Preservation comes not in competition," "to preserve the rest of Mankind."[7]

Moreover, each individual possesses an executive power to enforce the law of nature, that is, to punish those who offend against the law of nature. Locke says of his account of private executives, though not of his account of natural law, that it "will seem a very strange Doctrine to some men," but he suggests it is necessary to explain how governments have the right to punish foreigners within their realms.[8] Nor is executive power an absolute license to destroy, any more than the law of nature is a perfect license to do as one pleases: Punishment must be tailored to its ends, which are reparation and restraint. Thus he assigns punishment to one power—the executive—but he grants that it involves *"two distinct Rights,* the one of *Punishing* the Crime *for restraint,* . . .* the other of taking *reparation,*"[9] suggesting perhaps a distinction between executive and judicial concerns. This idea is no sooner raised than dropped, however, for "no Reparation can compensate" the loss of life, and like murder, all lesser crimes ought to be punished "as will suffice to make it an ill bargain to the Offender." As in Hobbes, punishment has more to do with looking forward than with looking back.

Though Locke argues that the law of nature that measures proper punishment is "possibly plainer" to anyone who reasons than the positive laws of commonwealths (which typically "put into Words" "the Phancies and intricate Contrivances of Men, following contrary and hidden interests"), he acknowledges the objection to his doctrine of private executives "That it is unreasonable for Men to be Judges in their own Cases, that Self-love will make Men partial to themselves and their Friends."[10] Here one must follow Locke very closely, for if assigning each man judgment over himself is "unreasonable" and reason is the law of nature, then the state of nature no sooner arrives than it must be supplanted by some form of government, by some common judge. After all, for Sir Edward Coke and the common lawyers, the principle that no man ought to be judge in his own cause is of a piece with their Aristotelian premise that government exists by nature; and for the patriarchalists Locke addresses, the step from the injustice of judging one's own cause to the supposition that God has appointed some judge for every man is short indeed.

Locke replies, "I easily grant, that *Civil Government* is the proper Remedy for the Inconveniences of the State of Nature, which must certainly be Great, where Men may be Judges in their own Cases"; and several chapters hence he admits that the state of nature is "very unsafe, very unsecure, . . . full of fears and continual dangers."[11] But the inconveniences of the state of nature are not resolved simply by the remedy of government, for if the form of government is absolute monarchy, there is still one person judging his own cause, and the evil entailed in a single self-judge, if less widespread, is more intense. Between absolute monarchy and the anarchy of the state of nature there must be an accounting of inconvenience. Locke supplies one: "Much better [than Absolute Monarchy] it is in the State of Nature wherein Men are not bound to submit to the unjust will of another: And if he that judges, judges amiss in his own, or any other Case, he is answerable for it to the rest of Mankind."[12]

The counsel of reason against a man's being judge in his own case does not, then, establish a law of nature that makes man by nature subject to government. It is perhaps a rule of convenience, but in that case, it must enter a calculation of conveniences and inconveniences before it can be accepted. Only upon such a calculation can government be established, according to Locke, and thus only by "their own Consents [do men] make themselves Members of some Politick Society."[13] Again, Locke does not deny that the calculation of convenience will drive men toward government. His point is that the sums are not so overwhelmingly on one side that men have no room to consider what sort of government it is to which they are consenting—and thus can never afterward question their initial choice. In practice, the state of nature is likely to degenerate into a state of war, he admits, but analytically the two conditions can be kept distinct: *"Want of a common Judge, with Authority, puts all Men in a State of Nature: Force without Right, upon a Man's Person, makes a State of War,* both where there is, and is not, a common Judge."[14] Locke's argument, then, is that the state of war can subsist not only in the state of nature but under government—that anyone who claims absolute power over another puts himself in a state of war with that person, whether the claimant be king, thief, or slaver and whether or not the violence be "colour'd with the Name, Pretences, or Forms of Law." Locke provides a standard of right independent of government, though it is a standard that, unless the injustice be temporary, lacks enforcement beyond what private executives can secure.

Still, in the absence of a common judge, the private executives do have a court: They may "appeal to Heaven," as Jephtha did in his controversy with the Ammonites over property in the land of Israel, and let "the Lord the Judge be Judge" (Judges 11:27). That apparently means they may do as Jephtha when, "relying on his appeal, he leads his Army to Battle." Locke explains that the judgment of when to make an appeal by battle lies in the conscience of every man who makes it, "as I will answer it at the great Day, to the Supream Judge of all Men." Locke's mention of conscience and the Day of Judgment here draws attention to their entire absence in his chapter on the state of nature, where he said simply, "if he that judges, judges amiss in his own, or any other Case, he is answerable for it to the rest of mankind."[15] By calling the power to enforce the law of nature in the state of nature executive rather than judicial, Locke suggests that at issue is a choice of when to fight, when to challenge, not a determination of who is right or wrong. All judgment, at least in the state of nature, is rendered in one's own case. Such judgment is not "to administer justice," to use Locke's modern term, but a matter of prudence, of assessing one's chances and risks.

LOCKEAN PRUDENCE

As described thus far, Locke's state of nature and natural law bear a remarkable resemblance to the equivalent concepts in the writings of Hobbes. This is not the place to conduct an in-depth review of the scholarly debate that has arisen in the past generation on the relation of the doctrines of Hobbes and Locke, but a few observations on this score are critical to the present task.[16] One difference between the two appears beyond dispute: Locke is willing to accept rebellion against a despot or tyrant, while Hobbes is not. Perhaps this can be expanded: Locke denies the legitimacy of absolute monarchy (or later, "absolute Arbitrary Power"), while Hobbes thinks that all sovereignty is by its nature absolute, that all legislation is in a sense arbitrary, that monarchy is the best form of government, and that tyranny is merely a word that breathes displeasure.[17] Between Locke and Hobbes, then, is no small difference, especially when the question at hand concerns the nature of law and judgment. Still, it is important to consider how deep the rift might run.

Suppose for a moment that Leo Strauss is correct in his conclusion: Hobbes's and Locke's doctrines of natural right diverge not in principle but in presentation; apparent fundamental differences disappear or fade away once one reads Locke with an eye alert to equivocation, expecting less frankness from the "eminently prudent man" than from "that imprudent, impish, and iconoclastic extremist, that first plebian philosopher."[18] One need hardly think esoteric writing the universal science of political prose to accept its plausibility in Locke's case, for his reader confronts not only the anomaly of manifold contradictions in a work by an author who scrupulously corrected his texts, but also the strange history of Locke's refusal ever to acknowledge publicly his authorship of the *Two Treatises,* even after the fact was generally known. Certainly the account of the natural law that Locke offers at the outset of the *Second Treatise* begs revision, even on its own terms.[19] For example, he first presents natural law as imposing a duty—not just allowing a right—

of self-preservation, since human beings are God's property. By chapter 4, however, he notes without objection that the slave has the power, "whenever he finds the hardship of his Slavery out-weigh the value of his Life . . . to draw on himself the Death he desires," and in the next chapter he grounds the right to acquire property in the fact that "every Man has a *Property* in his own *Person*."[20] Hobbes admits his "natural laws" are improperly called laws, "for they are but Conclusions, or Theoremes" of reason, so that without a sovereign, "they bind to a desire they should take place: but *in foro externo*; that is, to the putting them in act, not alwayes."[21] Locke, in contrast, omits mention of natural right before natural law, and he speaks of natural law as strict law, providing the natural executive power for its enforcement. But as his argument unfolds, moving from duty to possessiveness, his natural law becomes more difficult to distinguish in practice from Hobbesian natural right, and his natural executive power grows to resemble the Hobbesian liberty "of doing any thing, which in his own Judgement, and Reason, hee shall conceive to be the aptest means thereunto."[22]

Now, still granting a similarity in principle, from whence would arise the difference between Locke and Hobbes on the questions of absolute sovereignty and justifiable resistance? Perhaps it results from a difference of judgment about the relative evils of anarchy and tyranny, or in other words, from a different calculation of the relative inconveniences of the state of nature on the one hand and absolute, arbitrary despotism on the other. We have seen already Locke's accounting of this sum; he repeats it metaphorically when he writes that to support an absolute ruler "is to think that Men are so foolish that they take care to avoid what Mischiefs may be done them by *Pole-Cats*, or *Foxes*, but are content, nay think it Safety, to be devoured by *Lions*." Turning more mathematical, Locke asserts that a person is

> in a much worse condition who is exposed to the Arbitrary Power of one Man, who has the Command of 100000. than he that is expos'd to the Arbitrary Power of 100000. single Men: no Body being secure, that his Will, who has such a Command, is better, than that of other Men, though his Force be 100000. times stronger.[23]

Hobbes appears to agree that the matter is one of weighing inconveniences, acknowledging that "the estate of Man can never be without some incommodity or other." However, he thinks that the condition of subjects

> as being obnoxious to the lusts, or irregular passions of him, or them that have so unlimited a Power in their hands . . . is scarce sensible, in respect of the miseries, and horrible calamities, that accompany a Civill Warre; or that dissolute condition of masterlesse men, without subjec-

tion to Lawes, and a coercive Power to tye their hands from rapine, and revenge.[24]

Do the different politics of Hobbes and Locke, then, derive merely from their different reports of life in the state of nature and under despotism, from different empirical judgments about the dangers posed by tyranny and anarchy, despite agreement on the fundamental matters of how to frame the question and where to look for a reply? The issue cannot be so simple, for their respective accounts of the incommodities in the state of nature and under a despot are similar enough. Rather, the break between the authors is most evident not on the facts of political life but on the questions of how to weigh human facts and how to ameliorate human circumstances. The various differences between Hobbes and Locke form a pattern, and that pattern relates to the status of judgment or prudence in their theories. Strauss's own distinction between the scientific Hobbes and the prudent Locke suggests as much, at least if one allows, as Strauss surely would, that a philosopher's choice of how to present his teaching is itself philosophically informed.

Hobbes defines both judgment and prudence as capacities of what he calls human beings' natural wit: Judgment is the ability to discern and distinguish, while prudence is the frame of mind that puts judgment to work, with some target to hit and with memory and experience as ammunition. Though Hobbes favors the choices of judgment and prudence to the vagaries of fancy and dogma for the government of one's own affairs, and perhaps even for the government of a state, he thinks prudence can be largely supplanted by science in the business of politics. The civil philosophy he develops in *Leviathan* aims to do just that, and he recommends its official adoption, although science must still be supplemented by prudence when applied to a particular situation. The absolute authority of Hobbes's sovereign at once depends upon the certainty of the new political scientist and improves upon his skepticism. The laws of a commonwealth are commands of the sovereign: In the best case, these need be little more than a reenactment, with specified punishment for violation, of the "natural laws" that reason constructs, but because reason can never fully overcome the inevitable arbitrariness of naming, the certainty that reason cannot achieve must be supplied by command.[25]

Now Locke too distinguishes judgment from knowledge—not in the *Second Treatise,* however, but in the *Essay Concerning Human Understanding*. The passage I have in mind goes as follows:

The Faculty, which God has given Man to supply the want of clear and certain Knowledge in Cases where that cannot be had, is *Judgement*: whereby the Mind takes its *Ideas* to agree, or disagree; or which is the same, any Proposition to be true, or false, without perceiving a demonstrative Evidence in the Proofs. The Mind sometimes exercises this *Judgement* out of necessity, where demonstrative Proofs, and certain Knowledge are not to be had; and sometimes out of Laziness, Unskilfulness, or Haste, even where demonstrative and certain proofs are to be had.[26]

Whether for reasons of necessity or because most men are lazy, unskilled, and hurried, politics appears for Locke to belong to the realm of judgment, not science.[27] Its coin, then, would not be certainty, but assent and dissent—or, when men are taken together, as in political life we are, consent. To be sure, in a noted passage in a minor work, Locke does suggest a distinction between theoretical and practical knowledge of political matters— "Politics contains two parts very different the one from the other, the one containing the original of societies and the rise and extent of political power, the other, the art of governing men in society"—and he recommends his *Two Treatises* as an example of the former.[28] Yet the *Treatises* have quite a bit to say about the art of governing, just as they refrain from explicit demonstration of every principle involved in the origin of government and the extent of its power; Locke himself does not compose separate political works that speak only to one or the other part. Precisely because politics swims in uncertainty, Locke cannot announce that fact in the work on politics itself. Hobbes pursues one project that begins with epistemology and builds toward politics; Locke divides epistemology and politics so thoroughly that he refuses to sign his name to both books. His celebrated prudence, then, is no mere stratagem, nor is Hobbes's frankness a naive oversight. For each, his understanding of the nature of politics shapes not only the political doctrine but the discourse itself.

These differences of approach and doctrine appear in the styles of their respective works, in their attitudes toward sovereignty and revolution, and also in what they have to say about justice. For Hobbes, justice is a theme of no little importance: He lists it as a natural law; he defines it on the model of thought itself, as "somewhat like" adherence to the principle of noncontradiction; and he vests it squarely in obedience to the sovereign. He rails against those by whom "Succesfull wickednesse hath obtained the name of Vertue," and he insists that "All Punishments of Innocent subjects, be they great or little, are against the Law of Nature."[29] Locke, in contrast, seems to treat the theme of justice only in passing, and in several of his more Machiavellian passages, he appears willing to write off "some few private Men" and "some private Mens Cases" when need be for the sake of stability.[30] Hobbes characterizes his sovereign as supreme judge, while Locke locates the final word in the executive's prudent use of prerogative or the people's choice to appeal.

THE SEPARATION OF POWERS AND THE RULE OF LAWS

My arguments thus far seem to point toward this conclusion: Locke thinks both that judgment is the principal faculty of mind at work in political life and that it consists rather in a guess about what proves convenient or useful than in discernment of right and wrong according to law. Yet law and the principle of the rule of law play a critical role in Locke's theory; indeed, to borrow the phrase (if not the context) of one commentator, Locke's achievement is to constitutionalize the political philosophy of liberalism, to hedge political power in by law.[31] While Hobbes defined laws as the sovereign's commands, Locke says many times, though characteristically never in a definition, that laws are "settled standing rules." Ordinary laws are the products of a legislative power, but that power itself is constituted by laws made by a sovereign people—or to adhere to Locke's language, by the *"Community* [which] perpetually *retains a Supream Power* of saving themselves from the attempts and designs of any Body, even of their Legislators."[32] Locke calls a government with a legislative power a "Constituted Commonwealth," and he refers to the conditions of its establishment as its "original Constitution," though he does not deny that there was legitimate preconstitutional government. Primitive government was monarchical, arising almost naturally from the paternal government of the family and consisting almost wholly of the rule of one man's will. Experience with selfish rulers, however, taught men the necessity of confining government by certain rules and thus the necessity of a legislative power in order to help secure the public good. Settling the form of this power is a great political achievement, according to Locke, and he almost concludes, "Where-ever Law ends, Tyranny begins"—almost, but not quite, for reasons soon to be considered.[33]

To ensure the efficacy of standing rules, Locke adopts the doctrine of the separation of powers, or at least the separation of legislative and executive powers. Though distinct, the powers are set in a clear hierarchy; the legislative power is supreme over the executive, which is "ministerial and subordinate" in that it is charged merely with carrying out the laws the legislature has made. Locke avoids the embarrassment of making the king an "errand boy" by not requiring that the separation between institutions be perfect if the distinction of functions is clear; sharing as he does in Parliament, in that his consent is necessary to make a law, the king "in a very tolerable sense may also be called Supream," or more precisely, "the Supream Executive Power."

Actually, though the legislative power is called supreme, as it must be if the laws it makes are to bind, Locke offers none of the encomiums on the power of Parliament typical in either his common law predecessors, such as Coke, or his eighteenth-century successors. No sooner does he proclaim the supremacy of the legislative than he asserts its subordination to the residual power of the people. No sooner does he even define the legislative power as "that which has a right to direct how the Force of the Commonwealth shall be employ'd for preserving the Community and the Members of it" than he speaks of the need to create a separate executive because

> it may be too great a temptation to humane frailty apt to grasp at Power, for the same Persons who have the Power of making Laws, to have also in their hands the power to execute them, whereby they may exempt themselves from Obedience to the Laws they make, and suit the Law, both in its making and execution, to their own private advantage, and thereby come to have a distinct interest from the rest of the Community, contrary to the end of Society and Government.[34]

The implication here is that executives were invented to limit legislatures, not the reverse. W. B. Gwyn notes of Locke's consequent praise of limiting the sessions of the legislative that "we seem to be left with the strange conclusion that men are secure and free only when their legislatures, themselves necessary for security and freedom, are not in session." But the strangeness of the doctrine is abated when one recalls the emphasis Locke places on seeing the rules that govern society as "settled" and "standing," which they cannot be if they are subject to immediate or continuous amendment.[35] Besides, as Locke likes to point out, legislatures that regularly disband can be better trusted, since members out of session must live by the laws and pay the taxes they voted while inside.[36]

Locke's continued stress on the limits on the legislature, in relation not only to society but to the other branch, prepares his readers for a strengthening of the executive. The new muscle is Locke's well-known doctrine of prerogative, the executive's "Power to act according to discretion, for the publick good, without the prescription of the Law, and sometimes even against it."[37] Though Locke denies that the people, by making laws, encroach upon the king's prerogative, the point becomes moot by his including in the definition of prerogative the power to go against the laws. What gives prerogative its justification and its limit is "this Fundamental Law of Nature and Government, *viz*. That as much as may be, all the Members of the Society are to be preserved." What keeps it in check is the ultimate judgment of the people as to whether the laws have been surpassed or transgressed to their good.

Locke's explicit reference to natural law here recalls that the executive power itself exists in the state of nature (unlike the legislative power, incidentally), as does the federative power by which a commonwealth defends itself abroad—a power "really distinct" from but "always almost united" with the executive.[38] Though the executives in the state of nature were private men while the executive in question here is a public official, the distinction is not definitive, since an unwarranted exercise of prerogative makes the executive or his deputies vulnerable to prosecution as private individuals.[39] An exercise of prerogative becomes a public act when it is ratified by the people, that is, by their reluctance to declare "they have just Cause to make their Appeal to Heaven." To make such an appeal, of course, is to act outside the constitution, since "the *People* cannot be *Judge,* so as to have by the Constitution of that Society any Superior power, to determine and give effective Sentence in the case," but this illustrates rather than undermines Locke's constitutionalism. If he called "*the establishing of the Legislative* Power" "the *first and fundamental positive Law* of all Commonwealths," it is nevertheless itself clearly subordinate to "*the first and fundamental natural Law*" of self-preservation.[40] As Harvey Mansfield has observed, in Locke's doctrine of prerogative, the end of government overrides its form; the separation of powers in Locke is not so much a mechanism to balance government as an expression of this basic political fact.

I noted at the outset that the doctrine of separation of powers as formulated by Locke omits the judicial power as an independent branch or function of government. That Locke had available to him a tripartite scheme distinguishing legislative, executive, and judicial functions was noted before, and an intimation of this division appears in the text of the *Second Treatise*. Locke begins chapter 9 by discussing a threefold lack in the state of nature, of "*established,* settled, known *Law,*" of a "*known and indifferent Judge,*" and of "*Power* . . . to give [a sentence] due *Execution,*" and he ends the chapter speaking in terms of the same three functions.[41] Yet when he differentiates the powers of government explicitly, the division not only omits a separate judiciary but adds a federative power which is quickly assimilated to the executive. Since the point of separation is to distinguish the making of "settled standing rules" from their execution, judges in the courts of law would apparently belong to the executive. Yet when Locke first discusses the setting up of a commonwealth, he calls it the establishment of "a Judge on Earth," and he writes that that "Judge is the Legislative, or Magistrates appointed by it."[42] Since Locke denies that legislative power can be delegated, the "Magistrates appointed by it" must again be the executive and its subordinates. The remaining ambiguity over whether the judicial task belongs primarily to legislative or executive perhaps reflects Locke's theory of political development: Though the legislative appears prior to the executive analytically, governments historically begin with the immediate execution of judgments, with rules and laws getting established after primitive prerogative is abused. What does seem clear is that, as the argument of the *Second Treatise* unfolds, the importance of judicial matters in relation to individuals diminishes, though Locke takes a growing interest in the people's judgment of government.

Again, this judgment, though described in quasi-judicial language, takes place by revolution, not by process at law.

MODERN PROPERTY AND MODERN LAW

The evolution of the meaning of judging is not unique in Locke's argument. Throughout the *Second Treatise,* he seems typically to give terms their meanings not by actual definition but by repeated, slightly varied use, so that words move almost imperceptibly from their traditional contexts to Locke's own. He does, however, explicitly define law early on in the *Treatise* and in a surprisingly classical way:

> For *Law,* in its true Notion, is not so much the Limitation as *the direction of a free and intelligent Agent* to his proper Interest, and prescribes no farther than is for the general Good of those under that Law. . . . So that, however it may be mistaken, *the end of Law* is not to abolish or restrain, but *to preserve and enlarge Freedom*: For in all states of created beings capable of Laws, *where there is no Law, there is no Freedom.*[43]

The traditional appearance, though, is deceptive, for the sentence omitted by ellipsis and the sentence that follows the quotation make plain that the relation of law and freedom Locke has in mind is altogether consistent with the doctrine of Hobbes, who defined law and liberty as opposites but recognized that "The Greatest Liberty of Subjects, dependeth on the silence of the Law."[44] Law, for Locke as for Hobbes, is not reason's command to the individual about how to live and act, but reason's contrivance to allow free movement in a crowded world. Freedom is achieved not by fulfilling the law but by staying clear of its prohibitions, by walking between its hedges. Locke continues:

> Freedom is not, as we are told, *A Liberty for every Man to do what he lists*: (For who could be free, when every other Man's Humour might domineer over him?) But a *Liberty* to dispose, and order, as he lists, his Person, Actions, Possessions, and his whole Property, within the Allowance of those Laws under which he is; and therein not to be subject to the arbitrary Will of another, but freely to follow his own.[45]

"Freely to follow his own arbitrary will," the passage seems to beg to be completed: Not instruction in virtue but protection of property is the end Locke assigns to law.

This principle so pervades Locke's theory of government that my neglect of it thus far has made my account somewhat more abstract than Locke would have it. His theory of property and its importance in politics merits and receives much comment. Whatever else is ignored in Locke, most readers remember his definition of property as including "life, liberty, and estate"; his argument that a right of property naturally arises from the labor a human being invests in something; and his standard pitch that the end of government is the preservation of property.[46] Locke's difference from Hobbes on this score is probably exaggerated. Though Hobbes admits no right of property that can exclude the sovereign, he clearly recognizes in the possibility of property and prosperity one of the principal benefits of civil society and compensations for the loss of natural liberty.[47] Locke's assignment to property of a special place is demonstrated in his accounts of its origin, of its function as the end of government, and of the limit its security imposes on the power of taxation. However, he also suggests that legislation can substantially determine the rules by which property is recognized, thereby seeming to undermine the case he constructs on behalf of its claim to protection under natural law.

The power of legislation over property appears in a sentence toward the end of chapter 5. After noting that gold and silver get their value by tacit consent, Locke explains that "in Governments the Laws regulate the right of property, and the possession of land is determined by positive constitutions." Indeed, "settled standing rules" seem designed precisely to give property its definition and thus a large measure of security.[48] The undermining of the case by natural law has been noted by several scholars and requires exposition at greater length than is possible here; let it suffice to note the contradiction between the condition of appropriation (in Locke's phrase, that "enough and as good" be left for others, which presumes natural plenty) and the prohibition of spoilage (which presumes natural scarcity). Not natural law but a judgment of utility defends the right of property; not so much the labor men have done as the future plenty they can produce supports private appropriation of the naturally common.[49]

Still, if Locke leaves ample room for the regulation of property, its centrality to his political theory is undeniable. For my purposes, several points about Lockean property deserve remark. First, the priority Locke assigns to property reinforces the importance he attributes to human judgment and common consent. The realm of private property gives each individual who can master the arts of acquisition a locus for the exercise of his judgment, while the rise and use of money demonstrates the human capacity for uncoerced consent, a capacity on which Locke's doctrine of the origin and repair of government stands or falls. Second, property makes visible people's rights and thus makes recognizable their peril or invasion. Instead of Hobbes's visible sovereign that frightens malefactors, tames the proud, and reassures the complaisant, Locke develops a visible standard that offers all some hope of benefit, perhaps seducing the ambitious to the pursuit of wealth, if reserving their irascibility for its occasional defense.⁵⁰

Third, the account of property and its origin that Locke outlines allows him to escape having to argue against absolute power by appealing to the ancient constitution of England. Commentators have noted that Locke, almost alone among Whigs of both centuries in which he lived, eschewed any such appeal; his silence is, in retrospect, all the more mysterious since Locke's influence on English politics is undeniable, despite his having dropped its favorite idiom.⁵¹ His peculiar—indeed, peculiarly successful—manner of referring to England in the *Two Treatises* almost never directly by name, but almost always recognizably, reflects his desire to defuse appeals to antique precedent. His story of the prototypical origin of government in the people's attempts to limit abused prerogative by new laws, though it prefigures the "Whig interpretation of history," surely cuts against the claim of parliamentary antiquity; his barbs at popular inertia in revolutionary situations suggest that the "ancient Names, and specious Forms . . . that . . . are much worse, than the state of Nature or pure Anarchy"⁵² are the names and forms of the English constitution—which, again, Locke rarely uses, preferring "legislative" and "executive" to "Parliament" and "king." Finding the origin of property in labor dismisses the feudal case, that property originates in exchange for military service,⁵³ while it also weakens the claim of common law to settle inheritances according to its custom and logic.

Locke's neglect of Coke fits his rejection of antiquity. He does not mention Coke as an authority in the one passage on political right in the *Second Treatise* where he directs his readers to common law authors such as Bracton and Fortescue. In the essay "Concerning Reading and Study" in which he draws a syllabus of "ancient lawyers" to read, he includes "My Lord Cook on the second *Institute,* and the *Modus Tenendi Parliamentum,*" thus recommending Coke's commentaries on parliamentary statutes and procedure but conspicuously omitting Coke's famous *First Institutes,* the *Commentary on Littleton,* which discusses at length the common law of property.⁵⁴ Like Hobbes, who appropriates the term *common law* for his own theory of equity, Locke speaks of "the common law of Nature" in his definition of prerogative.⁵⁵ Hobbes takes Coke to task for his account of criminal law, while Locke apparently intends to redesign Coke's view of the law of property. Still, Coke's failure in the minds of both philosophers is identical: Like Hobbesian punishment, Lockean property looks forward, not back.

The titles alone of Locke's chapters "Of the Extent of the Legislative Power" and "Of the Subordination of the Powers of the Commonwealth" suggest that for Locke the purpose and power of government are limited. Indeed, the specification of the end of government as the protection of property does as much, for it not only limits government to a determinate end, but in particular to an end outside of politics itself. Modern liberalism takes the principle of limited government so much for granted that we often neglect to reflect on the insight it expounds. Government ought to be limited, the liberal concludes, not only because we distrust this or that office-holder but because we doubt how much any human being or collection of human beings can know about human affairs: about human motives, human interests, human ends.[56] If politics is characterized by judgment rather than knowledge, the need for limits becomes plain—if also the difficulty of fashioning limits that will last.

For Locke, the decisive limit upon governmental authority is what we have come to call revolution. People are slow to leave their established ways, he says, so in practice this check is no license. Indeed, he calls his doctrine "the best fence against Rebellion," since he holds, with Hobbesian optimism, that a government that anticipates the possibility of revolt will be least likely to overstep its bounds. Still, one wonders if the doctrine is as conservative as Locke makes it appear.[57] To set as the end of government the preservation of property might seem to shackle innovation, but to argue thus would be to miss the dynamic nature of property as Locke defines it. If property is creative, building further and further beyond the scantiness of nature's provision, government that exists to preserve it—or that claims to exist to preserve it—must change to keep up: The people must be ready to "erect a new Form."[58] If there is no limit to the advance of production, is government really limited, or can we say only that it is limited for the time being? This ambiguity in Locke's revolutionary constitutionalism—whether it aims primarily to restore or to progress—reflects the ambiguity noted before in the application of Locke's definition of judgment in the *Essay* to politics in the *Second Treatise*: Is political knowledge "not to be had" or yet to be got? Locke's fence against rebellion, it seems, opens a gate for innovative reform. Depending on no ancient constitution for its authority and on no ancient order for wise counsel, a constitution of "settled standing rules" is subject to revision as prudence dictates and judgment allows.

9

MONTESQUIEU'S LIBERAL SPIRIT

Any detective searching through the texts of the modern political philosophers for the sources of judicial review would soon enough fix attention
on the Frenchman Charles Louis de Secondat, Baron de Montesquieu. His
masterpiece, *The Spirit of the Laws,* is the only text of any stature cited in
Alexander Hamilton's *Federalist* No. 78, and critics concur that Montesquieu
deserves credit for revision of the doctrine of the separation of powers to
include the power of judging as an independent branch alongside the legislative and the executive. Moreover, *The Spirit of the Laws* was widely cited by all
sides at the time of the Founding, not only for its classic account of the
English constitution but for its teachings concerning federalism and commerce, matters of no small importance in the debate. But a good detective
would soon recognize that the baron is not a suspect but a witness, and a
witness not easy to cross-examine. Montesquieu's influence on the Framers is
undeniable, as is his importance for Blackstone. He does not, however, imagine a judiciary in a republic enabled to declare statutes void for unconstitutionality, though he does offer clues to one who searches for the origins of
legal institutions, as well as advice to judges with discretion to employ.

A SINGULAR BOOK

Montesquieu writes in the preface to *The Spirit of the Laws* that the book
contains an "infinite number of things," and at the risk of sounding absurd,
one cannot help but say that he understates its magnitude. Not only are the
details about which he writes practically innumerable—the laws of all known
and even some imagined societies, whether ancient or modern, Eastern or
Western, primitive or developed—but he more often recounts stories than
composes arguments, more often relates surprising facts or telling maxims
than derives their principles or spells out their consequences. At the end of
the most commonly cited book in the work, Book XI, in which he has discussed the English constitution and the separation of powers, Montes-

quieu writes: "It is not necessary always to so exhaust a subject that one leaves the reader nothing to do. It is not a question of making him read, but of making him think."[1]

Of course Montesquieu does make us read, and at great length,[2] for he apparently holds that thought, or at least political thought, proceeds best not by the inexorable march of abstract propositions but by reflection upon details and the relations among them. He writes in the preface, "Many truths will not make themselves felt until after one will have seen the chain that links them to others. The more one will reflect on the details, the more one will feel the certitude of the principles."[3] As these remarks suggest, though Montesquieu makes reference to human nature throughout his work, often enough as a standard for judgment, and offers now and again a "general maxim," his political philosophy is not constructed upon a system of natural law. In the first book he speaks briefly of "relations of equity anterior to the positive law that establishes them" and devotes a chapter to the laws of nature; the relations of equity seem to be dictates of abstract reason, while laws of nature are the stirrings of sentiment or feeling. Nevertheless, by far the bulk of laws that interest human beings in society are positive laws, and to the immense variety of these he devotes the rest of the work.[4]

Montesquieu's extensive concentration on actual details betrays his interest in teaching not only specific maxims but a certain "manner of thinking," to borrow a phrase he employs. He seems not to mean by this phrase, as we might today, a process of thought independent of its discoveries; every page of the work speaks against attributing to him a methodologically driven frame of mind. Through reflection on details, links appear between particular observations, and these come together to form a whole; where the links or relations in question involve human laws, the whole is called "the spirit of the laws." Laws themselves, defined at the outset of Book I as "necessary relations that derive from the nature of things," are by the end of the same book defined in human terms: "Law, in general, is human reason, inasmuch as it governs all the peoples of the earth; and the political and civil laws of each nation must only be particular cases where this human reason applies itself."[5] The laws form a whole because they issue from reason, but reason itself in Montesquieu's understanding appears principally, if not exclusively, in relation to particular circumstances. Perhaps one should note right away that Montesquieu sees this truth about reason in prescriptive as well as descriptive terms: He thinks reason ought to act with awareness of particulars if it is to avoid the temptation to severity or the assumption of despotic sway typical of abstract thought when it tries to rule directly.

The "particulars" with which Montesquieu is concerned are not only particular circumstances, events, and actors, but also "les particuliers," perhaps best translated as "particular individuals." There is, of course, something problematic in speaking of "particular individuals" abstractly, and in a sense Montesquieu's treatment of individual rights and judicial procedures is intended to address the actual evils that arise from this difficulty. In Books II through V of *The Spirit of the Laws* he develops a theory of the threefold nature of governments (republican, monarchical, and despotic), their corresponding principles or springs (virtue, honor, and fear), and the relations of specific laws to these natures and principles, culminating in a book entitled "That the laws which a legislator gives must be relative to the principle of the government." In Book VI, he begins to modify the initial scheme as he draws attention to "the simplicity of civil and criminal laws, the form of judgments and the establishment of penalties." Simple laws are despotic laws, possible because in despotisms the subjects "are nothing";[6] even republican laws begin to appear suspect, as they are apt to subject the individual to the willfulness of the people. The best protection for the individual is a series of judicial procedures, not devised abstractly, but developed through historical change from the manner of judging practiced by the Germanic tribes "in the woods." The telling of this tale occupies, on and off, no small part of the remainder of the work. General attention to particular individuals appears possible through particular procedures that developed in a particular way.[7]

In my earlier description of Sir Edward Coke's articulation of the reason of the common law, I mentioned his emphasis on its particularities; lest his views be unthinkingly assimilated to Montesquieu's, I should note the contrast between them. Though both were judges and thus by experience familiar with the detail of law, in their writings they look at the law from very different perspectives. Coke writes as a judge or a lawyer, from within the orbit of the common law and its authority. His reason works upon that law, either in the practical circumstances of a particular case or in the assembling of doctrine in *Reports* or *Institutes*. Montesquieu, in contrast, writes from outside the laws of any particular country, perhaps above them all. His cosmopolitan outlook detaches him from the authority of any law; he seeks reason in laws as evidence of the workings of the human mind, not for any immediate practical end. But if the whole difference were one of perspective, the contrast need not go deep. What sets their thought at odds is that Montesquieu does not merely describe law from outside but seeks to influence its development and more especially to moderate its force. The difference between Coke and Montesquieu thus is not that of practice and theory but of practice defined in different ways, the first in the spirit of Aristotelian practical science, the latter as an archetype of modern liberal social science, universal in its claims if not always its reach. The particular in Montesquieu has no transcendent meaning. But it can serve to illustrate to both theory and practice the possibilities available for human use.[8]

MONTESQUIEU'S CONSTITUTION
OF ENGLAND AND INVISIBLE JUDGES

The discovery of a general model in a particular case appears most strikingly in Montesquieu's renowned discussion of the English constitution in Book XI, chapter 6. Commentators who notice that this account does not describe with perfect accuracy English government in his time have mistaken the author's intention if they mean their observation as critique. Montesquieu introduces the chapter with a conditional statement, fills it with similarly tentative remarks, and after the title never mentions England by name until the third paragraph from the end, where he writes: "It is not for me to examine whether or not the English enjoy this liberty at present. It suffices for me to say that it is established by their laws, and I search into the matter no further."[9] The particular facts themselves apparently do not tell their own story but must be mediated by an intelligence that can view them in light of other facts, that can see them "as in a mirror." Montesquieu prepares the chapter by suggesting that England is the "one nation in the world that has for the direct object of its constitution political liberty,"[10] and the book in which the chapter appears is entitled "Of the laws which form political liberty in its relation with the constitution." Still, a free constitution is not sufficient for political freedom in Montesquieu's scheme, so he follows Book XI with a book devoted to "laws which form political liberty in its relation with the citizen," then another about the relation of taxes to freedom simply.

The chapter on the English constitution figures in the history of American constitutionalism for its formulation of the doctrine of the separation of powers and in particular for its addition of the judicial power to the doctrine. Montesquieu is cited as authority and quoted at some length in the number of *The Federalist Papers* in which the separation of powers is introduced, and as mentioned, his remarks in this context on the judiciary figure in the first pages of *Federalist* No. 78, where Hamilton proceeds to sketch the developing practice of judicial review.[11] As W. B. Gwyn has noticed, the distinction of the three powers in the first sentence of Book XI, chapter 6, corresponds almost precisely to the division of powers made in chapter 12 of Locke's *Second Treatise,* though Montesquieu reverses Locke's order of the executive and federative powers and calls the latter not federative but "the executive power of things that depend on the law of nations."[12] While Locke treats the executive and federative powers as analytically separate but in practice coincident, Montesquieu adopts the opposite strategy, renaming Locke's federative power "simply the executive power of the State" and calling the executive power over things at civil law "the power of judging."

That more is involved here than semantics becomes clear in Montesquieu's reformulation soon after: The three powers are "that of making the laws, that of executing public resolutions, and that of judging crimes or disputes among particular individuals."[13] "Public resolutions," it seems, can involve either foreign or domestic matters; when the latter are at issue, the executive may prosecute suspected criminals and later punish those convicted, but executive resolution must submit to the power of judging. Throughout the discussion of the separation of powers, the power of judging appears special: It is named with a form of the verb, not with an adjective (i.e., "judicial"), as are the other powers; it is accented as Montesquieu's distinctive contribution to separation of powers doctrine; and it is said enigmatically to be, in the English constitution, "so to speak, invisible and nothing."[14] The question of where to locate the power of judging becomes the leading theme in the subsequent discussion of the distribution of powers in ancient Rome, and in a chapter on the ancient Greeks that prepares the section on Rome, Montesquieu writes, "The chief work [chef d'oeuvre] of legislation is to know how to place the power of judging well."[15]

Since the division of powers in the American Constitution follows Montesquieu's threefold scheme, one might suppose that the power of judging described in *The Spirit of the Laws* provides a clue to the subsequent ordering of the American judiciary. On inspection, however, Montesquieu's account of the English constitution seems nowhere more curious than on this point. The power of judging he describes is lodged not in a judiciary but in juries. He says of the English judges that they are "only the mouth that pronounces the words of the law; inanimate beings who can moderate neither its force nor its rigor."[16] The genius of the English system seems to be that juries sit only for the moment, then disband: "In this way, the power of judging, so terrible among men, being attached neither to a certain estate, nor to a certain profession, becomes, so to speak, invisible and nothing. One does not have judges continually before one's eyes; and one fears the magistracy, not the magistrates."[17]

The passage that seems enigmatic when quoted out of context—as, incidentally, it is in *Federalist* No. 78—resolves itself quite clearly once one notices that English juries, not English judges, are in question. Yet as Montesquieu's chapter on the English constitution proceeds, the power of judging indeed becomes invisible. The "three powers" in the constitution are soon the executive and the two houses of the legislature, with the body of nobles in the (unnamed) House of Lords serving to balance the government between king and commons; the two-party system that results is described in relation to the "two visible powers" in the reprise eight books later (Book XIX, chapter 27), where the power of judging is almost entirely absent. With characteristic subtlety, Montesquieu slips from the constitutionalism of separation of powers to the constitutionalism of mixed and balanced government. At least in the constitution dedicated to political freedom, the place for judging is quickly found and quietly left.

THE "DEPOSITORY OF THE LAWS"

Montesquieu does, however, treat at some length a strong and visible judiciary, in the discussion not of the common law judges of England but of the aristocratic parlements of France. Himself the president of the parlement of Bordeaux, he describes a powerful judiciary as characteristic not of a republic—as he seems to have classified England—but of monarchies. His original definition of monarchy suggested as much: "Intermediate, subordinate, and dependent powers constitute the nature of monarchical government, that is to say that in which one alone governs by fundamental laws."[18] Fundamental laws are possible only if there is a "depository of the laws," that is, "political bodies, that announce laws when they are made and recall them when they are forgotten." The reference is apparently to the French parlements; it is explicitly not to the English judiciary, for Montesquieu criticizes the English Parliament for having abolished the prerogatives of lords, clergy, nobility, and cities, especially the courts of the lords. Though the common law courts were the king's courts and though Montesquieu recognizes that in England, "on the foundation of a free government, one would often see the form of an absolute government,"[19] he apparently takes his model for a judiciary—if not for every judicial procedure—from monarchical France.

Still, his description of the judicial task in a monarchy often draws upon maxims or practices familiar also in the common law. What he says at the outset of Book VI about the importance of following precedent, of securing the property and life of each citizen, of knowing the immense variety in kinds of property, and of recognizing diversity in the customs of different provinces is, except perhaps on the last point, as applicable to England as to France. Indeed, his claim that the complexity of law in monarchies "seems to make an art of reason itself" resonates of Coke's "artificial reason of the law." In the third and fourth chapters of Book VI, Montesquieu writes of "the manner of judging" in despotisms, monarchies, and republics: "In despotic States, there is no law: the judge is himself his rule. In monarchical States, there is a law: and where it is precise, the judge follows it; where it is not, he searches for its spirit. In republican government it is of the nature of the constitution that judges follow the letter of the law." In this echo of the work's title, knowing the spirit of the laws belongs especially to judges in a monarchy; in forming judgments, "they deliberate together, they communicate to each other their thoughts, they reconcile themselves." In contrast, republican judges declare simply guilt or innocence, and the examples he offers are from Rome and

England; in the latter, juries decide guilt or innocence, and if they find guilt, "the judge pronounces the penalty that the law inflicts for this deed; and for that, he only needs eyes."[20]

The different manners of judging in different forms of government, however, begin to fade in importance after the initial chapters in Book VI. More precisely, the classification of governments begins to reshuffle, as the distinction between moderate government and despotism comes forward and the threefold scheme recedes. The shift is suggested in chapter 6, "In which government the sovereign can be judge," where Montesquieu corrects Machiavelli on the law of treason: "I would gladly adopt the maxim of this great man; but as in these cases the political interest forces, so to speak, the civil interest (for it is always an inconvenience that the people itself judges its offenses), it is necessary, to remedy this, that the laws provide, as much as it is in them, for the security of particular individuals."[21] Despots can themselves be judges, but monarchs never can, for several reasons, while the people in a republic must have their power of judgment limited in some way or another by laws. Four chapters later, in "Of the severity of penalties in the different governments," the only difference in question is between despotic and moderate governments. Though monarchies are always accounted moderate, republics seem sometimes moderate, sometimes left in the company of despots, an issue clouded by Montesquieu's reference to England as "a nation where the republic hides itself under the form of monarchy."[22]

The form of government becomes less urgent as the security of the individual becomes more so. As the question of where to place the power of judging is "the chief work of legislation," so knowledge of sound procedures in criminal law "interests humankind more than anything else that there is in the world"; in later words, the proper sort of judicial formalities is "the thing in the world that is most important for men to know."[23] By implication, these are also matters that previous liberal political philosophers overlooked, thinking they could find security for individuals in the proper derivation of political power. For Montesquieu, as prosperity develops from commerce, which reaches around regimes, so security of persons depends upon a kind of commerce in sound judicial practices—with philosophers as merchants and their writings as bills of exchange.[24] More than mere collection and transfer is at issue, however, for the reformer must understand the relation between political and civil law, a distinction first established in Book I and still under examination in the concluding books. Learning how to balance these two orders of law, perhaps to moderate each with the other, is critical for the legislator. Indeed, by the end of the work, Montesquieu seems to have demonstrated what he asserted in its preface—"that proposing changes only belongs to those who were happily enough born to be able to penetrate with a stroke of genius the whole constitution of a State."[25] The reader is given no program or method for reform but is invited to imitate the author's efforts or assimilate his judgments.

LAW, LEGISLATION, AND LIBERALISM

The account offered thus far of reason, law, liberty, and government in Montesquieu might seem so distant from the theory of Thomas Hobbes as to make assigning to both philosophers the name of liberal appear capricious. In fact, in the opening pages of his work, Montesquieu takes Hobbes to task for his view that the state of nature is a state of war: "The desire that Hobbes gives at the outset to men of subjugating each other is not reasonable. The idea of empire and domination is so complex, and depends on so many other ideas, that it cannot be that which he would have at the outset."[26] But the weakness of Montesquieu's criticism quickly becomes apparent, for he finds human beings soon enough in the condition Hobbes described, and within several books he describes the "idea of despotism"—cutting down a tree to harvest its fruit—in terms that hardly feature its complexity and dependence.[27] It was a favorite strategy of early liberals to insinuate themselves among their likely opponents by joining the latter in openly disowning Hobbes, even while accepting his leading principles, and Montesquieu is no stranger to this technique. He gives the right of self-defense a pride of place equivalent to what it earns in Hobbes, if with his own distinctive color: Where for Hobbes self-defense had been inalienable natural right, for Montesquieu it becomes the key to Germanic criminal procedure. Likewise he follows Hobbes in avoiding dependence upon religious principle, in seeking a cure for prejudice, in defending the integrity of individual thought, and in relying upon scientific reason, though he goes about each task in his own way. For Hobbes, the faculty of reason is at once general in its discourse and particular in its source; reason speaks in universals, but no general right reason can be identified apart from men's agreement to accept the language of some particular individual or body of individuals. This paradox generates fundamental oppositions in Hobbesian theory: absolute power versus inalienable right, state of nature versus civil society, and the like. Montesquieu is less confident than Hobbes in the generalizing power of reason but more sanguine about finding in existing laws a general spirit shared by those who live under them. Accepting Hobbes's views about first things and last things, he finds the work of reason to take a different form—and from this modification of reason's work arise various doctrines of government, liberty, and law.

The Spirit of the Laws concludes with a string of books that have been characterized as introducing a historical jurisprudence: the two books on the origin of feudal law (XXX – XXXI), a short book on the development of the

Roman law of inheritance (XXVII), and a very long book on the history of French civil laws, with special attention to the rise and decline of trial by battle (XXVIII). Between the books on civil law and those on feudal law, Montesquieu includes one "On the manner of composing the laws" (XXIX), evidently aimed at fulfilling the design he set out in Book I to treat of the relation of the laws "with the object of the legislator." By this stage of the text, it has become clear that that relation is by no means direct. Legislation is a subtle art, consisting in the adjustment of procedures, the inspiration of morals, attention to particulars, a knack for finding balance, and as he writes at the beginning of Book XXIX, the legislator's "spirit of moderation," "which it seems to me that I have written this work only to prove." As the historical books show in exhausting detail, laws are changed "little by little," usually by indirection, intended or not. Indeed, by the final chapter of Book XXIX, Montesquieu seems to suggest that the true legislators are philosophers, not because they ought to be given a Platonic crown or a Hobbesian license, but because laws, if they are not to be tyrannical commands, must conform to the human spirit. The inspiration of the proper spirit is essential to law giving, and philosophers, if not themselves capable of such inspiration, can at least advise those in authority as to what sorts of circumstances and practices encourage a moderate and free spirit among men.[28]

If all of this appears a bit vague, that is not entirely foreign to Montesquieu's intention, for a treatise on how to legislate would contradict his account of the nature of law—or at least of moderate law, of law worthy of the human spirit. It does seem clear that when Montesquieu speaks of the business of the "legislator," he means something more comprehensive than the day-to-day activities of the "legislative power" he discusses in Book XI; the legislator may need the legislative power to enact certain laws, but the drift of the argument is that legislation is generally unsuccessful in its attempt to make law or is at any rate quite limited in what it can accomplish. Since law is best made little by little, with attention to particulars, one wonders whether Montesquieu does not tacitly suggest a special role for judges in reforming the laws, at least in those governments where they serve as depository. Of course, he says explicitly that the legislative power must not be joined to the power of judging, and it seems obvious enough that a depository of the laws must not consume the fortune it is meant to guard. Still, no depositors complain if the sums they stowed are returned with interest, and most expect it. At least in the matter of judicial procedure, that "most important thing to know," it is difficult in retrospect not to find intimations in *The Spirit of the Laws* of a judiciary quietly instructed in reform.

What do these reflections on Montesquieu's teaching import for the question of his influence on American constitutionalism? Certainly these last speculations do not establish that Montesquieu is the father of today's judicial activism. Nor, given his concentration on English juries rather than judges, can his account of the power of judging in the English constitution be taken as a pattern for the federal judiciary under the Constitution of the United States. The American Framers adopted from Montesquieu a formula for the separation of governmental powers, just as they found convenient his account in Book IX of a federative republic; but the arrangements they established corresponded to the philosopher's descriptions no more precisely in the matter of the separation of powers than in the matter of federalism. His influence on the Founding is at most indirect, but since this is precisely the mode of influence he seems to have sought, it hardly determines the larger issue. Before the question can be addressed of how similar in spirit his work is to American constitutionalism, we owe attention to another channel through which that influence has run.

10

BLACKSTONE'S
LIBERALIZED COMMON LAW

In the conclusion to his widely read essay, *The "Higher Law" Background of American Constitutional Law,* Edward S. Corwin attributes to the influence of William Blackstone the challenge posed against the nascent practice of judicial review by the doctrine of legislative sovereignty. He borrows with evident relish several of Thomas Jefferson's shots aimed at the young lawyers reared on the "honeyed Mansfieldism of Blackstone . . . [who] began to slide into Toryism," and to these he adds his own indictment of the master: "Eloquent, suave, undismayed in the presence of the palpable contradictions in his pages, adept in insinuating new points of view without unnecessarily disturbing old ones, [Blackstone] is the very model of legalistic and judicial obscurantism."[1]

Corwin himself risks historical obscurantism, however, in reducing Blackstone to a snarl of contradiction and an implicit foe of American constitutionalism. If Blackstone's influence on pre-Revolutionary polemicists is only now coming to light, suggesting the reputed Tory to be in fact a closet Whig,[2] his popularity among lawyers in the young American republic has long been well known. Jefferson himself frequently cited Blackstone's authority in his legal writings and always recommended the *Commentaries* to fledgling law students—though typically reminding his charges of their incompleteness. James Wilson drew heavily on Blackstone in his lectures on law at the University of Pennsylvania, delivered while he was a justice of the newly established Supreme Court, though with explicit attention to the need to adapt Blackstone to the American situation.[3] Chancellor James Kent of New York took it upon himself to refashion the *Commentaries* for the new nation, and when Lincoln was asked the proper syllabus for a legal education, he always began with Blackstone—and omitted Jefferson's caveat.[4] Indeed, Corwin's enlistment of Jefferson for the cause of judicial review in opposition to Blackstone forges a curious alliance, since the lawyers that irked Jefferson were likely friends, not opponents, of John Marshall and his constitutional doctrines.

Since Blackstone's influence in the early republic suggests some similarity of principle between the American Founders and the English professor, the apparent tangle on the surface of his volumes should not surprise. The *Commentaries* are a subtle work because their author has undertaken a difficult task: to reconcile not just in theory but in detail the principles of liberal political theory and the practices of English common law. No doubt Blackstone's popularity in the United States derived in part from his providing in relatively succinct and straightforward form a summary of English common law, which the newly independent states generally claimed as their inheritance.[5] Still, the reasons for his importance to American constitutionalism go beyond handiness: Even why a book is thought handy deserves some thought, especially when the work in question is complex enough to earn the epithet "obscurantist" and when the matter it treats is, like the common law, a realm where Ockham's razor was rarely the tool of choice. The *Commentaries* merit our attention because American constitutionalism is largely built of the same materials as they, though with different form—a difference that allows no place in Blackstone for judicial review as we know it or even as his admirer, Alexander Hamilton, was to conceive it.

My argument throughout has been that the joining of the common law mind and liberal political philosophy is problematic. I have shown in some detail the opposition between Coke and Hobbes; I have noted how Hobbes's attempt to subsume common law within his theory failed to convince the common lawyers of his time almost as much as his theology failed to persuade the divines; and I have suggested that Locke's reconciliation of liberal principle and a tacitly reformed English political practice was purchased with the deliberate neglect of the common lawyers' notions of the English constitution, just as his theory of property can and must ignore the common law of inheritance, entail, dower, and the like. Despite modern expectation, Blackstone is not a common lawyer who spices his legal knowledge with a little philosophic learning. Rather, he aims to perfect liberal doctrine as he reforms English law, beginning from liberal principles and using common law practice to develop and correct them. He was the first in England to undertake this enterprise, but the project of improving liberal theory with extensive legal learning was not without precedent: This was among the designs of Montesquieu's *Spirit of the Laws*. Blackstone draws both explicitly and silently on Montesquieu throughout the *Commentaries*. The two works are quite different in scope and intended audience, but they share a certain sympathy of spirit—and a certain influence on American constitutionalism.

LIBERAL EDUCATION IN THE LAW

Montesquieu is the first modern author cited in the *Commentaries,* as an authority for the proposition that "political or civil liberty is the very end and scope of the [English] constitution."[6] However, Blackstone takes his cue rather than his doctrine from the Frenchman, in part because their works are undertaken with different designs, in part because Montesquieu, despite his vast learning in continental law, has almost nothing to say about English common law and evinces no familiarity with its literature. Writing a book for a general readership, comparing himself at the outset to Plato and, somewhat less explicitly, to modern political theorists and publicists, Montesquieu celebrates his homeland but addresses legislators generally, practicing, he writes, "this general virtue that comprehends the love of all."[7] Blackstone, in contrast, has a specific audience in mind, as befits a work that began as a course of lectures and indeed is published in that form. Whatever their later influence on American lawyers, the *Commentaries* are addressed to English university students, aiming to acquaint them not so much with law generally but with English law, and to teach them law not in the detail necessary for legal practice—as, for instance, Coke's *Institutes* were intended to do—but with sufficient precision to help them both in their own affairs and in their political careers. Insofar as Blackstone's introduction of the study of English law to the university is designed to open the minds of common lawyers, it reproduces the spirit of Montesquieu's work; insofar as he undertakes to focus academic attention on English law, Blackstone necessarily gives his work a different scope and obliges that it address different traditions.

Today the study of law in the university is so taken for granted that it is easy to overlook the novelty of Blackstone's lectures; indeed, the enormous success of his curricular reform is no small indication of his influence.[8] Delivered at Oxford initially in 1753 and repeated annually, then formalized with Blackstone's appointment as the first Vinerian Professor in 1758, the lectures published between 1765 and 1769 as the *Commentaries* were, according to the historian William Holdsworth, "the first lectures ever given on English law at any university in the world."[9] Blackstone himself highlights the importance he attached to this achievement by beginning his introduction with a section "Of the Study of the Law" and indeed by printing this in the form of his inaugural lecture as Vinerian Professor. English law, hitherto studied only by lawyers at the Inns of Court, ought to be within the province not only of the legal profession but of every gentleman in England. After all, he is the one who will be called to sit on juries, may be appointed justice of the peace, and might find himself in Parliament, among the "guardians of the English constitution; the makers, repealers, and interpreters of English law," since "most gentlemen of considerable property, at some period or other in their lives, are

ambitious of representing their country in parliament."[10] The university had
been home to the study only of the Civil Law, derived from the *Institutes* of
the Emperor Justinian and in force generally on the Continent but employed
in only a few specified areas of English law, such as the law of admiralty and
ecclesiastical law. The connection of Civil Law and canon law accounts, in
Blackstone's view, for the longstanding exclusion of English common law
from the universities, which had been of course under the province of the
clergy. The distrust of clergy (not to mention the outright hostility toward
"monkish superstition"[11]) that permeates the pages of the *Commentaries* animates as well his project as a whole.

John W. Cairns has argued in a recent article that Blackstone's enterprise
must be understood within the context of what he calls the Institutist tradition in early modern Europe: the gradual introduction in the universities in
one country after another of teaching about national law in addition to Civil
Law, a development that coincided with the rise of the nation-state and involved use of the general categories of Civil Law in the analysis of national
legal customs.[12] Acceptance of this thesis, however, does not excuse one from
inquiring what led men of intelligence and learning to endorse the nation-
state, and this question moves beyond matters of law narrowly conceived to
raise issues of political theory. Whatever might be said of Cairns's continental
examples, what needs accounting first in Blackstone is not his attention to the
national—for the English common lawyers before him had spared few words
in their celebration of the magnificently national character of the common
law[13]—but rather his attempt to improve both the education of English
lawyers and the common law itself by bringing to bear upon it not only the
categories of Civil Law but also the insights of liberal political theory and the
general character of liberal science, of "genuine, experimental, philosophy."[14]
Himself trained in the university and at the Inns of Court, Blackstone undertakes a reconciliation between the common law and liberal theory to the improvement, he thinks, of both.

The pose or attitude of reconciliation and balance indeed pervades the
Commentaries, as several recent scholars have noticed, not always in their eyes
to Blackstone's credit. Daniel Boorstin's book-length study, *The Mysterious
Science of the Law,* finds in Blackstone one who means to develop a science of
law but who, unawares if unavoidably, merely dresses his prejudices favoring
private property and civil society in the rationalist's suit; the contradictions
and obscurities result from the impossibility of a perfect fit.[15] Duncan Kennedy, less forgiving of mere prejudice and therefore more attentive to
Blackstone's reasoning, also considers Blackstone's project an extended apol-
ogy for the status quo. Kennedy rightly recognizes the problems inherent in
the attempt to reconcile an ancient aristocratic order with modern commercial society, and he correctly names such reconciliatory politics liberal, but in

the end he attributes Blackstone's difficulties to the impossibility of any effort to overcome the fundamental chaos he posits in all social reality.[16] Truer to Blackstone's intention is the interpretation tersely sketched by Herbert Storing in an essay couched in a textbook: Blackstone's premises and his ends are fundamentally those of modern liberal political philosophy, but it was his special prudence to endow these with the familiar if resplendent garments of the English common law (though Storing does not explain why Blackstone did not find liberal theory and English practice adequately reconciled by the prudence of John Locke).[17] Another generally sound assessment of the *Commentaries* appears in an article by Richard Posner, but his perspective is the obverse of Storing's: Blackstone's achievement was to start from the laws of his society and "demonstrate how those laws operated to achieve the economic, political, and other goals of the society."[18]

The following sketch of what might be called Blackstone's constitutionalism will not match the learning behind those and other studies on substantive details of English law. I do hope to indicate the self-conscious astuteness of Blackstone's attempt to meld liberalism and common law and to outline the sort of constitutional and legal practice he appears to recommend.

BLACKSTONE'S CONSTITUTION OF ENGLAND

Blackstone's attention to the particulars of common law might be Montesquieuean in inspiration and in occasional detail, but the doctrine he sets down in the second section of the *Commentaries,* "Of the Nature of Laws in General," is remarkably Hobbesian, though he avoids the risky compliment of a citation. After a nod at Justinian's summary of natural law as the command "that we should live honestly, should hurt nobody, and should render to every one it's due," Blackstone passes by any doctrine of natural law that depends upon "a chain of metaphysical disquisitions." He discovers that God "has been pleased so to contrive the constitution and frame of humanity, that we should want no other prompter to enquire after and pursue the rule of right, but only our own self-love, that universal principle of action." In fact, self-love is not only the means to natural law but in a way its object, for God "has graciously reduced the rule of obedience to this one paternal precept, 'that man should pursue his own happiness.' "[19] Moreover, not to revise natural law but to help us discover it, God has added by revelation the divine law, whose "precepts, when revealed, are found upon comparison to be really a part of the original law of nature, as they tend in all their consequences to man's felicity"—not, evidently, ever to his damnation, much less his felicity in another life. To these two must be added the law of nations, since "man was born for society" but all mankind cannot fit into one society, though this law too "depends entirely upon the rules of natural law." In other words, before "the principal subject of this section, municipal or civil law," there exists only the natural law that man pursue his own good, the other forms of law proving upon inspection merely to confirm or apply the "law of nature."[20] Remembering the grounding of Hobbes's natural right in the principle that human beings necessarily act for their own good, one can see that, except for the terminology, Blackstone's account is coincident with Hobbes's.

More like Montesquieu than like Hobbes, Blackstone does not go on to develop a long doctrine of natural law but rather proceeds to the treatment of positive or human law, rarely to return to what was strictly preliminary. Still, the definition of positive or municipal law he gives is not without a clear Hobbesian resonance: "Municipal law . . . is properly defined to be 'a rule of civil conduct prescribed by the supreme power in a state, commanding what is right and prohibiting what is wrong.' " Each term in this definition is then subjected to precise explication, during the course of which Blackstone's indebtedness to liberal theory becomes clear. That law is a rule makes it "permanent, uniform, and universal," dependent "upon the maker's will," not on counsel, compact, or agreement; that law concerns civil conduct means it leaves natural law, moral conduct, revelation, and "the rule of faith" to other contexts; that law is a prescribed rule ensures that those bound by it are notified, though the people "may be notified by universal tradition and long practice, which supposes a previous publication, and is the case of the common law of England."[21]

The command of right or wrong is partly declaratory of natural rights and duties, prohibiting offenses against natural and revealed law, and partly determinative of things indifferent, whether or not they will be allowed. This distinction between natural rights and wrongs on the one hand and freely legislated rights and wrongs on the other, however, is thrown into question almost as soon as it is made. The declaratory part of the law, Blackstone writes, "depends not so much upon the law of revelation or of nature, as upon the wisdom and the will of the legislator."[22] How wide is the latitude and how narrow the principle within which the legislator can act appears several sections later, in the account of what Blackstone calls "the absolute rights of individuals." Though "natural liberty consists properly in a power of acting as one thinks fit, without any restraint or control, unless by the law of nature," political or civil liberty "is no other than natural liberty so far restrained by human laws (and no farther) as is necessary and expedient for the general advantage of the publick." More precise standards of what can or cannot properly be legislated are unavailable, it seems, as Blackstone rests his confidence in "the vigour of our free constitution," through which "the ballance of our rights and liberties has settled to it's proper level."[23] Since legislators act with latitude, the obligation to obey their rules cannot be absolute:

It rests in the sanction attached to the law; it is not imposed on the consciences of subjects.[24] The account of legislative latitude, the recommendation of substantial individual freedom, and the unwillingness to acknowledge a human claim upon others' consciences are all consistent with the underlying liberalism to which Blackstone subscribes.

The critical step in Blackstone's definition of positive law is his attribution of the source of law to "the supreme power in the state." Elaborating upon this phrase allows him at once to spell out the basic tenets of his political theory and to describe in general terms the English constitution. He denies that the notion of the social contract has historical accuracy, but he readily admits that the concept "in nature and reason must always be understood and implied," since "it is their sense of their weakness and imperfection that keeps mankind together."[25] As in Hobbes, the substance of the contract is the establishment of a sovereign power, and as "legislature . . . is the greatest act of superiority that can be exercised by one being over another," "Sovereignty and legislature are indeed controvertible terms." What exactly qualifies the sovereign for rule is a bit more complex. Though in the absence of a common superior men "would still remain as in a state of nature, without any judge upon earth to define their several rights, and redress their several wrongs," the argument takes a less Hobbesian turn when Blackstone adds that "the natural foundations of sovereignty" are "wisdom, goodness, and power."[26] Ancient writers found these attributes in the three different kinds of government—aristocracy, democracy, and monarchy—but it is the good fortune of England to collect wisdom, goodness, and power in the three branches of Parliament, its legislative power. The balance noted, Blackstone can make clear that the authority of Parliament does not derive from its symmetry but rather from "the consent of all persons to submit their own private wills to the will of one man, or of one or more assemblies of men, to whom the supreme authority is entrusted."[27]

As Blackstone's treatment of the English constitution develops in Book I of the *Commentaries,* one recurring theme of particular interest to this study is his apparent critique of John Locke. At the conclusion of the opening chapter on individual rights, Blackstone outlines what is needed for their security: "To preserve these [rights] from violation, it is necessary that the constitution of parliaments be supported in it's full vigor; and limits certainly known, be set to the royal prerogative."[28] The chapters that follow expand on parliamentary authority and royal limits, treating, like Locke, the relation between Parliament and king as a relation between legislative and executive powers. Locke's name surfaces in the context of Blackstone's statement of the "sovereign and uncontrolable authority" of Parliament in legislation and its practical "omnipotence"; in making this assertion, he is obliged to reject

Locke's view that the people "retain a supreme power to remove or alter the legislative, when they find the legislative act contrary to the trust reposed in them"—not because it is inaccurate in theory but because it is inconsistent "under any dispensation of government at present actually existing." Revolution cannot always be avoided, Blackstone understands, but neither can the right of revolution be built into the constitution without dissolving government, social hierarchy, and "all positive laws whatsoever before enacted."[29] In the introductory description of the English constitution Blackstone cites Locke as authority on the "entire dissolution of the bands of government" should the legislative power be altered, noting that Locke "perhaps carries his theory too far"; in the subsequent treatment, Blackstone quietly suggests that Locke is insufficiently attentive to the detailed requirements of settled law, though the search for "settled standing laws" or for the conditions that bring these about was central to his treatise.[30]

The ramifications of Blackstone's position appear in his account of the Glorious Revolution of 1688. He calls this "an entirely new case in politics, which had never before happened in our history; the abdication of the reigning monarch, and the vacancy of the throne thereupon."[31] As his discussion proceeds, he makes it clear that whatever may have been the justice of the Convention Parliament's fiction of a vacancy on the throne after the king was driven from England for his "endeavours to subvert the constitution by breaking the original contract, his violation of fundamental laws," the matter is now settled. Its legality is less to be admired than "that it was conducted with a temper and moderation which naturally arose from it's equity." Once again Locke comes in for a thrashing, since Blackstone thinks that accepting his doctrine of a dissolution of government would have left the country in "the wild extremes into which the visionary theories of some zealous republicans would have led them," since, again, it

> would have reduced the society almost to a state of nature; would have levelled all distinctions of honour, rank, offices, and property; would have annihilated the sovereign power, and in consequence have repealed all positive laws; and would have left the people at liberty to have erected a new system of state upon a new foundation of polity.[32]

Blackstone acknowledges that from the Glorious Revolution "a new aera commenced, in which the bounds of prerogative have been better defined, the principles of government more thoroughly examined and understood, and the rights of the subject more explicitly guarded by legal provisions, than in any other period of the English history," but in his mind the novel gains do not vindicate Locke's theory. In good Montesquieuean fashion, Blackstone is reluctant to acknowledge a thorough restructuring of society, preferring rather that reforms be undertaken little by little or at least be thought to proceed step by step.

Locke's name emerges again, as might be suspected, in the discussion of prerogative. While Locke defined prerogative abstractly, as the executive's right to act in the silence of the laws, or even against them for the public good, Blackstone appears to treat of the prerogative in a more traditional way, by listing the various powers of the king and celebrating the limits on prerogative and the very freedom that allows their discussion. As he acknowledges a carefully limited right of the people to go outside the constitution in a crisis, so he draws a distinction between prerogative "in the ordinary course of law" and "those extraordinary recourses to first principles."[33] Here Blackstone praises Locke, not so much for his definition of prerogative as for his principle that "if that discretionary power be abused to the public detriment, such prerogative is exerted in an unconstitutional manner." Still, the prerogative that "Mr Locke has well defined" is in Blackstone's account only half what it is in Locke's, since Locke includes the power to act not only in law's silence but, when the need arise, even against it. Whether this is meant as a tacit correction of Locke, or only to show that within the system of law such matters must remain tacit, will grow clearer as we turn from Blackstone's constitutional theory generally to his specific statements about courts and common law.

REFINING THE COMMON LAW

Having begun the introductory section on laws in general with a discussion of the law of nature and having followed this with the general definition of law as a rule prescribed by the sovereign power, Blackstone concludes with "a few observations concerning the interpretation of laws." Since he, like Hobbes, defined law generally on the model of the statute, it comes as no surprise that his observations on interpreting laws are rules for reading statutes and thus for discerning the legislative intent. Lest his readers overlook this point, he prefaces the discussion with a brief critique of the Roman practice of giving "the force of perpetual laws" to emperors' rescripts (or answers in particular disputes) rather than adopting only "those general constitutions, which had only the nature of things for their guide." Criticized also by Montesquieu as a "bad manner of giving laws," rescripts are, according to Blackstone, "Contrary to all true forms of reasoning, [since] they argue from particulars to generals,"[34] but he passes silently over whether the rule of *stare decisis* at common law does not to some extent proceed in the manner of rescripts. Blackstone then sketches the common sense of interpreting statutes and closes the section with brief remarks on equity, notable for their strong caution against carrying too far the equitable consideration of "the particular circumstances of each individual case," since this would "destroy all law, and leave the decision of every question entirely in the breast of the judge."

> And law, without equity, tho' hard and disagreeable, is much more desirable for the public good, than equity without law; which would make every judge a legislator, and introduce most infinite confusion; as there would be almost as many different rules of action laid down in our courts, as there are differences of capacity and sentiment in the human mind.[35]

In short, the section "Of the Nature of Laws in General" concludes in the same spirit with which it began, endorsing the priority of legislation and the subordination of the power to judge.

Once this is grasped, the transition to the next section, "Of the Laws of England," appears especially problematic. One might expect this section to parallel its predecessor, only filling in details where matters before had been necessarily general, and to some extent this expectation is fulfilled: Section 3, like section 2, ends with a discussion of the interpretation of statutes and an account of equity, this time adding to general principles of interpretation and equity specific rules and maxims accepted in English law. Still, the organization of the section is determined by a distinction introduced in its first sentence, between "the *lex non scripta,* the unwritten or common law; and the *lex scripta,* the written, or statute law," with most attention devoted to the former.[36] That the difference between sections 2 and 3 involves more than a division between general principle and particular instance should have been evident already in Blackstone's choosing to discuss the constitution of the English Parliament in the former, not the latter. The gap between section 2 and section 3 is between the theory of sovereign legislation and the way of thinking of the common law judiciary; in drawing the distinction as he does, Blackstone defines the task of reconciliation he proceeds to undertake.

His examination of common law begins with a brief foray into its history, a project completed at somewhat greater length in the last chapter of the final book of the *Commentaries.* Common law descends from the Saxon law and thus antedates the Norman Conquest; this opinion, as seen in Coke and in Hale, was accepted doctrine among common lawyers and common law historians. Blackstone adds his own twist, by comparing common law, as digested by Edward the Confessor from Alfred's original code, to similar bodies of law in early Portugal, Sweden, and Spain. The ability of Alfred's laws to withstand the shock of Civil Law, which came in the Conqueror's wake—not to mention feudal law, which came with his army—seems to be the secret of

English "political liberties," of "the free constitution of England." Blackstone does not make entirely clear whether this secret success consists in some special property in the laws themselves or in the mere fact of their existence, as they give those who would resist despotism a post on which to nail their claim and thus provided a balance against Norman force; his statement that the English constitution "has been rather improved than debased" implies the latter, as does indeed his high praise of the same in the *Commentaries'* final pages.[37] There he also contrasts "the narrow rules and fanciful niceties of metaphysical and Norman jurisprudence" to the "pristine simplicity and vigour" of common law, and he finds in English law in his own day "an elegant proportion of the whole," mixing "noble monuments of ancient simplicity, and the more curious refinements of modern art."[38] Though this last phrase probably refers to the fictions employed to soften feudal remnants, it might extend as well to Blackstone's own undertaking, for its scientific aim does not at all deter him from spinning elaborate metaphors or fictions of his own. Indeed, the self-consciously literary character of the *Commentaries* rarely escapes mention among his own commentators, not to mention among critics such as Jeremy Bentham who would make a sparer science of the law.[39]

Though Blackstone is interested in the history of common law, he defines common law as customary law, "of higher antiquity than memory or history can reach"; that is, a custom counts as common law if it has been followed as law "time out of mind; or, in the solemnity of the legal phrase, time whereof the memory of man runneth not to the contrary." Coke had defined common law as including not only custom but also writs, records, maxims, and natural law itself, all collected together by legal reason. Characteristically, Blackstone's definition is much neater: The common law is composed of customs and maxims, "But I take these to be one and the same thing. For the authority of these maxims rests entirely upon general reception and usage; and the only method of proving, that this or that maxim is a rule of the common law, is by shewing that it has always been the custom to observe it."[40]

The validity of custom and customary maxim is established "by the judges in the several courts of justice. They are the depositary of the laws; the living oracles," he writes in unmistakably Montesquieuean tones—but of course against Montesquieu's own characterization of the English judiciary.[41] What bridges the gap between what in the Frenchman's terms would be an aristocratic judiciary and the quasi republic in which it sits is the strict adherence to precedent:

> For it is an established rule to abide by former precedents, where the same points come up again in litigation; as well to keep the scale of justice even and steady, and not liable to waver with every new judge's

opinion; as also because the law in that case being solemnly declared and determined, what before was uncertain, and perhaps indifferent, is now become a permanent rule, which it is not in the breast of any subsequent judge to alter or vary from, according to his private sentiments: he being sworn to determine, not according to his private judgment, but according to the known laws and customs of the land; not delegated to pronounce a new law, but to maintain and expound an old one.[42]

By definition the common law might be custom, but as this passage suggests, in reality the origin of customary law is lost to memory in part because its establishment is undeclared; new cases yield new law, if not by necessity at least through solemnity. The common law "is a positive law, fixed and established by custom, which custom is evidenced by judicial decisions."[43] Blackstone does not say outright that judicial decisions establish law by giving such evidence, though one might glean that from the drift of what he says and from his subsequent treatment of particular legal matters. What he does insist upon explicitly is that both judges and common law be tamed of their pride.

There appears to be one limit on the rule of precedent (in addition, that is, to the power of statutory law to override common law). That is the doctrine that precedents against reason, "flatly absurd or unjust," do not bind: "Hence it is that our lawyers are with justice so copious in their encomiums on the reason of the common law; that they tell us, that the law is the perfection of reason, that it always intends to conform thereto, and that what is not reason is not law."[44] Blackstone sets a mild standard for measuring the reason of the law, however: That which is not unreasonable is good enough. The distance here from Coke's description of the "artificial perfection of reason" in the law is at once easy to overlook and yet precisely signaled. Coke holds the perfection of law to arise from the wisdom of generations of judges, "fined and refined" through experience, not merely subject to an occasional purge. The maxims of law are a part of that reason, perhaps the critical premises of practical reasoning, not simply customary forms of words no more cogent in themselves than ancient rhymes. Blackstonian reason aims not so much to determine particular cases as to give the variety of things existent an orderly form in the whole; to achieve this, it is enough, to borrow a phrase of Hobbes's, to take off "the rude and cumbersome points."

Blackstone assembles and retains many forms of common law thinking, and in the section on English law he makes Coke his authority, not Justinian, Pufendorf, Locke, or Hobbes. Still, he constrains Coke rather than defers to him, calling him "a man of infinite learning in his profession, though not a little affected by the quaintness of the times he lived in, which appear strongly in all his works." Blackstone confines Coke's doctrine, as for example when he takes Coke's general words about the artificial reason and perfection of law and applies them, not to common law as a whole, but to particular customs in particular situations.[45] Blackstonian reason searches for a comprehensive vision, capable of tying together separate threads; in this sense, Boorstin is correct to describe his work as attempting to develop a rational science, a social science. One can also see why, if his reason works generally, not in application to particular cases, he earned his reputation rather as professor and author than as judge.[46]

Significantly, Blackstone's differences from Coke appear most sharply on the question of whether the common law judiciary can limit parliamentary acts. He concludes his reprise of "rules to be observed with regard to the construction of statutes" with a rejection of the broad reading given to Sir Edward Coke's opinion in *Doctor Bonham's Case*:

> Acts of parliament that are impossible to be performed are of no validity; and if there arise out of them collaterally any absurd consequences, manifestly contradictory to common reason, they are, with regard to those collateral consequences, void. I lay down the rule with these restrictions, though I know it is generally laid down more largely, that acts of parliament contrary to reason are void. But if the parliament will positively enact a thing to be done which is unreasonable, I know of no power that can control it: and the examples usually alleged in support of this sense of the rule do none of them prove, that where the main object of a statute is unreasonable the judges are at liberty to reject it; for that were to set the judicial power above that of the legislature, which were subversive of all government.[47]

Though Blackstone proceeds to explain in what circumstances "collateral consequences" might be disregarded, drawing in fact on an example proposed by Coke in *Bonham's*, he makes clear that judicial discretion is strictly limited and judicial invalidation of legislative acts foreclosed: "There is no court that has power to defeat the intent of the legislature, when couched in such evident and express words, as leave no doubt whether it was the intent of the legislature or no." For all the praise he heaps upon the common law, in the end he holds to his general principle that "the legislature, being in truth the sovereign power, is always of equal, always of absolute authority: it acknowledges no superior on earth."[48] Throughout the *Commentaries* Blackstone quietly gives reforming judges plenty to do. As once they limited military tenures, now they can enhance commercial property, and the criminal law is in serious need of reform. Still, he insists they work behind the mask of legal fictions. Blackstone perhaps offers a general lesson when he speaks of the modern executive power of the Crown: The monarchy's "instruments of power are not perhaps so open and avowed as they formerly were, and therefore are the less liable to jealous and invidious reflections," but a king is no less energetic on that account.[49]

In the midst of the book on the complex system of remedial writs, Blackstone draws his most quoted metaphor. Discussing how reliance on common law, prudently subject to development, secures the public good far more effectively than would attempts "to begin the work of legislation afresh," he offers the following "clew" to pervade his "labyrinth":

> We inherit an old Gothic castle, erected in the days of chivalry, but fitted up for a modern inhabitant. The moated ramparts, the embattled towers, and the trophied halls, are magnificent and venerable, but useless. The inferior apartments, now converted into rooms of convenience, are chearful and commodious, though their approaches are winding and difficult.[50]

Yet even this image, though it nicely suggests the relation of reform to conservation in Blackstone's thought, does not fully unfold his view of his larger project. He intends not simply changing the common law in its substance and details but first of all changing what common law itself means, defusing its pride in its justice and antiquity, expanding its horizons so that genuine improvement can be conceived. Through the combination of a skillful rhetoric of encomium and an extensive knowledge of the detail of English law, Blackstone is able to succeed where Hobbes failed in taming common lawyers—indeed, in a way by going beyond Hobbes, for he envisions a society that is not only peaceful but progressive. Kennedy writes that it was Blackstone's "intention to vindicate the common law against the charge that it was inconsistent with the enlightened political thought of his day, and especially with emerging liberalism,"[51] but it might better be said that he aims to modify common law so that it becomes consistent with advanced liberal doctrine. The riddle of Blackstone in America is whether the pattern might be inverted: Could liberal principles have been put to work within a regime in some ways dedicated to the maintenance of the spirit of common law?

PART FOUR
RECOVERING
CONSTITUTION AS LAW

My discussion thus far of the sources of American constitutionalism in the tradition of common law and in liberal political philosophy has attempted first to unfold the two schools of thought and their initial opposition, then to suggest the ways in which liberalism sought to accommodate common law constitutionalism. In the essays that follow, I try to bring the analysis to bear upon several aspects of the American Founding. First, I examine the interacting roles of common law politics and liberal principles in the constitutional debate that defined the Revolution. Next I offer a reading of those numbers of *The Federalist Papers* that concern the new federal judiciary; I suggest that the general liberalism of the papers must itself be tempered when the judicial power is analyzed and defended, or at least that an interpretation of *The Federalist* exclusively in terms of liberal political theory needs to be revised. Finally, I look briefly at the interplay of liberal and common law understandings at the Philadelphia Convention and in the First Congress as it drafted the Bill of Rights, proposing that the common law context of the debate helps explain certain choices the Framers made and thus the character of their intent.

In speaking of common law in a sense beyond its narrowly technical meaning in a contemporary court of law, I will allude to a common law way of thinking about politics; before showing it at work in the Founding, let me clarify what I take that way of thinking to be. The common law approach to politics involves the citizen or legislator conceiving his task as judge or advocate within a legal frame: viewing each controversy as a matter, not for free invention or for fresh deduction from first principles, but for judicious choice, with attention to precedent always in order but authoritative solution always elusive. The common law proceeds by reason, but by reason that collects and judges particulars—by a sort of Aristotelian practical reason—rather than by reason in the modern, Enlightenment, analytical sense—the reason that breaks apart and reassembles. It stresses continuity rather than novelty, though it demands some reason greater than custom alone, for by common law, unreasonable customs have no legal force.

Though the essays in this part are assuredly suggestive, not exhaustive, I think they begin to show that in the founding of American law and the establishment of the Constitution as law, it is more accurate to say that liberal insights are assimilated into a common law context than to argue the reverse. It bears repeating that I do not intend by this to belittle the importance of liberal political theory in instructing the Founders, especially those whose names are most familiar to us today, much less to deny the eventual preponderance of liberal doctrines and institutions in the regime—indeed, in the judicial power as it subsequently develops. Still, as Ellis Sandoz has reminded us in reference to the religious as well as the common law heritage enjoyed by the founding generation, if at question is not the most radical thoughts of the most progressive thinkers but the national consensus that underlay consent, the foundation of the American regime was laid on classical ground, not modern premise.[1] In the language if not precisely on the terms of Harvey Mansfield (whose analysis of the most distinctively modern element of the regime, the executive, also shows its essential dependence upon an ambivalence facilitated by the persistence of premodern ways), the Founding was the act of a sovereign people who were already in fact, not only in prospect, a constitutional people[2]—a people, in the old phrase from Bracton, "under God and the law."

11

BEHIND THE "FACTS SUBMITTED TO A CANDID WORLD": CONSTITUTIONAL ARGUMENTS FOR INDEPENDENCE

What is the source of the inalienable rights asserted in the Declaration of Independence, and how did Americans of the Revolutionary age know what their rights were? To one familiar with the text of the document or to one who merely pauses to read its introductory paragraphs, these questions seem unfit for serious inquiry, since the answers leap out from the page. The rights are given to all men equally by their Creator, "Nature's God"; this fact and the theory that governments are established by consent to preserve the people's rights, with a right reserved to change a government that fails its charge, are known as self-evident truths. The singularity of the term *self-evident* has been often noted, if never satisfactorily resolved. It gives the doctrine an aura of philosophic rigor, though perhaps the phrase should be read in light of the appeal in the first paragraph to "the opinions of mankind"—or more precisely, the expressed desire to show to those opinions a "decent respect," the variability of human opinion no doubt foreclosing a more exacting standard of proof. As others have noted, the claim of self-evidence is admittedly an assertion: "We hold these truths to be . . . ," the sentence begins, not "These truths are. . . ." Jefferson himself, though he includes authorship of the Declaration on his epitaph, denied he had devised anything original: "It was intended to be an expression of the American mind. . . . All its authority rests then on the harmonizing sentiments of the day, whether expressed in conversation, in letters, printed essays, or in the elementary books of public right, as Aristotle, Cicero, Locke, Sidney, etc."[1]

If the modern mind today holds anything to be self-evident, it is that "Laws of Nature," "inalienable rights," and "self-evident truths" are essentially nothing other than fictions, perhaps created by ingenious men, widely spread among members of a particular generation in a certain society. They are not principles about which people hold opinions and seek knowledge but are at most the currency of a common life, always changing in value. The question posed at the outset regarding the source of "inalienable rights" thus takes on an entirely different meaning than the naive reader would suppose. At issue is not the legal or philosophic grounding of those rights but a question in the history of ideas. Actually, since the principles at issue present themselves in a public document with a political purpose, the inquiry belongs even more to the history of ideologies. This is not where we will end our search, but it is at any rate where we are today obliged to begin.

IDEOLOGY AND IRONY: BAILYN'S REVOLUTION

The sentiments of the preceding paragraph seem to be the characteristic assumptions, if not conclusions, of Bernard Bailyn's *Ideological Origins of the American Revolution*. After more than twenty years it is still generally accounted the authoritative study of the meaning of the thought of those whose deeds precipitated the War of Independence. Drawing upon an exhaustive familiarity with the enormous pamphlet literature of the era, Bailyn finds five contenders for the title of founding doctrine—classical antiquity, Enlightenment rationalism, the tradition of the English common law, New England Puritanism, and radical Whiggism or republicanism. The last wins the prize, for the radical Whig theory of liberty against power, virtue against corruption, and country against court provides the framework, Bailyn thinks, which the other traditions merely fill or dress. This theory supplied the "intellectual switchboard" that so programmed the minds of colonials that the bumbling efforts of successive British ministers were read as conclusive evidence of despotic design, triggering the demise of the first British empire and the establishment of the independent United States. Somehow in the process was spawned "the most creative period in American political thought."[2]

What draws Bailyn's attention to the radical Whigs is the "logic of rebellion" they provided. A host of writers, including especially the Englishmen John Trenchard and Thomas Gordon, whose *Cato's Letters* were widely reprinted in colonial papers throughout the eighteenth century, taught the colonists to see in every exercise of power a possible encroachment upon liberty, to look for traces of conspiracy to reduce free citizens into slavery, and to guard jealously every privilege against invisible but entrenched enemies bent upon subversion. Rejecting the view that colonial printers and pamphleteers were propagandists of an emerging nation or for an ambitious merchant class, Bailyn finds in the ideology of conspiracy an explanation for the vehemence of the colonists' language, so unrestrained to modern ears, as well as for the apparent disproportion between threat and reaction—rebellion for a tax on legal paper, revolution for a tax on tea! Indeed, implicit in his account is a doubt as to the necessity of the Revolution, in the sense not only of economic or demographic causation but of political necessity: With cooler hearts or clearer minds, the crisis might have been successfully weathered.

The ideology of conspiracy—the colonists' "peculiar inheritance of thought"—made what was theoretically avoidable politically inevitable:

> They saw about them, with increasing clarity, not merely mistaken, or even evil, policies violating the principles upon which freedom rested, but what appeared to be evidence of nothing less than a deliberate assault launched surreptitiously by plotters against liberty both in England and in America. . . . This belief transformed the meaning of the colonists' struggle, and it added an inner accelerator to the movement of opposition. For, once assumed, it could not be easily dispelled: denial only confirmed it, since what conspirators profess is not what they believe; the ostensible is not the real; and the real is deliberately malign.[3]

The precision in Bailyn's choice of his book's title thus becomes clear: He does not merely weigh the claims of intellectual ancestry but shows that ideology in the precise sense—not just any collection of opinions, but doctrine impassioned, systematic, and self-verifying—was the principal cause of American independence. "Ideas," not only money and intrigue, have power in the world, though less on account of their wisdom than of their fury.[4]

These last remarks go further than Bailyn would like to allow, although not necessarily further than he can be coaxed. Despite the book's title, he writes in its foreword that his is a "rather old-fashioned view that the American Revolution was above all else an ideological, constitutional, political struggle and not primarily a controversy between social groups undertaken to force changes in the organization of the society or the economy."[5] Indeed, the second half of the book is devoted to constitutional and political questions, as Bailyn explains how colonists weaned on the radical Whigs' unrelenting distrust of power and motive nevertheless developed sober constitutional arrangements and pursued the logic, not of paranoia, but of their principles. "The radicalism the Americans conveyed to the world in 1776 was a transformed as well as a transforming force," he writes; "words and concepts had been reshaped in the colonists' minds in the course of a decade of pounding controversy— strangely reshaped, turned in unfamiliar directions, towards conclusions they could not themselves clearly perceive."[6] Although he treats the story of collapse apart from the story of reconstruction, he knows they are coincident, for he draws upon the same pamphlets in both tales. The interpretation, then, presents an elegant paradox. The modern historian, having "no stake in the outcome," can "now embrace the whole of the event, see it from all sides." What he sees is "the tragedy of the event," but at least in the study of the American Revolution, it is not a sad scene— though perhaps no historian who sees that the agents of the past "were all equally real, equally bound by the circumstances of the time" can resist a twinge of sadness at having lost that sense of speaking to the ages and acting for posterity that was professed and practiced by Jefferson, Adams, and their kind.[7]

The reach of Bailyn's scholarship has nevertheless left room for doubt of his conclusion. First, the radical Whigs are not alone in their tendency to see conspiracy beneath all action, to suppose evil intention behind every inconvenient outcome. As Bailyn himself notes, the colonial governors and the ministry in England were apt to see conspiratorial ambition in the colonists' protests every bit as much as the colonists found tyrannical design behind official acts. The roots of conspiratorial thinking are "elaborately embedded in Anglo-American political culture," he says, and rightly so: There was surely something close to this mentality at work a century-and-a-half before in Sir Edward Coke's invectives against recusants and especially "Papists," in the English Parliament's distrust of the Stuart kings' favorites, and then in its distrust of the kings themselves. From a different political corner, similar tones echo in the writings of Thomas Hobbes as he warns of the designs of orators and clerics; and John Locke's elaborate metaphor comparing a people heading toward despotism to a ship secretly sailing toward the slave market in Algiers—resuming its course after every storm so as to leave no doubt of its nefarious destination—could serve as ideal type for the whole genre, not to mention as a reminder that not all voyages are innocent.[8]

Though Bailyn might respond that allegation not of conspiracy alone but of conspiracy by power against liberty is the mark of the radical Whig, this proves too much, for if one can find in the literature the intransigent accuser, one also typically discovers the phrases of obeisance—after all, not the king but his ministers are to blame. By Thomas Paine's *Common Sense* in 1776 (indeed, in many respects by Thomas Jefferson's *Summary View of the Rights of British America* in 1774), the king is either chief, or co-conspirator. But such republicanism comes late in the progress toward Revolution, or at least it openly proclaims itself only when rebellion has begun. Meanwhile, theorists such as Locke, whom Bailyn is apparently reluctant to count among the radicals, have a substantial republican bent. The conspiratorial style, in other words, is not a reliable test of radical Whiggism, much less a proof of its predominance.

These remarks suggest a second, perhaps more comprehensive observation concerning Bailyn's definition of the candidates for influence, that is, with the marking of categories of thought. The modern historian, seeking to write without taking sides, is apt to find himself without a principle by which to distinguish idea from ideology or clear thought from muddled opinion. Facing a stream of words competing to define and explain the very events they cause, he is driven to take refuge in an admission of the inevitable arbitrariness of classification. However he might wish to start from the self-understanding of the parties, the historian's own contribution, if he is to be more than a chronicler, is usually to show how historical individuals and peoples failed fully to understand themselves or their situations. Surely this is Bailyn's ambition: Not only to call attention to sources often neglected but also to show how what had been discounted was in fact determinative.

This type of historical argument, however, unravels when the classification upon which it rests begins to tear. Bailyn runs into difficulty, as noted, in the matter of John Locke. Apparently cited by almost all parties, it is difficult to deny Locke a place among Bailyn's Enlightenment rationalists; nor can one escape the problem by claiming the hero of the Enlightenment was the author rather of the epistemological *Essay Concerning Human Understanding* than of the political *Two Treatises,* for the *Letter on Toleration,* which bridges the gap between politics and first principles, is classic Enlightenment fare. But would Locke, author of *The Reasonableness of Christianity* and an authority widely cited in the colonial pulpit, not also fit in with the awakened Puritanism Bailyn discusses, at least in regard to its social and political doctrines? Or would the man who calls the state of nature one of perfect liberty and equality, who criticizes the concept of paternal power for its male bias, and who made little effort to conceal in his teachings the right of revolution not deserve a place among radical Whigs? In short, although neither classicist nor common lawyer, Locke qualifies as a member of many parties in Bailyn's scheme, showing either his own mind hopelessly confused or the scheme of classification too narrow for his genius.

If Bailyn's scheme is too confining for Locke, it also seems to underestimate the role of the common law and the common lawyers. Edmund Burke, whom one might think the last person to overlook the reach of radical Whiggism, compiles in his "Speech on Conciliation with America" a somewhat different list than Bailyn's relating to what he calls the "temper and character" of Americans, their "fierce spirit of liberty."[9] Burke includes among the causes of this spirit the colonists' English heritage, which made them not only devoted to liberty, but to liberty according to English ideas, and on English principles. Abstract liberty, like other abstractions, is not to be found . . . Their love of liberty, as with you, fixed and attached on this specifick point of taxation.

Going on to note the popular character of American assemblies, the dissenting Protestantism in the northern colonies, the pride in liberty natural to slaveholders in the south, and the effect of distance in weakening government, Burke proceeds to add mention of

another circumstance in our colonies, which contributes no mean part towards the growth and effect of this untractable spirit. I mean their education. In no country perhaps in the world is the law so general a study. The profession itself is numerous and powerful; and in most provinces it takes the lead. The greatest number of the deputies sent to the congress were lawyers. But all who read, and most do read, endeavor to obtain some smattering in that science. . . . This study renders men acute, inquisitive, dextrous, prompt in attack, ready in defense, full of resources. In other countries, the people, more simple, and of a less mercurial cast, judge of an ill principle in government only by an actual grievance; here they anticipate the evil, and judge of the pressure of the grievance by the badness of the principle. They augur misgovernment at a distance; and snuff the approach of tyranny in every tainted breeze.

Burke is examining the same characteristics that Bailyn was later to notice, but he attributes them to a different tradition or perhaps puts Bailyn's tradition within a larger frame. One can sense in what Burke says of the colonists no little admiration—he was, after all, among their friends in Parliament, he praised their spirit of liberty, he himself was educated as a lawyer, and he was to use famously the lessons of anticipation—but his own position was not exactly theirs. As he makes plain later in the speech, "The question with me is, not whether you [Parliament] have a right to make your people miserable; but whether it is not in your interest to make them happy." Even accounting for the imperatives of his difficult rhetorical situation, Burke not only makes his case but forms his judgment on the basis of policy rather than right.[10] He had, after all, supported the Rockingham policy in 1766 of both repealing the Stamp Act and passing the Declaratory Act, thus removing the special grievance while maintaining the Parliament's entire claim of legislative authority. Yet precisely this distance from American opinion makes his testimony more telling: To understand the thought, even the spirit of the American Revolution, one must try to grasp the case at law.

THE CONSTITUTIONAL CASE IN THE DECLARATION

The classic scholarly account of the colonists' constitutional case is Charles Howard McIlwain's 1923 essay, *The American Revolution: A Constitutional Interpretation*.[11] Drawing upon the Irish precedent—an analogy made almost explicit by Parliament in the Declaratory Act, largely copied from the similar Act of 1719 declaring parliamentary supremacy over Ireland—McIlwain suggests that the American colonists were basically correct in asserting that they had never consented to the sovereignty of Parliament, accepted in Great Britain through the Glorious Revolution of 1688. Maintaining their connection to England through the Crown, they argued that they had held their legislatures to be independent of, if parallel to, the English Parliament. The assertion of parliamentary supremacy over the dominions, McIlwain finds, in fact began in 1649, the year of the regicide, under the Long Parliament, and if corrected at the Restoration and left untested after the Glorious Revolution, it was still, when asserted in the 1760s at ministerial initiative, an innovation on the part of the metropolis from the colonists' point of view. In short, as Jefferson was to argue in his *Summary View*, Parliament had misunderstood the nature of the British empire: As determined in *Calvin's Case* in 1607, with rare unanimity among Coke, Bacon, and Ellesmere, the various dominions of England are necessarily united in the king, but they may remain separate jurisdictions, and thus subject to separate legislatures, by fundamental law.

McIlwain realizes that the "reputation of the revolutionary statesmen" depends upon the plausibility of their constitutional arguments, and unlike Bailyn he is not satisfied that intellectual reputations are secure if their claims are uncovered as "only the creation of heated imaginations or uninstructed minds."[12] Still, McIlwain thinks the constitutional case confined to the imperial argument; no cogent case can be made, though it was surely attempted, that the colonists ought to be free from Parliament's reach on the basis of colonial charters (these were easily revocable by law and could not run against prerogative), or on the basis of the rights of Englishmen founded in natural law and embodied in the English constitution (this fundamentally Whig argument was ultimately a doctrine of parliamentary supremacy). As for the case from natural rights and consent of the governed, it is revolutionary and thus no longer constitutional—a matter of politics and political theory, not of law. The Revolution, notes McIlwain, "was a political act, and such an act cannot be both constitutional and revolutionary; the terms are mutually exclusive."[13]

But McIlwain discounts too quickly the importance of the arguments from the charters and from English common law rights and accepts too soon the Blackstonian view that constitutional and revolutionary principles are incompatible. Consider the argument of James Wilson, who pamphleteered before the Revolution, sat in the Congress that passed the Declaration, distinguished himself at the Philadelphia Convention eleven years after, and was appointed by George Washington to the first Supreme Court. In his lectures on American law, begun in 1789, Wilson asserted that, contrary to the doctrine of the *Commentaries,* revolutionary principles in the United States are the very basis of fundamental law, not its antagonist.[14] What is in a sense the reverse is also true: that the colonists' understanding of fundamental or constitutional law was the basis of their revolutionary principles. Perhaps it would be more precise to say that they did not really distinguish the one from the other, maybe thinking little would be gained and much lost by trying to sever bedrock and foundation. A historian of legal and political thought rightly separates the traditions of English common law, with its idea of an ancient constitution, from the tradition of modern liberal political philosophy—and thus the claims of the rights of Englishmen from the doctrine of the rights of nature and revolution. But from the standpoint of those who shared what Jefferson later called the "one opinion" of 1776, the traditions were intermixed and continuous.

Both the distinction and the continuity between these two moments in the colonists' thought appear in the pamphlets and in the Declaration itself. In the latter, one sees the American complaint against British policy as a constitutional grievance if one reads beyond the famous introduction and does not immediately skip down to the end. Of course, they understood that in dissolving their political bands with England they could not appeal exclusively to English rights. This matter had been debated in Congress already, and the political choice to "assume, among the Powers of the earth, [a] separate and equal station" required that their claim be grounded on "the Laws of Nature and of Nature's God," not only for the sake of logic but to declare to the British and pledge among themselves that the time for reconciliation had passed. The theoretical discussion of the origin of government and the right "to alter or to abolish" a destructive form, then to choose the organization and principles of its replacement, makes clear that the appeal must run beyond tradition to natural right; indeed, custom is alluded to with a hint of impatience, as that which makes most people a little too hesitant to seek their own improvement. The old order has failed; "their former Systems of Government" must be altered; Americans must find themselves "new Guards." Still, there is, to use Jefferson's own word, a "prudent" restraint in both dealing with the old and boasting of the new: The causes for change ought to be serious and permanent, and the change itself, though by right either abolition or alteration, is in the case at hand called the latter. Jefferson's draft had had the people not only "throw off" absolute power but "expunge" the former systems; his editors in Congress made "absolute Despotism" the object thrown off and had the former systems merely altered. Indeed, more than prudence seems at work here. As no ear that catches rhythm can forget, the throwing off of despotism is not only a right, "it is their duty," while the alteration itself is called a matter of necessity and constraint.

Anyone who has sat on committees and spent endless hours quibbling over meaningless terms in wasted memoranda might recoil from so close a reading of a collective text, but that overlooks the seriousness of the political choice the men in Philadelphia understood they were making. Still, the argument for seeing in the Declaration not only a revolutionary but a constitutional case need not hang upon inference from precisely chosen words. For the bulk of the Declaration, if often slighted today, is a bill of indictment against the king and Parliament, measuring misdeeds against specific maxims and practices of Anglo-American constitutionalism, inferring from these "abuses and usurpations" "a design to reduce them under absolute Despotism"—in other words, to subvert the free constitution, or as is said in a more particular context, to abolish "the free System of English Laws." To review the entire list is beyond the scope of the present essay but perhaps also beyond what is needed, for it is almost enough just to read.

As befits the conclusion of a long struggle over the respective powers of Parliament and the colonial assemblies, the opening objections concern the legislative power, though their focus is upon the king's role. Beginning with an objection to his use of the veto—an objection more political than constitutional, perhaps, though it was not lost on the colonists that no acts of Lords and Commons had been refused by the monarch since the Glorious Revolution—the list turns to abuses of prerogative: the refusal to allow representation of newly settled areas, the irregular calling and dissolving of colonial assemblies. Complaint is then made of neglect of judiciary powers and the absence in the colonies of judicial independence, which had been fixed in English law by the Act of Settlement in 1701. The Declaration registers the concern about keeping, "in times of Peace, Standing Armies, without the Consent of our legislatures," and this charge is reiterated: "He has affected to render the Military independent of and superior to the Civil Power." The reader might then expect to see the accusations relating to the fighting under way, but those are quite properly saved until later, for they detail, under the heading of abdication (again an echo of the Glorious Revolution), how the separation has in effect already been made and by the king's own deeds.

Between the initial constitutional charges and the closing catalogue of acts of war, there is embedded another list, not of acts of the king but acts of Parliament. Having accepted the doctrine of imperial order related by McIlwain, thereby acknowledging connection to England only through the Crown, the authors of the Declaration consistently direct their objections against the king, as it is the ultimate band to him that they sever. He then must be held responsible for Parliament's Intolerable Acts, Navigation Acts, and the various acts of taxation, from the Stamp Act to the Townshend duties, which lay at the heart of so many of the colonists' grievances over the previous thirteen years. In this catalogue the constitutional objections are unmistakable: taxation without consent, deprivation of trial by jury, forced quartering of troops, suspension of colonial charters and legislatures. Indeed, it is apparent from the embedded list (if not from the entire bill of particulars) why McIlwain's divorce of the imperial question from the question of the charters and fundamental laws and rights is too refined. In the mind of the Continental Congress, the various issues fit together in a whole.

How they might characterize that whole is hinted at in the sentence that makes the transition from the principal list to the sublist: "He has combined with others to subject us to a jurisdiction foreign to our constitution, and unacknowledged by our laws; giving his Assent to their Acts of pretended Legislation." The "others" referred to of course are the British Parliament, but worthy of note is that the exercise of parliamentary authority is declared "foreign to our constitution." The phrase "our constitution" needs interpretation, for though the term if used today would seem self-evident, quite obviously it could not mean to Congress in 1776 what it does to Americans after 1789. The "our" apparently refers not to the English constitution in which the colonists might have been said to have a part but to the "us" in the same sentence, presumably that same "one people" of America mentioned at the Declaration's start. But that is the easy word to liquidate. The meaning of "constitution" is complicated by a textual irregularity of no small interest. As far as I can determine, in all of Jefferson's drafts that scholars have found, the word is "constitutions," in the plural. This is hardly surprising, since the word is plural in the passage in Jefferson's *Summary View* from which the phrase is copied verbatim.[15] But in the Declaration passed by Congress, the word is in the singular; the source of the change is apparently unknown, though the existence of the singular form in a copy of Jefferson's early draft made by John Adams is suggestive.[16] In any event, what the singular form makes clear is that the Congress could not have meant by the term anything so narrow as the particular colonial charters. Rather, I think it must be taken to mean, as the term then meant when used in reference to the British, the whole amalgam of offices, principles, and fundamental laws that give the polity its form. The Declaration does not here say of the unconstitutional acts, as Jefferson had in the *Summary View*, that "we declare these acts void," but the opinion is obvious in referring to them as "pretended legislation." At the moment of separation, the question of voiding particular acts becomes moot, but that does not make the issue uninteresting. What the whole sentence suggests is that independence, though necessarily a step beyond the existing constitution and thus necessarily based on the most fundamental political principles, still proceeds down a well-trod path.

If Burke after 1776 had been at liberty to analyze the American situation as freely as he had been the year before, he might well have repeated his observation about the influence of lawyers on the proceedings; the Declaration's bill of particulars does read like an indictment, and the document as a whole has been maligned as a lawyers' brief. But if he had repeated the opinion that the Americans made their case not on abstract principles but on British liberties, he would have been only partially correct, as perhaps he was even before. The influence of Locke on the doctrine of natural rights and revolution is unimpeachable, and Locke's theory, however much it echoed and then influenced English practice, begins as a theory of abstract right. But at least as much as Locke ever intended, into that theory were integrated doctrines and practices of English common lawyers and their notion of an ancient constitution—an unwritten constitution subject to development as well as decay but ultimately aimed at protecting English liberties. For when the question became whether the king was a tyrant or whether inconveniences were actually abuses or usurpations, reference was typically had to the heritage of liberties at English law. The specifics of the common law and the ancient constitution gave the abstract theory its distinctive form, while the theory made order of a mass of particulars in the extreme case, when the question of foundations was raised not just abstractly, but politically.

The question of which branch was grafted onto which—liberal theory onto common law, or the reverse—appears different today. To the political theorist, it might seem most useful to treat the common law constitutionalism of the age as fitting the details into a Lockean frame. But to the lawyers who helped make the Revolution—or who helped direct it, giving popular passion form and thereby at once making it effective and keeping it contained—the abstract doctrines were assimilated to the well-clothed frame of common law. It had, after all, long been a maxim at common law that it included nothing against reason and thus that it included natural law. A proverbial house with many rooms, the common law was inclined to admit or at least content to live alongside the Lockean right to revolution, even if it saw no necessity to draw from the doctrine of the state of nature a philosopher's radical conclusions about either legislative supremacy or executive prerogative. Jefferson, trained as a common lawyer, though by his graces and wit freed from the mercurial narrowness Burke found typical in the breed, illustrates the ability of the common law mind to assimilate that which demonstrates itself to be reasonable and applicable to settling particular issues of right. The previous quotation that included his list of "the elementary books of public right, as Aristotle, Cicero, Locke, Sidney, etc.," shows rather the mind that collects and judges than the intelligence that sorts and divides.

Of the revolutionaries he says, "All American Whigs thought alike on these subjects," but he would include among those of like mind not only Locke and the Whigs of 1688, but Sir Edward Coke—than whom "a sounder Whig never wrote, nor of profounder learning in the orthodox doctrines of the British Constitution, or in what was called British liberties."[17]

THE COMMON LAW POLITICS
OF THE REVOLUTIONARY PAMPHLETEERS

If the text of the Declaration and the context in which it squarely puts itself show the conjunction of common law constitutionalism and liberal political theory, something similar appears from the pamphlet literature in the decade or more preceding the Revolution, though the variety in perspective among the authors and over time reveals the complexity, if not the difficulty, of the mix. The pamphlets I have chosen briefly to discuss—James Otis's *Rights of the British Colonies Asserted and Proved* (Boston, 1764), John Dickinson's *Letters from a Farmer in Pennsylvania to the Inhabitants of the British Colonies* (Philadelphia, 1768), Thomas Jefferson's *Summary View of the Rights of British America* (Williamsburg, 1774), and Thomas Paine's *Common Sense* (Philadelphia, 1776)—were each in their time among the most popular and widely read of the genre throughout the colonies. The first three are by lawyers (though Dickinson's title conceals his background), but all address the public at large. If Paine's sparked the Revolution, the others kindled the dispute. Indeed, despite its proximity in timing and intent, *Common Sense* is in some respects the furthest of them all from the Declaration.

Otis wrote the *Rights Asserted and Proved* during the Stamp Act crisis, but he had unfolded one of its characteristic arguments a few years before in the celebrated *Paxton's Case of the Writ of Assistance*.[18] In this case Otis had argued against the power of a Massachusetts panel to issue a writ of assistance, which apparently would have enabled the sheriff to enlist help in searches for smuggled goods; though supported by the text of an Act of Parliament, the writ "is against the fundamental principles of Law," Otis claimed.

> As to Acts of Parliament. an Act against the Constitution is void: an Act against natural Equity is void: and if an Act of Parliament should be made, in the very Words of this Petition, it would be void. The Executive Courts must pass such Acts into disuse—8. Rep. 118. from Viner.—Reason of ye Com Law to control an Act of Parliament.

The citation here is to Coke's opinion in *Doctor Bonham's Case,* and the concluding words are taken almost directly from that source. Modern scholars have often seen in Otis's argument in this case the first request to an American court for the exercise of what would later become known as judicial review. John Adams, who was present as a young Boston lawyer and who recorded Otis's words, saw an even greater significance in them when he looked back at the case from the other end of his career: "Then and there the child Independence was born."[19]

In the pamphlet, Otis twice recounts the argument he made in *Paxton's Case*, in different forms of words:

> If the reasons that can be given against an act are such as plainly demonstrate that it is against natural equity, the executive courts will adjudge such act void.
> . . . .
> 'Tis hoped it will not be considered a new doctrine that even the authority of the Parliament of Great Britain is circumscribed by certain bounds which if exceeded their acts become those of mere power without rights, and consequently void. The judges of England have declared in favor of these sentiments when they expressly declare that acts of Parliament that are against natural equity are void. That acts against the fundamental principles of the British constitution are void. This doctrine is agreeable to the law of nature and of nations, and to the divine dictates of natural and revealed religion. It is contrary to reason that the supreme power should have the right to alter the constitution. This would imply that those who are entrusted with sovereignty by the people have a right to do as they please.[20]

But as the second passage, taken from an appendix, suggests, and as is apparent from the organization of the pamphlet as a whole, the role of the courts in ensuring the constitutionality of parliamentary acts is neither their principal business nor the ultimate check on Parliament.

Otis argues generally about the rights of the colonists and the power of Parliament, indeed about the natural rights of human beings and the powers of government, deriving the particulars of the colonists' situation from apparently universal principles. Attributing the origin of right to God, he nevertheless gives a Lockean account of the origin of government, though not a Lockean picture of a state of nature. He describes the history of the colonists' emigration and of colonial development, showing the peaceful and commercial intentions and practices of the English colonies and thus proving, he thinks, that the colonists gave up neither their natural rights nor their rights as Englishmen when they came to North America. Since among the English rights is the right to property and thus the right to consent to taxation, and since representation in Parliament is impossible for the

Americans, colonial legislatures are indispensable. Still, Otis is happy enough to admit that the colonial legislatures are subordinate to Parliament; the supremacy of Parliament, like the right to no taxation except by one's consent, is an undoubted part of the British constitution, at least since it was "re-established at the [Glorious] Revolution with a professed design to secure the liberties of all the subjects to all generations."[21] Parliamentary supremacy must not be understood to mean that Parliament is absolute and arbitrary: "The Parliament cannot make 2 and 2, 5; omnipotency cannot do it. The supreme power in a state is *jus dicere* only; *jus dare*, strictly speaking, belongs alone to God."[22] If Parliament oversteps its bounds, it can be checked by the executive through the courts, or petition can be made for repeal of the offending act—with the first method presumably effective in stopping injustice in a particular case, the latter in repairing systematic inequity. Throughout the pamphlet, Otis suggests the constitutional limits on Parliament and proposes several ways those limits might be enforced, but he sees no certain and general mechanism to prevent abuse.

Though he incorporates Locke, Montesquieu, and Emmerich von Vattel, Otis's attitude toward the relation between fundamental law and the institutions that embody it remains essentially that of Coke. Law can bind power, but it cannot always effectively enforce its command. Like Coke, Otis is more interested in determining what law is in any particular case than in devising a perfect political machine. When a practice can do some good and is fixed in precedent—like the doctrine that courts can limit or "control" legislative acts—then it ought to be employed in a case where it applies. Still, the absence of a guarantee of success ought not to squelch the quest for justice. When rights are threatened, all hands might be called upon for their protection, all different procedures recommended for redress. No one doctrine or device can secure the constitution; it depends upon a balance that for Otis, in contrast to some of his contemporaries, is not mechanical but moral in kind.

What makes Otis's pamphlet in the end so difficult is that its author aims at the universality of liberal theory—including an account of the origin of government and the equipoise of the constitution—but preserves Coke's posture of focusing on the numerous particular rights at law and comprehending by means of exhaustive collection, not by theoretical insight.[23] In his editor's introduction to the pamphlet, Bailyn argues most suggestively that "Otis' untenable subtleties—the result of an unsure, incomplete application of seventeenth-century doctrines to eighteenth-century issues—exposed the central problem of Anglo-American relations [the nature and extent of Parliament's power over the colonies], and dramatized in their failure the inescapable imperative of the colonists' claims."[24] It might also be said that, having accepted an eighteenth-century propensity to reason through political disputes abstractly, Otis attempted to preserve the subtle argument and complex doctrine of the common law.

Dickinson's *Letters from a Farmer* succeed where Otis's pamphlet fails. This may be due in part to the literary form he chooses—a series of essays rather than a treatise—but also because he takes the tack at which the lawyer's mind is expert, focusing upon a particular question of right and searching out the precedents and the reasons that would resolve it. Writing after the repeal of the Stamp Act, Dickinson sounds alarm at two recent parliamentary endeavors—the suspension of the New York legislature and the imposition of the Townshend duties, which apparently had been met with general acquiescence in sharp contrast to the reception of the earlier act. The *Letters* are carefully measured in tone and intention, ever respectful of the king's authority and of the inviolability of the colonies' link to the mother country, but Dickinson's good manners make him no less insistent on the particular point of right he examines. The power of Parliament over the colonies allows the former to regulate the latter's commerce. Though the consequences of the Navigation Acts are sometimes hard, limiting colonial trade with other countries and restricting local manufacture of goods available from the metropolis, these acts are made with ample precedent, going back to the early days of colonial settlement. Parliamentary taxation of the colonies in order to raise a revenue, however, no matter how little it might collect, has no precedent before the Sugar and Stamp Acts of the 1760s. Though occasional duties had been allowed for regulatory purposes, revenue from the colonies had always been obtained with the colonists' consent through their assemblies. Between these two powers, to regulate and to tax, a strict and unbreachable line ought to be maintained, Dickinson argues. Not only is the ancient principle of taxation by representation at issue, but there is the palpable danger that a Parliament that taxes goods it can also restrict will be able to levy unlimited burdens on items of necessary commerce. Though the present weight of the imposts is light, the precedent is fatal, so that if the colonists now acquiesce in the duties, they make themselves "slaves."[25]

With singular equanimity, Dickinson exemplifies the common law mentality at work, not in a particular case at law but in a specific political dispute. He investigates the question of right, then urges political action to ensure that precedent is kept straight in present policy; not discovery of some new principle but firm adherence to the old practices is his aim, though that adherence might require correction of a recent breach, since it distinguishes settled right from blind acceptance of the current. The temper of Dickinson's proposal and his prose—the acuteness and dexterity Burke attributed to lawyers, but with nothing mercurial—might be due to an education that obviously goes beyond the *Institutes* and *Reports* of Sir Edward Coke and other authors of public law. He introduces himself to his readers as a farmer, but a gentleman farmer of sorts, having "received a liberal education." Now, "Being generally master of my time, I spend a good deal of it in a library, which I think the most valuable part of my small estate." Beginning the *Letters* in a calm style with apparently moderate purpose, he gradually brings his readers by the seventh letter to more extravagant rhetoric: "We are taxed without our own consent, expressed by ourselves or our representatives. We are therefore—SLAVES." After introducing Machiavelli's *Discourses* (Book III, chapter 1), to show "that a state, to be long lived, must be frequently corrected, and reduced to its first principles," he exhorts the colonists to "incessantly watch, and instantly take alarm" at the encroachment of power; he then takes leave of his readers in the final *Letter* with his first invocation of Providence and an assurance of the Americans' "true magnanimity of soul." Indeed, the obvious subtlety of Dickinson's pamphlet suggests a mind that would have the fear of conspiracy deliberately cultivated in readers, not uncontrollably rampant in itself, and cultivated in the language, if not exclusively the spirit, of common law.[26]

The measured restraint of Dickinson's *Letters* is mostly absent from Jefferson's *Summary View*. Since its doctrine of the imperial constitution was discussed above and its contributions to the language of the Declaration noted, a few words here will suffice. Jefferson's rhetoric, if less subdued, is no less deliberate than Dickinson's; as William Hedges has recently noted, though Jefferson's argument in the pamphlet is that the king, not Parliament, receives the colonists' allegiance, the whole tenor of the pamphlet is to upbraid the monarch, as the apparently legal and historical discussion yields to the exhortation, "Open your breast, sire, to liberal and expanded thought."[27] Indeed, it is precisely a liberal and expansive argument he makes to justify removing the king by apparently promoting him. With the same theoretical clarity he later shows in the opening paragraphs of the Declaration—in fact, somewhat more clearly, since he did not have to put this writing to a vote—Jefferson treats the monarch as a mere executive, posits a legislative power in the people incapable of annihilation, and asserts a natural right of emigration, which is of course a sort of right of revolution on an individual scale.

Still, if the theory of Jefferson's pamphlet is soundly Lockean, the argument has a place for common law, not in providing particular rights and limits on prerogative but in the myth of the ancient Saxon constitution and laws, which "still form the basis, or groundwork, of the common law, to prevail wheresoever the exceptions have not taken place."[28] Writing alone without an assembly of lawyers to hold him to account, Jefferson's appeal to common law has more a literary than a legal character, as Hedges observes. But to Jefferson, common law and natural law actually do tell similar stories: Both look back to a past where the power of hereditary authority is limited, in the one case by settled custom and the other by popular consent, and both insist of law and constitution that they meet the test of reason. What Jefferson declined to see or refused to say was that common law and philosophy conceive of reason rather differently, and that if these differences are sometimes inconsequential, they other times determine opposite courses, if not opposite ends.

COMMON SENSE AND COMMON LAW

The language of Paine's *Common Sense* still shows its power two hundred years after its composition, in part, no doubt, because we hear its echoes in subsequent American political discourse. And despite the reservations of a recent editor, Paine is at his most cogent in the section of the tract in which he discusses not theory of government but the "present state of American affairs," arguing that, hostilities having begun and eventual separation universally thought inevitable, the time is ripe for independence.[29] But when Paine does write political theory, one sees clearly his distance from the constitutionalism of the dispute that preceded independence and also of the decades that followed.

The antimonarchism of the pamphlet's first pages strikes a theme that was incorporated into American political thought. A decade later, "Publius" would take as a necessary assumption in the design of government for the United States the republican "genius of the people of America," and he held this in accord with "the fundamental principles of the Revolution; or with that honorable determination which animates every votary of freedom to rest all our political experiments on the capacity of mankind for self-government."[30] But this did not stop the Framers from establishing a unitary executive, nor had the fundamental principles of the Revolution driven the authors of the Declaration to deny the legitimacy of a prince fit to be "the ruler of a free people," however far George III was from the mark and however much Americans' choice of independence and the success of their fight made a return to monarchy politically unimaginable. Paine, in contrast, denounces constitutional monarchs together with tyrants; indeed, he admits that absolute monarchy has certain advantages over the English constitution, namely, that the former is simple while the latter is "so exceedingly complex": "I draw my idea of the form of government from a principle in nature, which no art can overturn, viz. that the more simple any thing is, the less liable it is to be disordered, and the easier repaired when disordered."[31] The influence of this opinion on the Pennsylvania Constitution of 1776 is perhaps undeniable, as is certainly its pressure throughout the progress of American democracy. It is also undeniable that American constitutionalism, with intricacies like the separation of powers and a federal form, could never have grown from Paine's "idea."

To those who see the radical Whigs, whose perfect heir is Paine, as the principal force behind the American Revolution, the era of constitution writing, which began even before the Declaration was penned and reached a sort of culmination in the Bill of Rights, must appear as a sort of mystery. Historians' word for mystery, of course, is "creativity" or "creation," and when they see the readily identifiable tracks of colonial and British institutions in those of the republic, they posit unthinking habit or unreflective pragmatism, keeping at least the ideology pure. To be sure, no understanding of the American Revolution can be complete without appreciating the extent to which the Founders grasped the novelty of their experiments, a novelty encouraged not only by radical Whiggism but by its rather more sober parent, the liberal political theory of Locke and others. Still, if James Wilson meant, in finding the American Constitution to be built on Revolutionary principles, that it rested on nothing else than the free will of a sovereign people, he claimed a bit too much for himself and his fellows. For if the Founders helped form a nation, they too had inherited their character from the people and the law with which they broke political (though not always social or even legal) bands. One great legislator might be so thoroughly master of his own soul as to claim full credit for its products, but the genius of the American Founders, perhaps even more than that of the people they persuaded, was republican, shared in common.[32] The genius of the American Revolution—that, in defiance of so many previous examples and, more strikingly, in contrast to so many subsequent, it did not devour but exalted its children—owes no little debt to its having begun, as it was later to culminate, in the spirit of law.

CONSTITUTIONALISM AND JUDGING IN *THE FEDERALIST*

One can scarcely read the papers of *The Federalist* devoted to the judiciary—numbers 78 through 83—without thinking that they do not quite fit into the whole. David Epstein comments in his recent book that Publius's treatment of the judiciary "stands somewhat apart from the rest of the book, just as the judiciary stands somewhat apart from politics."[1] The publication history of the text bears out this observation. Unlike all preceding numbers, the papers on the federal courts did not first appear in the newspapers but in the second volume of the bound collection, which was published in May 1788;[2] perhaps this explains why Hamilton writes several essays of unusual length, including the longest single paper in the whole series. Despite their unusual appearance, these pieces serve practically to conclude *The Federalist*. Only two numbers follow the sequence on the judiciary, and one of them examines the issue of a bill of rights—a matter of no small consequence to the question of the courts' form and function.

As Epstein's quotation asserts, the distinctiveness of the text describing the judiciary only mirrors the uniqueness of the institution itself, or rather, its uniqueness in a republican government. Most obviously, judges, alone among officers of the federal government, hold their positions on tenure of good behavior.[3] Likewise, the judiciary is the only one of the major branches that owes selection of its members to the process of appointment rather than election and in which membership depends—albeit by general understanding, not constitutional command—upon certain professional qualifications.[4] Moreover, its structure is the least defined in the Constitution itself; only the Supreme Court is mandated, Congress being left discretion over how or whether to establish inferior courts, and even the size of the Supreme Court is

This chapter appeared earlier in *Saving the Revolution: The Federalist Papers and the American Founding,* edited by Charles R. Kesler. Copyright © 1987 by The Free Press, a division of Macmillan, Inc. Used with permission of the publisher.

left to legislative settlement.[5] And of course, what in Hamilton's account (and subsequent history) quickly appears as this branch's most remarkable authority—the power to declare legislative acts unconstitutional—receives no mention in the very document this authority is designed to uphold.

But it is not the style of the text or the particularities of the institution alone that mark the distinctiveness of the account of the judicial power. Implicit in Publius's treatment of the courts is the recognition of a constitutionalism that seems to cut against or go beyond the general thrust of the political theory of *The Federalist*. While *The Federalist* is written in defense of a proposed constitutional document, the guiding spirit of most of its papers is a distrust of "parchment barriers" and "constitutional shackles."[6] Publius holds a firm conviction of the necessity of lodging certain "objects" of politics in a central government whose means are adequate to its purposes; he pays respect to republican forms but insists that we ought to be ready to subordinate form to substance, at least once the basic authority of the people is secured. But the authority of courts rests on taking very seriously the forms, the means, the shackles, and the parchment. Hamilton's account of the judiciary surely seeks at many points to integrate that institution into the overall political theory of Publius, but he is only partially successful. It is my contention that the special character of the courts and the difficulty of fitting them neatly into the liberal frame that *The Federalist Papers* seem to build show the need to attend to the common law sources of American constitutionalism. Publius's concluding difficulties also point ahead toward the substantial modification of the Constitution made soon after its ratification (over the objections of Publius, though with the blessing of at least one of his creators): the addition of the Bill of Rights.

THE JUDICIARY AND THE FEDERALIST PROJECT

However eccentric the account of the judiciary may seem to the theory of politics that predominates in *The Federalist Papers,* it is important at the outset to make it clear that the establishment of a federal judiciary was essential to the whole project of constitutional reform. The "radical vice" of the Articles of Confederation, Hamilton writes in *Federalist* No. 15, "is in the principle of LEGISLATION for STATES or GOVERNMENTS, in their CORPORATE or COLLECTIVE CAPACITIES, and as contradistinguished from the INDIVIDUALS of whom they consist."[7] Such a legislature must either hope that, against "the true springs by which human conduct is actuated," the subordinate governments will obey federal law without a sanction, or it must be prepared to raise a military force against the offending government—or simply suffer the humiliation of seeing its law ignored. The corrective—granting the federal government authority to operate directly on individuals— involves an expansion of Congress's legislative powers to include the power to tax and to raise an army, rather than rely on requisitions of men and money from the states, as well as the addition of a power to regulate interstate commerce. But part of the corrective must be the establishment of a federal executive and judiciary charged with enforcing the law against the recalcitrant. Hamilton writes in *Federalist* No. 23 that "there is an absolute necessity for an entire change in the first principles of the system; . . . we must extend the laws of the federal government to the individual citizens of America."[8] This change in principles entails alterations not only in formal powers but in institutions. Congress can remain, though substantially changed in form; the feeble executive committee must become a strong, individual executive; and a federal judiciary, altogether new, must be supplied. Indeed, Hamilton writes in No. 22 that "the want of a judiciary" is "a circumstance which crowns the defects of the Confederation."[9]

Publius, especially Hamilton, defends the direct operation of the federal government upon individuals as a new but necessary means of fulfilling the ends of common defense and regulation of interstate commerce—ends established in or generally conceded to the federal government under the Articles, but without the powers needed to meet them. However, frequent passages in *The Federalist* suggest that not only the means but the ends themselves must be expanded. The preamble to the Constitution mentions first, after the general need to perfect the Union, the purpose "to establish justice." In *Federalist* No. 51, a paper that in many respects stands at the crux of the argument, Madison asserts categorically that "justice is the end of government. It is the end of civil society. It has been and ever will be pursued until it be obtained, or until liberty be lost in the pursuit."[10] The passage in No. 10 that Madison here restates specifies what he has in mind: "The protection of these faculties [i.e., the diversity of the faculties from which the rights of property originate] is the first object of government."[11] Throughout *The Federalist* the authors decry actions of the state governments that have "impaired the obligations of contract," released debtors from their debts, and undermined public confidence. While infringement of property rights appears as the foremost complaint, Publius often defines justice to include individual rights generally speaking. And of a justice so defined, the immediate guarantor must be the courts, since it is in court that individuals' obligations are determined and their rights vindicated.

Thus, whether the proposed reform is to the means or to the ends of general government, the judiciary appears at the heart of the project. It is, then, no surprise to find that the courts are involved in both of the principles that give the new government its form: federalism and the separation of powers.

FEDERALISM AND COURTS

In one respect the involvement of the judiciary in questions of the relation of the national and the state governments is clear from what has already been said, since the judiciary is an indispensable tool by which the federal government can act directly on individual citizens and, as sanctions cannot be avoided, can "substitute [for] the violent and sanguinary agency of the sword . . . the mild influence of the magistracy."[12] But this involvement remains ambiguous, for it is not clear from the constitutional text whether the enforcement of federal law is to be effected by a separate federal judiciary or entrusted principally to the state courts. Article VI explicitly binds state judges to the Constitution and the laws "made in Pursuance thereof," but Congress has discretion over whether and how far to constitute "inferior courts." Hamilton in *Federalist* Nos. 81 and 82 interprets this to leave open the possibility that Congress will choose to assign to state courts many matters of federal jurisdiction.

The ambiguity in the text of the Constitution may reflect in part the reluctance of the Convention to settle upon one scheme or another, but it is also, Hamilton suggests, due to the nature of judicial power. While separate sovereignties must clearly possess separate legislative powers, even in a complex scheme of concurrent and unequal sovereignty, such as that proposed by the Constitution, judicial power is less rigidly aligned. Publius writes:

> The judiciary power of every government looks beyond its own local or municipal laws, and in civil cases lays hold of all subjects of litigation between parties within its jurisdiction, though the causes of dispute are relative to the laws of the most distant parts of the globe. Those of Japan, not less than of New York, may furnish the objects of legal discussion to our courts.[13]

The judiciary, in other words, takes its orientation first from the parties to the dispute before it, then looks to see what law must be consulted to settle the case. Its jurisdiction is defined in the first place by who may sue before it and concerning what sort of dispute; then whatever law is needed must be applied. This characteristic of judicial power raises specific problems for the federal judiciary, since if that judiciary is to be limited so as not to subsume the state courts, it must be limited in terms of what law it can apply, at least when the parties to a dispute are from the same state. Where there is federal law, state courts will be bound to apply it and thus will have authority to interpret it. If there are federal courts, they must do the same with regard to the states. The potential for confusion and conflict here stems not only from the complexity of federalism but from the nature of judicial power in contrast to legislative power. In the spirit of common law, this argues the prudence of leaving the establishment of ordinary federal courts and the definition of their jurisdiction to legislative determination, rather than to the rigidity of constitutional command.

One point, however, is incontestable according to Publius: There must be a Supreme Court established as part of the national government, to ensure through its appellate jurisdiction uniformity in the interpretation of federal law throughout the land. This argument appears as early as *Federalist* No. 22, in the course of explaining why the lack of a judiciary power is a chief defect of the Confederation, and it is repeated in No. 80.[14] That the judicial power of the federal government must be "coextensive with its legislative" authority is a "political axiom," "if there are such things." "Thirteen independent courts of final jurisdiction over the same causes, arising upon the same laws, is a hydra in government from which nothing but contradiction and confusion can proceed." Likewise, in disputes involving foreign powers or between states or between citizens of several states, the need for federal authority is plain. Though it may be in the nature of the judicial power for any court to spread its scope as wide as law itself, the fallibility of human reason and the feebleness of human impartiality recommend a single court of last appeal in matters of national concern.

But the place of the federal judiciary in general, and of the Supreme Court in particular, within the scheme of federalism is still more complicated than appears so far, for any attempt to enforce federal laws upon individuals entails the responsibility of ensuring that federal law is not impeded by the law of the states. Once again, the nature of judicial power to see the law as a whole runs up against the tendency of men to be partial. The impossibility of distinguishing with certainty the bounds of federal and state authority makes it inevitable that conflicts between federal and state law will arise.[15] While both state and federal judges must resolve these difficulties whenever they arise in a dispute before them, the need for uniformity—and for protection of federal authority—dictates that decisions of this sort be reviewable in the Supreme Court.[16] Though it is impossible to ensure that no one is judge in his own cause in such disputes—since every court is constituted as an agency of one of the governments whose laws are in question—Publius seems to argue that the very generality of the national government is a guarantee, or at least the best available guarantee, of impartiality.

The structure of the judiciary in the federal system designed by the Constitution and defended in *The Federalist* is thus at the very least complex and perhaps more deeply problematic. The need for a single Supreme Court with appellate jurisdiction over disputes involving federal laws or conflicts between federal and state authority might be clear, but the organization of the courts of original jurisdiction is more difficult. Because the task of the federal courts, applying the laws to particular disputes, is "wholly national" in character and because the applicability of law in a case depends on the nature of the case, not the nature of the court, it seems impossible to develop a rule to separate the jurisdictions of federal and state courts with even the modest degree of clarity achieved by the distinction between federal and state legislative powers.

While pointing out the complexity of the question of jurisdiction and justifying saving it for Congress to determine, Publius is not unaware that much rides on the decision of what federal courts will be able to do. He writes in No. 17 that "the ordinary administration of criminal and civil justice" is the "great cement of society,"

> the most powerful, most universal, and most attractive source of popular obedience and attachment. It is this which, being the immediate and visible guardian of life and property, having its benefits and its terrors in constant activity before the public eye, regulating all those personal interests and familiar concerns to which the individual is more immediately awake, contributes more than any other circumstance to impressing upon the minds of the people affection, esteem, and reverence towards the government.[17]

Publius often notes that popular favor will fall upon that government which is best administered, but this passage makes plain that not only the quality of the administration but also its objects count. "Reverence for the laws" may depend upon the stability of the Constitution over time, but the success of the federal government will also rest, at least in part, upon the activities of its courts.

SEPARATION OF POWERS AND THE COURTS

If the place of the federal judiciary in the federal system is complex and problematic, its place within the general government in the scheme of separation of powers is no less so. This assertion might seem odd, for one characteristic that sets apart the judiciary proposed by the Constitution is its independence as a branch or department of government, apparently equal in status to the legislative and executive branches. As is well known, not every version of the separation of powers includes coequal status for the judiciary. We have seen that in Locke's *Second Treatise,* the judiciary is treated as part of the executive, and even Montesquieu, who formulated the threefold distinction the Framers adopted, speaks not of a judicial power but of a "power of judging," apparently having in mind the English jury and ignoring the English judge.

Blackstone is typically elusive, commenting on judicial independence in England, but finding the essential constitutional balance in the structure of Parliament.[18] *The Federalist* is not without remnants of the British view. In his early papers positing the need for direct operation of federal laws on individuals, Hamilton repeatedly makes mention of the role of "magistrates," and while the term seems usually to apply to judges, it is worth keeping in mind that Publius routinely refers to the president as the "Chief Magistrate."[19]

Yet the difficulty in assimilating the judiciary into the account of the separation of powers is only suggested by this ambiguity in drawing lines between the executive and judicial. It is more fully revealed in a comparison of the account of the separation of powers in No. 51 with the account of judicial independence and judicial review in No. 78. Of course, judicial review—the power of courts to set aside as unconstitutional the acts of the other branches of government, most particularly the legislature—presupposes the separation of the branches of government. Indeed, as W. B. Gwyn has argued, one of the original purposes of the theory of the separation of powers was to ensure the rule of law—more precisely, to transform the king into an executive who carries out a rule previously legislated by a separate body.[20] But the account of the separation of powers in *The Federalist* goes beyond the "rule of law" version of the doctrine. Likewise, the understanding of law implicit in judicial review goes beyond the positivistic concept of "rule of law," in which the question of accord between previous legislative will and subsequent executive act takes precedence over the question of the justice of the rule itself, not to mention the soundness of its results.

Publius often distinguishes the powers of government as if they involved different functions and displayed different characters: Consider, for example, Hamilton's contrast of the "vigor and expedition" needed by the executive with the "deliberation and circumspection" characteristic of the legislature.[21] But Madison's series on the separation of powers typically treats the branches as interchangeable. Whatever else they may be, the three branches are powers, particular institutions into which a "mass of power is distributed." Power itself "is of an encroaching nature," against which "parchment barriers between branches provide no security."[22] Madison's famous solution to the problem of making the separation of encroaching powers work is the mechanism by which "ambition [is] made to counteract ambition";[23] through institutional devices or "inventions of prudence" by which the partisans of separate kinds of power are distributed among dissimilar branches, the whole of each of the powers is kept distinct and free government ensured. As the mechanism of the extended sphere used the plurality of factions to obviate the danger of faction, so the separation of powers turns ambition against the dangers it poses.

Now to say of this account that it ignores the distinctiveness of each power would distort Madison's meaning. As he makes clear in No. 48 and as Hamilton seconds in later papers, in a republican government the power most likely to encroach is the legislative, "inspired by a supposed influence over the people with an intrepid confidence in its own strength."[24] Still, he claims that legislative overreaching "must lead to the same tyranny as is threatened by executive usurpation." In No. 51, the example of a device to ensure separation is the presidential veto, a power legislative in kind but given to the executive to help fortify him against legislative predominance—though given in qualified form, lest he become a full branch of the legislature. In all of this the judiciary is noticeably absent.[25] Its only mention in No. 51 is in the context of the argument that each branch should derive its appointment independent of the others but directly from "the same fountain of authority, the people"; the judiciary is of course excused from the requirement, "peculiar qualifications being essential in the members," and judges' dependence on the other branches for their origin is quickly erased by their permanent tenure.[26] To the naive reader familiar with the modern Court, Madison might seem to have the judiciary in mind when he speaks later in the paper of "creating a will in the community independent of the majority" as a means of "guard[ing] one part of the society against the injustice of the other part," but actually he is referring to "an hereditary or self-appointed authority," a monarch or an aristocracy. He has, naturally, no place for such an independent will, as it would be "at best . . . but a precarious security; because a power independent of the society may as well espouse the unjust views of the major as the rightful interests of the minor party, and may possibly be turned against both parties."[27]

When Hamilton moves to consideration of the judiciary in No. 78, he speaks in the spirit of structural engineering that Madison had adopted some thirty numbers before, though without losing sight of the distinction of functions. He sets out to discuss the permanent tenure conferred on the judiciary by the proposed Constitution and to explain its necessity in terms of strength and independence. The judiciary, he remarks in a much-celebrated phrase, is the branch "least dangerous to the political rights of the Constitution," lacking as it does "influence over either the sword or the purse," "ultimately depend[ent] upon the aid of the executive arm even for the efficacy of its judgments."[28] It is the power least able and thus least likely to encroach upon the others, and so the attention of the science of politics must be toward shoring it up, not keeping it down. But it quickly appears that while its strength is slight, its claims are bold, for in the context of discussing the need for judicial independence, Hamilton grants the courts the power to declare void statutes they find in violation of the Constitution and even to limit statutes which, though not infringing the document itself, nonetheless threaten justice or constrict rights. This disproportion between claim and strength suggests to Hamilton a guarantee of balance in the exercise of the judicial function; certainly the distinction between paper claim and practical power runs throughout *The Federalist*. But in the case of the courts, the distinction is misleading, for judicial power rests on the respect courts receive both from the governed and from the other branches. The political theory of *The Federalist* is eloquent in explaining the judiciary's theoretical weakness but is rather inarticulate on the question of accounting for its actual strength.

A COMMON LAW CASE FOR JUDICIAL REVIEW

Again, what I am suggesting is that the strength of the judiciary and its peculiar character must be understood in light of the common law background of the institution. This background is in some respects taken for granted in *The Federalist,* and it comes to the forefront only incidentally. For instance, at the end of No. 78, Hamilton adds, as a minor reason for permanent judicial tenure, the need to recruit men of "long and laborious study" whose knowledge of "strict rules and precedents which serve to define and point out their duty in every particular case that comes before them" will allow us "to avoid an arbitrary discretion in the courts." This need, he says, will be hard to meet, as it will involve enticing fine lawyers into "quitting a lucrative line of practice to accept a seat on the bench."[29] Though the federal courts will combine jurisdiction over law and equity and will in other respects differ from their English forebears, they nevertheless assume the basic structure of the old common law courts: respecting precedents as well as legislation, composed not of specially trained civil servants but of lawyers called to the bench.[30] While in an early paper Hamilton includes judicial tenure on good behavior among the "great improvement[s]" in the science of politics generally, by No. 78 he pays full tribute to its origin, noting that "the experience of Great Britain affords an illustrious comment on the excellence of the institution."[31] American law in the early years of the republic was to modify many particulars of the inherited common law, and federal law, with its limited objects, never adopted and hardly developed a common law, but the basic forms of common law adjudication were sustained.[32] The English judge in the United States may have lost his wig, but he kept his robe.[33]

With the establishment of a judiciary on the federal level that was more or less traditional in its form, the Constitution gave authority to certain ideas inherent in the institution, in particular the common law understanding of the nature of law. This understanding was not in every way compatible with the political theory that informed the other institutions of government, much less the interpretation given that theory in *The Federalist*. I alluded above to positivist elements in the rule of law as generally understood in American constitutionalism; indeed, conceiving the Constitution itself as a fundamental statute argues the origin of law in the people's sovereign will. But to add courts of the common law mode to a government with a strong legislature and an energetic executive alters the equation. Both the legislative and executive powers see their task as acting to achieve certain objects of government, and laws are means, perhaps *the* means, by which such objects can be achieved in a free government. From this perspective, the judiciary appears as a last check upon the government; it allows, as Epstein writes, "private men to dispute with the executive's decision about their case," with the consequence that "the executive cannot be quite so energetic" as he might otherwise have been, though since the disputes are undertaken individually and not collectively, they pose no immediate political danger.[34]

But the perspective of a court is quite the reverse. It begins not with a policy to enact and enforce but with a dispute brought before it for judgment; its task is to resolve that dispute by expounding applicable law. Judicial reasoning, then, starts from a particular instance and explores law for a purpose that is neither abstract nor political, but in order to resolve a dispute. To a court law is something not to be made but to be found, though moving from the case to the law and back to the case is something of an art. In a common law environment, the work of the judge is governed by the doctrine of precedent, according to which, as similar cases are to be decided similarly, prior cases are law to subsequent ones. Still, deciding under what precedent a new case falls is not much easier than deciding under what statutes; indeed, it is often more controversial. Again, in some areas of law statutes are not even the starting point of inquiry; in others, they are, like the statue of Glaucus in antiquity, so covered with the barnacles of precedent that they have assumed a new form.[35]

Now, the authors of *The Federalist* were lawyers or had studied law, and their common law orientation appears when they discuss the judiciary. In several passages Publius tempers his apparent positivism with a comment on the incompleteness of law and the need for judicial interpretation. After his remarkable account in No. 37 of the imperfection and imprecision in all human science, especially in politics and law, Madison continues:

> All new laws, though penned with the greatest technical skill and passed on the fullest and most mature deliberation, are considered as more or less obscure and equivocal, until their meaning be liquidated and ascertained by a series of particular discussions and adjudications.[36]

Hamilton later restates this claim, in the context of discussing the judiciary but with less emphasis on the judicial role:

The erection of a new government, whatever care or wisdom may distinguish the work, cannot fail to originate questions of intricacy and nicety; and these may, in a particular manner, be expected to flow from the establishment of a constitution founded upon the total or partial incorporation of a number of distinct sovereignties. 'Tis time only that can mature and perfect so compound a system, can liquidate the meaning of all the parts, and can adjust them to each other in a harmonious and consistent WHOLE.[37]

Though both of these statements suggest that no written constitution can settle of itself all the questions to which it will give rise, neither answers unambiguously the question of what body will serve to fill in the gaps that remain in the original. Hamilton's remark in particular, especially as rephrased in a quotation from Hume in the final paper,[38] appears to leave the matter to the political judgment of subsequent generations, or perhaps to the workings of what we today would call a self-correcting mechanism.

The most striking instance of common law reasoning in *The Federalist* is, significantly, the argument establishing judicial review itself. To associate judicial review with common law may seem preposterous on its face, especially since English courts at the time the Constitution was written were abandoning any notion that they could lay to rest an act of Parliament. There are two rejoinders to this charge: first, that scholarship has not closed the debate over whether something like judicial review existed in England from Sir Edward Coke's opinion in *Doctor Bonham's Case* in 1610 into the early eighteenth century; and second, that a written constitution changes the issue altogether. The first consideration has been examined at some length already; the second arises in the course of Hamilton's argument.

The case for judicial review in *Federalist* No. 78 is simpler than it appears. From the premises that "the interpretation of the laws is the proper and peculiar province of the courts" and that a "constitution is, in fact, and must be regarded by the judges as a fundamental law," Hamilton concludes that when a constitution and a statute conflict in a particular case, the courts must declare the latter void.[39] The common law character of the reasoning becomes apparent when he compares the judicial scrutiny of an act alleged to violate the Constitution with what judges do when two statutes clash. Not only are statute and constitution treated as analogous, but the rules for what to do in case of a conflict correspond. If two statutes of the same legislative authority clash, the more recent prevails "by a mere rule of construction, not derived from any positive law but from the nature and the reason of the thing"; by the same way of thinking, "the nature and reason of the thing" command preference for a constitutional rule over a statute should they conflict.[40] Here then is common law reasoning, not only in Hamilton's choice to argue by analogy but in the very rule to which his analogy is made. Judicial review, after all, rests on the need to enforce the limits of a written constitution, but the power is inferred from, not expressed in the document.[41] Consistent with this toleration of unwrittenness, Hamilton assigns to the courts the power of "mitigating the severity and confining the operation of [unjust and partial] laws," even in the absence of a constitutional provision.[42]

A legal argument against judicial review must begin by denying one or both of the premises Hamilton cites. In fact, the weak link seems to be the assertion that the Constitution is law and thus subject to a judicial reading. Hamilton himself opens the door to such an objection several pages later when he states that constitutions must be construed differently from technical rules.[43] The claim that a constitution is different in kind from law depends upon the claim that the constituent power of the people is unique; the object of the narrower legal argument against judicial review is thus to prepare the way for the republican argument, the claim that the striking down by unelected judges of acts of the people's representatives violates the principle that the authority of the government derives entirely from the people.[44] This theory was advanced with much prescience by the Anti-Federalist "Brutus" in a series of essays that appeared in the New York newspapers shortly before Hamilton wrote the papers on the courts.[45] Brutus argued that the meaning of tenure on good behavior is entirely transformed when transplanted from English monarchy to American republics. Whereas English judges need protection from the Crown while acknowledging parliamentary supremacy, American judges will be independent of the legislature as well as of the executive; having the power to declare void acts "inconsistent with the sense judges put upon the constitution," they will often prove superior to the legislature.[46] Instead, he advocated leaving constitutional construction with the legislature, who "would have explained it at their peril" as "an appeal will lie to the people at the period when the rulers are to be elected."[47]

Hamilton's defense of judicial review in No. 78 aims to refute Brutus's charge of judicial superiority, but without taking what I have called a common law perspective, the refutation remains unconvincing. Indeed, if one accepts his claims that the courts are "an intermediate body between the people and the legislature" and that "the power of the people" is superior to both representatives and judges,[48] it seems logically necesssary to place the courts above Congress. Hamilton goes on in fact to defend the power of the courts to frustrate not only congressional will but even the will of the majority of the people should it run against constitutional command. A "momentary inclination" of the people is no substitute for "some solemn and authoritative act" to change "the established form."[49] It is no argument against granting the courts such a power that they might abuse it: "If they should be disposed to exercise WILL instead of JUDGMENT, the consequence would equally be the substitution of their pleasure to that of the legislative body. The observation, if it proved anything, would prove that there ought to be no judges distinct from that body."[50]

Where does the argument for judicial review leave Publius's account of the separation of powers and his defense of the republican principle? As for the first, the preceding quotation hardly seems to square with the spirit of counteracting ambitions. On the contrary, if it is not to be dismissed as rhetorical excess, it must be understood as a comment on the integrity of the judicial function—the impossibility of chopping it up and distributing it among various institutions, as one can to some extent with the legislative, or of calling it to task, as one can with the executive. Rather, Hamilton appears to rely upon what he calls the "comparative weakness" of the judiciary, "its total incapacity to support its usurpations by force"; besides, the power of impeachment in Congress "is alone a complete security."[51] But both his underestimation of what judicial power would become and his exaggeration of the ease with which it could be curbed seem due to an inadequate confidence in the power of law, at least in the long run.[52] As he intimated in No. 17 and makes even more explicit in No. 27, a well-administered federal judiciary is bound to win public confidence, and this in turn might tempt it to usurpation. At the same time, if usurpation begins in small steps as misinterpretations of the law,[53] the power of impeachment is worthless to stop it precisely to the extent that there remains virtue in the legislature, for impeachment is, after all, a judicial proceeding and when responsibly used goes against malconduct only, not mistake or even inability. In short, the ethic of competing ambitions does not belong to impartiality—to judgment—and is thus relatively useless with regard to the judicial branch.

Hamilton's response to the objection from republicanism is that in voiding unconstitutional acts the courts serve as the people's champion. Yet one need not be a cynic to note that an appointed and permanent body charged with disciplining popular will to its solemn and authoritative acts is not everyone's idea of an advocate. The requirement that the people act by constitutional form surely limits the claim of the people to absolute sovereignty. And it would be out of step with the spirit of *The Federalist* to insist on formal limitations while denying substantive ones. It is indeed true that no court is strong enough to resist sustained popular resentment, but that is only an argument for prudence in the exercise of judicial power, not an argument of principle against its right. Hamilton is clear that, however much judges are "the bulwarks of a limited Constitution" and "faithful guardians of the Constitution," the people are its "natural Guardians," and "the general spirit of the people and of the government" is "the only solid basis of all our rights."[54] Far from contradicting the common law interpretation of judicial review here presented, these statements complete it, for it is of the essence of the common law and its unwrittenness that no particular statute nor the judgment of any court is the final word on what is just.[55] To be a guardian is not the same as to be a sovereign. The republican principle may, as Epstein argues, reflect an "honorable determination" on the part of the people to choose their government and order their lives.[56] But only the Machiavellian republican would deny the propriety of complementing the honor of choice with the humility that comes from recognizing the limits of human choice and the need for the guidance of law.

TOWARD A BILL OF RIGHTS

Let me try to collect my argument, then add a brief coda. The judicial power and Publius's discussion of it bring to light an aspect of American government that often remains hidden in practice and certainly only lingers in the background in the bulk of *The Federalist*. Epstein notes in the papers a commitment to and tension between republican government and good government, but my suggestion is that there exists as well a commitment to justice that is not reducible to public or private right, or in Epstein's account, public or private selfishness.[57] The maintenance of what I have somewhat loosely called a common law judiciary embodies this dedication, for such a judiciary is committed by its forms of proceeding to serious attention to the concrete disputes of individuals and the discovery of law through consideration of "the nature and the reason of the thing." The judiciary and what it stands for hardly give the American regime its whole character. American government is enormously diverse, not only in its structures but in the principles that inform them. But without the temper given to the regime by its judicial power, our constitutionalism would oscillate between the heirs of republicanism and those of "good government," between self-assertive populism and utilitarian realism.[58] Nor is the faculty of judgment, which Hamilton treats as specific to the judiciary, without appearance elsewhere in the regime: Madison uses the term in reference to legislators, and Hamilton refers thus to the people's evaluation of the proposed Constitution.[59] Indeed, in the faculty of judgment and the institutions that promote it, the "reflection and choice" Publius invokes in the first paragraph of *The Federalist* intertwine.

Still, Publius seems more explicitly bent on quieting republican jealousy and rallying the partisans of good government than on cultivating a general judiciousness, and though the form of *The Federalist Papers* may contribute to this end,[60] his ambiguity on the judicial power suggests the limits of either his attention or his theory. This is confirmed by his treatment of juries and a bill of rights. With respect to both he admits the principle but balks at the complaints of his opponents, hoping to preserve for the new government full flexibility. The issue of the right to trial by jury had achieved, according to Hamilton, the most success of any objection to the Constitution.[61] Whatever the merits of the particular complaints the Anti-Federalists voiced, one should hardly be surprised at the controversy: After all, what is at issue is the reverse side of the direct operation of the government on its citizens, namely, their direct participation in the federal government. While schemes of representation in an extended sphere can help ensure a national spirit in the federal government, a federal jury will be in its composition as local as a jury of the state. Likewise, Hamilton's objections to a bill of rights, contradictory though they are in first claiming that protection of particular rights is written into the Constitution and then arguing that to protect such rights in writing would be dangerous, reflect his tilt toward the importance of governmental power to the neglect of judicially protected right. Indeed, except obliquely through citing Blackstone on habeas corpus, he makes no mention of the judiciary in his entire discussion of a bill of rights, despite having just previously concluded his examination of the judicial power.[52]

I quoted before Hamilton's comment recognizing the necessary imperfection of the Constitution and perhaps by extension the imperfection of the account of politics provided by *The Federalist* or by any political theory. Though in many respects the maturing of the whole he speaks of was to take generations, and at least one terrible shock, in one sense the whole was quickly altered—through the addition, of course, of the Bill of Rights. Herbert Storing may indeed be correct in saying that the passage of only certain of the amendments originally proposed was a Federalist victory of sorts;[63] after all, they were initiated and guided through the House by an author of *The Federalist*. Still, it is worth noting that half of the ten amendments had to do with judicial matters, bringing protections of common law to bear upon citizens in their relations with the central government.[64] Nor, from the perspective of our century and in the wake of further amendments— especially the Fourteenth—can we ignore the extent to which the amendments have defined a preponderance of American constitutional law. *The Federalist* may be in some respects the authoritative commentary on the Constitution, but we ought to keep in mind that the document on which it comments was incomplete in a very real sense, especially with regard to the judiciary and hence with regard to constitutionalism itself.

13

NOT "BUILDERS OF BABEL": LEGISLATING A CONSTITUTION

On the final day of the Philadelphia Convention, 17 September 1787, Madison reports, "The engrossed Constitution being read, Docr Franklin rose with a speech in his hand," and as had been his practice all summer, on account of his age, Franklin gave the speech to James Wilson to read to the delegates. It was a plea for unanimity among the states present in signing the document, composed with characteristic wit, reminding his colleagues of the fallibility of human wisdom and urging them each to doubt their remaining objections to the common product. The middle of the speech includes this remark:

> It astonishes me . . . to find this system approaching so near perfection as it does; and I think it will astonish our enemies, who are waiting with confidence to hear that our councils are confounded like those of the Builders of Babel; and that our States are on the point of separation, only to meet hereafter for the purpose of cutting one another's throats.[1]

Franklin's reference to the biblical story of the confounding of tongues at the tower of Babel invites reflection when it is read today. Though the delegates left Philadelphia with sufficient unanimity in support of the plan and of a strategy to secure its ratification, in our own time we rarely read the Constitution as though it were written in a single language, much less framed with a common intent. Those who assert that the Framers' intent is the key to constitutional meaning often disagree when they come to specify what that intent might be for a particular case; others doubt, and some even ridicule, the notion that any such intention is intelligible or was ever existent, leaving those who read the Constitution in need of other authorities (usually themselves). A generation or so ago, books were written and courses designed on "American Political Thought," as though a coherent doctrine or at least a stable canon of books mights develop the Constitution's spare frame; but today no such course is likely to fly without attention to other voices, dissenting from or even antagonistic to the once-perceived consensus. Indeed, throughout the polity but especially within the university, in field after field across the humanities and the social sciences, the image of Babel—multiple languages in the wake of a collapsed orthodoxy—serves very well to describe the academic predicament. When I assert, then, that the Framers were *not* builders of Babel, I am suggesting that they did not experience our perplexity in the midst of multiple paradigms at once competitive and solipsistic. At the same time, of course, the mere assertion of a more coherent past is not an argument for its desirability or recoverability—much less a reason to exclude voices once left unheard.

A recent essay by Leon Kass invokes the image of Babel to make a related point.[2] Kass offers a lay reading of the biblical story in light of the insights provided by his study of classical political philosophy: The tower of Babel, reaching to the heavens, was the hubristic project of human beings who, sharing a single language and thus a way of thinking, were unaware of the limits of human power or of political possibility. In his concluding remarks, he notes that in symbolic mathematics humankind had found again "one language and one speech" and suggests that the technological society thus built threatens us with the fate of Babel's tower if we cannot learn to heed the ancient admonition. With Kass's reading in mind, the image of Babel assumes new meaning, especially in the mouth of *Doctor* Franklin, America's first scientist of world renown. For the Framers have often been interpreted as engineering a government based upon principles of modern political science, principles rooted in a modern psychology—as devising a system, fueled by human nature, securing peace and progress, if not promising perfect bliss. To assert in this context that they are *not* builders of Babel is to question such an interpretation of the founding project—and to suggest further that this is not such a bad thing.

THE CONVENTION AS A SUPERLEGISLATURE

In the course of determining what the Constitution means, every interpreter develops an attitude toward those who wrote it, and roughly speaking, these attitudes fall between two poles. At the one extreme, the Framers might be characterized as an "assembly of demigods" (to use Jefferson's phrase) or, more soberly, as Founders in the tradition of the founders of antiquity (e.g., Solon, Lycurgus)—or, more precisely, in that tradition as interpreted in the modern political philosophy of Machiavelli or Rousseau. At the other extreme, the Framers are seen as ordinary politicians, dealing more or less successfully with the political crises of their generation, gaining their sometimes exaggerated reputations by the fortuity of their opportunity or their effect, or by the encomiums of politicians who came after, encomiums composed for purposes other than dedication to historical truth.[3] The first attitude (demi-gods) has to recommend it the common-sensical recognition of the remarkable perseverance of the Constitution and the unprecedented growth and prosperity of the people whose union the Framers meant to perfect; moreover, any student of the Convention debates or of *The Federalist Papers* can see their care in reasoning and their elevation of purpose. The second attitude (ordinary politicians) is supported not only by our democratic inclinations but by the fact that, hardly a lifetime after the Constitution went into effect, their Union was broken by the Civil War—over issues anticipated but not resolved in Philadelphia. Furthermore, as any political theorist will observe, the debates and *The Federalist,* whatever their merits, appear time-bound and limited alongside the books of, say, Machiavelli and Rousseau.

Now, historians and political scientists and law professors who study the Founding often assume one or the other of these attitudes on methodological principle, and naturally enough they see only what they look for. Let me avoid for the present a reiteration of the various interpretations now current to propose instead that, at least in attempting to understand the Framers as they understood themselves and as they were likely to be understood by their contemporaries (and constituents), we ought to begin by viewing them as legislators engaged in a somewhat extraordinary task.

The Framers were certainly aware of the classical antecedents to the task of new-modelling the fundamental laws of a society—the Convention debates contain several references to Solon, for example—and they referred often enough to the novelty of their undertaking, even to its significance for peoples around the world. Through the experience of forming state constitutions (achieved state by state between 1776, when Congress called the states to the business, and 1784), they had come to appreciate the need for fundamental law to originate by a process outside the ordinary legislature, usually by the deliberation of a specially summoned convention, subsequently confirmed in some instances by town meetings (that is, by direct popular vote). The Philadelphia Convention was called to propose amendments to the Articles of Confederation—amendable on its own terms only by unanimous consent of the state legislatures—but it quickly settled upon an extraordinary mission. First, by establishing a rule of secrecy in its proceedings and a rule allowing easy reconsideration of points decided, the Convention departed from ordinary legislative practice and enabled, indeed encouraged, frank discussion and imaginative invention. Second, it agreed in the first few days to center its deliberations around a plan for a wholly new frame of government proposed by the delegation from Virginia (and apparently drafted by James Madison).

But in other ways, the Convention proceeded by ordinary, parliamentary means. In the first place, as Publius for one was quick to note, the Framers, unlike the fabled legislators of antiquity or the summoned founders of the modern political philosophers, were an assembly or congress of men, not a single individual; they were several, aware of differences in opinion and constituency, aware that their agreement would depend to some extent upon compromise or accommodation. Reviewing the Convention debates, one is struck by the obvious fact that the men who participated were on the whole practiced legislators, experienced either in the states or in the Congress under the Articles—or in even the Continental Congresses that first prepared and proclaimed the Revolution, then pursued its course in more routine ways. The operating procedures at the Convention—with the exceptions noted above—followed the well-known course of parliamentary law. Their skill, for example, in proceeding through committee of the whole or in the use of ad hoc committees for discrete but timely purposes was hardly improvised on the spot.

If the Framers thought in legislative form not only in their way of proceeding in the Convention but in the development of their product, then they offer up a first clue to their intent. To be sure, they kept in mind the differences in status between fundamental and ordinary legislation, and they show in Convention a reluctance to embody in the document too extensive detail; still, they went about writing the Constitution as legislators going about writing a statute, and this suggests that in some respects the Constitution ought to be read as one would read a statute. Now, at the time of the Founding, there were in English and American law fairly well-settled rules for the interpretation of statutes. The intent of the legislature was critical in this enterprise, but intent was to be construed not so much from detailed historical researches into the debates on the floor, much less into the private papers of the members, but rather from the statute itself and an understanding of the context in which it was made. According to the *Commentaries* of William Blackstone, recognized as an authority even more on this side of the Atlantic than on his own, statutes are understood to be either declaratory or remedial of common law.[4] Declaratory statutes are interpreted as continuous with established custom and precedent, while remedial statutes are to be interpreted by keeping in mind (a) the old law, (b) the mischief to be repaired, and (c) the remedy itself. Hence to discover the legislators' intent means to distinguish what is declaratory from what is remedial, and then to recall in regard to the latter the circumstances that occasioned the writing of the law and the attitude toward those circumstances (i.e., the definition of the mischief) among the authors.

What attitude does this perspective bring to the question of interpreting the Framers' intent in the Constitution? It suggests first of all that one must not rule out the possibility that parts of the Constitution are declaratory of unwritten law rather than originative of new law. This would seem to apply especially to certain provisions of the Bill of Rights, to analogous clauses of the original document (for instance, the habeas corpus clause, which limits the conditions for suspending habeas corpus while assuming the existence of the writ), and to the clauses introducing Articles I, II, and III, granting kinds of power that may carry implications not detailed in the subsequent text. Second, regarding the remedial character of the Constitution, it suggests that we read the document in comparison to the Articles of Confederation, remembering the mischiefs then thought to need correction. To be sure, the Framers, by the provisions they devised for ratification, effected a sharp break in legal continuity between the Articles and the Constitution: They silently dissolved the old bonds of perpetual obligation and substituted a new agreement brought into effect by super-majoritarian, not unanimous, consent of the states. Still, even political continuity was not entirely abandoned: The new Constitution was, after all, forwarded for distribution to the states through the Congress sitting under the Articles; the states themselves were left intact, despite proposals to dissolve or recarve them; and the argument was made that the Convention remained faithful, in substance if not entirely in form, to its initial charge to propose amendments to the Articles of Confederation.[5] In matters of a civil rather than a political nature, continuity was never thrown into doubt; the new government would of course assume the debts and property of the old.

What makes this reading of the document unusual today is the rather simplified notion of legislation now regnant—fostered, I believe, most especially by political scientists. We think of law-making as one part of a larger policy-making process, treating law as simply an instrument of policy and conceiving policy as the result of free political choice. Devised in the first half of the twentieth century to cut the Gordian knot of encumbered common law and statutes to meet the perceived imperatives of a modern economy of national scope, the policy perspective has in turn produced entangled webs of legislation and regulation, substituting one legalism for another, while making invisible older meanings of law and making arguments relating law and natural justice seem contrived. The more particular account of the Framers' view of law I now will sketch is intended as a step toward recovery of older perspectives, so that we do not ignore sources of wisdom that could inform us in our present predicament, or fail to consider what mischiefs the departure from older views might have been meant to cure.

THE INTERPLAY OF POLITICAL THEORY AND COMMON LAW

My argument about the Constitution is that it somehow combines the scientific reason of the modern political theorists and the common law reasoning of lawyers and judges. This combination is built into its structure as it persists and operates today, but to show this in detail is a task for another time. Here I wish to observe how the combination of opposite elements developed through dialogue and deliberation in Convention and in the First Congress, which wrote the Bill of Rights. In general, I suggest that the process of the Framing of the Constitution goes as follows: In Convention, the Virginia Plan appears as the theorists' assertion, which, as the summer wears on, is modified and refined by the common lawyers; then, as a sort of secondary treatment, the Constitution, still on the whole the theorists' assertion, is further modified and refined in Congress by the common lawyers through the addition of the Bill of Rights. In particular, I suggest that in both the Convention and the Congress, this process can be observed through the repeated disputes between James Madison, the best-prepared political theorist in regular attendance, and Roger Sherman, a Connecticut Superior Court justice and a common lawyer in the American mode. Speaking schematically, one might say that political theory supplied the doctrine of forming a government, while the common law way of thinking allowed the assimilation of power to law.

Madison is generally thought to have devised the Virginia Plan, introduced in the Convention by his fellow delegate Edmund Randolph, and he is known to have spent much of the year between the Annapolis Convention and Philadelphia studying books of history and public law in preparation for the latter. Nevertheless, though often called the "Father of the Constitution," Madison found himself defeated on three key proposals of the Virginia Plan, proposals he supported until the Convention's end (though of course he suppressed his reservations when the question came of signing). First, he advocated a Senate apportioned according to population and thus opposed the equality of the states in the Senate established by the Great Compromise. Second, he supported a Council of Revision, consisting of the executive and a number of the judiciary, to certify the constitutionality of acts of the national legislature before they became law. Third, he insisted that the national legislature be given the power to veto state laws that it thought violated the articles of union. On the first and third of these proposals, and eventually on the second, Madison was opposed by Sherman. The story of the Great Compromise being familiar, let me address the Council of Revision and the national veto—mechanisms designed to ensure the constitutionality of federal and state legislation, respectively.

The proposal for a Council of Revision was, in one form or another, discussed four times in the Convention.[6] Modeled upon a similar body established in New York, the council would have been composed of the president and a number of federal judges, and it would have had submitted to it for its approval all bills passed by the national legislature. The objection to the plan was raised immediately by Elbridge Gerry of Massachusetts. Since judges might later rule on the constitutionality of legislation in the course of their adjudicatory duties, Gerry thought it unwise to give them a prior screening. As he added later in the summer, he was against making judges statesmen or guardians of the rights of the people.[7] Madison recorded no immediate challenge to Gerry's presumption that judges might be called in the course of their ordinary duties to determine the constitutionality of legislation, although later several members expressed doubt as to the propriety of such authority. In any case, Madison's proposed council was quickly transformed into the executive veto familiar today, and the sharp separation of the executive and the courts was thus secured.

Interestingly, Madison did not give up the fight for a Council of Revision despite its quick transformation. As late as 21 July he joined James Wilson in seeking to revive the initial plan, arguing in the course of debate that the council would provide an "auxiliary precaution" in the scheme of separation of powers—indeed, using the debate over the council to formulate the theory of the separation of powers to which he gave classic expression the following year in *Federalist* No. 51. In that paper, the place of the judiciary in the scheme of checks and balances is left unspoken. From the *Debates* it is clear that Madison himself anticipated this observation: Conceiving the judiciary as a power of similar sort to the legislative and executive, he intended to give it explicit means of institutional self-defense. In any event, once the attempt to revive the Council failed, Madison worked to link the executive and the courts by other means, namely, by presidential rather than legislative appointment of judges. Moreover, he soon afterward apparently accepted the power of judges acting on their own to declare laws violating the Constitution null and void and used this doctrine as an argument in support of his case for popular ratification of the Constitution itself.[8]

Something like the Council of Revision surfaced again in mid-August, as a proposal that the executive and the judiciary *separately* certify the constitutionality of national legislation before it would take effect. The single executive now well established and the veto now to be given to the branches independently, Madison received the backing of several delegates who expressed their opposition to judges' having the authority subsequently to block the enforcement of legislation on the grounds of its unconstitutionality. He lost Sherman, whose previous support had apparently been based upon his advocacy of a plural executive and thus approval of some sort of executive council: If the judiciary was now to act on its own, Sherman "disapproved of Judges meddling in politics and parties."[9] Again the proposal failed, this time not to be revived. (No vote was taken, of course, on whether the judicial power to declare statutes unconstitutional ought to be explicitly recognized.) In sum, Madison's persistence in supporting a Council of Revision suggests the importance he attached to understanding the judiciary as a political body, and his failure to establish such a council suggests the strength of the Convention's sense that the judicial is different in kind from the political.

The contrast between a political and a legal sensibility appears again in the debate over whether the national legislature ought to have the power to review and to veto state laws. This power was first proposed in the Virginia Plan, as the power "to negative all laws passed by the several states contravening in the opinion of the National Legislature the articles of Union." Madison insisted that this power was crucial to the establishment of federal supremacy. While the model for the Council of Revision was a state constitution, the model for the national veto was the power of the British monarch to veto laws passed by the colonial assemblies—a surprising source, especially since the king's exercise of this power was the very first of the colonists' grievances expressed in the Declaration of Independence. (Indeed, Madison went so far in following the British model in his proposal as to suggest in debate that a federal agent, a sort of governor general, might be posted in each state to alert Congress of state legislative activity.) Clearly, Madison's proposal shows that he thought of federalism in terms of relations among sovereignties in a political (if not politic) frame.

Opposition to the national veto developed slowly. Unlike the Council of Revision, the resolution to establish the national veto was passed the first week of the Convention "without debate or dissent," only to be reconsidered and rejected later in the summer, after the Great Compromise was struck. Sherman expressed reservations early on, asking for the definition of cases in which it might be used.[10] What seems to have turned sentiment around on the national veto was the New Jersey Plan. Formulated in order to redefine the character of federalism as it stood in the Virginia Plan, the New Jersey Plan proposed the continuation of the Congress established under the Articles of Confederation. In formally countering the Virginia proposal of representation by proportion in the legislature, the reassertion of state equality set the stage for the Great Compromise. What is less often noted and still less understood is that the New Jersey Plan first devised the Supremacy Clause, which was adopted almost word for word in the final document. In other words, though the New Jersey proposal to restore state equality in Congress only partially succeeded, the transformation of federalism into a legal relationship, enforceable in the ordinary courts of law, carried the day: The Constitution was to be not only articles of union but proper law.

As with the Council of Revision, Madison sought to revive the national veto several times after its replacement with the Supremacy Clause, and in all instances he was answered by Sherman. In the first attempt, Sherman responded that the negative was unnecessary because disputes will be settled in the courts (including, of course, the state courts). In a subsequent attempt, now proposing a national veto by a two-thirds vote in Congress, Madison was again countered by Sherman, who thought any such veto superfluous as federal law was to be supreme.[11] Finally, in discussing the last draft of the Constitution as presented by the Committee of Style, in particular the passages restricting state powers over commerce, Madison complained again of the lack of a congressional veto over state laws, only to be answered yet again by Sherman, who asserted—in anticipation of nineteenth-century judicial doctrine—that federal and state jurisdiction would be concurrent in commercial matters. Actually, buried in Article I, section 10, in the limits placed upon the states' commercial powers, are the last vestiges of Madison's national veto: No state may tax imports or exports, lay duties of tonnage, keep troops, or make compacts with other states without the consent of Congress—or as one provision has it, the states may act in the matters under question "subject to the Revision and Controul of the Congress."

In sum, Madison's approach in Convention was typically to attempt to settle lines of authority by establishing appropriate institutions and relations of hierarchy among them. Sherman, in contrast, was much more apt to settle upon a declaratory clause in the Constitution and then leave detailed matters to disposition in particular cases in courts of law. Put this way, one can see the kinship of Madison's program to the liberal political theory that began with the philosophy of Thomas Hobbes, while Sherman's deeds recall the parliamentary practice of the common lawyer Edward Coke.

THE FORM OF THE BILL OF RIGHTS

The opposition between the institutional and legal approaches, or between political theory and common law, appears again in the debates in the First Congress over the Bill of Rights. It had been proposed at the Convention that a bill of rights be included in the Constitution, but outside of a few provisions, such as the protection of habeas corpus and the prohibition of ex post facto laws, the call for a bill of rights was quickly dismissed, not least by Sherman, who argued that rights were adequately protected by state law. After the Convention, apparently following the signals of George Mason and Elbridge Gerry, both of whom refused to sign the document, the Anti-Federalists made the lack of a bill of rights a rallying cry of their opposition. They were rebuffed by the Federalists, most notably in a widely circulated speech of James Wilson's and in *Federalist* No. 84, on the grounds that some rights were included while others were not endangered because the federal government had only delegated powers. Moreover, Hamilton in the same number of *The Federalist* asserted that the "Constitution is itself, in every rational sense, and to every useful purpose, a BILL OF RIGHTS."[12]

These arguments proved notoriously unpersuasive in crucial states, and a compromise that won over sufficient Anti-Federalist votes was finally settled on in Massachusetts and other key states: The Federalists promised that, if the Constitution was ratified without condition, amendments would be introduced in the First Congress under the provisions of Article V. As described by Herbert Storing and others, the Federalist strategy, commanded by Madison, was to select those amendments proposed by the several states that sought to secure individual rights, while rejecting proposals that would have altered the basic structure or power of the federal government.[13] By and large this strategy succeeded in Congress, and in fact, the two structural amendments proposed by Congress failed to achieve the three-quarters majority of the states necessary to ensure ratification. Indeed, so adept were the Federalists in their choice of provisions for the Bill of Rights that Anti-Federalists who had initially clamored for a bill of rights now and again found themselves in opposition to the proposals, while some Federalists who had once resisted amendments supported them.

The resistance in Congress, as in the Convention, was in some respects led by Sherman, though as in Convention he approved the final product.[14] I will not work through the proposals clause by clause, but I do want to make a general observation. Madison's initial proposal would have inserted the amendments into the document itself, clause by clause, as today a legislature amends a code. This was important, he asserted, in order to maintain the systematic character of the Constitution. But Sherman immediately objected to the changes, the first of which, incidentally, would have inserted in the Preamble, before the phrase "We the People," a brief statement of the principle that government is intended for the benefit of the people and must thus be established by their authority. No one, said Sherman and those who joined him, would amend an act once it had been passed; this would destroy "the whole fabric of the law." Rather, it would be easy to know the meaning of amendments by comparing the new clauses to the original—by engaging, in other words, in the activity of interpretation by the well-known course of reasoning at common law. Sherman failed at first in altering Madison's approach, but eventually his route was taken, and the amendments were added to the original as appendages.

Needless to say, the Bill of Rights was to attain its prominence in later days in no small part because of form: The rights were not embedded but numbered afresh. Moreover, the superlegislative character of the Constitution that I mentioned above remained visible by this manner of composition, so that today reading through the Constitution and its amendments supplies a brief course in the history of American constitutional development. In the Bill of Rights, as in the original Constitution, in other words, Madison's genius for system is balanced by a sensitive assimilation of the new, positive law of constitutional provision to the common law fabric of American law as a whole. Hamilton wrote in *Federalist* No. 84 that no bill of rights was necessary because the Constitution is a bill of rights—but in the event, a bill of rights was easily enough added because, rather than being an institutional substitute for parchment barriers, the Constitution had already been refined in its development by the discipline of common lawyers.

The story of the establishment of the Constitution and of its subsequent development shows—with the glaring exception of Civil War—that American constitutionalism has been able to avoid both the boastfulness of uniform language and a demise into a post-Babel world of incompatible difference. To the Framers and their successors, genuine differences were not immediately interpreted as fundamental conflicts of value but were resolved through deliberation in which even opposing conceptions of law and reason sought to contribute their share and yet—perhaps by remembering the limits of all human wisdom—kept to a modest place. Contemporary historians, sifting past records for coherent ideologies, find themselves so often at odds because they seek unwittingly for a kind of political doctrine known more in our age than in that of the Framers. The genius of the balance between political theory and law in American constitutionalism is now overlooked on both sides in practice, perhaps because it has rarely been appreciated in thought.

CONCLUSION

To end an analysis of an institution of American government with the Founding, indeed with a sketch of the Founding, might seem to leave a riddle hanging. I have sought in the preceding pages to draw attention to the common law background of American constitutionalism and to picture the force of liberal political theory for the Founding against that background. Exaggerating the influence of liberalism in American political life, I have suggested, fails to account for all of the strengths of the regime and deprives the American citizen of sources of wisdom and authority not foreign to national experience. At the risk of writing what I called "lawyers' history" in the manner of Sir Edward Coke, I have tried to look backward from the character of the American judicial power to discover its sources, not because those sources have in themselves the binding force of precedent, but in the hope that their light might reveal aspects of the regime now overlooked. Indeed, part of what one finds in the heritage of common law, at least going back beyond the modern gloss of Blackstone to the classic period represented by Coke, is that the law can be something else besides despotic precedent, abstracted theory, or "muddling through." I have aimed, in short, to help restore a sense of the virtue of common law still embedded in American constitutional forms and also to restore a proper sense of the virtue of liberalism—which lies in thinking through a particular problem to its solution or tempering righteousness gone astray, but within a form provided by an intelligence that transcends analytical insight and thus guides its use.

I conclude my inquiry before the establishment of judicial review in federal law—or, to speak more in the spirit of common law, before its declaration—and although I do not pretend that my scheme will solve every issue raised by the course of the constitutional law that the courts have unfolded, I think it might provide a useful heuristic. In some ways, Chief Justice Marshall's opinion in *Marbury v. Madison* might have formed as apt a close to the argument as Hamilton's papers on the judiciary in *The Federalist* or the brief account of the Convention and the drafting of the Bill of Rights. Marshall writes in *Marbury* of both the "theory . . . essentially attached to a written constitution" and of "the province and duty of the judicial department,"[1] echoing in a way the dual perspective I have sought to unfold; and the setting of his general argument in a particular and indeed particularly complex and delicate situation spells a drama reminiscent of encounters between King James and Lord Chief Justice Coke. Still, Marshall's words and deeds, like those of his great rival Jefferson, in some respects are a continuation of the Founding and in others address the problems of the early republic. It is worth remembering that he was the third chief justice (or fourth, depending how one counts), not the first, and of course the body of his opinions takes us well into the era of Jacksonian Democracy. The frame of institutions built by the authors of the Constitution and defended in *The Federalist* already poses the problem of judicial review, and Marshall's jurisprudence, however sound or brilliant, could not lay that problem to rest, if only because the Constitution itself is open to amendment and the American people have exercised their option in several decisive ways.[2]

Corwin begins his famous essay cited throughout this book by quoting Paine's statement in *Common Sense* "that in America the law is King," and he embellishes it with an even more remarkable statement of his own: "The Reformation superseded an infallible Pope with an infallible Bible; the American Revolution replaced the sway of a king with that of a document."[3] Leaving aside whether he has properly dated the doctrine of papal infallibility, one recognizes in his sentence what is often taken as the summary principle of constitutionalism—namely, that it secures, to use Marshall's phrase, "a government of laws, and not of men," that it enshrines the rule of law, not the sway of a sovereign.[4] Corwin proceeds to develop his meaning, distinguishing sovereignty from what he calls "higher law," that is, law in its nature "eternal and immutable" and in its application "discovered" or "declared"; but one ought to pause before snatching his dichotomy, if only because the term "higher law" seems to belong rather to the speeches of the Abolitionists than to the idiom of the American Founding. The characteristic American and British metaphor was "fundamental," pointing rather to the floor than to the ceiling. Too much can be made of metaphor either way, perhaps, but I think that earnest invocation of the sovereignty of law fits neither the tenor of American political thought nor the form of the American polity: A doctrine of sovereign law conceals a practice of sovereign judges or sovereign legislators, however much we squirm before confessing the fact.

The doctrine of the sovereignty of the people does not come as late as Corwin thinks, nor need it mean quite as much as those seem to fear who see in federal judges the only fence against injustice. The Revolution replaced the sway of the king with the sway of the people, and if their sway is sometimes exercised through constitutional statute, it is also tempered—as was monarchical rule at common law—by constitutional form and by the principles and practices of due process. At least in the ordinary business of government, the general demands of the state are met by particular individuals and particular corporate bodies with the right to have their particular claims heard and considered by a court of law, composed of a more or less independent judge and at times also of a jury of their peers. Without attention to the perspective of particular litigants and the judges who must decide their claims, our notion of public policy and of the political life devoted to its formation will be skewed. And without reflecting on why we allow judges to correct legislatures and executives—not sitting as commissioners of constitutionalism or as a Council of Revision but in the course of their ordinary business of determining particular controversies and cases—we will leave judicial review without sound defense or sensible exercise.

APPENDIX I

SUBTITLES IN IV *INSTITUTES*, CHAPTER ONE, "OF THE HIGH AND MOST HONOURABLE COURT OF PARLIAMENT"

— Of what Persons this Court consisteth. [1]
— Of what number. [1]
— The Names. [2]
— Parliaments in Scripture. [3]
— What properties a Parliament man should have. [3]
— Of Records of Parliament. [3]
— The Summons of Parliament. [4]
— Temporall Assistants. [4]
— Spiritual Assistants. *Procuratores cleri.* [4]
— The beginning of the Parliament. [6]
— What is to be done the first day of the Parliament. [7]
— The Election of the Speaker. [8]
— The presentment of the Speaker. [8]
— The matters of Parliament. [9]
— What the Speaker shall doe after his allowance. [10]
— The Writs of Summons of Parliament, which are to be found in the close Roll from time to time. [10]
— Petitions in Parliament. [10]
— Appointment of Committees of Grievances, etc. [11]
— Absents, Proxies. [12]
— Of the ancient Treatise called *Modus tenendi Parliamentum.* [12]
— *Lex & consuetudo Parliamenti.* [14]
— Of Writs of Error in Parliament. [21]

The numbers in brackets indicate on what pages the sections begin. The section titles in the original are generally in italic; those in roman in the original are here italicized.

OUTLINE OF COKE'S OPINION
IN *DOCTOR BONHAM'S CASE*

[Coke's praise of Cambridge, etc.]

[117a]   I. The censors lack the power to commit Bonham, because the clause granting authority to license is distinct from the clause granting authority to protect against malpractice (*non bene exequendo, faciendo et utendo facultate medicinae*), for . . .

[117b]   Five reasons:

1. there are two absolute, perfect, and distinct clauses, parallel to each other; the first specifies offense and punishment with four certainties, while punishment for malpractice is unspecified;

2. the offense involving harm to the body is reasonably punished by pain to the body, i.e., imprisonment, the other offense not;

3. unlicensed practice can be punished only after one month, while malpractice can be punished whenever it occurs;

[118a]   4. the college cannot be judges, ministers, and parties at the same time, without violating common right and reason, and when such a violation is threatened, the common law can "control and adjudge void" an act of Parliament (here four precedents and

[118b]   one hypothetical case are discussed);

5. two absurdities follow if the clauses are not distinguished: either a man can be punished several times for the same offense, or a month's unlicensed practice is punished only after thirty days while a single day's could be punished by discretion.

Two grounds or maxims in law prove all these reasons:

A. *Generalis clausula. . .*

The numbers in brackets are the standard page citations. Wilson's edition of the *Reports,* however, numbers both sides of pages, so to follow the case in this edition, the following translation is in order: [2 x (original page a)] − 2 = (Wilson page), or [2 × (original page b)] − 1 = (Wilson page). Hence, the famous passage from the case, at 118a, is in Wilson at 234.

[119a]   B. *Verba posteriora . . .*
        Objections and Answers:
        a. The second clause includes a broad grant of authority; BUT
            i. the sentence taken as a whole limits the grant to malpractice;
            ii. it would be absurd to give general power to punish but special definition of the fine;
            iii. an example of a grant to mayor and commonalty of London shows the distinction between the grant of authority to discover a wrong and the grant of authority to punish it.

[119b]   b. Every court can punish contempt; BUT
            i. the president and censors are not made a court, only an authority;
            ii. if it were a court, imprisonment could only be by the president and censors, but here only the censors imprisoned Bonham;
            iii. Bonham committed no contempt, but only raised a claim in law.

    II. If the president and censors had the power they claimed, still they did not pursue it correctly:
        1. only the censors have the power to issue a five pound fine, but here the president acted with them;
        2. again, only the censors may impose the ten pound fine for failure to appear for an examination, but the president joined them;
        3. fines not otherwise directed belong to the king, but they evidently kept half the ten pound fine for themselves;
        4. Bonham should have been arrested and imprisoned immediately, not made to wait upon the installation of a new president;

[120a]   5. the authority to imprison belongs only to courts of record, but the college proceeded by parol, without keeping record;
        6. the power to imprison should be taken strictly, so it can indeed be subject to review in the courts of law.
        Objection and Answer:
        The Act of I Mary enlarged the powers of the college? No, it only

[120b]   declared to jailers that they should receive those rightly committed by the college—"and that was not Bonham."

    Technical objection concerning the pleading in the case:
        Admitting that the grounds Bonham alleged do not carry the case, still the court is entitled to reach judgment on the record as a whole.

Seven things for the college to observe in the future for its better direction:

1. it shall punish none for unlicensed practice but by a five pound fine by the month, and prosecute in the courts;
2. unlicensed practice for less than a month cannot be punished;
3. malpractice can be punished within the month;
4. those who may be imprisoned should be imprisoned without delay;

[121a] 5. the fines they set (i.e., for malpractice) belong to the king;
6. they cannot fine or imprison without keeping a record;
7. the cause for which a penalty is imposed should be certain, for it can be appealed to the courts.

NOTES

INTRODUCTION

1. The origins of the modern debate over judicial review—or more precisely, the modern debate over modern judicial review—have been traced in a recent book by Robert Clinton, Marbury v. Madison *and Judicial Review* (Lawrence: University Press of Kansas, 1989), ch. 9–12.

2. See, e.g., Alexander Bickel, *The Least Dangerous Branch: The Supreme Court at the Bar of Politics* (Indianapolis: Bobbs-Merrill Company, 1962), and John Hart Ely, *Democracy and Distrust: A Theory of Judicial Review* (Cambridge, Mass.: Harvard University Press, 1980). Showing the practical harmony of people and court has been the project of political scientists, e.g., Robert Dahl, "Decision-Making in a Democracy: The Supreme Court as a National Policy-Maker," *Journal of Public Law* 6 (1957): 279–95; and William Lasser, *The Limits of Judicial Power: The Supreme Court in American Politics* (Chapel Hill: University of North Carolina Press, 1988).

3. Alexander Hamilton, James Madison, and John Jay, *The Federalist Papers* (New York: New American Library, 1961), No. 78, pp. 466–67; *Marbury v. Madison*, 1 Cranch 137 (1803). For a recent attempt to explain the paradox as a consequence of John Marshall's innovation, rather than of the original understanding of judicial review, see Sylvia Snowiss, *Judicial Review and the Law of the Constitution* (New Haven, Conn.: Yale University Press, 1990).

4. The distinction between interpretivism and noninterpretivism can be found in Ely, *Democracy and Distrust*, p. 1. Principal advocates of theories based on moral rights include Ronald Dworkin, *Taking Rights Seriously* (Cambridge, Mass.: Harvard University Press, 1978), Michael Perry, *The Constitution, the Courts, and Human Rights* (New Haven, Conn.: Yale University Press, 1982), and Laurence Tribe, *American Constitutional Law*, 2d ed. (Mineola, N.Y.: Foundation Press, 1988); Dworkin develops his thoughts on interpretation in *A Matter of Principle* (Cambridge, Mass: Harvard University Press, 1985), ch. 5–7. A revived constitutional jurisprudence based on property rights is presented in Bernard Siegan, *Economic Liberties and the Constitution* (Chicago: University of Chicago Press, 1980), and Richard Epstein, *Takings: Private Property and the Power of Eminent Domain* (Cambridge, Mass.: Harvard University Press, 1985). Widely cited theories based on inference from the structure of American democracy are found in Charles Black, *Structure and Relationship in Constitutional Law* (Baton Rouge: Louisiana State University Press, 1969), and Jesse Choper, *Judicial Review and the National Political Process* (Chicago: University of Chicago Press, 1980), as well as Ely, *Democracy and Distrust*.

5. See Robert Bork, *The Tempting of America: The Political Seduction of the Law* (New York: Free Press, 1990). The dean of original intentionalism is Raoul Berger, e.g., *Government by Judiciary: The Transformation of the Fourteenth Amendment* (Cambridge, Mass.: Harvard University Press, 1977). See also Walter Berns, *Taking the Constitution Seriously* (New York: Simon and Schuster, 1987).

6. "I have said more than once in the course of these hearings that my approach to the obligation of judging is to try to find an objective source of meaning that simply does not force the court into, in effect, giving free rein to its own predilections." Reported in the *New York Times*, national ed., 15 September 1990, sect. 1, p. 8.

7. Bickel, *The Supreme Court and the Idea of Progress* (New York: Harper and Row, 1970).

8. Rogers Smith, *Liberalism and American Constitutional Law* (Cambridge, Mass.: Harvard University Press, 1985); Christopher Wolfe, *The Rise of Modern Judicial Review: From Constitutional Interpretation to Judge-made Law* (New York: Basic Books, 1986); Clinton, *Marbury v. Madison and Judicial Review*, p. 18, the phrase itself adopted from a remark at the Philadelphia Convention by James Madison. Sylvia Snowiss's *Judicial Review and the Law of the Constitution*, analyzing variants of judicial review in the first decades of American independence, seems to confirm the consensus on change since the Founding, if also to move back the date of alteration.

9. Pangle, *The Spirit of Modern Republicanism: The Moral Vision of the American Founders and the Philosophy of Locke* (Chicago: University of Chicago Press, 1988), p. 7ff. Classic examples of the "old orthodoxy" include Edward S. Corwin, *The "Higher Law" Background of American Constitutional Law* (Ithaca, N.Y.: Cornell University Press, 1955), and Charles H. McIlwain, *Constitutionalism: Ancient and Modern* (Ithaca, N.Y.: Cornell University Press, 1947). A restoration of this scholarship is proposed in Ellis Sandoz, *A Government of Laws: Political Theory, Religion, and the American Founding* (Baton Rouge: Louisiana State University Press, 1990), with, however, a sensitivity to the importance of religion in the American Founding, a matter of relatively little concern to Corwin et al. See also Donald Lutz, *Origins of American Constitutionalism* (Baton Rouge: Louisiana State University Press, 1988).

10. Bailyn, *The Ideological Origins of the American Revolution* (Cambridge, Mass.: Belknap Press of Harvard University Press, 1967); Wood, *The Creation of the American Republic* (Chapel Hill: University of North Carolina Press, 1969). See also J. G. A. Pocock, *The Machiavellian Moment: Florentine Political Thought and the Atlantic Republican Tradition* (Princeton, N.J.: Princeton University Press, 1975).

11. A recent example of a political theorist who adopts the dichotomy between republicanism and liberalism is Michael Lienesch, *New Order of the Ages: Time, the Constitution, and the Making of Modern American Political Thought* (Princeton, N.J.: Princeton University Press, 1988). The line between classical and modern republicanism is drawn in Pangle, *The Spirit of Modern Republicanism*, and a similar break is elaborated in Harvey C. Mansfield, Jr., *Taming the Prince: The Ambivalence of Modern Executive Power* (New York: Free Press, 1989), and illustrated in Ralph Lerner, *The Thinking Revolutionary* (Ithaca, N.Y.: Cornell University Press, 1987); see also Leo Strauss, *Natural Right and History* (Chicago: University of Chicago Press, 1953). For a historian's account of the Founding that stresses its modern character, especially with regard to political economy, see Forrest McDonald, *Novus Ordo Seclorum: The Intellectual Origins of the Constitution* (Lawrence: University Press of Kansas, 1985).

12. The importance of the English constitutionalism associated with common law to the American Revolution has been noted recently in the work of a number of legal historians, e.g., John Phillip Reid, *The Concept of Liberty in the Age of the American Revolution* (Chicago: University of Chicago Press, 1988), and William E. Nelson, *Americanization of the Common Law: The Impact of Legal Change on Massachusetts Society, 1760–1830* (Cambridge, Mass.: Harvard University Press, 1975). Their recognition of the echoes of seventeenth- rather than eighteenth-century English constitutionalism among American patriots has been challenged by Shannon C. Stimson, *The American Revolution in the Law: Anglo-American Jurisprudence before John Marshall* (Princeton, N.J.: Princeton University Press, 1990), who, taking Blackstone as her authority on

English common law, contrasts it with American law, with its emphasis on the law-finding function of juries, which she traces to the influence of the epistemology of John Locke. Still, Nelson and Stimson would agree that by the nineteenth century, American law was liberal in its essentials. See also Morton J. Horwitz, *The Transformation of American Law, 1780–1860* (Cambridge, Mass.: Harvard University Press, 1977), esp. ch. 1. A challenge to the merely ancillary influence assigned to religion in the Founding is issued by Ellis Sandoz, *A Government of Laws*.

13. Mansfield, *Taming the Prince*, e.g., p. 290.

14. For the distinction between early and late moderns, see Joseph Cropsey, "Introduction: The United States as Regime and the Sources of the American Way of Life," in *Political Philosophy and the Issues of Politics* (Chicago: University of Chicago Press, 1977), pp. 1–15.

15. Recent discussions of what one author has called "classical common law theory" by historians of English law include A. W. B. Simpson, "The Common Law and Legal Theory," in *Oxford Essays in Jurisprudence*, 2d series (Oxford: Oxford University Press, 1973), pp. 77–99, and Gerald J. Postema, *Bentham and the Common Law Tradition* (Oxford: Clarendon Press, 1986), ch. 1.

16. Holmes's reformulation of common law as judge-made law, which can be found in *The Common Law* (Boston: Little, Brown and Company, 1881), and *Collected Legal Papers* (New York: Harcourt, Brace and Howe, 1920), is taken for granted in two recent books by law professors that treat common law as a topic for rediscovery today: Guido Calabresi, *A Common Law for the Age of Statutes* (Cambridge, Mass.: Harvard University Press, 1982); and Melvin Aron Eisenberg, *The Nature of the Common Law* (Cambridge, Mass.: Harvard University Press, 1988).

17. Gough, *Fundamental Law in English Constitutional History*, rev. ed. (Oxford: Clarendon Press, 1961), ch. 1.

18. Cf. *Swift v. Tyson*, 16 Pet. 1 (1842), with *Erie R. Co. v. Tompkins*, 304 U.S. 64 (1938).

19. See, e.g., *The Federalist Papers*, No. 78, p. 468. One finds a willingness to speak of common law in a general, if not technical, sense in relation to the federal judiciary in the Godkin Lectures that Justice Robert Jackson wrote shortly before his death: "The federal courts by the familiar judicial process are making a common law on federal questions, sometimes departing from the common law of the states because of the Federal Government's interest. And so, had the federal courts been confined to cases involving federal questions, they would have proceeded with little that was unique or perplexing to those familiar with the nature of the judicial process." Robert H. Jackson, *The Supreme Court in the American System of Government* (Cambridge, Mass.: Harvard University Press, 1955), p. 32.

20. See Edward Levi, *An Introduction to Legal Reasoning* (Chicago: University of Chicago Press, 1949).

21. Tocqueville, *Democracy in America*, trans. George Lawrence (New York: Harper and Row, 1966), p. 292

CHAPTER ONE. COKE'S LIFE AND LAW

1. *The Writings of Thomas Jefferson*, ed. Andrew Lipscomb (Washington, D.C.: Thomas Jefferson Memorial Association, 1903), XII: iv. The youthful invective is in IV: 3.

2. Ibid., XV: 57.

3. Samuel Thorne, *Sir Edward Coke, 1552–1952* [Selden Society Lecture] (London: Bernard Quaritch, 1957), p. 3; Theodore F. T. Plucknett, "Bonham's Case and Judicial Review," *Harvard Law Review* 40 (1926): 61. For Coke's influence on the founding

generation more generally, see H. Trevor Colbourn, *The Lamp of Experience: Whig History and the Intellectual Origins of the American Revolution* (Chapel Hill: University of North Carolina Press, 1965).

4. *Quincy* 51 (Josiah Quincy, Jr., *Reports of Cases Argued and Adjudged in the Superior Court of Judicature of the Province of Massachusetts Bay between 1761 and 1772* [Boston: Little, Brown and Company, 1865]) is the citation for *Paxton's Case*, with Otis's argument coming at p. 56. However, a more complete report of the argument, kept by the young John Adams, is the source for our knowledge of Otis's mention of *Bonham's Case*. This is printed in a lengthy appendix in Quincy's volume, by Horace Gray, Jr.; the passage in question occurs on p. 474.

5. 8 *Reports* 118a (George Wilson, ed., *The Reports of Sir Edward Coke, etc.* [Dublin: J. Moore, 1793]; see the note in Appendix II for the algorithm to relate Wilson's pagination to standard form). One indication of Coke's authority is that his *Reports* were often cited without the author's name, simply as *Rep.*, though sometimes they were cited simply as *Co.* The original folio pagination is indicated in subsequent editions and provides the standard citation. In Wilson's printing, unfortunately, Coke's prefaces are sometimes not paginated or are incorrectly numbered—hence the erratic nature of my subsequent citations from these.

6. Edward Coke, *Institutes of the Laws of England*, part I (London: Society of Stationers, 1628); part II (London: M. Flesher and R. Young, 1642); parts III and IV (London: M. Flesher, 1644). The work went through numerous editions; I have used the reprint of the originals in the series *Classics of English Legal History in the Modern Era*, selected by David S. Berkowitz and Samuel E. Thorne (New York: Garland Publishing, 1979). I will again follow the traditional mode of citation (simply *Inst.*), though I will cite the four parts uniformly (the first was often cited as *Co. Litt.*).

7. See III *Inst.*, ch. 5, 6, 10; II *Inst.* 506; Louis Boudin, "Lord Coke and the American Doctrine of Judicial Power," *New York University Law Review* 6 (1929): 225ff.; IV *Inst.*, passim.

8. Sir William Blackstone, *Commentaries on the Laws of England* (Oxford: Clarendon Press, 1765–69; facsimile reprint ed., Chicago: University of Chicago Press, 1979), I: 72. (Subsequently I shall use the traditional form of citation to the *Commentaries*, which would render the foregoing as: I. Bl. Comm. 72.)

9. Sir William Holdsworth, *Some Makers of English Law* (Cambridge: Cambridge University Press, 1938), p. 132. The grudging testimony of Maitland is quoted in the same chapter, p. 129.

10. Only two book-length biographies of Coke have been published, both aimed toward a general audience: Hastings Lyon and Herman Block, *Edward Coke: Oracle of Law* (Boston: Houghton Mifflin Co., 1929); and Catherine Drinker Bowen, *The Lion and the Throne: The Life and Times of Sir Edward Coke* (Boston: Little, Brown and Company, 1957). The principal nineteenth-century account is in John Lord Campbell, *The Lives of the Chief Justices of England* (New York, 1874). A fine summary of Coke's career can be found in Stephen D. White, *Sir Edward Coke and "The Grievances of the Commonwealth," 1621–1628* (Chapel Hill: University of North Carolina Press, 1979), ch. 1. Holdsworth also gives a brief life, *Some Makers of English Law*, pp. 114–19. The paragraph that follows is based on these sources.

11. But see his apparent denial of this exclusion at IV *Inst.* 48.

12. See Roland G. Usher, "James I and Sir Edward Coke," *English Historical Review* 18 (1903): 664. Several shorter works—*The Complete Copy-Holder* (London, 1641) and *A Little Treatise on Bail and Mainprize* (London, 1635)—appeared after his death, and a 1607 imprint of a speech he gave to the grand jury at the Norwich Assizes has recently been republished (*The Lord Coke His Speech and Charge* [London: Nathaniell Butter, 1607; reprint ed., New York: Da Capo Press, 1972]).

13. *The Lion and the Throne*, p. ix. Holdsworth makes a similar remark in his *History of English Law*, 3d ed. (London: Methuen & Co., 1945), V: 472.

14. I *Inst.* preface (unpaginated). See also 10 *Reports* vii [xvii?] for further praise of Littleton's *Tenures*.

15. The Latin verse, from Ecclesiasticus 38:24, is translated in *The Revised English Bible* (Oxford and Cambridge: Oxford University Press and Cambridge University Press, 1989).

16. I *Inst.* 394–95.

17. See generally, Stephen A. Siegel, "The Aristotelian Basis of English Law, 1450–1800," *New York University Law Review* 56 (1981): 18; and Enid Campbell, "Thomas Hobbes and the Common Law," *Tasmanian University Law Review* 1 (1958): 37.

18. *Nichomachean Ethics*, book VI, 1141b.

19. I *Inst.* 319b; II *Inst.* 588. Cf. *Black's Law Dictionary*, 2d ed. (St. Paul, Minn.: West Publishing, 1951), pp. 1054–55. I have consulted *Black's* throughout in translating Coke's Latin maxims.

20. See Sir John Fortescue, *De Laudibus Legum Anglie*, ed. and trans. S. B. Chrimes (Cambridge: Cambridge University Press, 1942; written 1468–71), ch. 2–6; Christopher St. Germain, *The Doctor and Student, or Dialogues between a Doctor of Divinity and a Student in the Laws of England*, ed. William Muchall (Cincinnati: Robert Clarke & Co., 1874), Dialogue I, esp. ch. 4–6.

21. See I *Inst.* 394; 6 *Reports* viii (preface).

22. This has not stopped several notable scholars from reading Coke's doctrine of natural law quite broadly. See Edward S. Corwin, *The "Higher Law" Background*, p. 45ff., and Raoul Berger, "*Doctor Bonham's Case*: Statutory Construction or Constitutional Theory?" *University of Pennsylvania Law Review* 117 (1969): 528ff. But cf. John Underwood Lewis, "Sir Edward Coke (1552–1634): His Theory of 'Artificial Reason' as a Context for Modern Basic Legal Theory," *Law Quarterly Review* 84 (1968): 338ff.

23. For the citation of Justinian as an authority, see 4 *Reports* viii. Cf. 10 *Reports* vii, where he says, "It is a desperate and dangerous matter for civilians and canonists (I speak what I know, and not without just cause) to write either of the common laws of England which they profess not, or against them which they know not"; also, 3 *Reports* xii-a, where he warns "the grave and learned writers of histories . . . [to] meddle not with any point or secret of any art or science, especially with the laws of this realm, before they confer with some learned in that profession."

24. For examples of all these arguments, see generally the prefaces to 3 *Reports* and 9 *Reports*.

25. J. G. A. Pocock, *The Ancient Constitution and the Feudal Law: A Study of English Historical Thought in the Seventeenth Century* (Cambridge: Cambridge University Press, 1957; reissue with Retrospect, 1987), p. 56. On reading "law of the land" as in the first place "land law," see Walter Ullmann, *Principles of Government and Politics in the Middle Ages* (New York: Barnes & Noble, 1966), pp. 166–67, and, more generally, Arthur R. Hogue, *Origins of the Common Law* (Bloomington: Indiana University Press, 1966; reprint ed., Indianapolis: Liberty Press, 1985).

26. Coke's most systematic discussion of "land law" is, of course, the commentary on Littleton (I *Inst.*). At IV *Inst.* 25 he distinguishes acts of Parliament into "generall," on the one hand, and "private and particular," on the other; but I have never found him distinguishing public and private law.

27. II *Inst.* 47. The first seventy-eight pages of the *Second Institutes* are devoted to commentary on Magna Charta, and a dozen of those to the twenty-ninth chapter alone.

28. 8 *Reports* pref.

29. IV *Inst.* 8.

30. The term *sources of law* is John Chipman Gray's, not Coke's, but it provides a useful heuristic. Cf. Gray, *The Nature and Sources of the Law* (New York: Macmillan, 1902).

31. See Lewis, "Sir Edward Coke," pp. 332—33. Even Corwin appears to slip into this assumption in *The "Higher Law" Background*, p. 51.

32. E.g., IV *Inst.* 25.

33. See the prefaces to I, III, and IV *Inst.* For Coke's celebration of the antiquity and excellence of the common law, see, e.g., 2 *Reports* pref., 3 *Reports* pref., 5 *Reports* pref., 8 *Reports* pref.

34. I Bl. Comm. 70.

35. I *Inst.* 97b.

36. 3 *Reports* ii-b. For a discussion of "understanding, authority, and will," see 4 *Reports* xiii.

37. 3 *Reports* iii.

38. III *Inst.* proeme.

39. The cross-references can be found in the margin at I *Inst.* 66a. It appears that the phrases "against reason" and "inconvenient" occur at least a dozen times in the *First Institutes*.

40. I *Inst.* 62a.

41. Ibid. 97a—b.

42. On reason in Coke as the principle of consistency, see Lewis, "Sir Edward Coke," p. 337.

43. E.g., I *Inst.* 284a.

44. Ibid. 140a.

45. Ibid. 81b.

46. Ibid. 141a.

47. Cf. H. L. A. Hart, *The Concept of Law* (Oxford: Clarendon Press, 1961), p. 121 ff., with Dworkin, *Taking Rights Seriously*, ch. 2—3.

48. See, e.g., 9 *Reports* xiii-b; I *Inst.* 395; and III *Inst.* proeme. Now and again he will speak of the law as the "absolute perfection of reason," not its "artificial perfection." Is the former a more expansive concept? At least one use of this phrase occurs in such a way as to suggest not. In discussing the ancient *paine fort et dure*, (II *Inst.* 178—79; cf. III *Inst.* 217), a "most grievous and fearfull" judgment upon a man or woman who refused to plead in answer to a felony charge but stood silent, the uncooperative accused was to be stripped nearly bare, chained on the floor of a dungeon, covered with as much stone or iron as the body can bear, and kept on a diet of bread and puddle water "untill they be dead." Though not without recognition of the severity of the sentence, Coke refused to interpret away the statute mandating it as intending merely that the accused be held in prison until an answer was elicited: "Let no man imagine that the Common Law, which is the absolute perfection of reason, could foster so unreasonable, and unjust a meane of encouragement of felons, that they by their own contumacy against the Common Law should suffer onely one of the lowest punishments, *viz.* imprisonment untill they would answer." One is tempted to say that this example shows better that the common law was absolute than that it was absolutely perfect. This Coke may well have admitted. It should be noted that the cruel punishment here described would have been distinct in Coke's mind from torture: The offense was not refusal to confess one's guilt but refusal to answer at all, even to plead "not guilty." (This distinction is confirmed by Blackstone, IV Bl. Comm. 320.) For Coke's comment that torture is against the law in England, see III *Inst.* 25, 35; he refers his readers to Fortescue (*De Laudibus Legum Anglie*, ch. 22), who had

made the absence of torture in England a chief argument of the superiority of common to civil law.

CHAPTER TWO. CONSTITUTION, KING, AND PARLIAMENT

1. "Bonham's Case and Judicial Review," pp. 30–31.

2. *Politics*, book III, 1281a.

3. Ibid., 1286a–1288a. This appears to be the passage Coke cites at 4 *Reports* xiv. It should be noted that Siegel, "The Aristotelian Basis of English Law," seems unaware of the difficulty in equating Coke's jurisprudential thinking and Aristotle's political science.

4. 4 *Reports* iii. In fact, though he begins the list of six things to consider in legislating with the question of the "form of government," by the sixth item he is already squarely within the commonwealth of England: "Sixthly, the mean, and that only is by authority of the high (that in troth is the highest) court of parliament." Ibid. iv.

5. Fortescue, *De Laudibus Legum Anglie*, esp. ch. 28–37. On the importance of the concept of the regime in Fortescue, see the comment in Leo Strauss, *What Is Political Philosophy? and Other Studies* (Glencoe, Ill.: Free Press, 1959), p. 277.

6. Statements asserting that the common law is fundamental occur every few pages in Coke's writings; see, for example, the passages cited in Chapter 1. Though Magna Charta is dubbed fundamental almost as frequently, the most emphatic statement occurs in I *Inst.* 81a, where it is called "the fountaine of all the fundamentall Lawes of the Realme"; lest this be read to mean that Magna Charta is the first origin of the fundamental laws, cf. II *Inst.* proeme, where Coke explains that Magna Charta "was for the most part declaratory of the principall grounds of the fundamentall Laws of *England*, and for the residue it is additionall to supply some defects of the Common Law." How fundamental Parliament is appears in the first chapter of the *Fourth Institutes*; cf. 9 *Reports* pref., where he calls it "the most supreme court of this realm." At IV *Inst.* 10 he explains that the writs summoning Parliament can be changed only by act of Parliament; at IV *Inst.* 2, he notes that "of ancient time both Houses sat together," suggesting the changeability of parliamentary form.

7. It is one of the ironies of the modern administrative state that the attempt to replace adjudication with administration, and thus rules with discretion, has resulted in bureaucracy that gives rule-following itself a bad name. Perhaps those who imported this form of state apparatus into the United States did not altogether understand, or perhaps just did not adequately respect, the distinctiveness of the common law. Cf. Woodrow Wilson, "The Study of Administration," *Political Science Quarterly* 2 (1887): 197, with A. V. Dicey, *Introduction to the Study of the Law of the Constitution*, 8th ed. (London: Macmillan, 1915; reprint ed., Indianapolis: Liberty Classics, 1982), ch. 12.

8. For the proceedings of the Parliament of 1628, see Robert C. Johnson et al., eds., *Commons Debates 1628* (New Haven, Conn.: Yale University Press, 1977–78). The parliamentary activities here described are recorded in III: 173, 310, 375. Yet even in what we call economic matters, Coke thinks legally; as we have seen, he considered monopolies violative of Magna Charta and worked hard in James's late parliaments to achieve the Statute against Monopolies. For Coke's work against monopolies, see White, *Sir Edward Coke*, ch. 4, and for the result of his labors, III *Inst.* 181. See also Donald O. Wagner, "Coke and the Rise of Economic Liberalism," *Economic History Review* (1st ser.) 6 (1935): 30, and Barbara Malament, "The 'Economic Liberalism' of Sir Edward Coke," *Yale Law Journal* 76 (1967): 1321.

9. 12 *Reports* 63. The following quotations are from this brief report. See also the discussion of this case by Roland G. Usher, "James I and Sir Edward Coke."

10. The quotation describing the incident can be found in Bowen, *The Lion and the Throne*, p. 305. The golden met-wand is employed again at IV *Inst.* 41. The comment concerning the king and his bench occurs at ibid. 71.

11. *Proclamations*, 12 *Reports* 74. Again, the following quotations can be easily found in this brief case.

12. 12 *Reports* 18. For a discussion of prerogative at common law in the context of a more general treatment of medieval ideas of kingship, see Ullmann, *Principles of Government and Politics in the Middle Ages,* p. 184ff.

13. IV *Inst.* 65.

14. For the discussion of the High Commission, see IV *Inst.* 324ff., esp. pp. 330—31. Discussion of praemunire can be found at III *Inst.* 119 and 12 *Reports* 37. Chancery is treated in IV *Inst.* 8. For the events surrounding Coke's dismissal as chief justice, see Bowen, *The Lion and the Throne,* ch. 28.

15. *Some Makers of English Law,* p. 129.

16. IV *Inst.* proeme, 53. The remainder of the paragraph is based on the discussion in ibid. 53—57. I retained the antiquated spelling here because it is a key for us today to help unlock Coke's thought: The distinction between "council" and "counsel," between an authoritative body and good advice, which we take for granted, cannot be so easily made in the old orthography and indeed was not made by Coke, for whom authority and wisdom are not, at least in principle, distinct. I suspect the same might be said concerning the use of "judicium" in the twenty-ninth chapter of Magna Charta, though Ullmann employs nineteenth-century German legal concepts to distinguish judgment and the court that gives it (*Principles of Government and Politics in the Middle Ages*, p. 163).

17. Blackstone's discussion of the prerogative appears in I. Bl. Comm. ch. 7. Coke's view of the nature of kingship, both limited by and apart from law, bears some resemblance to a number of theories about the double nature of kingship in medieval times. See McIlwain, *Constitutionalism: Ancient and Modern,* p. 78ff., for the distinction between *gubernaculum* and *jurisdictio*; for the concept of "double majesty," see Francis D. Wormuth, *The Origins of Modern Constitutionalism* (New York: Harper and Brothers, 1949), ch. 5, and Donald Hanson, *From Kingdom to Commonwealth* (Cambridge, Mass.: Harvard University Press, 1970); see Ernst H. Kantorowicz, *The King's Two Bodies: A Study in Medieval Political Theology* (Princeton, N.J.: Princeton University Press, 1957); and see Ullmann, *Principles of Government and Politics in the Middle Ages,* esp. part 2, ch. 3, for a different distinction between theocratic and feudal kingship. None of these, however, seems to correspond precisely to what Coke has in mind, perhaps because all of these analyses presume a kind of thought at the level of regime that Coke eschews.

18. 7 *Reports* iii, 7.

19. Ibid. 7.

20. Ibid. 18.

21. Ibid. 14.

22. Ibid. 18.

23. Ibid. 21—22. For the modern meaning of the "Crown" and its relation to the personal authority of the monarch, see Dicey, *Introduction to the Study of Law and the Constitution*, esp. p. 308ff., and S. B. Chrimes, *English Constitutional History,* 4th ed. (Oxford: Oxford University Press, 1967), ch. 4.

24. Ullmann, *Principles of Government and Politics in the Middle Ages,* p. 186ff., seems to argue that in Coke's time the distinction between the theocratic and the feudal king is transformed into a distinction between the theocratic king and the constitutional

monarch. But Coke conflates the theocratic and feudal elements in the king and regards the law to which he is subject less as a feudal contract than as part of the larger, "artificial and refined" whole.

25. 7 *Reports* 25. The following two quotations are from the same page. Cf. *Politics*, book I, 1252a–1253a, where Aristotle makes it clear that while the origin of the family and the city is in the need for preservation, their end is in something more.

26. 4 *Reports* xviii: "The King is under no man, but only God and the law; for the law makes the king. . . ." Cf. 3 *Reports* xxi, where Coke suggests that William the Conqueror took England claiming legal title, not right of conquest. At IV *Inst.* 36–37 Coke recounts the actions of Parliament in settling the course of succession and thus title to the throne.

27. IV *Inst.* 361.

28. Ibid. 363–64.

29. Smith, *De Republica Anglorum: A Discourse on the Commonwealth of England*, ed. L. Alston (Cambridge: Cambridge University Press, 1906), book 2, ch. 1, pp. 48–49.

30. IV *Inst.* 36. Cf. I Bl. Comm. 156.

31. *The High Court of Parliament and Its Supremacy: An Historical Essay on the Boundaries between Legislation and Adjudication in England* (New Haven, Conn.: Yale University Press, 1910), p. 148. This remark occurs in the midst of ch. 3, in which the discussion here summarized can be found.

32. Ibid., pp. 146–47.

33. II *Inst.* proeme. This remark is repeated throughout his work. For a generally sound assessment of Coke's views on legislation, see R. A. MacKay, "Coke—Parliamentary Sovereignty or the Supremacy of the Law?" *Michigan Law Review* 22 (1924): 215.

34. 4 *Reports* v–vi. A similar passage occurs in the preface to the *Ninth Reports*, together with an example of a pernicious alteration in the time of Edward I. Another example with a similar caution occurs in the *Second Institutes*, and yet another, in the course of a lengthy discussion of an act of Henry VII allowing indictment by information rather than by grand jury, in the chapter of the *Fourth Institutes* about Parliament. See II *Inst.* 210; IV *Inst.* 41.

35. 2 *Reports* pref.; IV *Inst.* 331.

36. IV *Inst.* 48.

37. 4 *Reports* ix–x. He does add the caution, however, that "certain statutes concerning the administration of justice . . . are in effect so woven into the common law, and so well approved by experience, as it will be no small danger to alter or change them."

38. III *Inst.* epilogue. In relation to Coke's thoughts on preventing idleness and encouraging the practice of the trades, see the few comments above in note 8—and many more in the articles referred to there—concerning monopolies, which Coke apparently viewed as a chief cause of idleness.

39. The subtitles within Coke's chapter are listed in Appendix I.

40. IV *Inst.* 1.

41. Ibid. 3.

42. Ibid. 9.

43. This means, incidentally, that in its proceedings Parliament is not subject to the common law; rather, *lex et consuetudo Parliamenti* (the law and custom of Parliament) governs. IV *Inst.* 15.

44. Ibid. 24–28.

45. Coke suggests the distinction of adjudicative and statutory activities also when he distinguishes between Parliament and the French parlements, 9 *Reports* vii and I *Inst.* 110b.

46. IV *Inst.* 35.

47. Ibid. 36 – 37. The distinction between general and private legislation occurs in ibid. 25.

48. Ibid. 37 – 38.

49. Ibid. 39, 41.

50. Ibid. 42 – 43.

51. Ibid. 42.

52. Ibid. 3.

53. Coke's many activities in the crucial parliaments of the 1620s are discussed at length in Stephen White's recent book, *Sir Edward Coke and "The Grievances of the Commonwealth," 1621 – 1628,* to which the interested reader is referred.

54. See ibid., ch. 7.

55. *Commons Debates 1628,* III: 494 – 95. The amendment under discussion appears at p. 452.

56. John Rushworth, *Historical Collections of Private Passages of State, Weighty Matters in Law, Remarkable Proceedings in Five Parliaments* . . . (London: D. Browne et al., 1721), I: 562 (emphasis added). Despite the eighteenth-century publication date, the volume was evidently prepared for publication in 1658 – 59, for its dedication is to "Richard, Lord Protector." An example of scholarly reliance on the now discredited text is Corwin, *The "Higher Law" Background*, p. 54.

57. Rushworth, *Historical Collections,* I: 503, 505.

CHAPTER THREE. *DOCTOR BONHAM'S CASE*
AND LAWYERS' HISTORY

1. This appears to be the underlying assumption in the otherwise excellent article on Coke's legal thought by MacKay, "Coke—Parliamentary Sovereignty or the Supremacy of Law?" esp. p. 216.

2. 3 *Reports* xx; I *Inst.* pref.

3. II *Inst.* 402 (misprinted as 204), 587—88, 561. The first two references are commonly noted in the literature on Coke, but the third is overlooked.

4. IV *Inst.* 251. Consistent with his opinion in the case, he does not call the college a court.

5. The citation for *Bonham's* is 8 *Reports* 107a. The facts of the case and the pleas entered are given in excruciatingly repetitive detail over some fourteen pages, from which the following summary is culled. Perhaps Coke includes these in such detail to fulfill the promise he makes in the preface to the *First Reports* of "better instruction of the studious reader in good pleading, which Mr. Littleton saith is one of the most honourable, laudable, and profitable things in the law." The case was continued from Michaelmas term (November) to Hilary term (January); a briefer statement of the facts can be found upon resumption (114a), immediately preceding the justices' opinions.

6. The arrest is mentioned not in Coke's but in Brownlow's report of the case, which was until recently the only other known source: *College of Physicians' Case,* 2 *Brownlow* 255, at 257.

7. A contemporary tract against Coke, "Observations on the Reports," attributed to the Lord Chancellor Ellesmere, asserted that Coke did not have the majority he claimed for the case, but John Farquhar Fraser's edition of the *Reports* notes an argument by Serjeant Hill of Lincoln's Inn, refuting the charge that Coke lacked a clear majority. The recent discovery by Charles Gray of a third report of the case confirms

Hill's position and thus Coke's claim. Charles M. Gray, "Bonham's Case Reviewed," *Proceedings of the American Philosophical Society* 116 (1972): 35. The following summary of positions is indebted to Gray's work.

8. Ever the loyal Cambridge man, however, Coke cannot resist the opportunity to deliver a panegyric to the university, as "no comparison was to be made between that private college, and the great universities of Cambridge and Oxford, no more than between the father and his children, or between the fountain and the small rivers that descend from it." But he does make it clear that this was delivered "before he argued the points in law." 8 *Reports* 116b.

9. To distinguish the various levels of argument, an outline of the case appears in Appendix II. The roman and arabic numerals that appear in the text refer to this outline. To avoid repetitive footnotes to consecutive pages, Coke's arguments are cross-referenced to page numbers only in the appendix. His opinion itself in the case runs from p. 117a to p. 121a.

10. Coke's listing of what the college can and cannot do, by the way, is clearly prospective, giving directions to the president and censors concerning their future behavior. It thus takes on some of the characteristics that commentators attribute to the modern public law judiciary. See Abram Chayes, "The Role of the Judge in Public Law Litigation," *Harvard Law Review* 89 (1976): 1281.

11. Gray has unearthed a report of this case as well: see "Bonham's Case Reviewed," p. 41. Apparently the case in King's Bench was decided in February 1609 (Harold J. Cook, "Against Common Right and Reason," *American Journal of Legal History* 29 [1985]: 312), thus before the decision by the Common Bench. How much before seems uncertain. Coke's report has the decision rendered in Hilary 7 James I (ca. Feb. 1610), over a year after the initial pleadings, which were in Michaelmas 6 James I (ca. Oct. 1608). But Brownlow dates the decision at Trinity 7 James I (ca. May 1609), closer to the pleadings and the other decision.

12. S. E. Thorne, "Dr. Bonham's Case," *Law Quarterly Review* 54 (1938): 543; Berger, *"Doctor Bonham's Case."* Thorne's opinion is accepted by J. W. Gough, *Fundamental Law in English Constitutional History*, p. 32.

13. "Bonham's Case Reviewed," p. 49.

14. "Coke—Parliamentary Sovereignty or the Supremacy of Law?" p. 230.

15. The embedded ellipsis covers citations to three cases from the Year Books and one from Dyer's Reports. Only raw citations are given, without names for the cases and without discussion; apparently the cases support the principle that no one can be judge in his own case. But cf. the discussion in Gray, "Bonham's Case Reviewed," p. 44ff.

16. Contrary to the common assumption that Coke's invocation of "common right and reason" is "gratuitous dictum," unnecessary for the decision of the case (see e.g., Corwin, *The "Higher Law" Background*, p. 50), Thorne argues that the fourth reason is essential to the decision, since "it was clear law that to every fine imprisonment was incident." "Dr. Bonham's Case," p. 548. He is surely correct in noting that Coke's fourth argument is tightly constructed and to the point; at the same time, however, the whole case seems to provide alternative grounds of decision, with the preponderance of the reasons settling the final outcome.

17. "Coke—Parliamentary Sovereignty or the Supremacy of Law?" pp. 222–23. See also Thorne's comment: "There is no conscious constitutional problem raised here, but only one of statutory construction." "Dr. Bonham's Case," p. 549.

18. Ellesmere's comments occur in a speech quoted below and recorded in *Moore* 826, at 828. Blackstone's discussion of *Bonham's Case* and the larger issue it raises appears in I Bl. Comm. 91.

19. Gray, "Bonham's Case Reviewed," p. 40.

20. See Edward Levi, *An Introduction to Legal Reasoning*. By our passion for simplification in legal rules, I allude to the modern tendency to make appeal to the most general constitutional clauses—e.g., due process, equal protection—in matters that a generation or two ago would never have been considered to fall under constitutional law.

21. The leading work on the subject is Theodore F. T. Plucknett, *Statutes and Their Interpretation in the First Half of the Fourteenth Century* (Cambridge: Cambridge University Press, 1922). See also MacKay, "Coke—Parliamentary Sovereignty or the Supremacy of Law?" p. 235ff.

22. 3 *Reports* iv; 10 *Reports* xxiii.

23. "Bonham's Case and Judicial Review," esp. pp. 35–48.

24. Ibid., p. 35. See also his *Statutes and Their Interpretation in the Fourteenth Century*, pp. 68–70. Cf. 8 *Reports* 118a. Coke's discussion of the precedents here in question extends from 118a to 118b; Plucknett's consideration follows Coke's order.

25. "Bonham's Case and Judicial Review," p. 45.

26. That Coke perfectly well understood Herle's actual ruling, precisely as Plucknett understands it, is clear from II *Inst.* 448, where he cites the case and gives its holding succinctly, with no mention of the offending sentence; cf. II *Inst.* 561, where *Tregor's* is mentioned again, this time with a citation to *Bonham's* in the margin.

27. 8 *Reports* 118b.

28. II *Inst.* 588. Presumably he alludes in *Bonham's* to this basis for decision in *Annuity 41* when he writes, "and if the statute should be observed, every common seal shall be defeated upon a simple surmise, which cannot be tried."

29. *Generalis clausula non porrigitur ad ea quae specialiter sunt comprehensa* (A general clause does not extend to those things which are previously provided for specially), and *Verba posteriora propter certitudinem addita ad priora quae certitudine indigent sunt referenda* (Subsequent words, added for the purpose of certainty, are to be referred to the preceding words which require the certainty). 8 *Reports* 118b–119a.

30. Ibid. 119b.

31. Ibid. 120a.

32. See II *Inst.* proeme.

33. See note 14 above and accompanying text. See also Berger, *"Doctor Bonham's Case,"* p. 537, where he argues that "Coke's advance" on his predecessors, who had "'quietly set aside' [parliamentary acts] for the protection of private rights," was "to make the tacit explicit"; and George L. Mosse, *The Struggle for Sovereignty in England, from the Reign of Queen Elizabeth to the Petition of Right* (East Lansing: Michigan State College Press, 1950), p. 144ff.

34. *Moore* 828.

35. Gibson's opinion is in *Eakin v. Raub*, 12 *Sergeant and Rawle* 330 (1825). See also the discussion of *Marbury* in Alexander Bickel, *The Least Dangerous Branch*, pp. 1–14. For a dissenting opinion on the widely assumed conflict between Gibson's opinion and Marshall's, see Clinton, Marbury v. Madison *and Judicial Review*, ch. 8.

36. It is an innovation in this direction that Blackstone has in mind in his barely veiled criticism of Coke's opinion in *Bonham's*; see I Bl. Comm. 91.

37. Again, the judgments of Holdsworth, *Some Makers of English Law*, pp. 127–32, should be consulted here.

38. Again, the restrictive reading of *Marbury* is elaborated in Clinton, Marbury v. Madison *and Judicial Review*.

39. See especially Pocock, *Ancient Constitution*, ch. 2–3. Though Pocock makes Coke's approach to history the explicit theme of the first part of his book, the legal historians have long taken for granted Coke's inadequacy as an historian. See, e.g., Thorne, "Sir Edward Coke, 1552–1952," p. 7ff. Holdsworth, who is often Coke's

champion, abandons him on this score, calling Coke's historical work "almost con-temptible." *History of English Law* V: 472.

40. See, e.g., Holdsworth, *Some Makers of English Law*, pp. 127–32; Pocock, *Ancient Constitution*, p. 45; Plucknett, "Bonham's Case and Judicial Review," pp. 68–69. Cf. Corwin, *The "Higher Law" Background*, p. 57, and Thorne, "Dr. Bonham's Case," p. 552, who argue that, at least with reference to *Bonham's Case*, Coke's contribution to judicial review was merely to supply a "form of words" that his successors themselves remade into something they originally were not.

41. *Ancient Constitution*, pp. 38, 46. The recent reissue includes a lengthy Retrospect that qualifies some of the statements here questioned, but the gist of Pocock's argu-ment remains the same.

42. Ibid., p. 63. Remarkably, he substantiates this statement on the previous page with an example from the writings of Coke's contemporary, Sir John Davies, which appears to prove rather that history is a product of law.

43. Ibid., p. 42.

44. Indeed, one wonders whether Pocock himself does not indulge in a little "backwards-reading," for instance, when he describes Coke's "famous concept of 'arti-ficial reason'" as "essentially Burkean" (ibid., p. 35); the paradox in Coke's thought he discovers on the next page results from dressing him in Burke's clothes. The book as a whole, it might be added, began as a study of the Brady controversy, an argument about the ancient constitution in the reign of James II—a time in which Pocock himself says "the common law mind. . .was far gone in ossification" (pp. viii, 191).

45. 3 Reports vii-b, xxi-a; Pocock, *Ancient Constitution*, p. 40.

46. See the beginnings of 8 *Reports* pref. and 9 *Reports* pref., and the middle of 10 *Reports* pref.

47. Polydore Vergil, 1470?–1555?, was chamberlain to Pope Alexander VI and the pope's emissary to England during the reign of Henry VII. Upon his return to Italy, he wrote his twenty-six-book *Anglicae historicae*, which the *Columbia Encyclopedia* calls "the first critical history of England," a judgment in which Pocock apparently would concur. Vergil was despised by the Parliament men of the 1620s, evidently for casting doubt on the antiquity of English law. In one debate on the floor of Commons (re-ported in *Commons Debates 1628* IV: 48), a Mr. Littleton exclaims, "There were but two Vergils, the one was a poet, the other, a liar."

48. On the relation of justice and law for Coke, see II *Inst.* 56, where, in comment-ing on the last phrase in ch. 29 of Magna Charta, Coke paraphrases as follows: "Wee shall not sell deny, or delay Justice and right. *Justitiam vel rectum*, neither the end, which is Justice, nor the meane, whereby we may attaine to the end, and that is the law."

49. *Ancient Constitution*, p. 35.

50. This phrase occurs in the famous passage on artificial reason, quoted earlier. Its Latin version serves as an epigraph to 6 *Reports*.

51. I have found in Coke only one reference to Plato, in 4 *Reports* viii, where he cites *Laws*, book VI, on the law forestalling innovation.

52. See, e.g., 2 *Reports* pref.; 4 *Reports* xv; IV *Inst.* epilogue. On Coke's own reputa-tion as incorruptible, see Bowen, *The Lion and the Throne*, pp. 389–90.

53. 10 *Reports* xxiii.

54. Vergil, cited repeatedly in Coke's works, earns the epithet "philosophicall" at II *Inst.* 54, for describing the judge in hell, who does not adhere to due process as specified in Magna Charta, ch. 29; Chaucer's "Canon's Yeoman's Tale" testifies that alchemy engenders poverty, at III *Inst.* 74. Coke's apologies for his writing—and for that of lawyers generally—appear at 3 *Reports* xxi; 6 *Reports* ix; 10 *Reports* pref. A nice comparison with Bacon can be gained from reading the latter's argument in *Calvin's*

Case, in James Spedding, Robert Leslie Ellis, and Douglas Denon Heath, eds., *The Works of Francis Bacon* (Boston: Houghton Mifflin, n.d.), XV: 189ff.

55. Coke himself is said to have been much admired for his wit. Bowen recounts that once, while reporting statistics on trade and coinage to the Lords, Coke broke for a joke, after which Prince Charles said he "was never weary with hearing him, he mingled mirth with business to so good purpose." Coke replied, "If it please your Grace, there is no danger in a merry man but only in a sullen and melancholy, as Caesar feared not Brutus, but pale and sad Cassius." Bowen does not tell whether the future king caught the wit in Coke's response, though subsequent events suggest he did not. See Bowen, *The Lion and the Throne*, p. 438. Writing about law, however, was serious business, as Coke explains in the epilogue to the *Fourth Institutes*, presumably among the last words he wrote: "Whilest we were in hand with these foure Parts of the Institutes, we often having occasion to go into the City, and from thence into the Country, did in some sort envy the state of the honest Plowman, and other Mechanicks; for the one when he was at his work would merrily sing, and the Plowman whistle some self-pleasing tune, and yet their work both proceeded and succeeded: But he that takes upon him to write, doth captivate all the faculties and powers both of his minde and body, and must be only intentive to that which he collecteth, without any expression of joy or cheerfulnesse, whilest he is in his work."

56. Cf. Pocock, *Ancient Constitution*, p. 42ff. He evidently means by the "myth of the confirmations" that the kings were confirming law whose antiquity was mythical; that the confirmations were indeed proclaimed is, he would apparently hold with Coke, a fact.

57. Coke's ignorance of continental law is the subject of Pocock's third chapter. But cf. 10 *Reports* 22 pref., where, in the context of chastising the Civilian Hotman for denouncing the common lawyer Littleton, he writes, "It were a ridiculous attempt and enterprise in me (that because I confess I have read some little part of the civil and canon laws, and that with good assistance and help) by and by to write either of them, or against them."

CHAPTER FOUR. THE SCOPE OF SCIENCE AND THE FOCUS OF LAW

1. See H. Trevor Colbourn, *The Lamp of Experience: Whig History and the Intellectual Origins of the American Revolution*, appendix II, for library catalogues; a compendium of citations in early pamphlets appears in Donald S. Lutz, "The Relative Influence of European Writers on Late Eighteenth-Century American Political Thought," *American Political Science Review* 78 (1984): 189–97.

2. Something like this is suggested by Leo Strauss, *Natural Right and History*, pp. 165–66. On the influence of Hobbes on Pufendorf, see Walter Berns, "Judicial Review and the Rights and Laws of Nature," *Supreme Court Review* 1982: 49; and Quentin Skinner, "The Ideological Context of Hobbes's Political Thought," *Historical Journal* 9 (1966): 291. For a similar genealogy, from opposite premises and toward different conclusions from Strauss's and Berns's, see C. B. Macpherson, *The Political Theory of Possessive Individualism: Hobbes to Locke* (Oxford: Clarendon Press, 1962); and Frank M. Coleman, *Hobbes and America: Exploring the Constitutional Foundations* (Toronto: University of Toronto Press, 1977).

3. Some measure of the sheer volume of studies of Hobbes appears from William Sacksteder, *Hobbes Studies (1879–1979): A Bibliography* (Bowling Green, Ohio: Philosophy Documentation Center of Bowling Green State University, 1982), which

cites over fifteen hundred books and articles. On Hobbes's inconsistencies, see, e.g., Leo Strauss, "On the Basis of Hobbes's Political Philosophy," in *What Is Political Philosophy?* p. 173; Don Herzog, *Without Foundations: Justification in Political Theory* (Ithaca, N.Y.: Cornell University Press, 1985), p. 31.

4. Respectively, in *De Cive*, in Bernard Gert, ed., *Man and Citizen* (Garden City, N.Y.: Doubleday and Co., 1972), p. 95; *Leviathan*, ed. C. B. Macpherson (Baltimore: Penguin Books, 1968), pp. 216, 715; *De Corpore*, in William Molesworth, ed., *The English Works of Thomas Hobbes* (London: John Bohn, 1839), I: ix, xiv.

Part of what makes the interpretation of Hobbes's political philosophy so variable is that he presented it in several versions: *The Elements of Law, Natural and Politic* (1640) (ed. Ferdinand Tonnies [Cambridge: Cambridge University Press, 1928]), *De Cive* (1642), and *Leviathan* (1651) are the principal texts, but some scholars consider the changes made in the Latin translation of *Leviathan* (1668) warrant counting it separately, and anyone interested in Hobbes's views on law cannot ignore the posthumously published *Dialogue between a Philosopher and a Student of the Common Laws of England* (ed. Joseph Cropsey [Chicago: University of Chicago Press, 1971]). Though the first three works just mentioned contain numerous parallel passages—often whole chapters that appear to change from version to version like manuscripts going through multiple drafts—the reader must resist leaping to the conclusion that Hobbes meant each successive book to be an improvement upon the previous one. Not only is there no record of his having ever indicated that any one of the books superseded another, but he saw their more or less simultaneous publication around 1650—the *Elements* for the first time (though circulated in manuscript at the time of its composition), *De Cive* for the first time in English (as *Philosophical Rudiments Concerning Government and Society*), and then of course *Leviathan*.

Scholars have noted differences in the doctrines of Christianity in the several works purporting to show the congruence of philosophic and religious doctrine. Attention might also be given to the different audiences addressed in the introductory epistles, perhaps suggesting that the *Elements* was intended to appeal to the aristocracy, *De Cive* to scholars, and *Leviathan* to the emerging middle class. These considerations recommend to Hobbes's modern readers a certain caution in jumping from text to text; if Hobbes's intention (or to use his own word, his "scope") varies from work to work, sentences and passages may not be simply interchangeable. At the same time, they establish a presumption that Hobbes did not think he altered his doctrines in any fundamental way throughout his career.

5. The parallel in Hobbes's treatment of clerics and lawyers is noted by Joseph Cropsey in his Introduction to Hobbes's *Dialogue*, pp. 13, 17, 25–26.

6. The criticisms of Coke appear in *Leviathan*, ch. 15, p. 204, and ch. 26, pp. 316–17. "Aristotelity" is coined in ch. 46, p. 688.

7. Ibid., ch. 26, p. 312. That natural law, strictly speaking, is not law appears in ch. 15, p. 217. It is no accident that Hobbes chooses as his generic term *civil law*, with its echo of Rome and the continent and its implicit challenge to the common lawyers, though he emphasizes on the same page that he is speaking generically and thus not of the Civil Law derived from Justinian's code.

8. Ibid., ch. 26, p. 314.

9. See Howard Warrender, *The Political Philosophy of Hobbes: His Theory of Obligation* (Oxford: Clarendon Press, 1957), ch. 4.

10. *Leviathan*, pp. 323, 326.

11. Ibid., p. 334.

12. On Hobbes's method and its relation to his political thought, cf. Leo Strauss, *The Political Philosophy of Hobbes: Its Basis and Its Genesis* (Chicago: University of

Chicago Press, 1952), esp. preface, ch. 1, 8; with J. W. N. Watkins, *Hobbes's System of Ideas: A Study in the Political Significance of Philosophical Theories* (London: Hutchinson and Co., 1965), esp. ch. 2–4.

13. That Hobbes's scientific method has an essentially rhetorical function is argued most elaborately by J. Weinberger, "Hobbes's Doctrine of Method," *American Political Science Review* 69 (1975): 1336. See also William Mathie, "Reason and Rhetoric in Hobbes's *Leviathan,*" *Interpretation: A Journal of Political Philosophy* 14 (1986): 281; and David Johnston, *The Rhetoric of* Leviathan: *Thomas Hobbes and the Politics of Cultural Transformation* (Princeton, N.J.: Princeton University Press, 1986). That Hobbes generates his politics through his view of science seems best expressed by Michael Oakeshott, *Hobbes on Civil Association* (Berkeley and Los Angeles: University of California Press, 1975), p. 16; cf. Strauss, *Natural Right and History*, p. 171ff.

14. *Leviathan*, ch. 43, p. 626.

15. See ibid., ch. 7, p. 132ff., and ch. 43, p. 614ff.

16. Ibid., ch. 46, p. 686; ch. 21, p. 267.

17. See Joseph Cropsey, "Hobbes and the Transition to Modernity," in Cropsey, ed., *Ancients and Moderns* (New York: Basic Books, 1964), p. 225ff. Cf. Strauss, *The Political Philosophy of Hobbes*, ch. 3, 8. Perhaps it would be accurate to say that Hobbes distorts Aristotle no more than Aristotle does Plato.

18. *Leviathan*, ch. 7, esp. p. 134: "If Livy say the Gods made once a Cow speak, and we believe it not; wee distrust not God therein, but Livy."

19. Ibid., ch. 5, p. 116.

20. Ibid., ch. 3, pp. 96–98; ch. 8, p. 138.

21. Ibid., ch. 5, p. 113.

22. Ibid., pp. 111, 115. Those who fancy themselves at the conceptual frontiers of what is called artificial intelligence today ought to acknowledge their debt to Hobbes, who, along with certain of his contemporaries, first defined reason in such a way as to make "artificial intelligence" conceivable.

23. Ibid., p. 117.

24. Ibid., ch. 4, pp. 102–3.

25. See Kerry H. Whiteside, "Nominalism and Conceptualism in Hobbes's Political Theory," *Commonwealth: A Journal of Political Science* 1 (1987): 1; and Weinberger, "Hobbes's Doctrine of Method," esp. p. 1338ff.

26. *Leviathan*, ch. 1, 4; *De Corpore*, ch. 2, 25.

27. *Leviathan*, ch. 21, p. 263. He elaborates the argument in "Of Liberty and Necessity: A Treatise. . . ," in *English Works* IV: 229ff.

28. *Leviathan*, ch. 7, p. 131; see also ch. 9, where he distinguishes knowledge of consequence from knowledge of fact.

29. *De Corpore,* ch. 25, p. 388; *De Homine,* in Gert, ed., *Man and Citizen,* ch. 10, pp. 41–42. Cf. the division of the sciences in *Leviathan*, ch. 9, p. 149.

30. *Leviathan*, ch. 26, p. 329.

31. *De Corpore,* ch. 1, p. 11; cf. the chart of the sciences in *Leviathan*, ch. 9, p. 149.

32. *De Homine,* ch. 10, pp. 42–43.

33. *Leviathan*, ch. 5, p. 110.

34. *De Cive*, pp. 103, 99. *Leviathan*, pp. 82–83; ch. 13, p. 186, ch. 6, pp. 118–19. See also *De Corpore*, ch. 6, pp. 73–74, and Gary B. Herbert, *Thomas Hobbes: The Unity of Scientific and Moral Wisdom* (Vancouver: University of British Columbia Press, 1989).

35. *De Corpore*, ch. 1, p. 7. Cf. *Leviathan*, ch. 46, p. 682.

36. *Leviathan*, Introduction, p. 81.

37. *Leviathan*, ch. 3, p. 96. See also Strauss, "On the Basis of Hobbes's Political Philosophy," pp. 176–77 and note.

38. *Leviathan*, ch. 18, p. 238; ch. 4, p. 106.

39. *De Corpore*, ch. 1, p. 8.
40. See Alan Ryan, "Hobbes and Individualism," in G. A. J. Rogers and Alan Ryan, eds., *Perspectives on Thomas Hobbes* (Oxford: Clarendon Press, 1988), pp. 81–105.
41. *Leviathan*, ch. 26, p. 317.
42. Ibid., p. 325.
43. Ibid., ch. 20, p. 261.
44. Ibid., ch. 11, pp. 165–66.

CHAPTER FIVE. THE ORIGINAL CONSTITUTION OF RIGHT

1. The formula, which perhaps overstates the matter, belongs to Arnold A. Rogow, *Thomas Hobbes: Radical in the Service of Reaction* (New York: W. W. Norton & Co., 1986).
2. *Leviathan*, ch. 13, p. 183. The parallel chapters in the other works are *De Cive*, ch. 1, and *Elements of Law*, part I, ch. 14.
3. *Leviathan*, ch. 13, p. 185. Though Hobbes says "man," he apparently means to include women as well; as he writes on the question of who governs the family in the state of nature, "there is not always that difference of strength or prudence between the man and the woman, as that the right can be determined without War" (ch. 20, p. 253). In "Considerations upon the Reputation, Loyalty, Manners, and Religion of Thomas Hobbes, of Malmesbury, written by himself, by way of a letter to a learned person (John Wallis, D.D.)," Hobbes excoriates his critic for doubting that the power sacerdotal belongs to the sovereign, "when the sovereignty is in a Queen. But it is because you are not subtle enough to perceive, that though man be male or female, authority is not" (*English Works* IV: 434). The terms *man* and *he* in Hobbes, it seems, ought generally to be read so as not to exclude females.
4. *Leviathan*, ch. 13, p. 186.
5. *De Cive*, ch. 12, p. 246.
6. Cf. a discussion of the passage of *Leviathan* here in question, as evidence of the importance of rhetoric in Hobbes's later work, in William Mathie, "Reason and Rhetoric in Hobbes's *Leviathan*," esp. p. 289ff.
7. *Leviathan*, ch. 15, pp. 203–5.
8. Mathie notes, ironically, "The case for equality of prudence is thus based on prudence or even common opinion, or that passionate refusal of men to admit any others wiser than themselves" ("Reason and Rhetoric in Hobbes's *Leviathan*," p. 291).
9. *Leviathan*, ch. 13, p. 183; cf. ch. 10, p. 151.
10. Ibid., ch. 15, p. 205.
11. Ibid., ch. 8, p. 137; ch. 27, p. 336; ch. 29, p. 366; ch. 46, p. 700. See also Strauss, "On the Basis of Hobbes's Political Philosophy," in *What Is Political Philosophy?* p. 193; Cropsey, "Hobbes and the Transition to Modernity," p. 229; Cropsey, Introduction to Hobbes's *Dialogue*, p. 38; and Alan Ryan, "Hobbes, Toleration, and the Inner Life," in David Miller and Larry Siedentrop, eds., *The Nature of Political Theory* (Oxford: Clarendon Press, 1983), pp. 197–218. Privacy of thought, however, does not entitle a man to make himself a private judge of good or evil, or at least to act upon his judgment, except of course in the state of nature. *Leviathan*, ch. 29, p. 365ff.
12. See *De Cive*, ch. 1, p. 123n.
13. As others have noted, Hobbes's confidence in the benevolence of science apparently leads him to overlook the destruction that advanced armaments can wreak. Of course it is possible that Hobbes keeps a prudent silence on this point; some passages suggest a deep pessimism about international war, as when he writes, "When all the world is overcharged with Inhabitants, then the last remedy of all is Warre"

(*Leviathan*, ch. 30, p. 387). However, his usual stance is to denounce warfare, unless for self-defense, and to show leniency toward those with no taste for soldiering (e.g., ch. 29, p. 375; ch. 21, p. 270).

14. Ibid., ch. 13, pp. 187, 188.

15. Ibid., ch. 14, p. 189; *De Cive*, ch. 14, p. 274; *Elements of Law*, part II, ch. 10, p. 148.

16. *Leviathan*, ch. 14, pp. 189–90; ch. 15, p. 214.

17. The text continues: "But yet if we consider the same Theoremes, as delivered in the word of God, that by right commandeth all things; then they are properly called Lawes." A. E. Taylor, in an influential article written in the 1930s, argues that the theorems must be thus considered in order to be coherent and for the moral theory to be independent of Hobbes's egoistic psychology: "A certain kind of theism is absolutely necessary to make the theory work" ("The Ethical Doctrine of Hobbes," in K. C. Brown, ed., *Hobbes Studies* [Cambridge, Mass.: Harvard University Press, 1965]; see also Stuart Brown's introduction to Taylor's article in the same). In an even more influential book, Howard Warrender (*The Political Philosophy of Hobbes: His Theory of Obligation*) develops Taylor's thesis, holding that natural law must be understood as binding law even in the state of nature, though a sovereign is needed to invalidate the excuse of fear for not keeping one's covenants. For philosophic rejoinders to Warrender, see Watkins, *Hobbes's System of Ideas*, and David Gauthier, *The Logic of Leviathan: The Moral and Political Theory of Thomas Hobbes* (Oxford: Clarendon Press, 1969); for a historical rejoinder, see Skinner, "The Ideological Context of Hobbes's Political Thought," esp. p. 313ff.

18. *Leviathan*, ch. 15, p. 215.

19. See Herzog, *Without Foundations*, p. 39ff. and notes. Cf. Gauthier, *The Logic of Leviathan*, p. 27ff.

20. *Leviathan*, ch. 14, p. 189; ch. 21, p. 263. Cf. J. Roland Pennock, "Hobbes's Confusing 'Clarity'—The Case of 'Liberty,'" in *Hobbes Studies*, pp. 100–116.

21. *Elements of Law*, part I, ch. 14, p. 55.

22. See Oakeshott, *Hobbes on Civil Association*, pp. 32–33.

23. *Leviathan*, ch. 14, p. 192; ch. 21, p. 268ff.

24. E.g., Richard Tuck, *Natural Rights Theories: Their Origin and Development* (Cambridge: Cambridge University Press, 1979), pp. 119–32, who argues that Hobbes begins in the *Elements of Law* with anarchic natural right but develops his theory so as to ensure that natural right is limited to self-preservation. Tuck correctly cites Strauss, *The Political Philosophy of Hobbes*, to corroborate the view that certain human actions can violate natural right, but he neglects to say that Strauss sees the development of Hobbes's theory moving in the opposite direction, from a clear moral attitude toward a scientific denial that any actions—in particular, actions done out of pride or glory—contradict natural right. See esp. ch. 2 in Strauss.

25. Warrender, *The Political Philosophy of Hobbes: His Theory of Obligation*, ch. 3; Gauthier, *The Logic of Leviathan*, ch. 4. Hanna Pitkin, "Hobbes's Concept of Representation," *American Political Science Review* 58 (1964): 328–40, 902–16, for example, has surprisingly little to say about covenant; cf. Clifford Orwin, "On the Sovereign Authorization," *Political Theory* 3 (1975): 26–52, who suggests what the function of the concept of authorization is.

26. *Leviathan*, ch. 14, p. 191.

27. Ibid., ch. 21, p. 268.

28. See Brian T. Trainor, "The Politics of Peace: The Role of the Political Covenant in Hobbes's *Leviathan*," *Review of Politics* 47 (1985): 347–69.

29. *Leviathan*, ch. 14, p. 191.

30. Ibid., p. 196.

31. Ibid., ch. 17, p. 227.

32. Ibid., ch. 15, p. 209; ch. 14, p. 200. In his extensive discussion of "first Founders and Legislators of Common-wealths amongst the Gentiles" in ch. 12, p. 177, however, the only obvious generosity is with the truth, for the actual institution of states seems riddled with fear and fable.

33. Ibid., ch. 29, pp. 364–68; ch. 30, pp. 376–85. See also Johnston, *The Rhetoric of Leviathan*, ch. 3, 5.

34. *Leviathan*, ch. 21, p. 264; ch. 47, p. 711. See also Richard Tuck, "Hobbes and Locke on Toleration," in Mary G. Dietz, ed., *Thomas Hobbes and Political Theory* (Lawrence: University Press of Kansas, 1990), pp. 153–71.

35. Cf. *Leviathan*, ch. 21, p. 263, with ch. 30, p. 388.

36. Ibid., ch. 29, p. 375; Review and Conclusion, pp. 718–19; ch. 21, p. 270. But cf. George Kateb's suggestion that war between nations actually counts more to Hobbes than he admits, in "Hobbes and the Irrationality of Politics," *Political Theory* 17 (1989): 355.

37. *Leviathan*, ch. 15, p. 203; ch. 26, p. 334; ch. 21, p. 266.

38. Ibid., ch. 29, pp. 364–65. See also Cropsey's Introduction to Hobbes's *Dialogue*, p. 22.

39. *Leviathan*, ch. 18, p. 237.

40. Ibid., ch. 14, pp. 192, 199–200. See also *De Cive*, ch. 2, p. 130.

41. *Leviathan*, ch. 21, p. 270. See Gregory S. Kavka, *Hobbesian Moral and Political Theory* (Princeton, N.J.: Princeton University Press, 1986), p. 433; and Cropsey, "Hobbes and the Transition to Modernity," p. 229.

42. *Leviathan*, ch. 28, p. 354.

43. Ibid., ch. 30, p. 376.

44. Ibid., ch. 26, p. 322.

45. Ibid., ch. 5, pp. 111–12.

46. On the anarchy of meaning in Hobbes's state of nature, see Sheldon Wolin, *Politics and Vision: Continuity and Innovation in Western Political Thought* (Boston: Little, Brown, and Company, 1960), p. 244ff.

47. To rise quickly to the surface, it might be noted that the substitution of the question of *whose* for *what* is characteristic of the liberal account of law, as appears in Alexander Bickel, *The Least Dangerous Branch*, p. 3. See also Mansfield, "Hobbes and the Science of Indirect Government," *American Political Science Review* 65 (1971): 97.

48. *Leviathan*, Introduction, p. 81.

49. See Mansfield, *Taming the Prince*, ch. 7.

50. *Leviathan*, ch. 26, p. 323. For Hobbes's location of the source of belief, which of course must not be confused with knowledge, see ch. 29, p. 366.

51. Ibid., ch. 31, p. 408. The discussion in the following paragraph is based upon the same text. For Hobbes's insistence on the importance of the universities, see ch. 30, pp. 384–85.

CHAPTER SIX. FROM GENERAL SCIENCE TO SINGULAR CASE

1. *De Cive*, pp. 93–94.

2. *English Works* VI: 422.

3. In addition to Cropsey's Introduction, see Susan Moller Okin, "'The Soveraign and His Counsellours': Hobbes's Reevaluation of Parliament," *Political Theory* 10 (1982): 49; J. H. Hexter, "Thomas Hobbes and the Law," *Cornell Law Review* 65 (1980): 471, from which the quotation is taken; D. E. C. Yale, "Hobbes and Hale on Law, Legislation, and the Sovereign," *Cambridge Law Journal* 31 (1972): 121; and a fine but generally neglected essay by Enid Campbell, "Thomas Hobbes and the Common Law."

4. *Leviathan*, pp. 75–76; ch. 47, p. 715.

5. Ibid., ch. 31, p. 408. Cf. Pitkin, "Hobbes's Concept of Representation," pp. 906–7.

6. See William Mathie, "Justice and the Question of Regimes in Ancient and Modern Political Philosophy: Aristotle and Hobbes," *Canadian Journal of Political Science* 9 (1976): 449; cf. Curtis Johnson, "The Hobbesian Conception of Sovereignty and Aristotle's Politics," *Journal of the History of Ideas* 46 (1985): 327.

7. Richard Schlatter, ed., *Hobbes's Thucydides* (New Brunswick, N.J.: Rutgers University Press, 1975), pp. 13–14.

8. *Leviathan*, ch. 19, p. 241.

9. Ibid., p. 240.

10. Mansfield, "Hobbes and the Science of Indirect Government."

11. *De Cive*, preface, p. 104.

12. *Leviathan*, ch. 30, p. 380.

13. Ibid., ch. 26, p. 316.

14. I adopt the term *intermediate wholes* from Weinberger, "Hobbes's Doctrine of Method," p. 1347.

15. *Leviathan*, ch. 46, p. 699.

16. On Hobbes's "economic libertarianism," see Cropsey, "Hobbes and the Transition to Modernity," p. 226; and C. B. Macpherson, *The Political Theory of Possessive Individualism*, pp. 53–68.

17. *Leviathan*, ch. 26, p. 317. For a modern critique of the command theory of law, see H. L. A. Hart, *The Concept of Law*, esp. p. 22.

18. "The constitutions therefore of the sovereign power, by which liberty is abridged, are written, because there is no other way to take notice of them. . ." (*Elements of Law*, part II, ch. 10, p. 151).

19. *Leviathan*, ch. 27, p. 354.

20. Ibid., ch. 23, pp. 291–93.

21. Ibid., ch. 26, p. 327.

22. Ibid., p. 328; ch. 23, pp. 292–93.

23. Ibid., ch. 23, pp. 291—92.

24. Ibid., ch. 26, pp. 328, 326.

25. Ibid., ch. 15, p. 212; ch. 26, pp. 326, 314.

26. William Mathie, "Justice and Equity: An Inquiry into the Meaning and Role of Equity in the Hobbesian Account of Justice and Politics," in C. Walton and P. Johnson, eds., *Hobbes's "Science of Natural Justice"* (Dordrecht, Netherlands: Martinus Nijhoff Publishers, 1987), pp. 257–76.

27. *Leviathan*, ch. 25, p. 303.

28. Ibid., Introduction, p. 81; see ch. 8, p. 138.

29. Ibid., ch. 25, p. 308.

30. Ibid., ch. 30, p. 385.

31. See ibid., pp. 388–89.

32. Introduction to Hobbes's *Dialogue*, p. 18.

33. Johnston, *The Rhetoric of Leviathan*, p. 184.

34. *Leviathan*, Review and Conclusion, pp. 717–18.

35. Ibid., ch. 29, p. 366.

36. Ibid., ch. 11, p. 160

CHAPTER SEVEN. THE *DIALOGUE* AND COMMON LAW

1. Cropsey, Introduction to Hobbes's *Dialogue*, pp. 1–8.

2. Frederick Pollock and W. S. Holdsworth, "Sir Matthew Hale on Hobbes: An

Unpublished Manuscript," *Law Quarterly Review* 37 (1921): 274. "Reflections by the Lrd. Cheife Justice Hale on Mr. Hobbes His Dialogue of the Lawe" was republished as appendix III to volume 5 of William Holdsworth, *A History of English Law*, pp. 499–513. Subsequent citations will be to Holdsworth's appendix.

3. E.g., Hexter, "Thomas Hobbes and the Law," pp. 472–73.

4. Oakeshott, *Hobbes on Civil Association*, p. 14.

5. Hexter, "Thomas Hobbes and the Law," pp. 472–73; Okin, "'The Soveraign and His Counsellours,'" p. 49; Cropsey, Introduction, p. 10.

6. St. Germain, *Doctor and Student*, ch. 1–20, but esp. ch. 1–4. The thrust of the work, according to Holdsworth (*History of English Law* V: 268), was the importation into English equity jurisprudence of canonist principles of equity, but this must have been achieved with great tact, since the anticanonist Coke cites *Doctor and Student* regularly as an authority.

7. *Dialogue*, p. 54.

8. Cropsey, Introduction, p. 10. The attack on Coke reaches its height when the Philosopher exclaims toward the *Dialogue*'s end, "Truly I never read weaker reasoning in any Author of the Law of England, than in Sir Edw. Coke's Institutes, how well soever he could plead" (*Dialogue*, pp. 156–57).

9. *Dialogue*, pp. 54–55, 61–62.

10. Ibid., p. 145, for Coke's error that the king could give away to judges jurisdiction that could then limit him; pp. 86, 91, on Chancery as the court of appeal; on the inadequacy of custom alone, see pp. 92–93, and with reference to criminal law, see the entire sections "Of Crimes Capital," "Of Heresie," and "Of Punishments"; against the force of precedent, see pp. 89–90, 115, 129. Indeed, these themes are found on nearly every page of the *Dialogue*.

11. Ibid., p. 71.

12. Ibid., p. 55.

13. Ibid., p. 143; cf. *Leviathan*, ch. 26, p. 316. See also *Dialogue*, p. 97, where the Philosopher argues the congruence of reason and statutory law too, echoing the treatment in *Leviathan*, ch. 26, pp. 326–27.

14. See above, Chapter 1.

15. The phrase is from *Leviathan*, ch. 5, p. 116.

16. *Dialogue*, p. 56.

17. Ibid., p. 58.

18. Ibid., p. 93.

19. Ibid., p. 70. Cropsey has recognized that there is some misordering in the speeches here, and he has juggled them a bit to correct for it. Let me suggest one further move, which as best I can determine reduces by one the number of misreadings we must attribute to the original printer: The section of a speech here quoted ought to follow what Cropsey makes the Philosopher's next speech, with "But perhaps" following immediately upon "suffer dammage." This reordering would also make the Lawyer's brief responses more apposite.

20. Ibid., p. 91. Cropsey relates Hobbes's championing of Chancery to the program of his one-time employer, Sir Francis Bacon, bitter rival to Sir Edward Coke. See Cropsey, Introduction, p. 14.

21. *Dialogue*, p. 68.

22. Ibid., p. 138.

23. Ibid., p. 102. See also Cropsey's perceptive remarks in his Introduction, p. 30ff.

24. *Dialogue*, p. 123. Again, Cropsey's commentary on this point is very helpful.

25. Ibid., p. 140ff.

26. *Leviathan*, ch. 15, p. 210; Cropsey, Introduction, pp. 40–41.

27. *Dialogue*, p. 73. Cf. above, Chapter 5.

28. *Dialogue*, pp. 116–17.

29. Ibid., p. 150.

30. Ibid., p. 151. Cf. I *Inst.* 373b.

31. *Dialogue*, p. 152.

32. See William Mathie, "Justice and Equity"; and Larry May, "Hobbes on Equity and Justice," also in *Hobbes's "Science of Natural Justice,"* pp. 241–51. Charles M. Gray, in his Introduction to Sir Matthew Hale, *The History of the Common Law of England* (Chicago: University of Chicago Press, 1971), goes so far as to say that Hobbes "asserted the fact and the desirability of judicial legislation" (p. xxxii).

33. *Dialogue*, p. 72. See Cropsey's comment in his Introduction, p. 26.

34. *Dialogue*, p. 97.

35. Ibid., p. 66; cf. *Leviathan*, ch. 18, p. 238; see Cropsey, Introduction, p. 24. *Dialogue*, p. 54; cf. *Leviathan*, ch. 18, p. 233.

36. Introduction, p. 14.

37. "'The Soveraign and His Counsellours,'" pp. 50, 70–71.

38. E.g., *Dialogue*, p. 89.

39. Ibid., p. 71.

40. Ibid., p. 166.

41. Okin, "'The Soveraign and His Counsellours,'" p. 61; *Leviathan*, ch. 25, pp. 308–10.

42. See, e.g., *Leviathan*, ch. 19, pp. 242–43; also, Johnston, *The Rhetoric of Leviathan*.

43. Okin, "'The Soveraign and His Counsellours,'" pp. 63–64.

44. *Dialogue*, pp. 60–61, on taxes; p. 131, on punishment. See also the Philosopher's reference to "King and [not "in"] Parliament," p. 146.

45. Ibid., p. 76.

46. Okin, "'The Soveraign and His Counsellours,'" pp. 67–68. Cropsey would seem to agree, though he does not stress the point in his Introduction, pp. 26–27.

47. *Dialogue*, p. 157.

48. "'The Soveraign and His Counsellours,'" p. 71.

49. Introduction, p. 13.

50. Ibid., p. 14. Cf. *Dialogue*, p. 159, where the Philosopher does speak of the right, if not the state, of nature and in the usual Hobbesian way, as that "which they had to preserve their lives."

51. "Hobbes and the Transition to Modernity," p. 235; Introduction, p. 15.

52. Introduction, p. 14.

53. *Dialogue*, pp. 94, 136.

54. Ibid., p. 166.

55. The Philosopher does once mention the fate of Stafford, without noting that parliamentary proceedings against him began as impeachment. He attributes, in the same passage, the regicide not to Parliament but simply to "Rebels" (ibid., p. 139).

56. Ibid., pp. 88, 91. The Lawyer first uses the term, p. 87.

57. Cropsey, Introduction, p. 48; cf. p. 11.

58. *Dialogue*, p. 141.

59. *Leviathan*, ch. 30, p. 388.

60. *Dialogue*, pp. 160–61. See Cropsey, Introduction, p. 42ff.; also Okin, "'The Soveraign and His Counsellours,'" pp. 66–67.

61. Fortescue, *De Laudibus Legum Anglie*, esp. ch. 9–14.

62. *Dialogue*, p. 162.

63. Introduction, p. 48.

64. See Gray, Introduction to Hale, *History of the Common Law*, p. xiiiff.

65. "Reflections," p. 501.

66. Ibid., p. 502.

67. Ibid., pp. 504, 502, 503.

68. Ibid., pp. 504–5.

69. Ibid., p. 508.

70. Ibid., p. 511.

71. Pollock and Holdsworth, "Sir Matthew Hale on Hobbes," p. 284.

72. "Reflections," p. 512. Cf. Strauss, *Natural Right and History*, p. 179.

73. Perhaps this is unfair to Hobbes. While a scientific architect of commonwealths cannot avoid all incommodity, he can apparently foresee every circumstance that might cause domestic collapse; *Leviathan*, ch. 29, p. 363.

CHAPTER EIGHT. THE REVOLUTIONARY CONSTITUTIONALISM OF JOHN LOCKE

1. See Mansfield, *Taming the Prince*, esp. ch. 8.

2. M. J. C. Vile, *Constitutionalism and the Separation of Powers* (Oxford: Clarendon Press, 1967), p. 59; W. B. Gwyn, *The Meaning of the Separation of Powers: An Analysis of the Doctrine from Its Origin to the Adoption of the United States Constitution*, Tulane Studies in Political Science, vol. IX (New Orleans: Tulane University, 1965), pp. 54–55. On the relation of Locke to the parliamentary constitutionalists of the Interregnum, see Mansfield, *Taming the Prince*, p. 182ff.

3. *Second Treatise*, in Peter Laslett, ed., *Two Treatises of Government*, rev. ed. (Cambridge: Cambridge University Press, 1988), ch. 19, sect. 240, p. 427.

4. The pervasiveness of the theme of judgment in Locke's *Second Treatise* has been noted recently by Shannon Stimson, *The American Revolution in the Law*, esp. p. 40ff., who argues that through the *Essay* Locke provided the epistemological basis for American colonial deference to juries' judgment of the law.

5. *Second Treatise*, ch. 1, sect. 3, p. 268.

6. Ibid., ch. 2, sect. 4 and 7, pp. 269, 272.

7. Ibid., sect. 6, p. 271.

8. Ibid., sect. 9, p. 272. But cf. ch. 8, sect. 122, p. 349, where Locke gives a somewhat different account of the obligation of denizens.

9. Ibid., ch. 2, sect. 11, p. 273.

10. Ibid., sect. 12, 13, p. 275.

11. Ibid., sect. 13, p. 276; ch. 9, sect. 123, p. 350.

12. Ibid., ch. 2, sect. 13, p. 276.

13. Ibid., sect. 15, p. 278. On the distinction between a law of nature and a rule of convenience, see his *Essay Concerning Human Understanding*, ed. Peter H. Nidditch (Oxford: Clarendon Press, 1975), bk. I, ch. iii, sect. 2 (p. 66).

14. *Second Treatise*, ch. 3, sect. 19, p. 281.

15. Ibid., sect. 21, p. 282; ch. 2, sect. 13, p. 276.

16. The principal studies assimilating the doctrines of the two philosophers are Leo Strauss, *Natural Right and History*, ch. 5; Richard H. Cox, *Locke on War and Peace* (Oxford: Clarendon Press, 1960); and, from a rather different perspective, C. B. Macpherson, *The Political Theory of Possessive Individualism*. See also a recent article by Patrick Coby, "The Law of Nature in Locke's *Second Treatise*: Is Locke a Hobbesian?" *Review of Politics* 49 (1987): 3; and generally, Thomas Pangle, *The Spirit of Modern Republicanism*, part 3. The opposite position is perhaps taken by John Dunn, *The Political Thought of John Locke: An Historical Account of the Argument of the "Two Treatises of Government"* (Cambridge: Cambridge University Press, 1969), p. 24n. Peter Laslett, in his generally thoughtful Introduction to the *Two Treatises*, is much im-

pressed by recent evidence that Locke had loaned his copy of the *Leviathan* to his friend James Tyrrell before writing the *Treatises* and did not get it back until after their publication. But isn't it possible that Locke read books, or at least read Hobbes, rather after the manner of Pascal, remembering all he had read? See *Essay Concerning Human Understanding*, bk. II, ch. viii, sect. 9 (p. 154).

17. Cf. *Second Treatise*, ch. 2, sect. 13, pp. 275–76, and ch. 11, sect. 137, pp. 359–60, with *Leviathan*, ch. 19.

18. Strauss, *Natural Right and History*, pp. 165–66ff.

19. Cf. *Essay Concerning Human Understanding*, book I, which is devoted to showing there are no innate principles of mind, such as laws of nature; this apparent conflict between the *Two Treatises* and the *Essay* is perhaps the classic problem in the interpretation of Locke.

20. *Second Treatise*, ch. 2, sect. 6, pp. 270–71; ch. 4, sect. 23, p. 284; ch. 5, sect. 27, p. 287. See also Coby, "Is Locke a Hobbesian?" p. 8.

21. See especially *Leviathan*, ch. 15, pp. 215–17.

22. Ibid., ch. 14, p. 189.

23. *Second Treatise*, ch. 7, sect. 93, p. 328; ch. 11, sects. 137, pp. 359–60.

24. *Leviathan*, ch. 18, p. 238.

25. See ibid., ch. 3, p. 97; ch. 5, pp. 111–12, 115; ch. 8, pp. 135–38; ch. 25, pp. 307–8; ch. 26, passim.

26. *Essay Concerning Human Understanding*, bk. IV, ch. xiv, sect. 3 (p. 653).

27. See ibid., bk. IV, ch. xxi, sect. 1–5 (pp. 720–21), the final chapter of the *Essay*, where he divides the sciences into *Physike*, *Practike*, and *Semiotike*, saying of the first that it involves things knowable, of the last that it orders knowledge, but of the practical (of "Ethicks") only that it treats of "*Actions* as they depend on us, in order to Happiness."

28. "Some Thoughts Concerning Reading and Study for a Gentleman," in James L. Axtell, ed., *The Educational Writings of John Locke* (Cambridge: Cambridge University Press, 1968), p. 400. This distinction is remarked on in Nathan Tarcov, *Locke's Education for Liberty* (Chicago: University of Chicago Press, 1984), p. 5; and David Resnick, "Locke and the Rejection of the Ancient Constitution," *Political Theory* 12 (1984): 98.

29. *Leviathan*, ch. 14, p. 191; ch. 15, pp. 201–8; ch. 28, pp. 359–60.

30. *Second Treatise*, ch. 18, sect. 205 and 208, pp. 402, 404. Significantly, Hobbes follows his passage on not punishing the innocent with the assertion that "the Infliction of what evil soever, on an innocent man, that is not a Subject, if it be for the benefit of the Common-wealth, and without violation of any former Covenant, is no breach of the Law of Nature" (*Leviathan*, ch. 28, p. 360). Yet Locke shows great solicitude for the innocent victims of a conqueror—or at least for their property—throughout the chapter "Of Conquest" of the *Second Treatise*. Only by defining justice in terms of social purpose rather than individual desert is Coby able to find Locke more devoted than Hobbes to justice; he might have done better to have found Locke's doctrine simply more productive of "domestic peace" ("Is Locke a Hobbesian?" pp. 15–23). On Locke as "Machiavelli's philosopher," see Laslett's Introduction to *Two Treatises*, p. 88.

31. Again, see Mansfield, *Taming the Prince*, ch. 8, whose account of Lockean prerogative I attempt to follow here.

32. *Second Treatise*, ch. 13, sect. 149, p. 367. On the distinction between constitutive and ordinary legislation as Locke's contribution to the doctrine of sovereignty, see Julian H. Franklin, *John Locke and the Theory of Sovereignty* (Cambridge: Cambridge University Press, 1978), esp. p. 124.

33. The terms *Constituted Commonwealth* and *original Constitution* can be found throughout *Second Treatise*, ch. 13; see also ch. 19, sect. 212, p. 407. On the origin of

rules, see, e.g., ch. 7, sect. 94, pp. 329–30; ch. 8, sect. 107, pp. 338–39; ch. 14, sect. 162, p. 376. "Where Law ends . . ." is from ch. 18, sect. 202, p. 400.

34. Ibid., ch. 12, sect. 143, p. 364; the preceding discussion relies on ch. 12–13, passim.

35. *The Meaning of the Separation of Powers*, p. 76.

36. *Second Treatise*, ch. 11, sect. 138, pp. 360–61.

37. Ibid., ch. 14, sect. 160, p. 375.

38. Ibid., ch. 12, sect. 147, p. 365.

39. Ibid., ch. 18, sect. 205–6, pp. 402–3.

40. Ibid., ch. 14, sect. 168, pp. 379–80; ch. 11, sect. 134, pp. 355–56.

41. Ibid., ch. 9, sect. 124–26, p. 351; sect. 131, p. 353.

42. Ibid., ch. 7, sect. 89, p. 325.

43. Ibid., ch. 6, sect. 57, pp. 305–6.

44. *Leviathan*, ch. 21, p. 271, marginal notation.

45. *Second Treatise*, ch. 6, sect. 57, p. 306.

46. Ibid., ch. 5 and 9, passim.

47. *Leviathan*, ch. 13, pp. 186, 188; ch. 15, p. 202; ch. 21, p. 264; ch. 22 and 24, passim.

48. *Second Treatise*, ch. 5, sect. 50, p. 302. See also ch. 7, sect. 87, pp. 323–24; ch. 11, sect. 136, pp. 358–59; ch. 19, sect. 222, p. 412.

49. Ibid., ch. 5, esp. sect. 27 and 31, pp. 288, 290. See also Strauss, *Natural Right and History*, p. 234ff.; and Coby, "Is Locke a Hobbesian?" p. 13.

50. See Harvey C. Mansfield, Jr., "The Right of Revolution," in his *Spirit of Liberalism* (Cambridge, Mass.: Harvard University Press, 1978).

51. On the absence of the "ancient constitution" in Locke, see Resnick, "Locke and the Rejection of the Ancient Constitution," and J. G. A. Pocock, *Ancient Constitution*, p. 353ff.

52. *Second Treatise*, ch. 19, sect. 225, p. 415.

53. See also ibid., ch. 16, sect. 177, pp. 386–87.

54. Axtell, ed., *The Educational Writings of John Locke*, p. 401; cf. ibid., p. 295, in "Some Thoughts concerning Education," where Locke suggests to gentlemen the study of English law.

55. *Second Treatise*, ch. 14, sect. 159, p. 374. Of course the term *prerogative* existed at common law, though it referred to particular privileges of the king, not a general executive power.

56. This is Stimson's point in drawing attention to Locke's epistemological influence on American politics (*The American Revolution in the Law*, p. 40ff). She never mentions, however, the implications Locke draws from it, not for jural but for executive action.

57. For a recent attempt to restore Locke's reputation as a radical, see Richard Ashcraft, *Revolutionary Politics and Locke's* Two Treatises of Government (Princeton, N.J.: Princeton University Press, 1986).

58. Again, see Strauss, *Natural Right and History*, p. 245. The quotation is from *Second Treatise*, ch. 19, sect. 243, p. 423.

CHAPTER NINE. MONTESQUIEU'S LIBERAL SPIRIT

1. *De l'Esprit des Loix*, ed. Jean Brethe de la Gressaye (Paris: Société les Belles Lettres, 1950), bk. XI, ch. 20 (II: 104). The translations in this chapter are my own.

2. Though perhaps our sense of length is foreshortened: A Marylander in 1783 called *The Spirit of the Laws* "this little book." Quoted in Paul Merrill Spurlin, *Montesquieu in America, 1760–1801* (Baton Rouge: Louisiana State University Press, 1940), p. 94.

3. *De l'Esprit des Loix*, preface (I: 12).

4. For discussion of Montesquieu on natural law, see Thomas Pangle, *Montesquieu's Philosophy of Liberalism* (Chicago: University of Chicago Press, 1973), ch. 3; also Mark Hulliung, *Montesquieu and the Old Regime* (Berkeley and Los Angeles: University of California Press, 1976), prologue and ch. 5.

5. *De l'Esprit des Loix*, bk. I, ch. 1 and 3 (I: 19, 26).

6. Ibid., bk. VI, ch. 2 (I: 148).

7. Ibid., bk. XI, ch. 6 (II: 76); cf. bk. XXVIII, ch. 15 (IV: 55).

8. See Mansfield, *Taming the Prince*, ch. 9.

9. *De l'Esprit des Loix*, bk. XI, ch. 6 (II: 76).

10. Ibid., ch. 5 (II: 62).

11. Alexander Hamilton, James Madison, and John Jay, *The Federalist Papers*, pp. 301—3, 466.

12. Gwyn, *The Meaning of the Separation of Powers*, p. 101.

13. *De l'Esprit des Loix*, bk. XI, ch. 6 (II: 64).

14. Ibid., p. 65.

15. Ibid., ch. 11 (II: 81).

16. Ibid., ch. 6 (II: 72). This passage, and its reference back to book VI, was brought to my attention by Karl M. Schoenfeld; it is developed in his dissertation, "Montesquieu en 'la bouche de la loi'" (University of Leyden, 1979).

17. *De l'Esprit des Loix*, bk. XI, ch. 6 (II: 65).

18. Ibid., bk. II, ch. 4 (I: 45). The quotations that follow are from the same chapter.

19. Ibid., bk. XIX, ch. 27 (III: 34).

20. Ibid., bk. VI, ch. 1, 3, and 4 (I: 143, 148, 149).

21. Ibid., ch. 5 (I: 150).

22. Ibid., bk. V, ch. 19 (I: 133).

23. Ibid., bk. XII, ch. 2 (II: 111); bk. VI, ch. 2 (I: 146).

24. See ibid., bk. XXII, esp. ch. 10 (III: 151ff.).

25. Ibid., preface (I: 12).

26. Ibid., bk. I, ch. 2 (I: 23).

27. Ibid., bk. V, ch. 13 (I: 118).

28. Cf. Christopher Kelly, "'To Persuade without Convincing': The Language of Rousseau's Legislator," *American Journal of Political Science* 31 (1987): 321.

CHAPTER TEN. BLACKSTONE'S LIBERALIZED COMMON LAW

1. Corwin, *The "Higher Law" Background*, p. 85. See *The Writings of Thomas Jefferson* 12: iv.

2. Gerald Stourzh, "William Blackstone: Teacher of Revolution," *Jahrbuch für Amerikastudien* 15 (1970): 184.

3. See *The Works of James Wilson*, ed. Robert Green McCloskey (Cambridge, Mass.: Belknap Press of Harvard University Press, 1967), I: 76—80.

4. See *The Collected Works of Abraham Lincoln*, ed. Roy Basler (New Brunswick, N.J.: Rutgers University Press, 1953), III: 344, IV: 121. More generally, see Daniel Boorstin, *The Mysterious Science of the Law: An Essay on Blackstone's* Commentaries . . . (Cambridge, Mass.: Harvard University Press, 1941), pp. 3—4.

5. Somewhat ironically, incidentally, since Blackstone himself denied that the common law applied in the American colonies, as they had been acquired by conquest, he thought—and perhaps also because they allowed slavery, which common law forbade. I Bl. Comm. 104—5. A defender of the power of Parliament over the colonies, Blackstone voted in Parliament against the repeal of the Stamp Act.

6. I Bl. Comm. 6. Cf. *De l'Esprit des Loix*, bk. XI, ch. 5 (II: 62), where Montesquieu says *political* liberty is the direct object of the constitution of England, though it is true that the baron is more interested in distinguishing political and civil law than political and civil liberty.

7. *De l'Esprit des Loix*, preface (I: 13).

8. See A. V. Dicey, "Blackstone's Commentaries," *Cambridge Law Journal* 4 (1932): 300ff.

9. See W. S. Holdsworth, "Some Aspects of Blackstone and His Commentaries," *Cambridge Law Journal* 4 (1932): 262.

10. I Bl. Comm. 9.

11. II Bl. Comm. 456.

12. John W. Cairns, "Blackstone, An English Institutist: Legal Literature and the Rise of the Nation State," *Oxford Journal of Legal Studies* 4 (1984): 318.

13. See, for example, the prefaces to Sir Edward Coke's *Reports*, especially the preface to the *Third Reports*.

14. I Bl. Comm. 33.

15. Passim.

16. "The Structure of Blackstone's Commentaries," *Buffalo Law Review* 28 (1979): 209.

17. "William Blackstone," in *History of Political Philosophy*, 2d ed., ed. Leo Strauss and Joseph Cropsey (Chicago: Rand McNally, 1972).

18. Richard Posner, "Blackstone and Bentham," *Journal of Law and Economics* 19 (1976): 572.

19. This phrase, made famous by the Declaration of Independence, apparently originated in Locke; see *Essay Concerning Human Understanding*, bk. II, ch. xxi, sect. 47, (p. 266). See the discussion in Pangle, *The Spirit of Modern Republicanism*, pp. 177–78, 186–87, 205–9.

20. I Bl. Comm. 40–44.

21. Ibid. 44–45.

22. Ibid. 54.

23. Ibid. 121, 123. See also the discussion of the foundation of the rights of property in II Bl. Comm. 1–15, where Blackstone mocks as "too much of nice and scholastic refinement," the dispute between Grotius and Locke over whether property originates in occupancy or labor. Starting with a right to use things, but suggesting the injustice that lies beneath all original taking, Blackstone apparently justifies the right of property by the leisure it makes possible, though the legislative settling of property rights is explained as necessary to secure or maintain the peace.

24. I Bl. Comm. 57; see also Posner, "Blackstone and Bentham," p. 578.

25. I Bl. Comm. 47.

26. Ibid. 46, 48.

27. Ibid. 52.

28. Ibid. 140.

29. Ibid. 156–57.

30. Ibid. 52.

31. Ibid. 204.

32. Ibid. 205–6.

33. Ibid. 243.

34. Ibid. 58–59. Cf. *De l'Esprit des Loix*, bk. XXIX, ch. 17 (IV: 144–45). Blackstone's use of the terms *general constitutions* and *the nature of things* suggests he had Montesquieu open on his desk as he wrote, since in the chapter on rescripts Montesquieu recommended distinguishing rescripts from "Senatus-consulta, plebiscites, general

constitutions of the emperors, and all laws founded on the nature of things, the frailty of women, the weakness of minors, and the public utility."

35. I Bl. Comm. 61–62.

36. Ibid. 63.

37. Ibid. 66–67; IV Bl. Comm. 435–36.

38. IV Bl. Comm. 411, 436.

39. See Dicey, "Blackstone's Commentaries," p. 290ff., who has some sharp things to say about Bentham's relation to Blackstone. Cf. Posner, "Blackstone and Bentham," and Rupert Cross, "Blackstone v. Bentham," *Law Quarterly Review* 92 (1976): 516.

40. I Bl. Comm. 67–68.

41. Cf. ibid. 258–59, where Blackstone calls the judges "the grand depositary of the fundamental laws of the kingdom," mentioning that they hold their tenure on good behavior, and he suggests that the "administration of common justice be in some degree separated from the legislative and also from the executive power."

42. Ibid. 69.

43. Ibid. 70.

44. Ibid.

45. Ibid. 72, 77.

46. Boorstin, *The Mysterious Science of the Law*, preface, ch. 1; Stanley Katz, Introduction to vol. I of the 1979 Chicago reprint of the *Commentaries*, p. v.

47. I Bl. Comm. 91. Coke's pronouncement in *Bonham's Case* can be found in 8 *Reports* 118a. Corwin discusses several subsequent cases that invoked the doctrine in *The "Higher Law" Background*, pp. 51–53.

48. I Bl. Comm. 90.

49. Ibid. 324–25.

50. III Bl. Comm. 268.

51. "The Structure of Blackstone's Commentaries," p. 234.

INTRODUCTION TO PART FOUR

1. Sandoz, *A Government of Laws*, e.g., p. 38.

2. See Mansfield, *Taming the Prince*, p. 290.

CHAPTER ELEVEN. BEHIND THE "FACTS SUBMITTED TO A CANDID WORLD": CONSTITUTIONAL ARGUMENTS FOR INDEPENDENCE

1. *The Writings of Thomas Jefferson* XIV: 118 (letter to Henry Lee, 8 May 1825). See also Harvey C. Mansfield, Jr., "Thomas Jefferson," in Morton J. Frisch and Richard G. Stevens, eds., *American Political Thought: The Philosophic Dimension of American Statesmanship* (New York: Charles Scribner's Sons, 1971), p. 23ff.

2. *The Ideological Origins of the American Revolution*. For the array of sources, see ch. 2, p. 22ff.; the quotation is from p. 21. Other studies that highlight the importance of the radical Whig strand in the development of English and American political thought include Caroline Robbins, *The Eighteenth-Century Commonwealthman: Studies in the Transmission, Development and Circumstance of English Liberal Thought from the Restoration of Charles II until the War with the Thirteen Colonies* (Cambridge, Mass.: Harvard University Press, 1959); Gordon Wood, *The Creation of the American Republic, 1776–1789*; J. G. A. Pocock, *The Machiavellian Moment*.

3. *Ideological Origins,* p. 95.

4. On "ideology" in the specific sense, see ibid., p. 158.

5. Ibid., p. vi.

6. Ibid., p. 161.

7. The quotations are from the preface to Bailyn's *Ordeal of Thomas Hutchinson* (Cambridge, Mass.: Belknap Press of Harvard University Press, 1974), pp. ix—x.

8. *Second Treatise,* ch. 18, sect. 210. Stimson goes so far, in a similar critique of Bailyn on this point, to assert that the "paranoid style. . .was the intellectual gift of the Enlightenment, and in no small way a direct bequest of Locke." *The American Revolution in the Law,* p. 37.

9. Burke's speech, delivered less than a month before the shooting began at Lexington, can be found in *The Works of the Right Honourable Edmund Burke* (London: C. and J. Rivington, 1826), III: 23–132. The passages referred to in this paragraph are on pp. 49–57.

10. Ibid., p. 75. See also pp. 110–11.

11. Reissued by Cornell University Press, 1958. The imperial question has recently been reopened, though with a sociological rather than constitutional wedge, by historian Jack Greene, *Peripheries and Center: Constitutional Development in the Extended Polities of the British Empire and the United States, 1607–1788* (Athens: University of Georgia Press, 1986).

12. *The American Revolution: A Constitutional Interpretation,* pp. 186, 196–97. Actually it is a bit unfair to see in this quotation an anticipation of Bailyn's thesis, for Bailyn acknowledges the "essentially decorous and reasonable" character of the pamphlet literature he treats (*Ideological Origins,* p. 17). It would be more precise to say he finds the American imagination to have been instructed in getting heated.

13. *The American Revolution: A Constitutional Interpretation,* ch. 3; the quotation, however, is from p. 1.

14. "Of the Study of Law in the United States," in Robert McCloskey, ed., *The Works of James Wilson* I: 79ff.

15. For a reprint of several of the texts, photographic facsimiles, and discussion of the various drafts, which, however, does not comment on the errant "s," see Julian P. Boyd, *The Declaration of Independence: The Evolution of the Text as Shown in Facsimiles of Various Drafts by Its Author, Thomas Jefferson* (Princeton, N.J.: Princeton University Press, 1945); several of these versions are reprinted in Boyd, ed., *The Papers of Thomas Jefferson* (Princeton, N.J.: Princeton University Press, 1950), I: 413ff. The plural version is not infrequently included in what purport to be final texts of the Declaration, especially by editors whose principal interest is Jefferson. See, for example, Garry Wills, *Inventing America: Jefferson's Declaration of Independence* (Garden City, N.Y.: Doubleday and Company, 1978), p. 376; Merrill D. Peterson, ed., *The Portable Thomas Jefferson* (New York: Penguin Books, 1977), p. 237. A text of the *Summary View* appears in the latter, with the passages quoted at pp. 9, 13. The temptation to see in Jefferson's plural a glimmer of his later authorship of the Kentucky Resolutions is almost irresistible.

16. This is noted, without further comment, in Carl L. Becker, *The Declaration of Independence: A Study in the History of Ideas* (New York: Vintage Books, 1942), p. 145n.

17. *The Writings of Thomas Jefferson* XVI: 118–19; XII: iv. For a case that the Jefferson of the Declaration ought to be understood as a common lawyer and little else, see Daniel J. Boorstin, *The Genius of American Politics* (Chicago: University of Chicago Press, 1953), ch. 3.

18. *Paxton's Case of the Writ of Assistance,* reported in Josiah Quincy, Jr., *Reports,* p. 51; Otis's argument is printed in the appendix, p. 469ff.

19. See Edward S. Corwin, *The "Higher Law" Background,* p. 77.

20. Otis, *The Rights of the British Colonies Asserted and Proved,* in Bernard Bailyn, ed., *Pamphlets of the American Revolution, 1750–1776* (Cambridge, Mass.: Belknap Press of Harvard University Press, 1965), I: 449, 476–77.

21. Ibid., p. 446.

22. Ibid., p. 454.

23. The most striking instance of his invocation of universal principle, together with a common lawyer's almost casual assumption that what is right is also law, is his discussion of the injustice of black slavery, in ibid., p. 439ff. He also chides social contract theorists for what he takes to be their oversight of the female sex: "Are not women born as free as men? Would it not be infamous to assert that the ladies are all slaves by nature?" Ibid., p. 420.

24. Ibid., p. 410.

25. *Letters from a Farmer in Pennsylvania . . . ,* in Paul Leicester Ford, ed., *The Writings of John Dickinson,* vol. I, *Political Writings, 1764–1774* (Philadelphia: Historical Society of Pennsylvania, 1895).

26. Ibid., pp. 307, 357, 386, 390, 405–6. To one who has read the *Letters* with some care, it is interesting but not surprising to learn both that Dickinson studied law in England at the Inner Temple and that it was he who, in the first days of July 1776, made the final motion to delay a vote for independence.

27. William Hedges, "Telling Off the King: Jefferson's *Summary View* as Imaginative Fantasy," *Early American Literature* 22 (1987): 166.

28. *The Portable Thomas Jefferson,* pp. 21, 18.

29. *Common Sense,* ed. Isaac Kramnick (New York: Penguin Books, 1976). Kramnick remarks in his Introduction that "it is in the realm of common sense that the pamphlet bogs down" (p. 45).

30. Hamilton, Madison, and Jay, *The Federalist Papers,* No. 39, p. 240.

31. *Common Sense,* p. 68.

32. Cf. *The Federalist Papers,* No. 38, p. 231ff.

CHAPTER TWELVE. CONSTITUTIONALISM AND JUDGING IN *THE FEDERALIST*

1. *The Political Theory of* The Federalist (Chicago: University of Chicago Press, 1984), p. 186.

2. See Albert Furtwangler, *The Authority of Publius: A Reading of the Federalist Papers* (Ithaca, N.Y.: Cornell University Press, 1984), p. 58.

3. Since the Pendleton Act a century ago, judges have been joined more or less by civil servants, but the latter can still be removed by procedures rather less formidable than impeachment; besides, they are presumed to take their orders from political appointees.

4. The distinction of appointment versus election was somewhat less pronounced at the time the Constitution was proposed than it is today, now that senators are elected directly by the people and the electoral college has become little more than a mechanical device for tallying presidential votes by state.

5. The number and kind of the executive departments under the president were also left to legislative determination, but the choices involved in structuring the subordinate executives are less fundamental than those at issue in constituting lower courts; the question with regard to the former is which departments to establish, while regarding inferior federal courts the question is not only which but whether.

6. All notes refer to the 1961 edition of *The Federalist Papers,* edited by Clinton Rossiter. The two phrases here are from *Federalist* No. 48, p. 308, and No. 23, p. 153.

7. *Federalist* No. 15, p. 108.

8. Ibid, No. 23, p. 154; cf. No. 39, where Madison admits, in the context of distinguishing national and federal features of the plan, that in its operation the government will be entirely national (p. 245).

9. Ibid., No. 22, p. 150.

10. Ibid., No. 51, p. 324.

11. Ibid., No. 10, p. 78.

12. Ibid., No. 15, p. 108.

13. Ibid., No. 82, p. 493.

14. Ibid., No. 22, p. 150; No. 80, p. 476.

15. Ibid., No. 37, p. 227ff.

16. Ibid., No. 39, pp. 245–46.

17. Ibid., No. 17, p. 120.

18. I Bl. Comm. 258; cf. III Bl. Comm. 23–24.

19. E.g., *Federalist* No. 77, p. 464.

20. *The Meaning of the Separation of Powers*, p. 35. See also M. J. C. Vile, *Constitutionalism and the Separation of Powers*, ch. 2, and Francis Wormuth, *The Origins of Modern Constitutionalism*, ch. 20.

21. *Federalist* No. 70, p. 427.

22. Ibid., No. 47, p. 301, and No. 48, p. 308.

23. Ibid., No. 51, p. 322.

24. Ibid., No. 48, p. 309.

25. This is also noted by Epstein, *The Political Theory of The Federalist*, p. 186. Madison, of course, had in the Convention proposed a Council of Revision, which would join the president and "a convenient number of the National Judiciary" in exercising the veto over legislation. The debate that led to rejection of such a council provides some of the best evidence that the Framers intended, or at least expected, judicial review. See Max Farrand, ed., *The Records of the Federal Convention of 1787* (New Haven, Conn.: Yale University Press, 1911), I: 21, 97–98, and Chapter 13, below.

26. *Federalist* No. 51, p. 321.

27. Ibid., pp. 323–24.

28. Ibid., No. 78, p. 465.

29. Ibid., p. 471.

30. On the combination of law and equity, as in Scotland but in contrast to England, see Gary L. McDowell, *Equity and the Constitution: The Supreme Court, Equitable Relief, and Public Policy* (Chicago: University of Chicago Press, 1982), ch. 1.

31. *Federalist* No. 9, p. 72, and No. 78, p. 472.

32. See generally, William Nelson, *The Americanization of the Common Law;* also Horwitz, *The Transformation of American Law, 1780–1860*, ch. 1. Cf. Stimson, *The American Revolution in the Law*, who defines common law by the increasingly professional and technical norms of eighteenth-century British practice and thus stresses what is distinctively American, in particular a widened use of juries.

33. See Nathan Glazer, "Towards an Imperial Judiciary?" in *The American Commonwealth 1976*, ed. Nathan Glazer and Irving Kristol (New York: Basic Books, 1976), p. 104, quoting Bryce.

34. Epstein, *The Political Theory of* The Federalist, p. 186.

35. In England, of course, the common law began as unwritten law, and statutes were interpreted to be either declaratory of it or remedial to it. It became settled by about the time of Blackstone (and hence Publius) that in case of a conflict between statutory law and common law, the statute was to prevail, though this rule is itself a rule of common law. On the subsequent development of a rigid doctrine of precedent in English law, in conjunction with the triumph of the doctrine of parliamentary

sovereignty, see Rupert Cross, *Precedent in English Law* (Oxford: Clarendon Press, 1961). In the United States, where the origins of government were within memory and usually inscribed in written documents, the legal status of the common law itself could depend on statutory provision, but since courts continued to do their work of construing laws and applying them in particular cases, a sort of common law would develop.

36. *Federalist* No. 37, p. 229.

37. Ibid., No. 82, p. 491.

38. Ibid., No. 85, p. 526.

39. Ibid., No. 78, p. 467.

40. Ibid., p. 468.

41. Cf. *Federalist* 33, p. 205, where Hamilton cites the Supremacy Clause in a somewhat oblique reference to judicial review, an argument he does not repeat in number 78.

42. Ibid., No. 78, p. 470.

43. Ibid., No. 83, p. 497. Alexander Bickel notes the same conflict in the opinions of John Marshall: *Marbury v. Madison* depends upon the analogy of constitutional law to ordinary law, but in a famous passage in *McCulloch v. Maryland* Marshall draws a line between a constitution and a legal code. See *The Least Dangerous Branch,* ch. 1.

44. For Publius's assertions of the wholly popular or republican character of the government proposed by the Constitution, see *Federalist* No. 14, p. 100, and No. 39, pp. 240–42; cf. No. 51, p. 321.

45. A complete text of Brutus's letters can be found in Herbert Storing, ed., *The Anti-Federalist: Writings by the Opponents of the Constitution* (abridged by Murray Dry) (Chicago: University of Chicago Press, 1985), pp. 103–97. Ann Stuart Diamond argues that Hamilton's papers on the judiciary are a direct response to Brutus; "The Anti-Federalist 'Brutus,'" *Political Science Reviewer* 6 (1976): 249–81. While this view somewhat underrates the systematic character of Hamilton's treatment of the judiciary, he surely does begin with a response to Brutus's central charge, and his comment at the beginning of *Federalist* No. 81 on the power of construing laws according to their spirit appears a direct reply to Brutus's Essay XI.

46. Storing and Dry, *The Anti-Federalist,* p. 185.

47. Ibid., p. 187.

48 *Federalist* No. 78, p. 467.

49. Ibid., pp. 469–70.

50. Ibid., p. 469.

51. Ibid., No. 81, p. 485.

52. Or perhaps what appears to be an underestimate is in fact a sly silence. Charles Kesler notes that of the four attributes of legislative and executive powers mentioned by Hamilton at the beginning of No. 78, only sword and purse are excluded, perhaps leaving to judges some power to dispense "honors" and to prescribe "rules by which the duties and rights of every citizen are to be regulated" (p. 465).

53. See Brutus, Essays XII and XV, for an account of how the judiciary can do its work quietly, in Storing and Dry, *The Anti-Federalist,* pp. 168ff., 186–87.

54. *Federalist* No. 78, pp. 469, 470 (first clause); No. 16, p. 117 (second clause); No. 84, p. 515 (third clause).

55. The most vivid illustration of this way of thinking I know is the criticism of the Supreme Court's decision in *Dred Scott* by that great common lawyer, Abraham Lincoln. See Robert Johannsen, ed., *The Lincoln-Douglas Debates of 1858* (New York: Oxford University Press, 1965), passim.

56. *The Political Theory of* The Federalist, esp. ch. 4.

57. Ibid., pp. 6–8.

58. For a characterization of constitutionalism in contrast to both legalism and

realism, see Harvey C. Mansfield, Jr., "Constitutionalism and the Rule of Law," *Harvard Journal of Law and Public Policy* 8, no. 2 (1985): 323–26.

59. For Madison, see *Federalist* No. 53, p. 332; for Hamilton, see No. 1, p. 35, and No. 85, p. 522.

60. See Furtwangler, *The Authority of Publius*, ch. 2–3.

61. *Federalist* No. 83, p. 495.

62. His contemporaries were not so reserved about the connection between a bill of rights and judicial review. Madison cites the possibility of judicial enforcement in introducing on the floor of the House the amendments that were to become the Bill of Rights, and Jefferson had spoken of this possibility in his letter to Madison of 15 March 1789.

63. "The Constitution and the Bill of Rights," in M. Judd Harmon, ed., *Essays on the Constitution of the United States* (Port Washington, N.Y.: Kennikat Press, 1978), pp. 32–48.

64. "Consider Amendments IV–VIII, which have to do with judicial procedure and include among their provisions the privilege against self-incrimination, the guarantee of due process, and the right to a jury trial.

CHAPTER THIRTEEN. NOT "BUILDERS OF BABEL": LEGISLATING A CONSTITUTION

1. Adrienne Koch, ed., *Notes of Debates in the Federal Convention of 1787 Reported by James Madison*, rev. ed. (Athens: Ohio University Press, 1984), pp. 653–54 (hereafter cited as *Debates*).

2. Leon R. Kass, "What's Wrong with Babel?" *American Scholar* 58 (Winter 1989): 41.

3. See John Roche, "The Founding Fathers: A Reform Caucus in Action," *American Political Science Review* 55 (1961): 799.

4. 1 Bl. Comm. 86–87. Of course Blackstone adopts this distinction from the common law tradition, for we saw it figure in the writings of Sir Edward Coke.

5. See *Federalist* No. 40.

6. *Debates*, pp. 61, 79, 336, 461.

7. Ibid., p. 338.

8. Ibid., p. 352.

9. Ibid., p. 464.

10. Ibid., pp. 44, 304ff. Sherman's reservations were expressed in the first debate over the negative, which occurred when Charles Pinckney, with Madison's support, moved unsuccessfully to expand the veto to allow Congress to reject not only laws that contravened the articles of union, but all laws "which they should judge to be improper" (pp. 88ff.).

11. Ibid., p. 304 (first attempt); p. 518 (subsequent attempt).

12. Hamilton, Madison, and Jay, *The Federalist Papers*, p. 515.

13. Storing, "The Constitution and the Bill of Rights."

14. The debates in the First Congress over the amendments that became the Bill of Rights can be found in Bernard Schwartz, ed., *The Bill of Rights: A Documentary History* (New York: Chelsea House Publishers, 1971), 2: 1006–1166.

CONCLUSION

1. 1 Cranch 137 (1803), at 177.

2. Also passsed over in this study, because largely a development of the nineteenth

century, is the use of common law adjudication to encourage the growth of the American economy, a subject of much scholarly interest today in two leading, if opposing, movements of legal-historical thought: "law and economics" and "critical legal studies." From the point of view of my account of common law, it should be noted that both schools already accept the marriage of common law and liberalism effected by Blackstone; it is no accident that I have cited law review articles on Blackstone by a principal representative of each school—respectively, Richard Posner, "Blackstone and Bentham," and Duncan Kennedy, "The Structure of Blackstone's Commentaries."

3. *The "Higher Law" Background*, p. 1.

4. *Marbury v. Madison*, 1 Cranch 137 (1803), at 163; see also Charles H. McIlwain, *Constitutionalism: Ancient and Modern*, ch. 1; cf. Judith N. Shklar, *Legalism* (Cambridge, Mass.: Harvard University Press, 1964), p. 111ff., on the inevitability of politics behind the mask of rule of law.

SELECTED BIBLIOGRAPHY

PRIMARY SOURCES

Aubrey, John. *Aubrey's Brief Lives.* Edited by Oliver Lawson Dick. Ann Arbor: University of Michigan Press, 1957.

———. *"Brief Lives," Chiefly of Contemporaries, set down by John Aubrey, between the Years 1669 & 1696.* Edited by Andrew Clark. Vol. I. Oxford: Clarendon Press, 1898.

Bacon, Francis. *The Elements of the Common Lawes of England.* London: I. More, 1630; reprint ed., New York: Da Capo Press, 1969.

Bailyn, Bernard. *Pamphlets of the American Revolution, 1750–1776.* Cambridge, Mass.: Belknap Press of Harvard University Press, 1965.

Blackstone, Sir William. *Commentaries on the Laws of England.* Oxford: Clarendon Press, 1765–69; facsimile reprint ed., Chicago: University of Chicago Press, 1979.

Boyd, Julian P. *The Declaration of Independence: The Evolution of the Text as Shown in Facsimiles of Various Drafts by its Author, Thomas Jefferson.* Princeton, N.J.: Princeton University Press, 1945.

Brutus [pseud.]. Essays. In *The Anti-Federalist: Writings by the Opponents of the Constitution.* Edited by Herbert Storing. Abridged by Murray Dry. Chicago: University of Chicago Press, 1985.

Burke, Edmund. *The Works of the Right Honourable Edmund Burke.* Vol. II–III. London: C. and J. Rivington, 1826.

Coke, Sir Edward. *Institutes of the Laws of England.* First part, London: Society of Stationers, 1628; second part, London: M. Flesher and R. Young, 1642; third and fourth parts, London: M. Flesher, 1644. Reprinted in *Classics of English Legal History in the Modern Era.* Edited by David S. Berkowitz and Samuel E. Thorne. New York: Garland Publishing, 1979.

———. *The Lord Coke His Speech and Charge.* London: Nathaniell Butter, 1607; reprint ed., New York: Da Capo Press, 1972.

———. *The Reports of Sir Edward Coke, etc.* Parts I–XI, edited by George Wilson. Dublin: J. Moore, 1793. Alternatively, parts I–XIII. London: E. & R. Nutts and R. Gosling, 1727.

Dickinson, John. *The Writings of John Dickinson.* Edited by Paul Leicester Ford. Vol. I, *Political Writings, 1764–1774.* Philadelphia: Historical Society of Pennsylvania, 1895.

Farrand, Max, ed. *The Records of the Federal Convention of 1787.* Vol. I. New Haven, Conn.: Yale University Press, 1911.

Fortescue, Sir John. *De Laudibus Legum Anglie.* Translated and edited by S. B. Chrimes. Cambridge: Cambridge University Press, 1942.

Hale, Sir Matthew. *The History of the Common Law of England.* Edited by Charles M. Gray. Chicago: University of Chicago Press, 1971.

———. "Reflections by the Lrd. Cheife Justice Hale on Mr. Hobbes His Dialogue of the Lawe." In William Holdsworth, *A History of English Law,* V: 499–518. London: Metheun & Co., 1945.

Hamilton, Alexander, James Madison, and John Jay. *The Federalist Papers*. Introduction by Clinton Rossiter. New York: New American Library, 1961.

Hobbes, Thomas. *De Cive (Philosophical Rudiments Concerning Government and Society)*. In *Man and Citizen*. Edited by Bernard Gert. Garden City, N.Y.: Doubleday and Company, 1972.

———. *A Dialogue between a Philosopher and a Student of the Common Laws of England*. Edited and with Introduction by Joseph Cropsey. Chicago: University of Chicago Press, 1971.

———. *The Elements of Law, Natural and Politic*. Edited by Ferdinand Tönnies. Cambridge: Cambridge University Press, 1928.

———. *The English Works of Thomas Hobbes*. 11 vols. Edited by William Molesworth. London: John Bohn, 1839–45.

———. *Hobbes's Thucydides*. Edited by Richard Schlatter. New Brunswick, N.J.: Rutgers University Press, 1975.

———. *De Homine*. Translated by Charles T. Wood, T. S. K. Scott-Craig, and Bernard Gert. In *Man and Citizen*. Edited by Bernard Gert. Garden City, N.Y.: Doubleday and Company, 1972.

———. *Leviathan, or The Matter, Forme, & Power of a Common-wealth Ecclesiastical and Civill*. Edited by C. B. Macpherson. Baltimore: Penguin Books, 1968.

———. *Opera Philosophica Quae Latine Scripsit*. 5 vols. Edited by William Molesworth. London: John Bohn, 1839–45.

James I. *The Political Works of James I*. Edited by Charles Howard McIlwain. Cambridge, Mass.: Harvard University Press, 1918.

Jefferson, Thomas. *The Papers of Thomas Jefferson*. Edited by Julian Boyd. Vol. I. Princeton, N.J.: Princeton University Press, 1950.

———. *The Writings of Thomas Jefferson*. 20 vols. Edited by Andrew A. Lipscomb. Washington, D.C.: Thomas Jefferson Memorial Association, 1903.

Johnson, Robert C., et al., eds. *Commons Debates 1628*. Vols. II–IV. New Haven, Conn.: Yale University Press, 1977.

Koch, Adrienne, ed. *Notes of Debates in the Federal Convention of 1787 Reported by James Madison*. Rev. ed. Athens: Ohio University Press, 1984.

Locke, John. *The Educational Writings of John Locke*. Edited by James L. Axtell. Cambridge: Cambridge University Press, 1968.

———. *An Essay Concerning Human Understanding*. Edited by Peter H. Nidditch. Oxford: Clarendon Press, 1975.

———. *Two Treatises of Government*. Edited by Peter Laslett. Rev. ed. Cambridge: Cambridge University Press, 1988.

Montesquieu. *De l'Esprit des Loix* [The Spirit of the Laws]. Edited by Jean Brethe de la Gressaye. 4 vols. Paris: Société les Belles Lettres, 1950.

Otis, James. *The Rights of the British Colonies Asserted and Proved* [1764]. In *Pamphlets of the American Revolution*. Edited by Bernard Bailyn. Vol. I. Cambridge, Mass.: Belknap Press of Harvard University Press, 1965.

Paine, Thomas. *Common Sense* [1776]. Edited by Isaac Kramnick. New York: Penguin Books, 1976.

Peterson, Merrill D., ed. *The Portable Thomas Jefferson*. New York: Penguin Books, 1977.

Quincy, Josiah, Jr. *Reports of Cases Argued and Adjudged in the Superior Court of Judicature of the Province of Massachusetts Bay between 1761 and 1772*. Boston: Little, Brown and Company, 1865.

Rushworth, John. *Historical Collections of Private Passages of State, Weighty Matters in Law, Remarkable Proceedings in Five Parliaments. . . .* Vol. I. London: D. Browne et al., 1721.

Saint Germain, Christopher. *The Doctor and Student, or Dialogues between a Doctor of Divinity and a Student in the Laws of England.* Edited by William Muchall. Cincinnati: Robert Clarke & Co., 1874.

Schwartz, Bernard, ed. *The Bill of Rights: A Documentary History.* 2 vols. New York: Chelsea House Publishers, 1971.

Smith, Sir Thomas. *De Republica Anglorum: A Discourse on the Commonwealth of England.* Edited by L. Alston. Cambridge: Cambridge University Press, 1906.

Wilson, James. *The Works of James Wilson.* Vol. I. Edited by Robert Green McCloskey. Cambridge, Mass.: Belknap Press of Harvard University Press, 1967.

SECONDARY SOURCES—BOOKS

Agresto, John. *The Supreme Court and Constitutional Democracy.* Ithaca, N.Y.: Cornell University Press, 1984.

Ashcraft, Richard. *Revolutionary Politics and Locke's* Two Treatises of Government. Princeton, N.J.: Princeton University Press, 1986.

Bailyn, Bernard. *The Ideological Origins of the American Revolution.* Cambridge: Belknap Press of Harvard University Press, 1967.

Becker, Carl L. *The Declaration of Independence: A Study in the History of Ideas.* New York: Vintage Books, 1942.

Berger, Raoul. *Congress v. the Supreme Court.* Cambridge, Mass.: Harvard University Press, 1969.

Berns, Walter. *Taking the Constitution Seriously.* New York: Simon and Schuster, 1987.

Bickel, Alexander. *The Least Dangerous Branch: The Supreme Court at the Bar of Politics.* Indianapolis: Bobbs-Merrill Company, 1962.

Boorstin, Daniel J. *The Genius of American Politics.* Chicago: University of Chicago Press, 1953.

———. *The Mysterious Science of the Law: An Essay on Blackstone's* Commentaries. . . . Cambridge, Mass.: Harvard University Press, 1941.

Bork, Robert. *The Tempting of America: The Political Seduction of the Law.* New York: Free Press, 1990.

Bowen, Catherine Drinker. *The Lion and the Throne: The Life and Times of Sir Edward Coke.* Boston: Little, Brown and Company, 1957.

Brown, K. C., ed. *Hobbes Studies.* Cambridge, Mass.: Harvard University Press, 1965.

Cairns, Huntington. *Legal Philosophy from Plato to Hegel.* Baltimore: Johns Hopkins Press, 1949.

Cappelletti, Mauro. *Judicial Review in the Contemporary World.* Indianapolis: Bobbs-Merrill Co., 1971.

Chrimes, S. B. *English Constitutional History.* 4th ed. Oxford: Oxford University Press, 1967.

Clinton, Robert Lowry. *Marbury v. Madison and Judicial Review.* Lawrence: University Press of Kansas, 1989.

Colbourn, H. Trevor. *The Lamp of Experience: Whig History and the Intellectual Origins of the American Revolution.* Chapel Hill: University of North Carolina Press, 1965.

Coleman, Frank M. *Hobbes and America: Exploring the Constitutional Foundations.* Toronto: University of Toronto Press, 1977.

Corwin, Edward S. *The Doctrine of Judicial Review: Its Legal and Historical Basis and Other Essays.* Princeton, N.J.: Princeton University Press, 1914.

———. *The "Higher Law" Background of American Constitutional Law.* Ithaca, N.Y.: Cornell University Press, 1955. First published in *Harvard Law Review* 42 (1928–29): 149–85; 365–409.

Cox, Richard H. *Locke on War and Peace*. Oxford: Clarendon Press, 1960.

Cranston, Maurice, and Richard S. Peters. *Hobbes and Rousseau: A Collection of Critical Essays*. Garden City, N.Y.: Doubleday and Company, 1972.

Cross, Rupert. *Precedent in English Law*. Oxford: Clarendon Press, 1961.

Dicey, A. V. *Introduction to the Study of the Law of the Constitution*. 8th ed. London: Macmillan, 1915; reprint ed., Indianapolis: Liberty Classics, 1982.

Dietze, Gottfried. *The Federalist: A Classic on Federalism and Free Government*. Baltimore: Johns Hopkins Press, 1960.

Dunn, John. *The Political Thought of John Locke: An Historical Account of the Argument of the "Two Treatises of Government."* Cambridge: Cambridge University Press, 1969.

Dworkin, Ronald. *A Matter of Principle*. Cambridge, Mass.: Harvard University Press, 1985.

———. *Taking Rights Seriously*. Cambridge, Mass.: Harvard University Press, 1978.

Eidelberg, Paul. *The Philosophy of the American Constitution. A Reinterpretation of the Intentions of the Founding Fathers*. New York: Free Press, 1968; reprint ed., Lanham, Md.: University Press of America, 1986.

Eisenberg, Melvin Aron. *The Nature of the Common Law*. Cambridge, Mass.: Harvard University Press, 1988.

Ely, John Hart. *Democracy and Distrust: A Theory of Judicial Review*. Cambridge, Mass.: Harvard University Press, 1980.

Epstein, David F. *The Political Theory of* The Federalist. Chicago: University of Chicago Press, 1984.

Franklin, Julian. *John Locke and the Theory of Sovereignty*. Cambridge: Cambridge University Press, 1978.

Friedrich, Carl Joachim. *Constitutional Government and Democracy*. 4th ed. Lexington, Mass.: Blaisdell Publishing Co., 1968.

———. *The Philosophy of Law in Historical Perspective*. 2d ed. Chicago: University of Chicago Press, 1963.

Furtwangler, Albert. *The Authority of Publius: A Reading of the Federalist Papers*. Ithaca, N.Y.: Cornell University Press, 1984.

Gauthier, David. *The Logic of Leviathan: The Moral and Political Theory of Thomas Hobbes*. Oxford: Clarendon Press, 1969.

Goldsmith, M. M. *Hobbes's Science of Politics*. New York: Columbia University Press, 1966.

Gough, J. W. *Fundamental Law in English Constitutional History*. Rev. ed. Oxford: Clarendon Press, 1961.

Greene, Jack. *Peripheries and Center: Constitutional Development in the Extended Polities of the British Empire and the United States, 1607–1788*. Athens: University of Georgia Press, 1986.

Gwyn, W. B. *The Meaning of the Separation of Powers: An Analysis of the Doctrine from Its Origin to the Adoption of the United States Constitution*. Tulane Studies in Political Science, vol. IX. New Orleans: Tulane University, 1965.

Haines, Charles Groves. *The American Doctrine of Judicial Supremacy*. 2d ed. Berkeley and Los Angeles: University of California Press, 1932.

Hanson, Donald. *From Kingdom to Commonwealth*. Cambridge, Mass.: Harvard University Press, 1970.

Hart, H. L. A. *The Concept of Law*. Oxford: Clarendon Press, 1961.

Hartz, Louis. *The Liberal Tradition in America: An Interpretation of American Political Thought since the Revolution*. New York: Harcourt, Brace and Company, 1955.

Herzog, Don. *Without Foundations: Justification in Political Theory*. Ithaca, N.Y.: Cornell University Press, 1985.

Hogue, Arthur R. *Origins of the Common Law*. Bloomington: Indiana University Press, 1966; reprint ed., Indianapolis: Liberty Press, 1985.

Holdsworth, Sir William. *A History of English Law*. 3d ed. Vols. IV–VI. London: Metheun & Co., 1945.

———. *Some Makers of English Law*. Cambridge: Cambridge University Press, 1938.

Holmes, Oliver Wendell, Jr. *Collected Legal Papers*. New York: Harcourt, Brace and Howe, 1920.

———. *The Common Law*. Boston: Little, Brown and Company, 1881.

Horwitz, Morton J. *The Transformation of American Law, 1780–1860*. Cambridge, Mass.: Harvard University Press, 1977.

Hulliung, Mark. *Montesquieu and the Old Regime*. Berkeley and Los Angeles: University of California Press, 1976.

Johnston, David. *The Rhetoric of Leviathan: Thomas Hobbes and the Politics of Cultural Transformation*. Princeton, N.J.: Princeton University Press, 1986.

Kantorowicz, Ernst H. *The King's Two Bodies: A Study in Medieval Political Theology*. Princeton, N.J.: Princeton University Press, 1957.

Kavka, Gregory S. *Hobbesian Moral and Political Theory*. Princeton, N.J.: Princeton University Press, 1986.

Lasser, William. *The Limits of Judicial Power: The Supreme Court in American Politics*. Chapel Hill: University of North Carolina Press, 1988.

Levi, Edward H. *An Introduction to Legal Reasoning*. Chicago: University of Chicago Press, 1949.

Lienesch, Michael. *New Order of the Ages: Time, the Constitution, and the Making of Modern American Political Thought*. Princeton, N.J.: Princeton University Press, 1988.

Lutz, Donald. *Origins of American Constitutionalism*. Baton Rouge: Louisiana State University Press, 1988.

McDonald, Forrest. *Novus Ordo Seclorum: The Intellectual Origins of the Constitution*. Lawrence: University Press of Kansas, 1985.

McDowell, Gary L. *Equity and the Constitution: The Supreme Court, Equitable Relief, and Public Policy*. Chicago: University of Chicago Press, 1982.

McIlwain, Charles Howard. *The American Revolution: A Constitutional Interpretation*. New York: Macmillan, 1923; reprint ed., Ithaca, N.Y.: Cornell University Press, 1958.

———. *Constitutionalism: Ancient and Modern*. Ithaca, N.Y.: Cornell University Press, 1947.

———. *The High Court of Parliament and Its Supremacy: An Historical Essay on the Boundaries between Legislation and Adjudication in England*. New Haven, Conn.: Yale University Press, 1910.

Macpherson, C. B. *The Political Theory of Possessive Individualism: Hobbes to Locke*. Oxford: Clarendon Press, 1962.

McWhinney, Edward. *Judicial Review in the English-speaking World*. Toronto: University of Toronto Press, 1956.

Mansfield, Harvey C., Jr. *The Spirit of Liberalism*. Cambridge, Mass.: Harvard University Press, 1978.

———. *Statesmanship and Party Government: A Study of Burke and Bolingbroke*. Chicago: University of Chicago Press, 1965.

———. *Taming the Prince: The Ambivalence of Modern Executive Power*. New York: Free Press, 1989.

Merryman, John Henry. *The Civil Law Tradition: An Introduction to the Legal Systems of Western Europe and Latin America*. Stanford, Calif.: Stanford University Press, 1969.

Mintz, Samuel I. *The Hunting of Leviathan: Seventeenth-Century Reactions to the Materialism and Moral Philosophy of Thomas Hobbes.* Cambridge: Cambridge University Press, 1962.

Mosse, George L. *The Struggle for Sovereignty in England, from the Reign of Queen Elizabeth to the Petition of Right.* East Lansing: Michigan State College Press, 1950.

Nagel, Robert F. *Constitutional Cultures: The Mentality and Consequences of Judicial Review.* Berkeley and Los Angeles: University of California Press, 1989.

Nelson, William E. *Americanization of the Common Law: The Impact of Legal Change on Massachusetts Society, 1760–1830.* Cambridge, Mass.: Harvard University Press, 1975.

Oakeshott, Michael. *Hobbes on Civil Association.* Berkeley and Los Angeles: University of California Press, 1975.

———. *Rationalism in Politics and Other Essays.* London: Methuen, 1962.

Ogilvie, Sir Charles. *The King's Government and the Common Law, 1471–1641.* Oxford: Basil Blackwell, 1958.

Pangle, Thomas. *Montesquieu's Philosophy of Liberalism.* Chicago: University of Chicago Press, 1973.

———. *The Spirit of Modern Republicanism: The Moral Vision of the American Founders and the Philosophy of Locke.* Chicago: University of Chicago Press, 1988.

Pennock, J. Roland, and John W. Chapman, eds. *Constitutionalism.* Nomos Vol. XX. New York: New York University Press, 1979.

Peters, Richard. *Hobbes.* Harmondsworth, England: Penguin Books, 1956; reprint ed., Westport, Conn.: Greenwood Press, 1979.

Plucknett, Theodore F. T. *A Concise History of the Common Law.* 5th ed. Boston: Little, Brown and Company, 1956.

———. *Statutes and Their Interpretation in the First Half of the Fourteenth Century.* Cambridge: Cambridge University Press, 1922.

Pocock, J. G. A. *The Ancient Constitution and the Feudal Law: A Study of English Historical Thought in the Seventeenth Century.* Cambridge: Cambridge University Press, 1957; reissue with Retrospect, 1987.

———. *The Machiavellian Moment: Florentine Political Thought and the Atlantic Republican Tradition.* Princeton, N.J.: Princeton University Press, 1975.

Posner, Richard. *The Federal Courts: Crisis and Reform.* Cambridge, Mass.: Harvard University Press, 1985.

Postema, Gerald J. *Bentham and the Common Law Tradition.* Oxford: Clarendon Press, 1986.

Robbins, Caroline. *The Eighteenth-Century Commonwealthman: Studies in the Transmission, Development and Circumstance of English Liberal Thought from the Restoration of Charles II until the War with the Thirteen Colonies.* Cambridge, Mass.: Harvard University Press, 1959.

Rogow, Arnold A. *Thomas Hobbes: Radical in the Service of Reaction.* New York: W. W. Norton & Co., 1986.

Sandoz, Ellis. *A Government of Laws: Political Theory, Religion, and the American Founding.* Baton Rouge: Louisiana State University Press, 1990.

Sacksteder, William. *Hobbes Studies (1879–1979): A Bibliography.* Bowling Green, Ohio: Philosophy Documentation Center of Bowling Green State University, 1982.

Shackleton, Robert. *Montesquieu: A Critical Biography.* Oxford: Oxford University Press, 1961.

Shklar, Judith N. *Legalism.* Cambridge, Mass.: Harvard University Press, 1964.

Skinner, Quentin. *The Foundations of Modern Political Thought.* 2 vols. Cambridge: Cambridge University Press, 1978.

Smith, Rogers. *Liberalism and American Constitutional Law.* Cambridge, Mass.: Harvard University Press, 1985.

Snowiss, Sylvia. *Judicial Review and the Law of the Constitution*. New Haven, Conn.: Yale University Press, 1990.

Spragens, Thomas A., Jr. *The Politics of Motion: The World of Thomas Hobbes*. Lexington: University Press of Kentucky, 1973.

Spurlin, Paul Merrill. *Montesquieu in America, 1760–1801*. University: Louisiana State University Press, 1940.

Stimson, Shannon C. *The American Revolution in the Law: Anglo-American Jurisprudence before John Marshall*. Princeton, N.J.: Princeton University Press, 1990.

Storing, Herbert J. *What the Anti-Federalists Were For*. Chicago: University of Chicago Press, 1981.

Strauss, Leo. *Natural Right and History*. Chicago: University of Chicago Press, 1953.

———. *The Political Philosophy of Hobbes: Its Basis and Its Genesis*. Chicago: University of Chicago Press, 1952.

———. *What Is Political Philosophy? and Other Studies*. Glencoe, Ill.: Free Press, 1959; reprint ed., Westport, Conn.: Greenwood Press, 1973.

Sutherland, Arthur E. *Constitutionalism in America*. Lexington, Mass.: Blaisdell Publishing Co., 1965.

———, ed. *Government under Law*. Cambridge, Mass.: Harvard University Press, 1956.

Tarcov, Nathan. *Locke's Education for Liberty*. Chicago: University of Chicago Press, 1984.

Thorne, Samuel. *Sir Edward Coke: 1552–1952*. Selden Society Lecture. London: Bernard Quaritch, 1957.

Tribe, Laurence. *American Constitutional Law*. 2d ed. Mineola, N.Y.: Foundation Press, 1988.

Tuck, Richard. *Natural Rights Theories: Their Origin and Development*. Cambridge: Cambridge University Press, 1979.

Ullmann, Walter. *Principles of Government and Politics in the Middle Ages*. New York: Barnes & Noble, 1966.

Vile, M. J. C. *Constitutionalism and the Separation of Powers*. Oxford: Clarendon Press, 1967.

Walton, C., and P. Johnson, eds. *Hobbes's "Science of Natural Justice."* Dordrecht, Netherlands: Martinus Nijhoff Publishers, 1987.

Warrender, Howard. *The Political Philosophy of Hobbes: His Theory of Obligation*. Oxford: Clarendon Press, 1957.

Watkins, J. W. N. *Hobbes's System of Ideas: A Study in the Political Significance of Philosophical Theories*. London: Hutchinson and Co., 1965.

White, Stephen. *Sir Edward Coke and "The Grievances of the Commonwealth," 1621–1628*. Chapel Hill: University of North Carolina Press, 1979.

Wills, Garry. *Explaining America: The Federalist*. New York: Penguin Books, 1982.

———. *Inventing America: Jefferson's Declaration of Independence*. Garden City, N.Y.: Doubleday and Company, 1978.

Wolfe, Christopher. *The Rise of Modern Judicial Review: From Constitutional Interpretation to Judge-made Law*. New York: Basic Books, 1986.

Wolin, Sheldon. *Politics and Vision: Continuity and Innovation in Western Political Thought*. Boston: Little, Brown and Company, 1960.

Wood, Gordon. *The Creation of the American Republic, 1776–1787*. Chapel Hill: University of North Carolina Press, 1969.

Wormuth, Francis D. *The Origins of Modern Constitutionalism*. New York: Harper and Brothers, 1949.

———. *The Royal Prerogative, 1603–1649. A Study in English Political and Constitutional Ideas*. Ithaca, N.Y.: Cornell University Press, 1939.

SECONDARY SOURCES—ARTICLES

Berger, Raoul. *"Doctor Bonham's Case:* Statutory Construction or Constitutional Theory?" *University of Pennsylvania Law Review* 117 (1969): 521–45.

Berns, Walter. "Judicial Review and the Rights and Laws of Nature." *Supreme Court Review* 1982: 49–83.

Boudin, Louis. "Lord Coke and the American Doctrine of Judicial Power." *New York University Law Review* 6 (1929): 223–46.

Cairns, John W. "Blackstone, An English Institutist: Legal Literature and the Rise of the Nation State." *Oxford Journal of Legal Studies* 4 (1984): 318–60.

Campbell, Enid. "Thomas Hobbes and the Common Law." *Tasmanian University Law Review* 1 (1958): 20–45.

Coby, Patrick. "The Law of Nature in Locke's *Second Treatise*: Is Locke a Hobbesian?" *Review of Politics* 49 (1987): 3–28.

Cropsey, Joseph. "Hobbes and the Transition to Modernity." In *Ancients and Moderns.* Edited by Joseph Cropsey. New York: Basic Books, 1964.

———. Introduction to *A Dialogue between a Philosopher and a Student of the Common Laws of England,* by Thomas Hobbes. Chicago: University of Chicago Press, 1971.

Cross, Rupert. "Blackstone v. Bentham." *Law Quarterly Review* 92 (1976): 516–27.

Diamond, Ann Stuart. "The Anti-Federalist 'Brutus.'" *Political Science Reviewer* 6 (1976): 249–81.

Diamond, Martin. "Democracy and *The Federalist*: A Reconsideration of the Framers' Intent." *American Political Science Review* 53 (1959): 52–68.

Dicey, A. V. "Blackstone's Commentaries." *National Review* 54 (1909): 653–75; reprinted in *Cambridge Law Journal* 4 (1932): 286–307.

Glazer, Nathan. "Towards an Imperial Judiciary?" In *The American Commonwealth 1976.* Edited by Nathan Glazer and Irving Kristol. New York: Basic Books, 1976.

Gray, Charles M. "Bonham's Case Reviewed." *Proceedings of the American Philosophical Society* 116 (1972): 35–58.

Grey, Thomas C. "Do We Have an Unwritten Constitution?" *Stanford Law Review* 27 (1975): 703–18.

———. "Origins of the Unwritten Constitution: Fundamental Law in American Revolutionary Thought." *Stanford Law Review* 30 (1978): 843–93.

Hedges, William. "Telling Off the King: Jefferson's *Summary View* as Imaginative Fantasy." *Early American Literature* 22 (1987): 166–74.

Hexter, J. H. "Thomas Hobbes and the Law." *Cornell Law Review* 65 (1980): 471–90.

Holdsworth, W. S. "Some Aspects of Blackstone and His Commentaries." *Cambridge Law Journal* 4 (1932): 261–85.

Johnson, Curtis. "The Hobbesian Conception of Sovereignty and Aristotle's Politics." *Journal of the History of Ideas* 46 (1985): 327–47.

Kass, Leon. "What's Wrong with Babel?" *American Scholar* 58 (Winter 1989): 41–60.

Kateb, George. "Hobbes and the Irrationality of Politics." *Political Theory* 17 (1989): 355–91.

Kennedy, Duncan. "The Structure of Blackstone's Commentaries." *Buffalo Law Review* 28 (1979): 205–382.

Lewis, John Underwood. "Sir Edward Coke (1552–1634): His Theory of 'Artificial Reason' as a Context for Modern Basic Legal Theory." *Law Quarterly Review* 84 (1968): 330–42.

Lutz, Donald S. "The Relative Influence of European Writers on Late Eighteenth-Century American Political Thought." *American Political Science Review* 78 (1984): 189–97.

MacKay, R. A. "Coke—Parliamentary Sovereignty or the Supremacy of Law?" *Michigan Law Review* 22 (1924): 215—47.

Malament, Barbara. "The 'Economic Liberalism' of Sir Edward Coke." *Yale Law Journal* 76 (1967): 1321—58.

Mansfield, Harvey C., Jr. "Hobbes and the Science of Indirect Government." *American Political Science Review* 65 (1971): 97—110.

———. "Thomas Jefferson." In *American Political Thought: The Philosophic Dimension of American Statesmanship*. Edited by Morton J. Frisch and Richard G. Stevens. New York: Charles Scribner's Sons, 1971.

Mathie, William. "Justice and Equity: An Inquiry into the Meaning and Role of Equity in the Hobbesian Account of Justice and Politics." In *Hobbes's "Science of Natural Justice."* Edited by C. Walton and P. Johnson. Dordrecht, Netherlands: Martinus Nijhoff Publishers, 1987.

———. "Justice and the Question of Regimes in Ancient and Modern Political Philosophy: Aristotle and Hobbes." *Canadian Journal of Political Science* 9 (1976): 449—63.

———. "Reason and Rhetoric in Hobbes's *Leviathan.*" *Interpretation: A Journal of Political Philosophy* 14 (1986): 281—98.

May, Larry. "Hobbes on Equity and Justice." In *Hobbes's "Science of Natural Justice."* Edited by C. Walton and P. Johnson. Dordrecht, Netherlands: Martinus Nijhoff Publishers, 1987.

Nelson, William E. "The Eighteenth-Century Background of John Marshall's Constitutional Jurisprudence." *Michigan Law Review* 76 (1978): 893—960.

Okin, Susan Moller. "'The Soveraign and His Counsellours': Hobbes's Reevaluation of Parliament." *Political Theory* 10 (1982): 49—75.

Orwin, Clifford. "On the Sovereign Authorization." *Political Theory* 3 (1975): 26—44.

Pitkin, Hanna. "Hobbes's Concept of Representation." *American Political Science Review* 58 (1964): 328—40, 902—18.

Plucknett, Theodore F. T. "Bonham's Case and Judicial Review." *Harvard Law Review* 40 (1926): 30—70.

Pollock, Frederick, and W. S. Holdsworth. "Sir Matthew Hale on Hobbes: An Unpublished Manuscript." *Law Quarterly Review* 37 (1921): 274—85.

Posner, Richard. "Blackstone and Bentham." *Journal of Law and Economics* 19 (1976): 569—606.

Powell, H. Jefferson. "The Original Understanding of Original Intent." *Harvard Law Review* 98 (1985): 885—948.

Resnick, David. "Locke and the Rejection of the Ancient Constitution." *Political Theory* 12 (1984): 97—114.

Roche, John. "The Founding Fathers: A Reform Caucus in Action." *American Political Science Review* 55 (1961): 799—816.

Ryan, Alan. "Hobbes and Individualism." In *Perspectives on Thomas Hobbes*. Edited by G. A. J. Rogers and Alan Ryan. Oxford: Clarendon Press, 1988.

Schoenfeld, Karl M. "Montesquieu en 'la bouche de la loi.'" Ph.D. diss., University of Leyden, 1979.

Siegel, Stephen A. "The Aristotelian Basis of English Law, 1450—1800." *New York University Law Review* 56 (1981): 18—59.

Skinner, Quentin. "History and Ideology in the English Revolution." *Historical Journal* 8 (1965): 151—78.

———. "The Ideological Context of Hobbes's Political Thought." *Historical Journal* 9 (1966): 286—317.

Smith, George P., II. "Dr. Bonham's Case and the Modern Significance of Lord Coke's Influence." *Washington Law Review* 41 (1966): 297—314.

Storing, Herbert J. "The Constitution and the Bill of Rights." In *Essays on the Constitution of the United States*. Edited by M. Judd Harmon. Port Washington, N.Y.: Kennikat Press, 1978.

———. "William Blackstone." In *History of Political Philosophy*. 2d ed. Edited by Leo Strauss and Joseph Cropsey. Chicago: Rand McNally College Publishing Company, 1972.

Stourzh, Gerald. "William Blackstone: Teacher of Revolution." *Jahrbuch für Amerikastudien* 15 (1970): 184–200.

Thorne, S. E. "Dr. Bonham's Case." *Law Quarterly Review* 54 (1938): 543–52.

Trainor, Brian T. "The Politics of Peace: The Role of the Political Covenant in Hobbes's *Leviathan*." *Review of Politics* 47 (1985): 347–69.

Tuck, Richard. "Hobbes and Locke on Toleration." In *Thomas Hobbes and Political Theory*. Edited by Mary G. Dietz. Lawrence: University Press of Kansas, 1990.

Usher, Roland G. "James I and Sir Edward Coke." *English Historical Review* 18 (1903): 664–75.

Wagner, Donald O. "Coke and the Rise of Economic Liberalism." *Economic History Review* (1st ser.) 6 (1935): 30–44.

Weinberger, J. "Hobbes's Doctrine of Method." *American Political Science Review* 69 (1975): 1336–53.

Wheeler, Harvey. "Constitutionalism." In *Handbook for Political Science*. Edited by Fred I. Greenstein and Nelson W. Polsby. Vol. V, *Governmental Institutions and Processes*. Reading, Mass.: Addison-Wesley Publishing Company, 1975.

Whiteside, Kerry H. "Nominalism and Conceptualism in Hobbes's Political Theory." *Commonwealth: A Journal of Political Science* 1 (1987): 1–25.

Yale, D. E. C. "Hobbes and Hale on Law, Legislation, and the Sovereign." *Cambridge Law Journal* 31 (1972): 121–56.

INDEX

Wars, 95–96, 100
Washington, George, 186
Westminster, 13
Whig(s): Coke as, 13, 190; Locke as, 150, 183; Blackstone as, 162; and American Revolution, 5, 180, 182, 190, 196
Will, 93
William the Conqueror, 63–64
Wilson, James, 162, 186, 196, 212, 218, 220

Wisdom, 44–45, 65, 168
Wolfe, Christopher, 3
Women, 21
Wood, Gordon, 5
Writ of Assistance, 190
Writs, 175
Written law: in Hobbes, 108, 123; constitution as, 98, 207, 211

www.ingramcontent.com/pod-product-compliance
Lightning Source LLC
Chambersburg PA
CBHW032112040226
39204CB00021B/100